MW00736325

# Hitchcock and the Making of *Marnie*

## Revised Edition

Tony Lee Moral

THE SCARECROW PRESS, INC.
*Lanham • Toronto • Plymouth, UK*
2013

Published by Scarecrow Press, Inc.
A wholly owned subsidiary of The Rowman & Littlefield Publishing Group, Inc.
4501 Forbes Boulevard, Suite 200, Lanham, Maryland 20706
www.rowman.com

10 Thornbury Road, Plymouth PL6 7PP, United Kingdom

Copyright © 2013 by Scarecrow Press, Inc.

British Library Cataloguing in Publication Information Available

**Library of Congress Cataloging-in-Publication Data**

Moral, Tony Lee.
  Hitchcock and the making of Marnie / Tony Lee Moral. — Revised edition.
      pages cm
  Includes bibliographical references and index.
  ISBN 978-0-8108-9107-4 (cloth : alk. paper) — ISBN 978-0-8108-9108-1 (ebook)
  1. Marnie (Motion picture)  2. Hitchcock, Alfred, 1899–1980—Criticism and interpretation.  I. Title.
  PN1997.M2635M67 2013
  791.4302'33092—dc23                                                    2013010922

∞™ The paper used in this publication meets the minimum requirements of American National Standard for Information Sciences—Permanence of Paper for Printed Library Materials, ANSI/NISO Z39.48-1992.

Printed in the United States of America.

# Contents

# Acknowledgments

In the writing of this book, I have had the pleasure of interviewing many of *Marnie*'s production team, who have affirmed to me that filmmaking is a collaborative art. I would like to thank Jay Presson Allen, Diane Baker, Kimberly Beck, Robert Boyle, James Hubert Brown, Linden Chiles, Sean Connery, Virginia Darcy, Winston Graham, Hilton Green, Mariette Hartley, Tippi Hedren, Evan Hunter, Paul Jacobsen, Louise Latham, Jim Linn, Harold Mendelsohn, Harold Michaelson, Rita Riggs, Howard Smit, Joseph Stefano, and Lois Thurman for sharing their memories of working with Alfred Hitchcock. In many cases they donated photographs for this book.

Permission to reproduce the storyboards is in a contractual agreement with Universal Studios, the Alfred Hitchcock Estate, and the Margaret Herrick Library, Academy of Motion Picture Arts and Sciences. Letters from François Truffaut are quoted with the kind permission of Laura Truffaut, and Grace Kelly's letter is reprinted by agreement with the Archives Audiovisuelles de Monaco. Permission to quote from the novel *Marnie* was provided by Winston Graham, in addition to his correspondence with Hitchcock. I thank the late Mr. Graham for acknowledging this work in his autobiography *Memoirs of a Private Man*, published posthumously in 2003.

Letters, certain information concerning *The Birds* and *Marnie*, and other material from Evan Hunter's memoir *Me and Hitch* have been used with the kind permission of the author's estate, copyright © 1997 by Evan Hunter. Permission to quote from the Edith Head seminars was provided by the American Film Institute and the Motion Picture & Television Fund, Woodland Hills, California. The late Robert Boyle kindly consented to quoting from his seminar at the American Film Institute.

I also thank Patricia Hitchcock O'Connell, Leland H. Faust, and Steven Kravitz for allowing me to publish from the *Marnie* files from the Alfred J. Hitchcock Trust. In addition, I thank Barbara Hall, Kristine Krueger, and the staff of the Margaret Herrick Library Academy of Motion Pictures Arts and Sciences, for their professionalism and dedication in allowing me access to them. I also thank the American Film Institute and Universal Studios, both their legal and archive departments, for their support in this project.

For the revised edition of this book, I also thank the Harry Ransom Center, University of Texas in Austin for giving me access to Jay Presson Allen and Lewis Allen's files, and to Brooke Allen for giving me permission to publish. I also thank Richard Allen for allowing me to quote from his 1999 Hitchcock Centennial interview with Jay Presson Allen at NYU, the V&A museum archives in London, and the Haymarket theatre. Special thanks to Peter Bogdanovich, who so generously allowed me to quote from his series of interviews with Hitchcock, and Bill Krohn, who shared his roundtable discussion on *The Birds* and *Marnie*, which was originally published in *Cahiers du Cinema* in 1982. Individuals I owe thanks to include Brooke Allen, Andrew Birkin, Andrew Graham, Gabrielle Kelly, and Bob Leuci. Finally, thank you to my mother and father.

# Introduction

What is the trouble with *Marnie*?

Fifty years since the making of Alfred Hitchcock's psychological thriller, that question is still being asked. Released in the summer of 1964, *Marnie* has generated more controversy than any other Hitchcock film. Less well known than its immediate predecessors, *North by Northwest*, *Psycho*, and *The Birds*, *Marnie* is commonly cited as the turning point in Hitchcock's career, being either his last great masterpiece[1] or the start of his decline.[2] When it was first released, *Marnie* was a commercial as well as a critical failure, causing the director to lose a great deal of confidence.

Early reviewers declared *Marnie* old fashioned and technically naive. Many were critical of Hitchcock's use of a highly expressive mise-en-scène, which included painted backdrops, the dependency of studio-bound sets, conspicuous rear projection, stylized acting, and red suffusions of the screen. These devices alienated audiences and critics alike, in what amounts to a constant assault on the boundaries of cinematic realism. Later biographical assessments attributed these faults to Hitchcock's own emotional turmoil, causing him to lose interest in the project.[3] This viewpoint has been resurrected in the recent portrayal of Hitchcock in TV and cinematic films, being tied to biographical assertions that he physically abused and sexually harassed his lead actress Tippi Hedren during the making of *The Birds* and *Marnie*.

*Marnie* still divides critics and audiences today, just as it did on initial release. The film's controversy is far more wide-ranging than that of *Vertigo*, which is often seen as a companion piece, in its exploration of obsession, fetishism, and domineering love. *Vertigo* is widely accepted as Hitchcock's masterpiece and in 2012 was named the number-one film of all time in a *Sight & Sound* poll, thus reaching the apex of its critical canonization. *Vertigo*'s popularity has been steadily rising in the last fifty years, having entered the top ten in 1982, eventually surpassing such greats as *Citizen Kane* (1941) and *Tokyo Story* (1953).

Two thousand and twelve was a watershed year for Hitchcock scholarship and for the director's reputation in the media. As well as *Vertigo* being voted number one, two dramatized biographies were released, placing the director directly in the spotlight. The first film, *Hitchcock*, starring Anthony Hopkins in the title role and Helen Mirren as Alma, charts the relationship between the director and his wife and is based on Stephen Rebello's book *Alfred Hitchcock and the Making of* Psycho. The second was a made-for-TV movie titled *The Girl*, a BBC/HBO collaboration about Tippi Hedren's recollections making *The Birds* and *Marnie*. With the latter drama, *Marnie* was re-introduced to a whole new generation of modern-day audiences, for better or worse, giving a unique opportunity to see how a fifty-year-old film, not widely known outside film scholars, Hitchcock fans, and auteurists, is perceived by a contemporary audience.

With the continual release and preservation of Hitchcock's films on DVD and Blu-Ray, *Marnie* is available to a discerning group of home entertainment viewers. Where does the film stand in relation to Hitchcock's greatest works such as *Vertigo, Psycho, North by Northwest*, and *The Birds*? Often it's classified as a late, flawed masterpiece, which is a particular source of fascination in the Hitchcock canon. For the release of the DVD in 2000, preeminent Hitchcock scholar Robin Wood declared, "If you don't like *Marnie*, you don't really like Hitchcock. I would go further than that and say if you don't love *Marnie* you don't really love cinema." Wood was being provocative and controversial for sure, but he was one of the first to recognize the virtuosity of Hitchcock's concept of pure cinema, his use of the subjective camera to evoke feelings, and how both reach a creative peak in *Marnie*.

More recently, another Hitchcock scholar, William Rothman, in his second edition of his seminal book *The Murderous Gaze*, published in 2012, says, "It does not bode well for our world, for the future of the 'art of pure cinema' within it, or for the field of film studies, that, after almost half a century, *Marnie* is still more widely dismissed or disparaged than acknowledged." Rothman's words may well refer to recent assessments of *Marnie* in 2012, resulting from the dramatized Hitchcock biographies. Less academically minded reviewers have called it a "terrible film,"[4] "misogynistic," "old fashioned," and "simple-minded," claiming that it promotes violence against women and suggests that a woman's sexual frigidity could be cured by rape. A caption at the end of *The Girl* stating that *Marnie* was Hitchcock's last masterpiece also provoked much controversy, but whatever one thinks of the merits of that particular drama, its acknowledgment of *Marnie* as a masterpiece brought the film back into the public spotlight.

In an attempt to grasp the complexities and Hitchcock's reasoning behind *Marnie*, it is fundamental to understand the film's origins. *Marnie* was intended as a vehicle to bring Grace Kelly back to the screen. Kelly had retired from Hollywood after making only eleven films, when she met and married Prince Rainier of Monaco in 1956. She remained close friends with the Hitchcocks and they would often visit her when in Europe. Kelly kept her agents, such as Jay Kanter, and although motherhood and monarchy preoccupied her in the first five years of life as a princess, she always entertained the possibility of returning to the silver screen.

By 1961, when Hitchcock received a pre-publication copy of Winston Graham's intriguing novel *Marnie*, he thought it would be an excellent book for Kelly's return and was anxious to secure her for the title role. *Marnie* was about a frigid and strange young woman named Marnie Elmer, who is blackmailed into marriage by Mark Rutland, one of her employers she robs. The novel featured many elements of kinkiness, fetishism, and sadomasochism that intrigued Hitchcock. In his eye, it was the perfect showcase for Grace Kelly's return.

Hitchcock was also fascinated by psychoanalysis. He wanted to expand the psychiatrist scene at the end of *Psycho* and there are many obvious parallels between that film and *Marnie*, especially the characters of Norman and Marnie. Both are affected in adulthood by a childhood trauma. "After all it stands to reason that if one were seriously doing the *Psycho* story, it would be a case history," said Hitchcock. "You would never present it in forms of mystery or the juxtaposition of characters, as they were placed in the film. They were all designed in a certain way to create this audience emotion. Probably the real *Psycho* story wouldn't have been emotional at all; it would've been terribly clinical."

With typical Hitchcock perversity and mischievousness, he delighted in finding subject matter about a sexually inhibited thief to mark Grace Kelly's return to the screen. The star of three films for Alfred Hitchcock, *Dial M for Murder*, *Rear Window*, and *To Catch a Thief*, Kelly would round out a quartet of films, with *Marnie*, highlighting his concept of the icy blonde with fire under her ice. "She used to joke about being called the ice princess," says hairstylist and friend Virginia Darcy.[5]

In a previously unpublished excerpt from a 1963 interview with Peter Bogdanovich, Hitchcock spoke about his reasoning for favoring Grace Kelly as his ideal heroine. He agreed with Bogdanovich's assessment that Kelly's portrayal of her character Frances Stevens in *To Catch a Thief* was a rather frightening example of the American debutante, but with one important exception: "In her case she wasn't frigid like the typical American debutante," said Hitchcock. "A typical American woman, I feel, is basically what we call a cockteaser. She dresses for sex, and doesn't give it. A man puts his hand on her she runs screaming for mother immediately."[6]

Hitchcock went on to say that he believed that "the English women are the best, the opposite to that; they look nothing, they look like school mistresses. They will tear your fly buttons open, off even." This was his viewpoint in every film; he liked women who behaved very ladylike in public but who were whores in the bedroom. He harboured this image of Kelly, and later said to his assistant director Howard Kazanjian on *Family Plot* (1976), "Did you know that Grace Kelly was a nymphomaniac?"[7] Naturally it was very bold for Hitchcock to propose that Grace Kelly, now Princess of Monaco and mother to the heirs to the throne, could play a frigid, compulsive thief on the screen. But this was all part of Hitchcock's perversity.

So certain was Hitchcock in his belief, he said that Kelly's character Frances Stevens was like the English women, her externals epitomizing cold ice. This is exemplified in the hotel corridor scene where, after Kelly is escorted to her bedroom by Grant, she very boldly plants a kiss on his lips. "She drags him and kisses him, she tore his flies open. I based her on the English type." Hitchcock also made a point that Grace Kelly was not a true American girl, so she couldn't be called a cockteaser, as her mother Margaret Majer was German, and her father Jack Kelly was Irish.

In fact, this scene when Grace Kelly walks down the hallway with Cary Grant and arrives opposite her bedroom door, then turns around and gives him a bold kiss, happened to Hitchcock in real life. Grace Kelly gave him a firm kiss on his lips.[8] Hitchcock was naturally delighted. "That could have happened," says Virginia Darcy. "Grace was playful and liked to play practical jokes." This was all part of Kelly's persona—she was playful, uninhibited, affectionate, and didn't take herself too seriously. She enjoyed joking with Hitchcock and indulge in repartee, answering back any quips that he had.

"Grace was his favorite actress," remembers Norman Lloyd, Hitchcock's longtime friend and producer on his television series *Alfred Hitchcock Presents*. "When she would come to this country [from Monaco] she would come straight up to Santa Cruz, to visit him in that beautiful place. She was a great girl, I knew her slightly. Even when she was the princess, there was something regular about her that was so easy to establish. He loved Grace, but not in a passionate way."[9] The assistant director on *To Catch a Thief*, Herbert Coleman said, "Of course he fell in love with her, but who didn't?" Virginia Darcy agreed, "You couldn't help but fall in love with Grace. We used to call her princess before she became a princess, and she acted like one."

Both Hitchcock and Alma loved Grace Kelly and she would often come around to their home and sit at the kitchen table to talk about her love life. Bearing in mind how important Kelly was to the development of *Marnie*, the genesis of the film went ahead. There are also shades of Kelly's character Frances Stevens, from *To Catch a Thief*, in Mark Rutland's character in *Marnie*. "It's more piquant that way," said Hitchcock; Kelly not only suspects Grant of being guilty but would prefer that he is. She's rather annoyed when she finds out that he isn't. "It's more in the nature of her fetish," said Hitchcock.

Hitchcock also saw something of Kelly in the character of Marnie. His main reason for making the film was that he saw Marnie as being representative of the American woman in the early 1960s, and he was fascinated by the social mores of the decade, played out on today's screens in the television series *Mad Men*. "Marnie is symptomatic of the American female: she is basically frigid," Hitchcock remarked. "There is a vast amount of difference between appearance and actuality in the American woman. She is schooled from childhood by magazines and advertisements to make herself seem alluring and sexy. But alas, her inhibitions are too great."[10]

Hitchcock went on to say, "There is in this country a long tradition of Puritanism. There is also a lack of sophistication. That is why there is so much divorce in America. When a wife suspects that her husband is having an affair, she immediately summons a lawyer. A European wife is more sophisticated. She says, 'Let him have his fling: he will come back to me.' And he generally does." Hitchcock's America in the 1960s, when it came to issues of sexuality and gender, was puritanical, repressed, and unsophisticated. This was in comparison to the freewheeling, uninhibited European woman of the 1960s, represented in films such as *La Dolce Vita* (1960), *Un Homme et une Femme* (1966), and *La Belle du Jour* (1967).

Indeed Hitchcock viewed the matter of female allure on a geographical basis. "Sexuality decreases as you travel southward on the European continent. That is only natural; when you have sophistication in literature, food, and other matters, you would expect a nation to be sophisticated about sex as well. That is certainly true of the Scandinavians. As for English women, they are the most promiscuous of all. Sexual enlightenment diminishes as you reach the Latin countries—and don't let the French preoccupation with nudes, etc. fool you. The French and the Italians have a schoolboy attitude towards sex."

It's worth noting at this point that Hitchcock and Alma enjoyed a fifty-four-year marriage. Thursday nights were always spent having dinner at Chasens. Weekends were spent in their Santa Cruz home. Christmas was in St. Moritz and vacations in Lake Como. The stability of the Hitchcock marriage was based on companionship, habit, and compromise. Alma may have allowed Hitchcock to indulge in his fantasies, but they were only that, fantasies. When Alma became ill in the 1950s and 1960s, colleagues remarked how deeply it affected Hitchcock, who rarely brought his emotional problems to the set.

With this background in mind, *Hitchcock and the Making of Marnie* is the first book-length study and its overall orientation is an attempt to explain the nature of this complex film. The methodology I employ takes into account previously unpublished production details, in addition to providing an oral history from several key participants. This single-film focus is an increasing common approach to film studies and history, offering a unique opportunity to see the process of filmmaking in action. Other Hitchcock films have received this treatment, notably *Psycho*[11] and *Vertigo*;[12] however, *Marnie* qualifies as a fascinating, if flawed, late-career work, around which there is much mystery and controversy. It continues to grow in reputation as one of Hitchcock's mature and intriguing films. This book has six main objectives:

1. I will suggest why *Marnie* has relevance for modem audiences, arguing that it is an important Hitchcock film because it addresses deeply pertinent human problems, issues of sexuality, and equality of men and women in the workplace. Hitchcock's preoccupation with sexual relationships evolves into a ruthless examination of gender expectations, which lead to violence within our culture. An attention to such universal human dilemmas is what gives *Marnie* a special degree of salience, which can account for both the initial response and the subsequent fascination with the film.

2. I will examine how *Marnie* fits into Hitchcock's overall thematic career, by underscoring the director's empathy with the woman's position; *Rebecca*, *Notorious*, and *Under Capricorn* are obvious forerunners. In the trailer for the film, Hitchcock said it was about "two very interesting human specimens," and *Marnie* is very much about the twentieth-century post-Freudian preoccupation with the battle of the sexes, not least because the Sean Connery character, Mark Rutland, is a zoologist.

3. Contrary to the auteurist view, I will highlight multivocality in the *Marnie* text, a product of the larger cultural and political forces that shape it. I will show how author Winston Graham and screenwriter Jay Presson Allen were major contributors to the narrative structure. The multiauthorship can also account for the various interpretations the Mark Rutland character has generated. The subversive complexities of Mark and his sadomasochistic qualities were part of the reason the film was rejected on its first release. Hitchcock also intuitively recognized that the critical dilemmas of society were class antagonism and child abuse, both sexual and psychological— subjects that were never broached during the time of *Marnie*'s release but that dominate contemporary news headlines today.

4. Hitchcock has been charged with neglect during the postproduction of *Marnie*. I will refute these allegations by detailing his active involvement throughout the production process. The preponderance of the evidence

suggests that *Marnie* was one of Hitchcock's most keenly felt and personal ventures. The lack of auteurist comments after the film was released highlights Hitchcock's sensitivity to criticism and his own disappointment in the public's refusal to accept a project that he had nurtured for three years. Moreover, I will show that rather than the charge of neglect, it was Hitchcock's predilection for total control that was the main cause of events going awry, for reasons I will expand upon.

5. I will unequivocally argue that the techniques employed were intentional and that *Marnie*, as an art film, is the culmination of Hitchcock's concept of "pure cinema." Furthermore, the utilization of such expressionistic devices was part of a larger campaign by Hitchcock to be taken seriously as an artist. Prior to filming *The Birds* in 1962, he watched a number of films by Jean-Luc Godard, Michelangelo Antonioni, and Ingmar Bergman. That same year, he met with the French director François Truffaut, who was preparing a book on Hitchcock's work, to elevate his reputation in the international art world of film. Together they talked about Hitchcock's plans for *Marnie* as a psychological character study, with which he would experiment with a looser narrative. Like the European art cinema of the early 1960s, *Marnie*'s focus on mental states was designed to appeal to a cultural elite. In correspondence with Giulio Ascarelli, who was the Universal head in Rome in the 1960s, Hitchcock received a letter dated April 13, 1965, indicating how the color in Antonioni's *Red Desert* was achieved. I show that with *Marnie*, Hitchcock was a forerunner in 1960s art cinema.

6. I will suggest that Hitchcock's *Marnie* was the most intensely personal of his films, and was the culmination of his career and his melancholy view of femininity. With *Marnie*, Hitchcock identified with his heroine more than any other. After the film's failure, Hitchcock had little else to say about female sexuality, and never again directly exposed his feelings so openly on screen. The films that follow—*Torn Curtain*, *Topaz*, *Frenzy*, and *Family Plot*—make no more open pleas for love and acceptance.

In achieving these aims, the book is divided into twelve chapters that chart the progress of Alfred Hitchcock's *Marnie*, from its conception, writing, phases of production, and marketing, to critical interpretation and assimilation within the art world. Events are presented chronologically and are based on two principal sources: archive material from Hitchcock's personal files held at the Margaret Herrick Library in Beverly Hills, and personal interviews with members of the production team, conducted between 1999 and 2000, and in 2012 and 2013 for the revised edition of this book, particularly Brooke Allen, Diane Baker, Kimberly Beck, Helen Colvig, Linden Chiles, Andrew Graham,

Virginia Darcy, Mariette Hartley, Paul Jacobsen, Louise Latham, Norman Lloyd, Rita Riggs, and Marshall Schlom. For the revised addition of the book, I was reliant on the Jay and Lewis Allen personal files held at the Harry Ransom Center at the University of Texas at Austin, Winston Graham's autobiography, and Peter Bogdanovich's series of interviews with Hitchcock.

The shape of this book also suggests how production and oral history, in addition to critical analysis, can be used to interpret a film's meaning. My own assessment of the research is then presented at the end of each chapter, which itself, of course, is subject to debate.

The first chapter investigates the behind-the-scenes events of how *Marnie* was conceived. Interviews with the author, Winston Graham, highlight his own sympathetic orientation toward women and the centrality of the feminine impulse in the book's conception. I reveal how the Marnie character was derived from real-life events involving the abjection of women in postwar Britain. Graham's attention to a psychological framework appealed to Hitchcock at a time when he wanted to be taken seriously as an artist. The chapter also chronicles Hitchcock's attempts to woo Grace Kelly for the Marnie role and how the film was intended as a vehicle for Kelly, a major reason for Universal's endorsement of the project. I examine the causal factors underlying Kelly's sudden withdrawal from the film. Also discussed is Hitchcock's attempt to manufacture a new star with Tippi Hedren, highlighting the qualities he saw in her that were in keeping with his own firmly imbibed Victorian notions of femininity.

Chapter 2 chronicles the development of plot and character between Hitchcock and his writers during the three years it took to bring *Marnie* to the screen. This production history is fascinating, as it demonstrates the often unpredictable and over-determined process by which ideas evolve during the adaptation of literary works to film. I trace how subversive elements such as sadomasochism, introduced by Joseph Stefano during the writing of *Psycho* and the *Marnie* treatment, impressed on Hitchcock throughout production. Moreover, I explore how these thematic anomalies were at odds with Hitchcock's next screenwriter, Evan Hunter, and why they were the causal factors leading to his dismissal. I also highlight how Hunter's experience as a novelist was a source for many crucial plot mechanics, despite Jay Presson Allen receiving sole credit for the final screenplay. Allen's attention and sensitivity toward issues concerning women and children, however, are also underscored as important narrative influences.

The preproduction phase described in chapter 3 demonstrates how Hitchcock's personal authorship, most substantially his concept of female portrayal, influenced others in their preparation for the film. Furthermore, Hitchcock's delineation of gender differences and its reduction to behavior and body language are shown to be instrumental in the casting of his principals. I show how Sean Connery's persona as James Bond was in alignment with the subversive elements Hitchcock had in mind for the character of Mark Rutland. Similarly, the casting and grooming of Tippi Hedren, a classic icon of 1960s femininity, whose physical and psychological assurance foregrounds a decade marked by women's liberation, are synchronized with the story's feminist appeal. Hitchcock's agenda for hiring Diane Baker in the part of Lil Mainwaring is also revealed.

Chapter 4 focuses on Hitchcock's working methods with his actors and how he created an atmosphere on the set that was specifically designed to elicit certain performances. I will argue that Hitchcock's desire to create an emotional response from the audience and deliberate use of highly expressive techniques have origins in the visual style of European art cinema, both German expressionism and Soviet montage. I also address the controversial events surrounding filming, based on an oral history with several key participants in the team and close analysis of the production archives held at the Margaret Herrick Library. Lastly, I surmise how Hitchcock's keen sense of control, a result of his Jesuit education, was responsible for many events and decisions that influenced the final outcome of the film.

Chapter 5, detailing the postproduction, illustrates how Alma Hitchcock's experience as an editor influenced key scenes in the overall tone of the film. Furthermore, I examine how changing audience tastes and film aesthetics urged Hitchcock to readjust his musical scores in keeping with those of European filmmakers. Conflicting objectives between Hitchcock, Universal Studios, and Bernard Herrmann during the scoring of *Marnie* are revealed to be determining factors eventually leading to the composer's dismissal.

Chapter 6 charts the marketing of the film and Hitchcock's own efforts to promote himself as a serious artist, through involvement with institutes such as the Museum of Modern Art in New York and with prominent figures in the film industry, most notably the French director François Truffaut. I examine how Truffaut's self-interested motivations persuaded Hitchcock to participate in what was to become the most famous book about himself, the series of interviews that appeared under the title *Hitchcock* in 1967. I address how studio publicity was also part of a concerted effort to manufacture for Hitchcock a new persona.

Chapter 7 outlines why Hitchcock's promotional efforts to alter his image from that of master showman to serious artist had a negative impact on journalistic review media when the film was released in 1964. I show that reevaluation of *Marnie* in the late 1960s and 1970s was dependent on the professional context of film study, notably the broad acceptance of the auteur theory within academic disciplines, in addition to the rise of feminist film

criticism. By addressing contextual issues of subjectivity, desire, and identification in Western cultural forms, I chart changing aesthetic standards on
the critical acceptance of Hitchcock and their influence on a film's meaning.
I also show how controversial biographical legends of Hitchcock after his
death have led to biased critical interpretations, which in turn have dictated
subsequent analysis in all media.

Chapter 8 assesses some of the broader themes of *Marnie* and how its
adoption by the auteur critics as a "lost child" facilitated its embrace by other
filmmakers, such as Truffaut and Martin Scorsese. I survey how *Marnie* has
influenced a range of artists in art, video, and theater, from Stanley Douglas,
one of the top contemporary artists in the world, to the British director Sean
O'Connor and his recent stage adaptation. The latter, for the first time, allows a comparison between Hitchcock's film and another reading of Winston
Graham's text.

For the four additional chapters in the revised addition of the book, I have
concentrated on new material that was not available when writing the first
edition in 1999 and 2000. Chapter 9 focuses on new biographical information on the two principal writers of *Marnie*, author Winston Graham and
screenwriter Jay Presson Allen. I argue through interpretation of this data
that neither Graham nor Allen were true feminists and that both may have
identified more with Mark Rutland than with Marnie. This may account for
the conflicting interpretations of the characters, and uneasiness about the film
from a woman's point of view.

Chapter 10 examines the production of Hitchcock's much-cherished
screenplay *Mary Rose*, the play's origins with playwright J. M. Barrie, the
premiere in London, and Hitchcock's lifelong efforts to bring it to the screen.
I suggest why Hitchcock had such a fascination with *Mary Rose* and how,
like *Marnie*, it was one of his most keenly felt and personal ventures. Also
discussed are Lewis and Jay Allen's efforts to bring the play to the screen in
the 1970s and 1980s and the reasons why the play was never filmed.

Hitchcock's cinematic style is detailed in chapter 11, and the importance
of his director of photography Robert Burks. The focus is on the techniques
of their subjective camera—their use of lenses, zooms, time distortions, montage, flashbacks, and filters that makes *Marnie* the most intensely personal of
all his films, where the audience feels the subjective state of the heroine. This
was all part of Hitchcock's plan for *Marnie* to be chiefly a character study,
showcasing his interests in psychoanalysis and subjective states.

In 2012 Hitchcock was prominent in the media. Chapter 12, the final
chapter, includes thoughts by Hitchcock's surviving crew from *Psycho*, *The
Birds*, and *Marnie*, as they remember the director and the man. Was he a sadistic Svengali or a sensitive collaborator? What's evident is that the portrait

of Hitchcock that emerges is multifaceted, that of a shy man, a perfectionist, someone generous in spirit but also very controlling.

As cinema is now recognized as the dominant art form of the twentieth century, I hope that the presentation of this research, and the oral history represented within it, bears testimony to one of the twentieth century's defining artists. The book also raises larger questions about the practice of filmmaking and the cultural factors that determine a film's reception.

## NOTES

1. Robin Wood, *Hitchcock's Films Revisited* (New York: Columbia University Press, 1989), 227.

2. Slavoj Zizek, ed., *Everything You Always Wanted to Know about Lacan (But Were Afraid to Ask Hitchcock)* (London: Verso, 1992), 5.

3. Donald Spoto, *The Dark Side of Genius: Life of Alfred Hitchcock* (Boston: Little, Brown, 1983), 508.

4. Alex Von Tazmann, "Do Hitchcock and *The Girl* Reveal the Horrible Truth about Hitch?" *The Guardian*, January 11, 2013.

5. Interview with Virginia Darcy, Santa Barbara, California, April 22, 2013.

6. Hitchcock to Peter Bogdanovich, February 13, 1963.

7. Interview with Howard Kazanjian, San Marin, California, April 12, 2013.

8. Interview with Norman Lloyd, Los Angeles, November 30, 2012.

9. Interview with Norman Lloyd, Los Angeles, November 30, 2012.

10. *Ottawa Citizen*, December 3, 1963, pg. 37.

11. Stephen Rebello, *Alfred Hitchcock and the Making of* Psycho (New York: St. Martin's Griffin, 1998).

12. Dan Aulier, Vertigo: *The Making of a Hitchcock Classic* (New York: St. Martin's, 1998).

*Chapter One*

# Genesis

I may be an instinctive feminist, but I think women on the whole have had a pretty rough deal.

—Winston Graham, author of *Marnie*

In the spring of 1961, the question on Alfred Hitchcock's mind posed by the world's media was how he would follow the success of *Psycho*. During its first year of release, *Psycho* had earned $15 million in domestic sales, and Hitchcock himself earned $7 million from the film. The challenge was to find a project that would match *Psycho* in its commercial appeal. Hitchcock's agent, Lew Wasserman, headed the MCA talent agency, and under his dynamic control it became one of the most powerful in Hollywood. Wasserman personified the power of the front office, the business end of filmmaking, and brandished the authority Hitchcock both respected and resented. The result was that both men endured a love-hate relationship, with Wasserman exercising a control over Hitchcock's career. The director often said when justifying his later projects, "Oh, well, I'm doing it for Wasserman."

When MCA bought Universal-International Studios in 1958 for $11.25 million, Wasserman's intention was to lure Hitchcock from Paramount Pictures to Universal by signing him to a lucrative five-picture deal. This involved relocating Hitchcock's main offices from the producers' building of Paramount at 5555 Melrose Avenue, Hollywood, to Universal Studios' main gate. A new bungalow complex housed Hitchcock's private office and outer offices for his secretary Suzanne Gauthier and assistant Peggy Robertson. There was also a hallway of production for the unit manager, the assistant director, and the art department; editing suites with a projection room; and a soundstage across the street. With such a prestigious power base, Hitchcock had ostensibly reached the pinnacle of his career.

## THE DIRECTOR

Alfred J. Hitchcock was born on August 13, 1899, in the London suburb of Leytonstone, the youngest of three children. His father, William Hitchcock, owned several grocery stores, both wholesale and retail. His mother, Emma, was a quietly dignified Victorian lady who instigated a strict education on her children but had a very warm and close relationship with them.[1] At eleven, Hitchcock was sent to Saint Ignatius College in London, a fee-paying school run by Jesuits. They taught him organization, control, and analysis and that guilt and fear were the driving forces of the human psyche. It was at the school that Hitchcock developed his self-discipline and orderly personal habits. "He is the tidiest man on God's earth," his wife would later remark. "I've never known him to leave a toothbrush or a tube of shaving cream out of place, or ever to walk out of a lavatory without making sure that the washbowl was immaculate."[2]

After his father died, Hitchcock, at fifteen, went on to study draftsmanship at the School of Engineering and Navigation, but dropped out when he became fascinated with the infant silent film industry. An individual life as a young adult was spent going alone to the theater and the cinema. In 1921, he met Alma Reville at the Famous Players-Lasky film studio in Islington, where she was working as a film editor on *Woman to Woman*. Hitchcock had been hired to design the film's title cards and asked her where the production office was. For the next two years he never spoke to Alma, but when the studio closed down, Hitchcock telephoned her one night and announced, "This is Alfred Hitchcock. I have been appointed assistant director for a new film. Would you work for me as a cutter?" He later confessed why he ignored Alma: "I'm very shy when it comes to women."[3]

When Hitchcock was sent to Germany for a collaboration at the progressive UFA film studios in Berlin, Alma came with him to assist. European visual style, particularly German expressionism, had a lasting impact on him. A central characteristic of the expressionistic style was an attempt to convey emotional states through the distortion of everyday objects and reality. By watching the directors Fritz Lang and F. W. Murnau at work, Hitchcock learned about the use of shadow, high- and low-angle shots, and off-camera framing, all of which he incorporated into his own cinematic grammar. During a pause in filming *The Princess and the Fiddler,* Hitchcock received a lecture from Murnau, who was filming *The Last Laugh* in the neighboring studio. How the décor looked on the set was of no importance, Murnau told him: "All that matters is what you see on the screen."[4] The bold expressionism of Fritz Lang's films such as *M* (1931), the story a psychotic child murderer who preys on small children in a German city also had a lasting impact. The studiously unreal and spatially distorted settings were enmeshed with a realistic emotional core. Peter Loire as the child murderer gives one of the most intelligent and extraordinary performances captured on film, in his portrayal of a diseased mind.

Hitchcock learned from the Russians that a film's meaning, its force and complexity, could be achieved by the juxtaposition of images, a technique known as montage. In a montage sequence, acting becomes a matter of stylized gestures and expressions, only becoming significant when applied to other images. The Russians believed that cinema was propaganda and that they could manipulate the audience through montage. It was this idea of manipulation that most appealed to Hitchcock, as he repeatedly spoke about the medium of pure cinema: "The assemblage of pieces of film to create fright is the essential part of my job."[5] He directed his first feature, *The Pleasure Garden,* in 1925, filmed on location in Germany and Italy. On the boat trip back to England, Hitchcock asked the sea-sickened Alma to become his wife. They were married in 1926 and had one daughter, Patricia. "He was a very kind and loving family man," says Patricia Hitchcock, "who taught me simplicity and honesty."

From 1925 to 1938, Hitchcock directed twenty-three feature films in England, which quickly earned him the title of the "Master of Suspense." The director elaborated on the meaning of suspense: "In many films there is a great confusion, especially in my particular genre of work, between the words mystery and suspense and the two things are absolutely miles apart. You see mystery is an intellectual process like in a 'who done it.' But suspense is essentially an emotional process. Therefore you can only get the suspense element going by giving the audience information."[6]

In 1938, Hitchcock signed a seven-year contract with the Hollywood producer David O. Selznick, who was in production for *Gone with the Wind* (1939). Hitchcock moved his family to California the following year and directed his first U.S. film, *Rebecca.* Whereas Selznick had respect for an original story when translating to film, Hitchcock often drew on particular themes or even, as in the case of *The Birds,* a single idea. He later described to the American Film Institute the type of story he was most interested in:

> I make many, many different kinds of pictures. I have no particular preference, to be quite honest: content I am not interested in at all. I don't give a damn what the film is about; I am more interested in how to handle the material to create an emotion in an audience. It would be like if one were painting a still life, I find, many people are interested in the content, but if you painted a still life of some apples on a plate, you'd be worrying whether the apples are sweet or sour. Who cares; I don't care myself. But a lot of films of course, live on content.[7]

During Hitchcock's most prolific period, from 1939 through 1960, he directed twenty-four feature films and fifteen television shows. Films such as *Notorious, Rope, Rear Window, The Man Who Knew Too Much, North by Northwest,* and *Psycho* firmly established Hitchcock as a popular entertainer and master of self-promotion. Although working within the confines of the thriller genre, Hitchcock demonstrated incredible range and versatility to create films that were uniquely personal to him, often using established stars within the studio system. However, Hitchcock's propensity to work within the suspense genre and established Hollywood conventions negated any estimation of him as a serious artist among the highbrow critics.

In 1961, while Hitchcock was contemplating future projects, Lew Wasserman and other Universal executives hoped that the director would return to the glossy thrillers of the 1950s that had become his trademark. Hitchcock was considering a film version of the Robert Thomas play *Piege pour un homme seul,* about a woman who returns from a mysterious disappearance to find her husband insisting she is not his wife. Another candidate was Paul Stanton's novel *Village of Stars,* set aboard a plane carrying an atomic bomb liable to detonate below a certain altitude. The story, focused on the pilot's attempt to get rid of the bomb after it had been loosened. Neither project was scripted to Hitchcock's satisfaction, and both were subsequently dropped. Also under consideration was an adaptation of Daphne du Maurier's short story "The Birds," as well as James Barrie's supernatural play *Mary Rose,* the latter being a project Hitchcock had long wanted to realize since seeing a stage version during his youth.

An agent named Shelly Wile, for the William Morris Agency in Beverly Hills, had been trying very assiduously for some time to find a property that might interest Hitchcock. She sent a prepublication copy of a novel called *Marnie* to his attention. The story was about a frigid kleptomaniac, Marnie Elmer, who is blackmailed into marriage by Mark Rutland, the wealthy man she robs. It possessed many of the ingredients that appealed to Hitchcock at a time when the sexual permissiveness of the 1960s was coming to the fore.

## THE AUTHOR

*Marnie* was written by the English novelist Winston Graham, who is best known for his *Poldark* series of twelve books, which were later televised by the British Broadcasting Corporation. Graham was born in Lancashire in 1908, and his storytelling prowess developed at school, where he read aloud or invented stories to a coterie of boys. When Graham was fourteen, his father had a stroke and the family moved to Perranporth, Cornwall. After his father died, Graham only wanted to write novels, so his mother offered to support him in his nascent career. He later married and had two children, continuing to write in Perranporth, where he lived for thirty years. Cornwall formed the inspiration for many of his stories, which were novels of suspense rather than thrillers, six of which were translated into feature films.

Graham conceived the character of Marnie from a combination of two women he knew in Cornwall. The first was a tall, good-looking young lady named Christine who took care of their youngest child when Graham and his wife were in London. "She seemed alright except that she was constantly taking baths, about three a day usually," Graham remembers, "and she was in constant communication with her mother. On one occasion, she left the letters lying about, and I found a letter from her mother warning her about the evils of men and that she must never consider having any connection with them at all. Why that was so, I never knew. She sublimated her interests in horses and spent all her spare time riding."[8]

The second woman was a young mother of three children who came down to Cornwall with other evacuees during the war. Her husband was at sea, and she decided that doing her part for the country was offering herself to any soldier that happened to take a fancy to her. Graham observes:

> She looked the absolute epitome of perfect behavior. She used to walk along the road with her legs curiously together all the time, and nothing could suggest that she would ever part them. Apparently, if the soldier wanted and knew about her, he'd come to the window and tap. She had her youngest child with her in bed, and she'd take the child out and put him in a cold bedroom next door. Then she'd open the window and let the soldier in.

An unwanted pregnancy resulted from the woman's behavior. As her husband was away at sea, she decided that under no circumstances could she ever admit to having a baby. A female neighbor came to assist during labor, but after she left, the mother strangled her newborn infant, wrapped it in newspaper, and hid it under the bed. Unfortunately for her, she began to have hemorrhages, and the neighbor had to call the doctor. Later, the woman was brought up for trial but was acquitted for temporary insanity. Graham used this ugly incident as the basis for the trauma that afflicts Marnie in later life, causing her to be terrified of sexual intercourse and the notion of childbearing.

The incident had further repercussions. After the war, the youngest child began to steal, and it seemed curious to Graham whether it was a consequence of the mother's deprivation. He derived the idea for Marnie stealing from this real-life event, together with an article he had read in the *Sunday Express* newspaper about a girl who kept stealing from her employers and reappeared in various guises: "She took jobs in restaurants or theaters and absconded with about £500 each time."

Graham chose to write *Marnie* in the first person, having experimented with two books written in such a style before. In doing so, he found that the first person was almost anonymous, in the sense that the character never seemed to reveal anything particular about him- or herself to the reader. It occurred to Graham what a great idea it would be if Marnie had a quirk, but she didn't reveal to the reader what that quirk was. Through her behavior it would become obvious to the reader that she was slightly odd. In Marnie's case her unusual behavior was her frigidity and stealing, which had its genesis from her upbringing.

"I don't think I necessarily approved of what Marnie did, but every author worth his name must have some feeling of sympathy for the person he is writing about, particularly when writing in the first person," claims Graham. "I may be an instinctive feminist, but I think women on the whole have had a pretty rough deal. I like women, I like their company apart from anything else; I like to take them out to dinner. I've had a lucky relationship with women; they've always been charming, intelligent, and nice. If a feminist slant was in the book, it was instinctive rather than purposeful."

When Graham had written about a hundred pages, he wrote a sentence: "Mark bent over me and kissed me." The identification seemed awkward to the male author, so Graham dropped the first-person narrative and started writing the novel again. Instead of writing "I came down the stairs, the policeman saying goodnight," Graham wrote, "She came down the stairs," but in doing so he found that he lost some kind of internal immediacy that only the first person can convey. So Graham resumed the first-person narrative, but most of his identification with Marnie was instinctive. Graham's insight into women later encouraged one New York female critic to proclaim that *Marnie* was the best book about a woman written by a man.

Another result of writing in the first person was that the reader exclusively saw the character of Mark Rutland through Marnie's eyes. In Graham's book, Mark was a perfectly straightforward stationer who had lost his previous wife and was immediately attracted by the charming young woman who came to work for him. Inevitably, a situation of class dissension arises between Mark and Marnie, at work and during their marriage. "I don't think I meant in any way to write about class; it was just a factor that was inherent in the story," says Graham. "I was fascinated in the relationship between a man and a woman, and with their particular inhibitions, and with her being trapped. She only agreed to marry him to prevent going to prison; therefore, the whole fusion of sexual relationships was quite different."

The absorption of psychoanalysis into literature, film, and theater has been popular ever since Sigmund Freud's theories emerged in the early twentieth century, and *Marnie* developed into a prime example of both a novelized case history and a mystery story. Graham himself had never been in psychiatry, so in preparation he read standard books on psychology such as *Deep Analysis*. He also consulted a Home Office pathologist friend on the habits of women thieves. The water imagery prevalent in the novel, which in Freudian terms is equated with sex, arose partly from Graham's own psychiatric studies and from the girl Christine, who was constantly taking baths. One of the states that exist within disturbed patients is to literally wash away their sins. The water concept also gave rise to the thunderstorms and Marnie's fear of them.

With the psychology and neuroses of Marnie firmly imbibed, Graham wrote the book over a relatively short period of fourteen months. All of his novels were handwritten in journals that the author then had transcribed. Like many writers, Graham impregnated the story with incidences from his own life, such as the death of his own mother. Graham's seven-year-old son Andrew was at the table coloring a picture book, and on hearing the news, he lay his head down on the book and started crying. The sudden sorrow and grief that comes from losing a loved one was used to write one of the novel's most poignant passages. Marnie remembers learning of her father's death, during one of her therapy sessions with the psychiatrist:

> When he died I had a picture book with an elephant on it and I didn't say anything but just put my head down on the book and let the three tears run onto the elephant. It was a cheap book because there was a sun behind the elephant and my tears made the color run until it looked as if I'd been crying blood. . . . Tears were running down my face and I grabbed my bag and took out a handkerchief. . . . This was the second time now I'd cried at these sessions—really, I mean, not for effect. I felt such a fool crying there because I'd remembered something I'd forgotten and because I felt again the twist of the grief inside me, remembering that day and how I knew I'd never have complete protection or shelter or love again.[9]

*Marnie* was published in the United States at the beginning of 1961. On January 8, the *New York Times* reviewed the book: "It is a tale of crime and pursuit, and retribution, but by no means a simple one. With what seems (at least to a male reviewer) a phenomenally successful use of a woman's view point, and a rare and happy balance of psychoanalytic and novelistic method. . . . It's a novel as rewarding as it is suspensefully readable." *The Hollywood Diary* on August 15 added, "This is one of the best suspense stories of this or any other year and if you are a devotee of the suspense story, this is an absolute must."

After *Marnie* was written, Graham took his family to the south of France, where they lived for twelve months. Graham had two agents in England who worked in close cooperation, Christopher Mann Ltd., who dealt with his film work, and A. M. Heath, who handled the literary side. In the States, the Mann office was represented by the William Morris Agency and Heath by Brandt and Brandt. When Graham returned to England, he heard from his agents that a director from Hollywood was interested in buying the film rights for his novel. On January 11, 1961, Ned Brown of the MCA talent agency made an offer by telephone "on behalf of an unnamed client for the motion picture and usual allied rights to the novel *Marnie*," to Graham's agent, Sylvia Hirsch of the William Morris Agency. A sum of $25,000 was offered. The fact that the client was anonymous led Graham and his agent to believe that one of Hollywood's leading ladies was interested in playing Marnie. Hirsch urged Graham to double the asking price to $50,000. A subsequent offer of that amount was then made with the client's authorization on January 15, providing that the full agreement was signed within three weeks.

Graham also requested that his credit on the film should be no less than the size type that the screenwriter would receive and that he gain credit in all paid advertising. He was advised by MCA that they could not agree to the credit request, but the client would make the final decision. Graham, of course, was delighted when he heard six weeks later that it was Alfred Hitchcock, the famed Master of Suspense, who was planning to make a motion picture from his novel. Graham wrote to the director on April 4, 1961: "I thought I would drop you a brief note to say how very delighted I am that you have bought my novel *Marnie.* I have been an admirer of your work for so very long, and I think I have seen every film you have made since *The Man Who Knew Too Much.* . . . I thought your last film *Psycho* was one of the most brilliant."

In 1947, when Graham's book *Take My Life* was being made into his first film translation, he went with the director and producer to the Old Bailey courthouse to absorb the atmosphere of a court scene. Graham just missed meeting Hitchcock, who had been there the previous day, on a similar mission for *The Paradine Case.* A number of Graham's novels, especially his earlier works, had a Hitchcockian flavor to them—namely, the explosion of the unusual on the commonplace. One such example occurs in the novel *Greek Fire,* when a wanted man takes refuge at a newspaper factory. A crowd of people arrive to view the printing press, and out comes a large picture of the man exclaiming that he is wanted for murder. Such a scenario may have been inspired by Hitchcock, but Graham, when writing *Marnie,* never thought the story was one that may have interested the director.

*Marnie* was published in the United Kingdom by Hodder and Stoughton in March 1961. Hitchcock, when acquiring the film rights, was intent to brand the book as a forthcoming Alfred J. Hitchcock Production. At his request, Ned Brown wrote to Doubleday suggesting an advertising campaign that would market the book as being firmly associated with Hitchcock. The idea was met with some resistance at first, as Doubleday felt that the life cycle of most novels was about three months in their original editions, and present sales on *Marnie* indicated that they would be no exception. The publishers expected to sell about ten thousand copies, and John Sargeant, the new chairman of the company, didn't think any additional advertising expenditure was justified, especially as the novel had been chosen as a *Reader's Digest* condensed book club selection, which in itself distributed 1.3 million copies.

When Hitchcock expressed his disappointment with Doubleday's lack of cooperation, Graham intervened by writing a firm letter to the company. After all, Doubleday would stand to keep one half of the receipts from the American *Reader's Digest* edition, which so far totaled $60,000, and would benefit from the sales of large foreign editions to be published separately in Canada, England, France, Germany, Italy, Sweden, Spain, Portugal, Holland, and Japan. Doubleday relented and initially offered $2,000. This sum was raised when Hitchcock proposed that $5,000 be jointly offered for the advertising campaign.

A portrait of Hitchcock's famous profile was used in the advertising campaign and on the book jacket. In July and August 1961, the campaign was targeted at many reputable book cities and newspapers. Large display ads appeared in major newspapers and book review media such as the *New York Times Book Review,* the *Herald Tribune,* the *New Yorker* and the *Los Angeles Times.* The English publishers Hodder and Stoughton took out similar ads for *Marnie* in the *Sunday Times* and the *Sunday Telegraph,* specifically mentioning that Hitchcock had chosen the book to make a film.

On July 10, 1961, a full-page ad in *Publisher's Weekly* posed the question "Why is Marnie the perfect Hitchcock heroine?" The section went on to describe Marnie as

> quietly attractive and efficiently dishonest. When "at work" (as Margaret Elmer, Mary Holland, or Mollie Jeffrey), her dresses are deliberately dowdy, so that few people notice her—especially men. Marnie is an accomplished liar, forger and embezzler. She is, in short, a highly successful professional thief who had made a career of changing identities and avoiding personal entanglements. One day Marnie gets caught, and is given a choice between prison and marriage to the man who finds her out. Her decision is based on a carefully planned exit—but is complicated by a climactic twist of events that makes her story one of the most compelling you will ever read. Marnie is the heroine of a brilliant suspense novel by Winston Graham, whose earlier books have delighted millions of readers. Alfred Hitchcock has just purchased the motion picture rights

to *Marnie* and will produce the film for release in 1962. Mr. Hitchcock is indeed enamoured of his new fictional friend and says: "Don't wait for the movie. It's going to be good, but the book is about one of the most unusual heroines I've ever encountered."

## THE PRINCESS

Aside from the character-driven plot, Hitchcock, when buying the story rights, had another reason for wanting to adapt Winston Graham's bestseller: he thought *Marnie* was a suitable vehicle to entice Grace Kelly back to film-making. Kelly had been Her Serene Highness, Princess Grace of Monaco, for six years and had already borne the principality two heirs to the throne. She had long expressed her interest in resuming her acting career, and who better to mastermind a comeback than Alfred Hitchcock, the director responsible for eliciting luminous performances from her in *Rear Window* and *To Catch a Thief?*

In 1961, Jay Kanter, an MCA agent, intimated to Hitchcock that Kelly was interested in returning to films under his aegis. "What happened is that he sent me the treatment," remembers Jay Kanter, who was Grace Kelly's agent while she was at MGM. "Hitch said to me, 'Do you think Grace will do it?' And I said, well let's ask. Grace was intrigued by the story and was interested in returning to the movies."[10]

Hitchcock's response to the *Boston Sunday Globe* was typically nonchalant: "I didn't hear a word from her at the time. In fact I have not communicated with her by letter or phone regarding the deal. But three weeks ago I was told that she wanted to play the role and please let the announcement come from the palace at Monaco instead of from my office."[11]

Emile Cornet, a palace spokesman, made the announcement to the world on March 19, 1962. There had been numerous reports during the marriage that the princess would resume her acting career. At one time Prince Rainier issued a formal denial stating that his wife was finished with filmmaking. As Rainier's wife, Grace had become one of the most titled women in the world. In addition to being the Princess of Monaco, she was the Princess de Chateau-Porcien, twice a duchess, nine times a countess, three times a marquise, and six times a baroness. Cornet concluded, "We are certain she won't make another film after this one."

That same day, Hitchcock's office issued the following press release: "A spokesman for the Prince of Monaco announced today that Princess Grace has accepted to appear in a motion picture for Mr. Alfred Hitchcock to be made in the United States this summer." London journalist Peter Evans of the *Daily Express* later interviewed Hitchcock in his limousine, en route to

Bodega Bay, where he was filming *The Birds.* "I never went after Grace you know," Hitchcock confided.

> I saw her and the prince several times over dinner in Paris. I am too much of a gentleman to mention work to a princess. That would be most uncouth. But I waited and finally she came to me. It happened this way. I brought this novel called *Marnie* and simply could not find an actress suitable for the part. So I sent it to her agents in New York—she always kept her agents, you know—and they passed it on to her. Then a week ago I was told that she would do it, just like that. I have not even spoken to her about it, not even a wire. I suppose I should send a wire, congratulations or something.[12]

"People, you know, have quite the wrong idea about Grace," the director continued. "They think she is a cold fish. Remote, like Alcatraz out there. But she has sex appeal, believe me. She has the subtle sex appeal of the English woman and this is the finest in the world. It is ice that will burn your hands, and that is always surprising and exciting too." When asked whether the princess would have any love scenes in *Marnie,* Hitchcock replied, "Passionate and most unusual love scenes, but I am afraid I cannot tell you anything beyond that. It is a state secret."

"Congratulations!" wrote Leonard Kaufman of the Lewin/Kaufman/Schwartz Agency in Beverly Hills. "I always said for years that this business needs more sex!" The news that Grace Kelly was returning to the cinema initiated tremendous excitement. Winston Graham remembers getting off a plane and reporters running toward him, asking whether the princess was going to be starring in the film version of his novel. There were journalists ringing his home in East Sussex from all over the world and knocking at the door for almost a week. Princess Grace's decision to return to filmmaking pleased Graham's literary agents. A large demand for the serial rights of *Marnie* from newspapers and magazines in London and abroad followed the announcement from Monaco. The novel had already been serialized in *Home* before publication. Only a star as big as Princess Grace could cause two serializations, remarked a spokesman for Graham's agents.

The announcement also started a studio contract row. Metro Goldwyn Mayor claimed that their contract with Kelly was merely suspended and not canceled when she left Hollywood in 1956; therefore, she could only make films for them. On March 23, Joseph R. Vogel, an MGM representative, sent a letter to Hitchcock pointing out that since Kelly's contract had not lapsed with the studio, they should have participation in the film. Previously, MGM had loaned Kelly to Hitchcock and Paramount Pictures for the films she had made with them before her retirement. Hitchcock's reply was that because the contract was made in 1953, by law it could only last seven years.

Kelly's salary for *Marnie* was another favorite angle for discussion. The princess would reportedly earn $1 million plus a percentage of the film's profits. According to Hollywood film circles, finance was the true reason that the Rainiers decided to participate. Prince Rainier dismissed the suggestion that Grace was making the film to help Monaco as "ridiculous nonsense." The simple fact was that Hitchcock agreed to schedule the filming with the Rainier's annual vacation to the United States: "My wife wanted to see her family, so we decided to spend a month in America with the children." He added that Princess Grace turned down Hitchcock's first offer to make *Marnie* but eventually agreed when the director changed the film schedule to coincide with her vacation plans.

On March 20, the *San Francisco Evening Standard* reported that Kelly would not be paid a definite salary but would receive a percentage of the finished film. Hitchcock stated that he did not know whether Grace had decided to return to Hollywood because of a shortage of money: "Personally, I don't think so, although many people will jump to this conclusion. How can she be accused of this when her own family fortune is supposed to be so large. I think the trouble is that too many people, including the English, love stories about failures."

The princess, possibly piqued by press criticism for her return to filmmaking, announced in a palace statement that she would use the money to establish a charitable fund. On March 23, her following words appeared in *The Times:* "In the same way as some priests or nuns perform common artistic, musical, or sporting tasks, for example, with the aim of raising funds for their work, I feel I am able to return to the cinema for a film with the charitable aim of aiding needy children and young sportsmen."

Everything seemed to be falling into place. Grace Kelly was genuinely tempted, and Prince Rainier, who was very fond of Hitchcock, favored the project. Then amid all the anticipation, on April 23, 1962, Hitchcock announced that filming of *Marnie* was postponed from August 1 of that year to the following spring or summer. He cited the reason for the delay as being the short time elapsing between the completion of his current film *The Birds* and the starting date of *Marnie*. It was hoped that the film would be shot during Princess Grace's annual vacation from the palace next year. Shortly afterward, on June 7, 1962, another statement was issued from the palace in Monaco announcing that the princess was withdrawing from negotiations to star in the film.

In an interview published by the newspaper *Nice Matin,* Grace said she had dropped plans to appear in *Marnie* because of the schedule difficulties. When asked whether she might appear in other films, the princess replied, "I don't like to say definitely, but it's obvious that the same problems as

*Marnie* would arise." She had planned to make *Marnie* while vacationing in the United States with her family, later in the year. Then Hitchcock found he could not begin the film until next year. "I could only have done it if my husband and the children had come with me. This was impossible. Going on with the plan created too many problems so I called Mr. Hitchcock and said I could not do it."

*Psycho* screenwriter Joseph Stefano, whom Hitchcock had contracted to start writing a treatment from the novel, remembers being called into the director's office: "He informed me that Miss Kelly has changed her mind. I think Hitch was more hurt than angry. He had invested his very special passion in something over several weeks. He was abruptly informed that she wasn't going to be involved, and his comment was, 'They probably got the money from somewhere else.'"[13]

What's evident from Stefano's testimony is that Hitchcock at the time believed that Kelly withdrew because Monaco's financial obligations were fulfilled through other means, rather than her acquiescing to the citizens of Monaco who had objected to the princess playing a thief on the screen. "I never heard that theory, and I doubt that Hitchcock ever did," Stefano stated. "He was just informed that she wasn't going to do it. He seemed to be under the impression that she was making the movie because Monaco needed the money, and all of a sudden they didn't need it and she wasn't going to make the movie. He was very disappointed and very angry." However, Hitchcock later publicly remarked, "I thought I had Grace for my new film, *Marnie,* the story of a girl who's a compulsive thief, and Grace wanted very much to play it, but the conservative element in Monaco—they didn't want their princess working in Hollywood, so Grace bowed out."[14] Hitchcock later said to Truffaut, "It was sad that Kelly couldn't do it. But her timing was very bad because of Rainier you know. He's in trouble huh. Yes with France, he's in a great deal of trouble."[15]

Stefano tried to persuade Hitchcock from shelving the project by suggesting that he could name five actresses who would be sensational in the title role: "I thought of Eva Marie Saint. I thought that she would have been even deeper than Kelly. But Hitchcock said, 'I'm not interested. Let's put this on the shelf and find something else.' I was disappointed because I thought it would be a very good movie."

The real reasons for Kelly's withdrawal, which Hitchcock later came to accept, can be found within the *Marnie* files of the Hitchcock Collection. An October 8, 1962, research memo, instigated by Hitchcock, reads, "Expiration date of treaty of friendship between France and Monaco. On April 11th, France renounced the 'Good Neighbor' Administration and Mutual Assistance Convention of December 23rd 1951, between the two countries.

This will affect taxation, customs, postal services, telecommunications and banking which could cease to exist in six months, as of October 11th 1962."

The French government was putting pressure on Prince Rainier over the prospect of heavier taxes on Monaco, and he didn't want to leave the country until the matter was settled. President Charles de Gaulle was irritated over Monaco's free and easy tax system, which included no income or corporation taxes. This subsequently lured many foreign firms and individuals, including Frenchmen, to the prince's sovereign soil. To make Monaco fall in line with the French tax system, de Gaulle ordered the withdrawal of the 1951 convention governing French-Monacan relations under an older treaty. Monaco had six months to negotiate a new one and otherwise faced economic loss of its French-controlled water supply and electrical and telephone services. To maintain these crucial links with France, the prince was forced to compromise and to make concessions that altered the privileged status of his principality. In the process, Grace Kelly had no choice but to abandon the cinema definitely.

## THE MODEL

Replacing Grace Kelly, the perfect incarnation of the Hitchcock blonde, appeared quite insuperable for the director to accomplish. Kelly possessed the exact combination of wit, poise, and sensual elegance the director sought in his heroines. Yet it was a feat Hitchcock hoped to win ever since Kelly left for Monaco in 1956. He first attempted with the actress Vera Miles, whom he spotted in a television show. Even at this time, Hitchcock was well aware of the difficulties of inventing new stars for the Hollywood film industry. Television had become the primary entertainment medium for the nation, and with a fall in demand and rising production costs, new talent could no longer be given the repeated exposure as when the studios were making fifty to sixty films a year. Hitchcock wanted to groom the wardrobe and appearance carefully for his new protégé, so he posed an embargo on further publicity shots of Miles. He planned to promote her in pictures of quality, such as his documentary style drama *The Wrong Man,* in which Miles was cast in a supporting role as Henry Fonda's wife, who suffers a nervous breakdown as a result of her husband being wrongfully accused. The director was ready to star Miles opposite James Stewart in *Vertigo,* as the mysterious blonde Madeline who epitomizes the Hitchcock woman of mystery and glamour. However, his plans were thwarted when Miles became pregnant. Although he gave her an undeveloped role as the second female lead in *Psycho*, Hitchcock couldn't resume the momentum with Miles again, and forever after he would exclaim the audacity of Miles becoming pregnant during preproduction of a Hitchcock film.

A number of actresses were very interested in attaining the coveted lead role. On March 1, 1961, George Weltner of Paramount Pictures in New York wrote to Hitchcock congratulating him on his Oscar nomination for *Psycho.* In the same letter, he suggested Lee Remick, "who seemed to have the sex appeal, the appearance of an early tough life hidden by her later maturity that seemed exactly the appearance that Marnie should have." Susan Hampshire handwrote a letter to Hitchcock on October 2, 1962, expressing interest in the part, and a letter from Walt Disney endorsed her shortly after. Agent Leonard Hirshan also contacted the director stating that Eva Marie Saint was interested in playing Marnie. But Hitchcock eschewed these suggestions, as if waiting for something portentous to happen.

The event occurred in early October 1961, while Hitchcock was watching NBC Television's *Today* show. A commercial for the diet drink Sego was airing every morning that week and featured a slim, elegant blonde who turns her head amiably in response to a little boy's whistle. Hitchcock waited to see a repeat of the commercial the following day before telephoning his agent Herman Citron to ask him to find out who the woman was. Her name was Tippi Hedren, a Minnesota-born thirty-one-year-old of Swedish descent. When she was a sophomore at Minneapolis West High, her family had moved to California because of her father's health. Hedren had completed her secondary education at Huntington Park before enrolling at Pasadena City College as an art major. After schooling, the cool, green-eyed, 5' 4" Hedren went to New York to begin professional modeling by joining the Eileen Ford agency.

During the time Hedren was modeling, she received several film offers, but they couldn't produce the same amount of money as modeling, which usually amounted to $60 an hour. She knew that the road to becoming an actress was a very difficult one and very difficult to succeed. Furthermore, modeling offered the prospects of travel, and Hedren's face appeared on the covers of *Life, Saturday Evening Post, McCall's, Glamour,* and other magazines. After seven years of marriage to the actor Peter Griffith, Hedren divorced and returned to California where her parents lived, because her daughter (the future actress Melanie Griffith) was at an age when she needed the kind of independence to go out and play. In New York City it wasn't possible to do that without a nanny.

Hedren rented a three-bedroom house in Sherman Oaks for $500 a month, hoping to continue the successful modeling career that she had enjoyed in New York. It didn't really happen for her, but Hedren possessed a great deal of self-confidence, so adapted her modeling to include commercials. On Friday the 13th of October 1961, Hedren began her own Hitchcockian adventure when she received a phone call from an agent asking, "Are you the girl in that commercial?" She said she was. "There's a producer who's interested in seeing you" was the reply. Hedren went along with her photographs and commercial reels to Universal Studios. On arrival she asked, "Who is this producer?" The man who met her smiled and didn't say anything. Later on in the car, Hedren asked again, but again the man smiled and didn't reply. He asked whether she would leave the photographs and film. Hedren said she would, but she needed them back, as they were an essential tool for her work.

The following Monday, Hedren returned to Universal, and all day long she was introduced to increasingly higher-ranked executives. To Hedren's vexation, nobody would tell her who the producer was. On Tuesday morning, she went to the MCA talent agency and met Herman Citron. He said, "Alfred Hitchcock wants to sign you to a contract." Hedren protested, "But he hasn't even seen me yet." Citron replied, "Yes, he has; he's seen your film and the commercials, and your photographs." Hitchcock later remarked, "I was that sure she had what it takes. I didn't even bother to interview her." Citron then discussed the money right there, which was a starting salary of $500 a week, guaranteed for a period of seven years, which was very appealing to Hedren, compared to the fluctuating work of modeling.

Citron took Hedren over to meet Hitchcock. They chatted about food and travel, and Hedren, who had traveled around the world as part of her modeling work, felt at ease and could contribute toward the conversation. Hitchcock was charming and polite but gave no clue about his plans for his new protégé. He thought he may have found a new star in Tippi Hedren and his quest was all part of the difficulty of finding new stars in the 1960s, as the decade before, television had taken over from the film industry as the dominant form. "It is no longer possible," Hitchcock says, "to build up stars. It takes about three years to create a star, and this depends on there being a regular succession of films for the new personality to appear in. Years ago a film company could tell its customers: 'We have two Garbos, three Barrymores, three Clark Gables, and a Ginger Rogers, and that could create a little boom, a promise of continuity. Now, with so little production going on, we must turn to other values and prescriptions."

At the beginning of the 1960s, the studios were suffering from the aftereffects of television. But the studios were making fewer films, and it was no longer possible to build up stars and submit them to the same kind of exposure. In Universal City, more than half of the thirty-two soundstages were devoted to television, and the studios were geared to a big program of expansion and modernization, while making successions of television Westerns and serials. Eight feature films were promised for 1964, with box office stars such as Cary Grant, Marlon Brando, and Deborah Kerr.[16] In the early 1950s,

Hitchcock was able to build up Grace Kelly, introducing her in *Dial M for Murder*, then *Rear Window*, and finally allowing her to fully blossom in *To Catch a Thief*. Hitchcock saw similarities in Kelly and Hedren. Hedren too was of Swedish and German descent. Hitchcock hoped that she, like Kelly, would have fire under the ice, as he liked women who were very ladylike on the surface, but had a sensuality beneath.

Hedren assumed that the director needed models like herself for his television work, but after she had been under contract for a month, she was asked to do an extensive screen test, which lasted three days and had a full Technicolor crew. Edith Head designed a beautiful wardrobe, and Martin Balsam was flown out from New York to be her leading man. "We filmed the test in Technicolor, in fully dressed sets on a sound stage and with a regulation crew," said Hitchcock. Hedren, who had a good basis of acting by working in commercials, had no qualms about being before lights and cameras. She not only learned dialogue quickly and played her prepared scenes well, but she kept her composure when Balsam deliberately threw ad-lib remarks at her while the camera rolled.

Hedren reenacted scenes from *To Catch a Thief*, *Notorious*, and *Rebecca*. Hitchcock later said to Truffaut:

> I did a test of Hedren as the girl in *Rebecca* . . . it was quite good. But I had to tear it up because, if Selznick had known I had used material from *Rebecca* to test, he would have sued. Because there's a copyright involved. . . . And I had Hedren do a scene from *Notorious* and she did that very well, but I didn't even photograph that. It was too risky. With the *Rebecca* test of Hedren, I took all her makeup off—completely and it was quite interesting.[17]

Later Hitchcock said:

> I was not primarily concerned with how she looked in person. Most important was her appearance on the screen, and I liked that immediately. She has a touch of that high-style, lady-like quality which was once well-represented in films by actresses like Irene Dunne, Grace Kelly, Claudette Colbert, and others but which is now quite rare. . . . I think the thing that struck me was the close-up in the commercial where she responded to the little boy's whistle. The toss of the head. The walk along the street impressed me as being . . . belonging to a person who had some positive quality. In, of course, my early talks with her and the early rehearsals, I told her that my idea of a good actor or good actress is someone who can do nothing very well. She naturally . . . that would bring out the question from her, "What do you mean by that?" You notice during the test she makes a reference to authority. I said, "That's one of the things you've got to learn to have . . . authority." Out of authority comes control and out of control you get the range. . . . Whether you do little acting, a lot of acting in a given

scene. You know exactly where you're going. And these were the first things that she had to know. Emotion comes later and the control of the voice comes later. But, within herself, she had to learn authority first and foremost because out of authority comes timing. You notice, if a man is a speaker—if you hear him racing his words he obviously is not paying any attention to the holding of his listeners and these were the earliest things she had to learn. The one thing she had not learned—and this was because she hadn't learned to exercise her emotions—was the sustaining of a mood. This was one of the things she hadn't got. And that's the thing I had to teach her as much as anything. That, if there was an emotional moment, she'd give it, but after fifteen seconds, it would die away and she would be gone. There's a lot to do with her still.[18]

Hitchcock surprised everyone around him, including Hedren, by offering her the lead role in his next motion picture, *The Birds*. (How Hedren fared is documented in the author's book, *The Making of Hitchcock's* The Birds.) For Hitchcock, the challenge was teaching a novice how to act, in addition to the numerous technical difficulties associated with making such a film. Hedren herself acknowledged:

To put a totally unknown into a major motion picture was fairly crazy. That's taking a very, very big chance, and all the executives at Universal, people close to him were saying, "Hitch what are you thinking? Every actress in Hollywood would want to do this movie." Oh, granted, I did years and years of commercial work; this gives you good stability in front of the camera—I wasn't camera shy. I didn't have to learn any of those things. But becoming a character is quite different to working with a product. Although the commercial that he saw was a story line.

Referring to the diet drink commercial that first brought Hedren to Hitch-cock's attention, the actress remembers, "Hitchcock said there was a particular reaction that I had when the little boy whistled at me and that's what got his attention. There may be more to this woman than in the commercial. . . . I was never told exactly why. I think he becomes obsessed with certain people."[19] When asked in an interview about his predilection for cool blondes, Hitchcock explained:

I'm only obsessed because I don't believe in stamping the woman with the word sex all over her, I think it should be discovered during the course of getting acquainted with her. And it's more interesting for this thing not to be apparent. In other words we don't have to have the sex hanging around her neck like baubles all over her. If you take the English woman, or the North German or the Swedish woman, sometimes they look like school marms but boy when they get going they are quite astonishing in their, shall we say perspicacity, in the sex. I believe its something to do with the climate. I believe the further south you go in Europe, the more obvious the sex is.[20]

Hitchcock was impressed enough to offer Hedren the demanding part of Marnie after Grace Kelly withdrew from the film. "When Hitch told me that I was playing the part, we were filming *The Birds*," Hedren remembers.

> I was stunned. I was amazed that he would offer me this incredible role and that he would have that kind of faith in me. Hitch wanted to film *Marnie* because there were so many interesting points about her that she was trying to hide. He liked to take women of strength who are pretty much together and put them in a situation and jumble them around and see how they come out. That was his method with almost every movie. I think it was the woman herself which attracted Hitch. I think it was Marnie, the fact that she was such a complicated character. And that was what Hitch loved, he loved contrast.

Hedren felt that she was extremely fortunate to be offered to play the range of scenes in *Marnie.* "I consider my acting, while not necessarily being method acting, but one that draws upon my own feelings. I thought Marnie was an extremely interesting role to play and a once-in-a-lifetime opportunity."

"I haven't publicized it, but I'm going to put this girl in the lead," confided Hitchcock to Truffaut in August 1962. "Because I feel that once you've started a girl you must make sure by not letting her go out to some other company. So I must complete my job as Svengali."[21]

## CONCLUSION

The genesis of *Marnie* suggests from the outset a very strong empathy with the woman's position, arising from the personal impulses of the principal artists. The character of Marnie was formulated by real-life incidences of the abjection of women within society. They are rendered sympathetic by the feminist sensibilities of Winston Graham, who throughout his life had enjoyed a balanced and healthy relationship with women. As a novelist, his focus was on human patterns of behavior and the mechanisms of gender construction and expectations. His attention to the psychological repression of women in the work and home environments proved to be a major source in the narrative's critique of social inequality.

Hitchcock's concept of femininity is tied to his own mother, the late Victorian milieu in which he grew up, a Jesuit education, his own relationship with female actresses (Carroll, Bergman, Kelly), and a deep-rooted need to manufacture, project, and control. *Marnie*'s story line firmly embodies his preoccupation with sexual relationships and patriarchal attempts (Strutt, Rutland) to control women. The latter impulse can then account for his relationship with Tippi Hedren, who as a professional model provided Hitchcock with inherent and malleable qualities, which he could cultivate into his concept of the feminine ideal. Hitchcock's own identification with women is dichotomous: his sympathy with the suffering heroine in his films is in opposition to his own patriarchal drives of trying to create a certain type of fantasy from his female stars.

Graham shared a number of affinities with Hitchcock, such as a specialization in suspense stories, a preference for female company, and a bourgeois, genteel lifestyle. Both lost their fathers when they were young men, and mothers played a prominent role in their lives. In Graham's case, his mother subsidized him in his early career as a novelist, while the centrality of the mother figure can be traced throughout Hitchcock's films, culminating in *Marnie.* The loss of his own mother led Graham to write one of the most poignantly moving passages in the book, when a young Marnie learns of her father's death at sea. The genesis of *Marnie* therefore is very much connected with loss: loss of the father figure, loss of an idealized actress, and the loss of maternal love coupled with childhood innocence.

## NOTES

1. Telephone interview with Patricia Hitchcock, Santa Barbara, California, July 11, 2000. A description of Hitchcock's life arises from this interview and the director's biography from the Alfred Hitchcock Collection, Margaret Herrick Library.

2. Mrs. Alfred Hitchcock as told to Martin Abramson, "My Husband Alfred Hitchcock Hates Suspense," *Coronet,* August 1964: 12–17.

3. Hitchcock and Abramson, "My Husband," 15.

4. John Russell Taylor, *Hitch: The Life and Work of Alfred Hitchcock* (New York: Panthean Books, 1978), 58.

5. Alfred Hitchcock, American Film Institute seminar, 1972.

6. Hitchcock, American Film Institute seminar, 1972.

7. Hitchcock, American Film Institute seminar, 1972.

8. Personal interview with Winston Graham at his home in Buxted, England, October 28, 2000. Unless stated, all other quotes originate from this interview.

9. Winston Graham, *Marnie* (London: Chapman's, 1961). Reproduced with the author's kind permission.

10. Interview with Jay Kanter, Los Angeles, September 24, 2012.

11. Marjory Adams, "Hitchcock Calls Grace Last of Great Ladies of the Screen," *Boston Sunday Globe,* March 25, 1962, 44N.

12. Peter Evans, "Grace Kelly: Ice That Burns Your Hands," *Daily Express,* March 21, 1962.

13. Personal interview with Joseph Stefano in New York, October 16, 1999, and Los Angeles, November 5, 2000. Unless stated, all other quotes originate from these interviews.

14. "Tippi Hedren: Can Hollywood Still Make a Star?" *Parade,* December 8, 1963.

15. Unpublished portion of interview with Hitchcock and François Truffaut, August 1962.

16. *Times*, November 26, 1963.

17. Unpublished portion of the Hitchcock-Truffaut 1962 interview, Alfred Hitchcock Collection, Margaret Herrick Library, 250.

18. Unpublished Hitchcock-Truffaut 1962 interview, 126.

19. Personal interview with Tippi Hedren at Shambhala animal preserve, Acton, California, June 19, 1999. Unless stated, all other quotes originate from this interview.

20. Unpublished Hitchcock-Truffaut 1962 interview.

21. Unpublished Hitchcock-Truffaut 1962 interview, 38.

## Chapter Two

# Writing

The fetish idea. A man wants to go to bed with a thief because she is a thief.

—Hitchcock to Truffaut on his reasons for making *Marnie*

Hitchcock was very involved in the writing for his films, but he never claimed screenwriting credit. Although he was literate, and his mastery of cinematic grammar unquestioned, growing up in a London borough at the beginning of the twentieth century made him very class-conscious. A sense of under-education may have prevented Hitchcock from taking on the task of writing himself, but this inevitably brought him into dissension with his writers. He once remarked:

> Well I've always had problems with writers because I find that I am teaching them cinematics all the time. You see, you've got to remember a lot of writers you have go by the page, and what is written on the page. I have no interest in that I only have that square white rectangle to fill. With a succession of im-ages—one following the other. Size of image and that's what makes a film. But merely to take words, you see I have no interest in pictures; that *[sic]* are what I call photographs of people talking. Nothing to do with the cinema or the use of it whatsoever. I mean just sticking a camera and photographing a group of people picking out the close ups and the two shots, well, I think that's a bore.[1]

The director believed that a combination of his cinematic mastery and hiring a sophisticated writer would do justice to the psychoanalytical perceptions in Winston Graham's novel. When it came to writing *Marnie*, Hitchcock was very sure of the story line he desired, while at the same time giving the impression that his writers were in control. The illusion of offering creative freedom was a particular skill Hitchcock had. Although he relied on his screenwriters for dialogue and plot, he worked with them throughout the writing process, sometimes bringing in a series of collaborators to achieve the overall effect he sought from the script. Often several writers would work on a treatment for his projects, and none of them would be aware of the others' involvement. Such was the case with the three screenwriters of *Marnie,* two of whom were initially working on a treatment simultaneously. In the final analysis, the film adaptation of the novel *Marnie* took three years and three writers to bring to the screen, and for one of the writers, the parting with Hitchcock turned out to be acrimonious.

## THE TREATMENT

When adapting a novel or a short story, Hitchcock began by contracting a writer to devise a treatment that set out the dialogue, describe the motivations and reactions of the characters, and outline the individual scenes. The story in which Grace Kelly would play a thief had to be handled delicately, especially if it was to mark her return to the cinema. In letters to Peggy Robertson, William Morris agent Shelly Wile recommended the following writers to take on the onerous task: Robert Thorn (*All the Fine Young Cannibals*), Clifford Odets (*The Country Girl*), Richard Nash (*The Rainmaker*), Marc Brandel (*Cleopatra*), Sidney and Muriel Box (*The Seventh Veil*), T. E. B. Clark (*The Lavender Hill Mob*), Blanche Hanalis (*The Hill Girl*), and Sidney Michaels (*The Voyage of the Beagle*).

However, Hitchcock chose to ask screenwriter Joseph Stefano, with whom he had just shared the success of *Psycho.* Stefano grew up as "a street kid in Philadelphia" and began his career as a songwriter in New York, writing for musicals and revues. He was introduced to Hitchcock by the MCA talent agency, when the director was seeking a writer for *Psycho.* "I wasn't in awe of Hitchcock when I first met him, and he loved that," Stefano remembers. "He didn't want the people who worked for him to be in awe of him but for the world to be in awe of him."

When Hitchcock intended to produce *Psycho* for under $1 million, he announced he would use his own television crew. It was kind of disappointing for Stefano initially, who wanted to do a "real" Hitchcock picture, with A-list stars like Cary Grant or James Stewart and filmed in grand Technicolor extravaganza. However, he was intrigued by the character of Norman Bates: "*Psycho* was a movie about sex—boys and mothers. It was Norman's interest in women which drove him to kill them. His mother dumped him for a real man."

Stefano also brought a young man's approach to the candid opening scene of Marion Crane (Janet Leigh) in the aftermath of lunchtime sex with her lover, Sam Loomis (John Gavin). Hitchcock later reasoned, "I felt the need to do a scene of that kind, because the audiences are changing, and you have to give them today, the way they behave themselves most of the time."[2] Stefano, like Winston Graham, identified with women, and over the years he has received many compliments for his portrayal of female characters. When writing about women, Stefano said that he drew on that part of himself that was too young to know the difference between the sexes. "Hitchcock was strongly attracted to women and told me one time that he was celibate. I'm surprised when creative men have totally successful relationships with women, because there is inevitably a competitive element."

During *Psycho's* filming, Hitchcock exercised an option for two additional projects with the screenwriter. Stefano, who was called into the director's office, remembers, "Hitch told me he had bought *Marnie* because Grace Kelly had informed him that she wanted to make another movie with him, and he thought that *Marnie* was an excellent book. He had never mentioned it to me before this time, though he had spoken about other books. I was very pleased and excited about it and thought that it would be great to have Grace Kelly back in the movies."

On February 23, 1961, a copy of *Marnie* was sent to the screenwriter to read. "Generally I liked the book," Stefano affirms.

> It had a couple of elements in it that were very similar to other Hitchcock movies; it had a triangle, two men and a woman. And not only had I seen that in many Hitchcock movies, but he himself had told me that's very fascinating to him, to deal with a triangle. In the book, the man who Marnie marries has a cousin who works in the same company and with whom he's very competitive, and the cousin falls in love with Marnie, too. So it's an interesting thing, Marnie being frigid and really wasn't very interested in either of them. My feeling was that it was an especially odd triangle, since there were cousins involved and a woman who was a thief and who was satisfying most of her compulsions by stealing.

The relationship in the novel between Marnie and the psychiatrist Roman was one that excited Stefano, who himself enjoyed writing scenes between a patient and a doctor. Moreover, Stefano was in psychoanalysis from 1950 until the time he began work on *Marnie.* During the writing of *Psycho,* Stefano came straight from his analyst in Beverly Hills to Hitchcock's Paramount office on Melrose. Hitchcock tried to guess whether it was a good or bad session, depending on Stefano's reaction. At this time, therapy was seldom talked about, so Hitchcock was very interested and curious about Stefano's frankness.

Stefano also had knowledge of an underground scene that Hitchcock had no direct experience of—the world of sadomasochism and fetishism, prevalent in New York art circles after the war and reaching predominance in the 1950s. Stefano was much more worldly than Hitchcock when it came to sexual practices, and that intrigued the director. When asked by Truffaut what were his reasons for making the film, Hitchcock replied, "The fetish idea, a man wants to go to bed with a thief because she is a thief, just like another man may have a yen for a Chinese or colored woman."[3] Hitchcock even considered constructing the story so that Mark would secretly watch Marnie rob the safe: "Then, he would have followed the thief, would have grabbed Marnie and made out he had just happened on her. He would have taken her by force, while pretending to be outraged. But you can't really put these things on the screen. The public would reject them. They would say, 'Oh no, that's not right. I don't believe it!'"[4]

After Stefano had read the book, he had another meeting with Hitchcock and told the director that it would make a wonderful film. Hitchcock informed him that he didn't want to send the book to Grace Kelly. He felt that what she needed was an intimation of how they were going to deal with the story. Hitchcock believed either that the princess wouldn't have time to read the whole book and therefore wouldn't, or that her understanding of the book would not be an accurate reflection of how they were going to translate the story to film.

Instead, Hitchcock suggested that Stefano write a detailed treatment. The structure of the film was the most important focus in discussions with his screenwriter, whereas dialogue was secondary. "In so much as we had worked on *Psycho* day after day, we began to work on *Marnie* the same way," Stefano recalls. "But I wasn't going to go home and write a screenplay like I had with *Psycho.* I would go home and write a treatment, but actually it turned out to be more of a sort of novel. Just about the time I had finished it four weeks later, I even included some dialogue. I wanted to give Grace Kelly the best possible explanation of the movie she was coming back to."

Stefano began writing the treatment on February 27 and was paid a salary of $1,500 a week. He interpreted Marnie as an angry, deprived human being who stole in order to compensate what had not been given to her in childhood. She was a strange, unlikable woman; men might not like her but they could fall in love with her. The two male characters, Mark Rutland and his cousin Terry Holbrook, were rivals both at work and for Marnie's attentions. The triangle that developed in many ways echoed that in *Notorious,* which Hitchcock later acknowledged to Peter Bogdanovich. Curiously, the character of Marnie also possessed many of the same qualities as the leads in *Psycho.* Like Marion Crane, Marnie is a thief, and like Norman Bates, she has a problematic relationship with her mother, arising from an absent father. In *Marnie,* Hitchcock and Stefano would extend the psychoanalysis they sketched out in *Psycho,* of how compulsive behavior could exist in both a normal person like Marion and a psychotic one like Norman.

"I never compared Marnie with anyone else. I have a rather strange reaction to movies that I write," Stefano states.

> When I finish, I go away, I forget them and put them in the past, and I'm only interested in what I'm doing today and what I might be doing next week. The images that came to my head when discussing the book with Hitchcock were all so different from *Psycho. Marnie* was going to be in color; this was going to be an expensive movie. I didn't know then who Marnie would be, but the riding scenes took it all so far away from where we had been with the depression era of *Psycho.* It was almost like suddenly I had moved into Park Avenue in this story. I felt this woman had no intention of being a victim and was being victimized by everyone around her and was being forced to go where she didn't want to go. Mark tried to blackmail her, and I found that a very interesting character, that to me had some of the resonance of Norman Bates, who seemed to be forced into the life that he began to lead.

On March 16, Stefano wrote a brief outline dividing the *Marnie* story line into parts. At this point, the story was firmly set on the East Coast, around Philadelphia, Washington, and Maryland, where most of the race tracks were located. Marnie's mother's house was sited in Baltimore and Rutland's office in Philadelphia. On May 3, Stefano transcribed from the novel nine sections between Marnie and her psychiatrist Roman. A copy was given to Hitchcock, who condensed the narrative into three visits. Stefano submitted the final pages of his 161-page treatment on June 9, having worked for fifteen weeks on the assignment.

At this time, Hitchcock was still hoping that Grace Kelly would return to filmmaking. In early November 1961, he asked John Boswell from Paramount Pictures to write a synopsis of Stefano's treatment, omitting the dialogue. Stefano's second commitment to revise the treatment began on April 26, 1962, for sixteen weeks. During the writing of *Psycho,* Hitchcock called Stefano into his office and expressed an interest in doing something about Daphne du Maurier's short story "The Birds." "I don't know if Hitchcock ever had a particular interest in birds," Stefano recalls. "I said to him one time that I hated zoos and would not go to them. And I remember him nodding in agreement. That was the closest we ever got to talking about animals." Stefano himself harbored no interest in birds or the story and remembered telling Hitchcock that he wanted to be far away from him when he was making that film.

Hitchcock must have taken Stefano's comments seriously because after Grace Kelly declined the Marnie role, Stefano didn't hear from the director until after production on *The Birds.* "The next time Hitch called me [in 1963] was when he decided to do *Marnie* with Tippi Hedren, but I was unavailable." Stefano declined with regret because he was producing the acclaimed science fiction television series, *The Outer Limits.* This was not well received, as Stefano subsequently heard via his agent that Hitchcock wanted to loan him out to Columbia. Stefano's response was to forget about the agreement until Hitchcock wanted him to do another film, but for Hitchcock a commitment was a commitment. The sadomasochistic and fetishistic ideas that Stefano had introduced, however, remained in Hitchcock's mind as elements he hoped to include in the screenplay.

## THE NOVELIST

During the spring of 1962, Hitchcock contracted Evan Hunter, the screenwriter for *The Birds,* to write a screenplay for *Marnie* in parallel to that of Stefano's. Hunter was a novelist and a writer of short stories, born and raised in New York, with a familiarity of the city's mean streets and uncompromising dialogue. His first success came in 1954 with the publication of *The Blackboard Jungle.* A year later, Hitchcock's television company, Shamley Productions, under the aegis of producer Joan Harrison, bought a short story of Hunter's titled "Vicious Circle" for *Alfred Hitchcock Presents.* The story was about the rise of a small-time hood, culminating in a gangland murder with a surprise twist.

Although *The Blackboard Jungle* garnered critical acclaim and the film version had been released, Hunter had only written a couple of teleplays and no screenplays at all. He classified himself as a novelist and a writer of short stories. It was therefore a surprise when he received a phone call from his agent saying that Shamley Productions had bought a story, *Appointment at Eleven* by Robert Turner, and wanted Hunter to adapt it for Hitchcock's television series. The story is told entirely in a young man's head as alternately he drinks at a bar and watches the hands of the clock. At eleven, the lights in the bar dim, and the reader learns that his father has just been electrocuted in the penitentiary nearby. "This was a difficult story to adapt," says Hunter, "because it all took place in the lead character's head, in a silent internal monologue."[5] Hitchcock later said that he specifically wanted a novelist to adapt the story because of its internal nature.

Hunter had yet to meet the Master of Suspense and finally did so during the summer of 1959, when Hitchcock was directing one of his television shows,

*The Crystal Trench.* Joan Harrison had invited Hunter and his then-wife, Anita, to view the final cut of *Appointment at Eleven.* Harrison took them onto the set to meet Hitchcock, and the director took an immediate liking to his guests and showed them around. By this time, Hunter had written four best-selling novels under his own name, and Columbia Pictures was adapting one of them, *Strangers When We Meet.* Furthermore, the *87th Precinct* novels, which Hunter wrote under his pseudonym Ed McBain, were scheduled for transmission that season. Two years later, in August 1961, Hitchcock asked Hunter to write the screenplay for *The Birds.* Hitchcock outlined his reasons for hiring Hunter to Truffaut:

> This man has written very few screenplays but, you see, I had a short story that needed expanding. So, I prefer to take a man who has a reputation for writing two or three kinds of stories so that I know that when I'm expanding the short story or re-writing it, whichever way you look at it, I'm adding something to it. Now I chose Hunter because he writes under two different names. He's written *Blackboard Jungle;* his last book was a successful one called, *Mothers and Daughters.* He is a good, all-round writer, and under another name, he writes about a New York police station, *87th Precinct.* He's Ed McBain. He's very successful. In choosing a writer, I choose someone who is, at least, a professional. Now, as professional though he is as a writer, he doesn't necessarily have the obliqueness of Hitchcock. But he's genial enough to accept my suggestions and, if I may say so, they are only suggestions . . . that cannot be changed.[6]

What is indicative of Hitchcock's reasoning for hiring Hunter is that he sought a writer of literary quality and professionalism, who would also be malleable to the director's specific requests. Hitchcock had complained to Truffaut that many writers only worked in the film medium for money. Writers who come out from New York, for example, attained a job at the Metro, with no particular assignment and simply awaited instructions. Hunter, however, was different. While he relished the chance to work with Hitchcock on a feature film, the novelist first asked to read Daphne du Maurier's original story, "The Birds," before making a commitment. On the day Hunter agreed, Hitchcock personally called him to say that they should forget the human story, which was set in Cornwall, but simply utilize the idea of birds attacking humans.

In the early 1960s, during the twilight years of the studio system, writers were paid a weekly salary and were required to do their actual writing in Los Angeles. Hunter, therefore, dutifully flew from New York to begin writing *The Birds,* for the sum of $5,000 a week. Later, he would bring out his wife and three young sons for an extended stay while he worked on the screenplay. "When I first met Hitch," Hunter recalls, "he was brimming with ideas and talking about future projects all the time. He told me he was entering the golden age of his creativity and that *The Birds* would be his greatest achievement."

To begin with, Hunter suspected that he was hired because of his ability to write suspense, evident in his *87th Precinct* novels. It never occurred to him that the real reason was for the serious critical appraisal *The Blackboard Jungle* had generated. One incident that Hunter remembers suggests that Hitchcock himself was on a quest for respectability. The writer had commented favorably on the paneled walls in Hitchcock's office, adorned with various awards. Hitchcock nodded and put his hand on Hunter's shoulder: "Always a bridesmaid, never a bride," he lamented. The director had been nominated for five Academy Awards, including one for *Psycho*—but recognition from his peers still eluded him. The quest for "true respect" was the impetus for making *The Birds* and later *Marnie,* starting with the hiring of Hunter himself.

On January 31, 1962, Peggy Robertson sent a copy of the book *Marnie* to Evan Hunter's home in Westchester, New York. Hunter thought that it was a good novel, not a murder mystery but a thriller, with suspense in it:

> I enjoyed the book and enjoyed the experience of working with Hitch on *The Birds* and wanted to continue the relationship. Hitch himself thought it was a fascinating story and also a showcase to mark Grace Kelly's return to the screen. I was trying to show a very troubled woman in seeming control, with a glacial exterior and a turbulent interior, which we only understand as the film progresses. I saw the audience asking the question, Why is this beautiful, intelligent, resourceful woman committing burglaries? What's wrong with her? I never thought of Marnie as hunted but as troubled—she needed help. There were two options for the screenplay to follow. One was of a vengeful society; the other was one of society trying to help the girl.

Hunter chose the latter, embodied in the character of Mark Rutland. "Mark's love increases for her as the movie goes on. He earns her trust as he learns about her. Hitch was always a stickler for plot development. He was very concerned with structure and that character should come out of plot. That was his working procedure."

During the first conversation they had about *Marnie,* Hunter expressed his concern for a particular scene in the book. Hitchcock feigned ignorance and asked, "What scene?" When Hunter mentioned the rape, Hitchcock replied, "Don't worry about—that'll be fine; we'll talk about it later." Hunter felt that he would have difficulty recovering a character after such a scene, for every woman in the audience would hate him, whether he be played by Sean Connery or Rock Hudson. In Hunter's mind, it wasn't heroic to rape a woman who was terrified, and it was also dramatically wrong. Hitchcock totally disagreed.

Hunter was sent a wire, care of his agent Scott Meredith in New York, detailing his hiring for twelve weeks at the sum of $5,000 per week. He was to begin work on March 14, 1962, at the Fairmont Hotel in San Francisco, where Hitchcock was staying during location filming of *The Birds.* During the sixty-mile location ride to and from Bodega Bay, the director and his writer discussed *Marnie,* as well as during lunch, dinner, and filming breaks. Schoolchildren would line the roads north with signs reading, "Mr. Hitchcock please stop." Hitchcock always graciously stopped, even up to half an hour, to sign autographs.

When Hunter asked Hitchcock who would be playing the role of Marnie, the director winked and mouthed the word *Grace.* A week later, Hunter returned to New York to write the *Marnie* screenplay, as Hitchcock was involved in the intricacies of directing *The Birds.* "It is the toughest assignment I have had," Hunter told London journalist Peter Evans. "For Marnie is a puzzlement. An enigma. A fearful, fascinating enigma. You see there are so many aspects of her character to balance and jiggle. She must be clever and witty and warm. But she is also afraid and mysteriously remote—and terrified of physical contact with men. If a man touches her she becomes violent."[7] When Hunter got off the plane at Kennedy Airport, a horde of reporters and photographers ran to the gate, asking him whether Kelly was indeed to play the lead role in *Marnie.* Hunter's response was, "You'll have to ask Hitchcock."

On his writing desk at home was an unframed picture of Grace Kelly, whom Hunter did indeed imagine as Marnie. Hitchcock and Hunter both agreed that Kelly was the first choice for the role and used the code word *HSH*—Her Serene Highness. Over the coming months Hunter sent letters to Hitchcock suggesting locations and adding notes on the script's progress. In a possible diffusion of the rather dubious character the Princess of Monaco would be playing, Hunter remarked, "Instead of being a thief, she will be a confidence trickster."

Like Winston Graham, Hunter consulted a psychologist friend to gain insights into the dynamics of the Marnie character. In a letter dated March 30, addressed to Hitchcock at the Fairmont, Hunter wrote:

> My session with our psychologist proved most rewarding. I now understand a great many of the things happening in the book (Winston Graham was either using a case history, or else was intuitively correct) and can cope with our dear Marnie very well indeed. You will be interested to learn that our psychologist felt the ending we worked out—concerning Marnie's trauma—was a more valid one than the one in the book. So it's full speed ahead with our drunken sailor and our intervening mother and, oh, all sorts of Oedipal undertones and overtones. I am picking up a book on screen memory this afternoon. I understand

the phenomenon quite well in its simplest terms, but I want to go into it a little more deeply just in case I decide to explain it to an audience at some point in the picture. In any case, I learned some exciting things which will provide us with a double twist on the trauma. I'm not anticipating any trouble at all.

The screen memory that Hunter referred to in his letter was a psychoanalytical term for a false memory that hides the real trauma a victim cannot face. Hunter explained this to the audience, in dramatic scenes Hitchcock never used in the film. The screen memory hid the real trauma of Marnie's mother killing the sailor, which Hitchcock and Hunter substituted for the strangling of the newborn child. Marnie tells the psychiatrist a memory, and just when the psychiatrist thinks they're reaching the truth, Marnie cuts the association short. This idea was later dropped by Hitchcock. Hunter, however, used the screen memory to good effect in his novel *Long Time No See,* under the pseudonym of Ed McBain.

On April 4, a year before Hunter would submit his final draft, the Writers Guild of America was informed by Peggy Robertson that Evan Hunter was employed by Alfred J. Hitchcock Productions, Inc., to write the screenplay of *Marnie.* No mention of Joseph Stefano's work was made. In fact, Robertson's letter specifically stated that no other writer had been employed. Hunter wrote a short note to Hitchcock on April 20 informing him that "*Marnie* is moving along nicely." Ninety polished pages were written, with only one possible problem—that of length. Hunter hoped to complete the Rutland robbery by page 120, leaving the remaining third of the script to the marriage, but seemed to be running long. He was delighted, however, with the way all the characters, even the minor ones, were shaping up.

Hunter sent another letter on May 24, again expressing concern of the screenplay's length: "It is now running a bit long (as did *The Birds* in its first draft), despite the fact that I have been cutting back even while working ahead. I believe its longishness is caused by the double-barreled necessities of complicated plot and complex character. I do not feel, however, that there are any no-scene scenes in this draft, and I would prefer discussing the screenplay with you before cutting any further."

When Hunter arrived in Los Angeles on June 6, he delivered a first draft of the *Marnie* script. The director was in production for *The Birds* and had yet to film what turned out to be the last bird attack on Melanie Daniels in the attic. It was during this visit that filming of the controversial sand dunes sequence occurred, when Melanie tells Mitch Brenner about her charity work and being abandoned by her mother at the age of eleven. The morning they were to film the scene, the actor Rod Taylor, who was playing the part of Mitch, presented Hunter with dialogue, asking him whether he had written it. A dismayed Hunter read the scene and said he hadn't, commenting on its amateurish nature. Hitchcock was in his production trailer with Peggy Robertson. Hunter requested to confer with Hitchcock privately and showed him the scene Taylor had just given him. Hunter said he didn't know who'd written it but that it was totally inept and devoid of any craftsmanship and that no single speech in it logically followed the speech preceding it. Hitchcock retorted, "Are you going to trust me or a two-bit actor?" The event marked the beginning of a number of disagreements between Hitchcock and Hunter.

Hitchcock postponed development on *Marnie* as he set to work on the complicated postproduction for *The Birds.* Hunter had hoped to have the final screenplay submitted by August, so that he could take a much-needed month's vacation in Europe before starting on his next novel in September. He wrote to his agent Scott Meredith expressing his frustration:

> Frankly, I was looking forward to the luxury of turning off everything but the telephone and beginning work on a book that is certainly long overdue from everyone's standpoint, including my own. The postponement of *Marnie* presents a dilemma, and I frankly don't know what to do about it. I think we both agreed a long time ago that the surest way to get sand trapped into all this Hollywood crap was to undertake one screenplay immediately after another. I don't buy the Hollywood Corruption idea except as a corruption of reality, and somehow or other we have slipped into screenplay, screenplay, screenplay—and this, Scott, is a corruption of reality. I am a novelist. If one more columnist calls me "screenwriter Evan Hunter," I think I'll climb the wall.

Twenty-four weeks elapsed before Hunter began revisions and rewrites on *Marnie.* He returned to Los Angeles on Sunday, November 25, to resume work with Hitchcock the following day. Again he was paid $5,000 per week, with a three-week break during the Christmas-New Year period. Hitchcock's working method began every weekday morning with the words "Tell me the story so far." After morning coffee, Hitchcock sat back in his black leather chair with his hands folded over his belly, while Hunter told him the story to date, beginning with where they had left off the previous afternoon. Hunter was keen to return to New York for Christmas.

The daily story conferences and the California climate left him little time or mood for Christmas shopping. During one story conference, when Hitchcock was relaying a long story about Charles Laughton and the filming of *Jamaica Inn,* Hunter grew impatient and reminded Hitchcock of how much he was being paid. "I know it's exorbitant," was Hitchcock's reply. Hunter remarked since that was the case, shouldn't they get back to the task at hand? Later that afternoon, Lew Wasserman stopped by the office to chat. He'd been in the office for only five minutes before Hitchcock interrupted him midsentence. "Excuse me, Lew," he said, "but we'll have to cut this short. Mr. Hunter is eager to get home for Christmas."

In his taped conversations with François Truffaut during the summer of 1962, Hitchcock voiced his intentions for *Marnie* to be primarily a character study:

> First you have to photograph the mind that steals. A calculating mind . . . and, of course, the questions of a psychiatrist bring out the gamin in her. He asks sex questions—she says, "You're a dirty old man." And it's a very . . . there are very amusing scenes in the way she resists the psychiatrist. But his probing brings out something of the child background. So here you have another area for the character to play and that is the area of the childhood pain which will transfer itself from a comedy scene into moments of fear because the psychiatrist touches raw spots . . . sore spots. And, of course, the childhood experiences when her mother had a man in with her and the man made an approach at her . . . four years of age. So there are a lot of angles for this character which will be quite a challenge for [Tippi Hedren], but more for me.[8]

Creating a plausible and psychologically valid central character was so important to Hitchcock that he asked Evan Hunter to write a letter to Hedren, dated December 10, 1962:

> To Tippi
> Hitch asked me to explain the psychological complex of the character Marnie. To do this we should first examine Marnie's childhood trauma which is the key to her subsequent adult behavior.
> At the age of four or five the Oedipal situation is at its strongest in all children. This means, in its simplest terms, that Marnie wants to go to bed with her father and considers her mother a rival for his love. Marnie's father, as we know, is a sailor aboard a ship somewhere in a battle zone. On the night of the incident that will shape Marnie's future life, a sailor whom her mother is entertaining enters Marnie's bedroom by mistake and approaches the bed. She mistakes him for her father at first and, frightened by the thunderstorm outside, succumbs to the sailor's gentleness and kindness. The sequence serves only to reaffirm her own fantasy concerning her real-life father. The fantasy achieves frightening reality when her mother enters the room and mistakes the sailor's friendliness for a sexual advance on the child. In short, Marnie, who wants her father, whose mother is her rival, is presented with a real-life situation in which a father figure displays affection toward her and is immediately attacked by the rival, her mother. The situation ends in the murder of the sailor. Unhappily, this coincides with the death of her father at sea—an event which is never adequately explained to Marnie. In the child's mind, the death of the sailor in her bedroom and the death of her real father at sea become one. The equation to her is clear and simple; "My father made love to me and my mother killed him for it."

How does this relate to Marnie's later behavior? The notion that her crimes are a substitution for sex is not a valid one. She does not rob safes because she desires men. Instead, her crimes are in effect a re-enactment of what happened to her that night in her bedroom. She commits the crimes in an attempt to find a different and more satisfactory solution to the situation. Long ago she stole her father and he was killed for it. Now, symbolically, she steals her father again every time she commits a crime and hopes that the solution will be a different one—he will not die.

Symbolically, the situation seems to change each time she commits a crime, because she then is allowed to enjoy the time honored symbol for father, The Horse. She is indeed ecstatic whenever she is with Forio. But, a temporary and seemingly satisfying solution to a deep psychological wound is never truly relieving unless someone understands what is causing the emotional disturbance to begin with. Marnie finds no relief. After her scenes with Forio she immediately seeks out her mother each time, and guilt ridden, gives her part of the money she had stolen, (In a sense, she is returning "father" to the person who rightfully owns him). The entire pattern is compulsive because she is desperately trying to work out an answer to her childhood experience. She is, if you will, emotionally arrested at the age of 4 or 5. The reason she so fears anything more than casual sexual contact with a man is because any man becomes a representation of her father. If she goes to bed with him, if she accepts his love, something dire and unimaginably horrible will happen. The scene wherein Mark forces himself upon her is graphic proof of this. It comes too close to the childhood trauma, and threatens the entire fabric of her life. She attempts suicide following it.

After Christmas, Hunter resumed discussions on Monday, January 28, 1963, in Hitchcock's office. A Smith-Corona electric portable typewriter was purchased by Hunter from the Beverly Hills Typewriter Company and delivered to the Hilton where he was staying. Hitchcock's appointment book showed that both he and his writer watched the film *Freud* (1962) by John Huston. The film depicts five years in the life of the psychologist Sigmund Freud (Montgomery Clift) and how he learned to use hypnosis to find out the reasons for his psychosis. His main patient (Susannah York) refuses to drink water and is plagued by the same nightmare. Hitchcock also viewed Federico Fellini's *La Dolce Vita* (1960), and although he was never given to discussing the work of other directors with his writers, he specifically mentioned *Freud* during the story conference for *Marnie*'s production design. A memo dated January 30 was sent to the Los Angeles Institute for Psychoanalysts asking whether a writer could go and make inquiries about case histories. Hitchcock had lunch with David Stafford Clark, a visiting fellow of the Royal College of Physicians in England, who had a diploma in psychological medicine; and Hunter spoke to Dr. Smaatama from the New York Psychoanalytical Institute.

On February 1, Hunter wrote a scene outline for *Marnie* that was divided into four parts under the headings "Marnie Is a Thief," "Rutlands," "Wedding and Honeymoon," and "Life with Mark." The succession of events remained faithful to Graham's novel. In the first part, the opening scenes of a railway station, Strutt's discovery of being robbed, the hotel room in New York, the bus terminal in Laurel, the old Colonial hotel, the visit to Mother's house, and the first hint of trauma are all clearly depicted: "Marnie, asleep, hears rattling at the window. She half-wakes, searches for sound, but the tapping stops. She drifts off into sleep again, but the tapping begins once more, and her sleep is disturbed and troubled."

Section 2, "Marnie Is a Thief," contained an elaborate scene at a movie theater, complete with a parody of an Italian film. Marnie's robbery of the theater is worked out in detail, but the robbery of Rutland's is not. Instead, Hunter sets up the question of whether Marnie will rob the Rutland safe because of her increasing involvement with Mark. He then simply cuts to the familiar pattern of events after Marnie's robbery (i.e., the riding of the horse Forio).

During the rape and suicide attempt, Hunter notes:

Pan from her face to open porthole and heaving sea. Dawn lightens the sky. Pan back to the bed with Mark in it alone. He awakes. The bedside clock tells us it is 5:00 a.m. Alarmed he leaves the suite, searches the empty witching-hour ship for Marnie, glancing over the side at the ocean, rushing past rows of deck chairs, empty decks, a gray sky and a gray sea. He finally comes upon the pool. Marnie is floating in it face downward. He drags her out, administers artificial respiration, and carries her back to the cabin.

Even the tag line is similar to what was used in the final film. Mark asks, "With all that ocean, why'd you pick the swimming pool?" Marnie replies, "I'm afraid of sharks." Hunter later dropped the tag line, which Hitchcock was fond of, in favor of the severity of the situation.

Hunter also wrote three analyst scenes that started three-quarters comic and one-quarter serious, in which the ratio is reversed during the last session. In Marnie's third and final visit to her mother's house, she arrives to discover that her mother has just died. The undertakers are waiting to claim the body, but Marnie asks them to wait. In searching for memorabilia of her mother in a black box under the bed, Marnie comes upon the single item that triggers memory of the trauma. This is a pearl of beads, which Hunter uses as the screen memory device. The trauma flashback was still to be worked out in detail but would be presented in terms of continuous and smooth-flowing present and past action interwoven with each other. Lucy Nye, an old woman who lives with Marnie's mother, tells of the terrible events that happened long ago. At the end of the flashback, Mark and the psychiatrist Roman are revealed to be present, and they have heard the whole confession. They take Marnie home, planning to bring her back for the funeral.

The final scene is beautifully depicted. When Mark and Marnie return to their house, Strutt, Terry, and a uniformed police officer are waiting in the doorway. Marnie and Mark play a love scene in the driveway, in which she offers herself freely and willingly for the first time, and the audience knows that Mark will wait for her. Then she walks toward the front door.

On February 4, Hitchcock met with Hunter and the production designer Robert Boyle to go over the story line and design for the film, producing three reels of taped conversation. Hitchcock's grasp of the film is encyclopedic; he tells the complete story of *Marnie,* scene by scene, whereas his collaborators contribute by either querying or clarifying a point. Hitchcock was very specific in what he envisioned for the rape scene:

> Each of the images must make a statement. . . . Now it's night in this scene. The cabin of the ship has to be a bedroom and a sitting room, a suite—and she's in a negligee. He's in shirt and pants. And he comes over to embrace her now. Now is the moment. And she turns on him and walks away and sits in a far comer of the room. He comes to the door and says, "What's wrong?" And in rather bold language, she says, "It's animal and the whole business is horrible"—and the language here will be quite outspoken—and he tries to talk her into being sensible about it, but she won't attempt it at all.

At this point, Hitchcock turned the tape recorder off and describes Marnie's rape in detail. Hunter knew better than to contradict the director in the presence of Boyle, a man whom Hitchcock had begun working with twenty years earlier. After the story conference, Hunter told Hitchcock that he did not wish to write the scene as the director had outlined. Hunter's view was that it would lose all sympathy for Mark if he rapes his own wife on their honeymoon. "I told him we can see the girl isn't being coy or modest; she's terrified, she's trembling, and the reasons for this all come out in the later psychiatric sessions. I told him if the man really loved her, he would take her in his arms and comfort her gently and tell her they'd work it out, 'Don't be frightened—everything will be all right.' I told him that's how I thought the scene should go."

Hitchcock's reply was to hold up his hands the way directors do when they're framing a shot: palms out, fingers together, thumbs extended and touching to form a perfect square. Moving his hands toward Hunter's face, like a camera moving in for a close shot, Hitchcock said, "Evan when he sticks it in her, I want that camera right on her face!" On hearing those words, Hunter knew there was going to be trouble ahead.

With this in mind, Hunter returned to New York on February 8, to begin further revisions and rewrites. In a letter dated February 14, Hunter requested from Peggy Robertson background details for a glass factory that would serve as the Rutland working environment, technical information for a conversation between an exhibitor and his projectionist in a movie theater, and the mechanics of stock transfer. On February 25, Robertson duly sent a transcription of dialogue between the manager of the La Reina theater in Los Angeles and his projectionist. The manager had a tiny microphone concealed on him as he talked to his projectionist, who knew nothing about the project. Robertson timed this dialogue just under five minutes. The scene, extrapolated from the novel, would provide the background for Marnie's theater robbery. That same day, Hunter wrote to Robertson, "I am very pleased with the way the script is going, and my only modest desire is that the movie will become another testimonial to the greatness of the man who wrote the novel."

In an odd coincidence, Hunter delivered what he hoped to be the final draft of *Marnie,* the day after April Fool's Day, exactly a year after delivering *The Birds.* The 189-page screenplay was sent to his agent, and a copy arrived at Hitchcock's office on April 5. Hunter's script contained three elaborate set pieces that he had cleverly adjusted from the novel. Marnie's robbery of the Rutland safe is preceded by the stealing of Susan's key, which offers access to the safe combination contained in Sam Ward's drawer. The robbery culminates with Marnie evading the cleaning woman, despite dropping her shoe. During the climactic flashback, Marnie looks through her deceased mother's trunk full of trinkets and finds a newspaper clipping telling of the sailor's death. A thunderstorm brews outside, and Lucy Nye appears and relates the story, causing Marnie to remember the events of long ago. The sailor has a mustache, and Marnie associates him with her father. His gestures are mistaken by Marnie's mother for sexual abuse, and in the ensuing struggle, it is she—not Marnie—who kills the sailor with an iron poker. A frightened Marnie, hiding under the bed, only remembers her mother's broken string of pearls rolling toward her.

Hunter submitted two versions of the honeymoon sequence, one with the rape and one without: "The rape scene always bothered me. I was uncomfortable with the Mark character—he seemed like a stuffed shirt, not sympathetic, especially with the notion of a girl who is deeply troubled." Hunter wrote a letter to accompany his submitted script:

Dear Hitch,
    Here is Marnie, which I believe has shaped up very well. There are a few things I would like to call to your attention, however, since they are deviations from the story as we discussed it. I found that some of our story line would not work in the writing, and I adjusted the screenplay accordingly.

The major change I have made concerns the honeymoon night. You will notice that there are two versions of this sequence in the script, one in white, one in yellow. The yellow version is the sequence as we discussed it, complete with poolside scene, and the rape. I wrote and rewrote it and polished and repolished this sequence, but something about it continued to disturb me. I finally wrote the white version—which is the version I would like to see in the film. I know you are fond of the entire honeymoon sequence as we discussed it, Hitch, but let me tell you what I felt was wrong with it, and how I attempted to bring it into a truer perspective.

To begin with, Marnie's attitude was misleading. We were asking an audience to believe that putting off Mark was on her mind from the top of the scene. This makes her frigidity a coldblooded thing (no pun intended) rather than something she cannot help. She can respond to warmth and gentleness, she can accept love-making—until it gets serious. Which brings us to a further examination. Why does Marnie marry him? The answer is simple: she loves him. She may think she is marrying him to avoid the police, but she really does love him (as we bring out at the picture's end). It is only her deep emotional disturbance that makes it impossible for her to accept or enjoy this love.

I have, therefore, written a rather playful honeymoon night scene, showing Marnie in a gay and likeable mood, a bit giggly (we have never seen her this way in the picture before), playing our entire Garrod's exposition as a warm love scene, which I think works. It is only when Mark's intentions get serious, only when his love-making reminds her of that night long ago, that she panics and pulls away. Her retreat is a curious thing, and the audience—for the first time—realizes that something is seriously wrong with this girl. The scene is frightening, and it also provides a springboard for the later scene in which Mark suggests psychiatric help. To me, it is believable and sound. The way we discussed it was implausibility bordering on burlesque.

*I firmly believe It is out of place in this story.* Mark is *not* that kind of a person. Marnie is obviously troubled, and he realizes it. Stanley Kowalski might rape her, but not Mark Rutland. Mark would do exactly what we see him do later—he would seek the help of a psychiatrist. And, without an out-of-character rape, there was no need for a poolside discussion. The entire honeymoon sequence now takes place on a single night. Marnie's panic is followed immediately by her suicide attempt. There is not a long stage wait. I am convinced that the rape has no place in this sequence, Hitch, and I hope you will agree and throw away the yellow pages.

Hitchcock replied on April 10, saying that he wanted to put the project aside until it was met with a fresh mind. Although Hunter was aware of the implications in these words, he professed ignorance, suggesting that they both reconvene at a later date. On May 1, Peggy Robertson called Hunter's agent to say that he was being replaced as the screenwriter of *Marnie*. Hunter, years later, admitted that his error was not including the rape scene as Hitchcock desired within the body of the script, but sidelining it within the throwaway yellow pages. He had held out on his opinion too long, and although Hunter saw Hitchcock socially some time after, the two never collaborated again.

## THE PLAYWRIGHT

With preproduction for *Marnie* beginning in earnest and filming slated for the coming fall, Hitchcock immediately began to seek a new writer. The director was quick to capitalize on Hunter's work, for he hired Allida Allen to write a sequence synopsis from the rejected script. Hitchcock asked Michael Ludmer, head of Universal Pictures story department, to contact the writer William Gibson, but a reply on April 23 from his agent said that Gibson was not available until he had finished his current book. Also under consideration was Edward Anhalt, who had written a script titled *Wives and Lovers.*

With news that Hitchcock was in need of a writer, many offers came in. Agent Ned Brown wrote to Hitchcock on May 17: "If you haven't decided on a writer yet for *Marnie,* I'd like to bring a writer by the name of Ray Russell out to meet you." Russell had read the book and was very keen to write the screenplay. As executive editor of *Playboy* magazine for seven years, he was, in his own words, "an authority on literary sophistication." Russell was also the author of *The Case against Satan,* a novel that intertwined modern psychiatry and demons in a story where man, the elements, and the spirits battled for supremacy.

Hitchcock still hoped to attain a writer of quality, like Hunter, but one who was more compliant to the director's wishes. In mid-May, he happened to read a play titled *The Prime of Miss Jean Brodie,* which had been sent to his office from one of the agencies. The story of an unconventional teacher in an all-girls school in Edinburgh was an adaptation from a book by Muriel Spark, published in London the same year as *Marnie.* Although postponed in the United States because the producer's wife became ill, the play opened in London to favorable reviews. Hitchcock was impressed enough to contact the playwright, whose name was Jay Presson Allen.

Born in San Angelo, Texas, in 1922, Allen was a self-confident child, with the responsibility that came from living in a frontier environment. After her education in Texas, Allen moved to New York with aspirations of becoming an actress. However, she quickly realized that although rehearsals were enjoyable, she didn't relish the performances. It was during her first marriage that Allen became a writer by default, when she wrote a novel titled *Spring Riot.* "I've always been interested in the why of human behavior," she remarked in an interview. "I think most writers are natural psychologists."[9] In

1955, Allen married her second husband, the stage and screen producer Lewis Allen, and had one daughter. Being an avid reader, a facile writer, and good talker, Allen started work as a scenarist in television before trying her hand at writing plays.

Hitchcock invited Allen to fly out to California on May 29 and join him and Alma for a couple of days at their home in Santa Cruz. Allen had an immediate rapport with the director: "We laughed. And I really liked Alma. I thought she was wonderful. And I think he began to very quickly trust me psychologically, knowing that I was skilled in that direction, which I am."[10] Allen returned to California on June 4 to begin work on *Marnie* for $26,500 for an unlimited time, having never read or known the existence of material written by Stefano or Hunter. "The only reason that I took the job was because of Hitchcock. I had no Hollywood ambitions at all," says Allen, who confesses to not being film oriented at the time. "In those days, not every theater graduate from junior high school wanted to be a screenwriter, though I thought I could be. I was just thrilled to be asked by *Hitchcock*, whose films had always entertained me, and I thought it would be fun to work with him. As it turned out he was the most extraordinary teacher—I couldn't learn as fast as he could teach."

Over the next few days, Hitchcock screened two of his favorite films for his willing apprentice, *The Trouble with Harry* and *Shadow of a Doubt.* They were followed by viewings of *Spellbound* and *Notorious,* films that echoed *Marnie*'s theme and content. At first, Hitchcock wanted to play and enjoyed talking endlessly about the characters Mark and Marnie, day after day. He wouldn't let Allen write for almost two months, as both became very involved in establishing some semblance of reality in the protagonists' relationship. As Hitchcock and Allen became friends, he would encourage her to direct, and later she interpreted his dreams: "He never ever told or exposed consciously what it meant to him. He never knew what a dream was about, not a clue; he didn't dig into himself. It was all instinctual, what we call talent."

Hitchcock skillfully offered Allen the illusion of creative freedom, which she found astonishing since she had never written a film before. "He made me feel extremely free," she says. "I never felt that anything was being imposed on me. I have no doubt that it was, but I never felt it. I felt that I was making it up for Hitchcock. He also did something very naughty. By union law, a writer is supposed to read the previous script—but Hitchcock never told me there was a previous script. I found out later when I met Evan Hunter." Although Allen doesn't recall, a distribution memo records that the ten-page synopsis of Hunter's script was given to her the day before she started work. A copy was also given from Peggy Robertson's file to Hitchcock, to discuss in the office with Allen. In doing so, Hitchcock was subtly guiding his new writer in structure and content, ensuring that the many months of discussion he had with Hunter were not wasted.

In the week beginning June 16, Allen had long story conferences with Hitchcock and Tippi Hedren, to discuss the character of Marnie. Allen's concern was to make everything rational and plausible, which Hitchcock favored. He was fond of Allen and wanted to film many of the scenes she wrote. "Maybe because his films were usually so plotty and convoluted, characterization escaped him more than he would have wished it to," Allen remarks. "Hitch was very concerned with characterization when he could get it, and basically that's what I do . . . that's what he loved."

Hitchcock also enjoyed socializing in equal measure to attending the script sessions. When Allen's husband joined her for a visit, the Hitchcocks took them to dinner at Perino's. In San Francisco they listened to the Philharmonic orchestra and dined at Ernie's, before spending a weekend in Santa Cruz, where they celebrated Patricia Hitchcock's birthday. Like Hitchcock, Allen read the English papers, the *Observer* and the *Times,* so daily copies were sent to her. Over the coming months, research on cruise liners *Leonardo da Vinci* and the SS *France*, horse racing and riding stables, and the criminal investigation process was assiduously undertaken by Peggy Robertson and Suzanne Gauthier to answer specific questions arising from the script.

During her time in California, Allen didn't work at home or in the office but at the Sportsmen's Lodge in North Hollywood, where she typed on an old Underwood 1949 typewriter. Unlike Graham or Hunter however, Allen did little background preparation for *Marnie*, apart from once consulting a psychiatrist, Dr. Judd Marmor. He was one of the top five psychoanalysts in Los Angeles, who deviated from pure Freudian psychology in that he stressed social and cultural factors in the development of the individual. A list of book titles of psychiatry with relation to stealing was given to Allen on August 2, with such names as *Psychiatry and the Law* and the *Psychopathic Delinquent and Criminal.* The title of the latter book was utilized in Allen's screenplay when Marnie mocks Mark during the free-association scene. Of the Graham novel, Allen says she didn't think it was very good but had possibilities of character that she developed. Indeed, Allen believes that women are more psychologically complex to write about than men; therefore, male writers have greater difficulty when fleshing out a female character. Allen professes to enjoy writing about children because they are exciting and challenging. Later, she was involved in an adaptation of *The Borrowers* (1973), and her husband Lewis produced the original and the remake of *Lord of the Flies* (1961 and 1990).

Allen saw Marnie as an underdeveloped woman, one who was deeply affected by her childhood. "I think child abuse was also quite significant in

1963. I was richly aware of all of that, absolutely. I had a child of my own; there was no way that I didn't know what was going on." Like Marnie, Allen was an only child: "Only children think a lot about their childhood, and it maintains interest. I liked Marnie and I felt sorry for her." Developing the relationship between Marnie and her mother more fully than in the book was one way of making the character more sympathetic and engaging to the audience. Specifically, Allen was pleased with a few good scenes between Mark and Marnie, which formed the framework for the film's themes of class distinction and feminism. She elaborated on these issues in her greatest critically acclaimed work, *Cabaret* (1967), and the underrated *Just Tell Me What You Want* (1980).

Hitchcock never voiced to Allen his attraction of the fetish idea. Indeed, she believed that his conception of the Mark Rutland character was the same as her own: "He was an extremely well-bred man from a Virginian family who had a dark streak. He was also a very good man." In transposing the adaptation of an English novel to the screen, Mark Rutland was made what Allen calls FFV—"First Family of Virginia." In the November 1961 *Marnie* treatment, revised by Hitchcock himself, Mark Rutland is described as a "good looking, quiet faced man in his early forties. . . . No one can hear the thundering thing happening to him; Marnie least of all. As she turns to go to her desk, he continues gazing at her, and finally has to make himself look away. It is obvious that she has hit him, as they say, where he lives." Allen's later shooting script characterized Mark Rutland as

> the American equivalent of an aristocrat. That is to say he has the rather uncommon twentieth century grace of identity. He has probably always been in rebellion against his stultifying background. Having quietly successfully broken so many rules and taboos of his own family and society, he would not hesitate long over breaking rules or even laws of a more general nature if he felt justified in his own judgement. He is a hero.

What is interesting about this description is that Allen unequivocally describes Mark as a hero, which a generation of later critics would dispute. The "dark streak" was much more prevalent in Hitchcock's mind than that of either of his writers, accounting for the different interpretations that the Mark character has generated, because of this anomaly between writer and director.

"I always thought that the man's character liked a hunt, a cat-and-mouse game, that he found it extremely intriguing and that's what I wrote," Allen observes. "He had a tremendous advantage over Marnie; it was a further kind of entrapment, where she was helpless and infant-like again." Hitchcock settled on establishing from the outset that Mark knows that Marnie is a thief and derives some perverse pleasure in the suspense of waiting for her to steal.

Confident that the script was being written to his specifications, Hitchcock traveled with Alma to Scotland on July 11 for a vacation and to begin research on a project he had long wanted to realize: *Mary Rose.* At the age of twenty, Hitchcock had watched the J. M. Barrie play premiere at the Haymarket Theater in London. The story was about a young woman who disappears on a haunted island during a belated honeymoon. Barrie was fascinated with ghosts and the belief that they were dead young mothers returning to the world to see how their youngsters have fared without them. Written in 1919, *Mary Rose* combined this idea with a folktale of children being kidnapped by fairies, which Barrie developed further in *Peter Pan.* The story is told in a flashback by the heroine's grown son. As a child, Mary Rose disappeared during a visit to the island, only to reappear with no memory of the intervening thirty days. The same thing happens to her when she visits the island three years after her marriage, but this time she stays away for eighteen years and returns to find her husband and parents have grown old. A trick set allows Mary Rose's family home to go from decrepit present to happy past and back again, while the audience watched. She remains in the house, an unhappy ghost looking for her lost child, until he returns to the empty house as a grown man. Although she doesn't recognize him, their reunion frees her to return to the island at the end.

From Mallaig, the Hitchcocks traveled to the Isle of Skye to investigate its filming potential as "The Island." *Mary Rose* was to conclude a trilogy, begun with *The Birds* and *Marnie.* It was to be billed as Hitchcock's *Mary Rose,* a ghost story, and even though Allen was later commissioned to write a first draft, Universal refused the project. Lew Wasserman didn't believe it was what film audiences expected from the Master of Suspense. In fact, Universal later stipulated in Hitchcock's contract that he could do any picture he chose for under $3 million, so long as it wasn't *Mary Rose.*

When Hitchcock returned to California, Allen submitted a first draft of the *Marnie* script on August 7, totaling 248 pages. Much of the script was overlong and warranted a great deal of cutting. Whereas plot was the hardest aspect of the story to write, because of Allen's theater training and natural articulation, dialogue came easy, which accounts for many of the long speeches. Over the next couple of days, Hitchcock worked at home with Allen, going over the script, pruning dialogue and adding camera direction. In the first draft, Marnie's mother is named Jessie, whereas the little girl is called Tommy Jean. The sequence where Marnie's mother brushes the girl's hair is used as a device to segue into a flashback of Marnie as a child. In this scene, Marnie steals from a store and is chased down an alley by three other girls, who tease her for having nits in her hair. The adult Marnie reflects on why her mother didn't wash her hair regularly with shampoo, as a result of their poverty.

Hitchcock needed an expressionistic device that reflected back to the childhood trauma, so together with Allen he devised the idea of the suffusions that afflict Marnie whenever she sees the color red. "I loved the idea, and he wanted to do it," remembers Allen. "So this was a little gift he was giving me." Hitchcock wanted to create the effect for the audience that Marnie has "a moment of nausea." Allen subsequently devised the idea of the red suffusions as a result of the gladioli, the red ink, and the red polka dots on the jockey's shirt. In the first draft, Mark gives Marnie a ticket to an automobile show, and she perspires when she sees a red compact car against a stark white background.

"He gave me the essence of what he wanted in a scene and gave me lots of options to interpret this," Allen says.

> Because I had no previous film experience, I wrote in a linear way, particularly during the honeymoon sequence from the marriage to the ship's bedroom. I phoned Hitch to say I didn't think this was working. Hitch said, "Why don't we have the church bells ringing, then people coming out, and they're throwing confetti, then cut to a bouquet of flowers in the honeymoon bedroom with a card saying congratulations, and water is sloshing in the basin." So from five scenes, Hitch reduced it to one scene. That was a masterful lesson in screenwriting he gave me.

Unlike Hunter, Allen didn't define the honeymoon scene as rape, and Hitchcock never used the term *rape* with her. She saw it as a trying marital situation, and it never became an issue, so the pivotal cause of Hunter's dismissal passed by Allen with no fuss. The rape scene as written is very specific in camera direction, suggesting that Hitchcock led his writer through the choreography. Little is changed from the initial draft to what was finally filmed:

> The violence of her rejection triggers an equally long controlled violence in Mark. In one cruel and brutal movement, his hand streaks out and tears the gown from her body. . . there is no outcry from her . . . only silence as the camera focuses on her bare feet and legs, and the violated gown that lies around them. When the camera cuts away, it comes up to include . . . close-up . . . both their faces . . . Marnie, her eyes closed, her face rigid and white . . . Mark, shocked, sorry . . . but terribly moved at the sight of her, naked and helpless before him. Slowly he takes off his own robe and covers her with it. Mark says "Marnie, I'm sorry."
>
> His hands, placing the robe around her bare shoulders, seem unable to leave her. Still she does not move from her icy stance. Gently, but compulsively, he pulls her to him, softly, coaxingly covers her face with kisses . . . it is not just his desire that has finally overflowed, but his very real love for her. And it is love that dictates the manner in which he takes her . . . not simply using her, but courting, caressing, desperately urging her response. Marnie, her fear and

revulsion manifest in her frozen face and body, yields only to his superior weight and strength and will. As she is pressed back onto the bed, the camera closes in on their heads. Mark's face, pressed first against her cheek and neck, and then against her breast, is hidden from our view, but Marnie's face, stark, staring blindly at the ceiling above her, is completely exposed to us, and on it is written . . . nothing. There is no flicker of expression, of emotion. It simply . . . endures.[11]

One of the important changes that Allen made from the original novel was dropping the Roman and Terry Holbrook characters. Both she and Hitchcock agreed that Mark Rutland should be the only male, and another female character was needed to be built up. Allen subsequently introduced Lil on page 44 of the original script: "A good looking young girl, about nineteen or twenty. She is casually, even carelessly dressed. She is not necessarily pretty, but scrubbed and fresh looking. Her eyes are bright and her expression is lively and intelligent. She has enormous self-assurance, and she is extremely good-humored and high-spirited, as these qualities show instantly. . . . Lil is obviously privileged."

By dropping the character of Roman the psychiatrist, the whole psychoanalytical aspect of the novel was simplified. Hitchcock instead may have wished to focus on the relationship between two people and the intricacies of a marriage that he had previously explored in *Under Capricorn.* All of Marnie's attempts to conceal her past and her real life, which amounted to the funny and tragic passages in the book, were telescoped into the single free-association scene, with Mark doing the analysis himself. In doing so, Mark had to be given credentials, so Allen made him a zoologist. The subsequent animal symbolism suggests philosophical inquiries into man's ancestry, evoking the work of Konrad Lorenz, Desmond Morris, and Robert Ardrey. "I wanted Mark to be very knowledgeable about animal emotions," says Allen. "Animals have the same emotions as we do; they're all from the same lower part of the brain. Pride, rage, all of those things are derived from other animals. . . . I thought I brought to *Marnie* a native instinct with psychology, and that was very primitive. The book was primitive, the story was primitive, and my work was primitive."

Despite the psychological framework Hitchcock took great pains in developing with his writers, Allen remains adamant that the sole purpose was commercial rather than striving for any art house status during the conception of *Marnie:* "Hitchcock always wanted to make psychological studies. I think that on a conscious level, very little of this came to the surface with Hitch. I think he set out to make entertaining, successful movies, and I think on a conscious level, he never deviated. And I do think I got to know him personally, certainly as well and much better than most writers." Although Allen was one of the few women who knew Hitchcock, the director may have kept his innermost feelings from even those closest to him. The flashback that Hunter devised was altered so that it is Marnie who kills the sailor:

> The child stands . . . not knowing what to do . . . how to help. The sailor shakes his heads, begins to crawl off the woman, but in doing so, he causes her even further pain and she screams. At this, the child is driven beyond her endurance. She grabs up the poker and strikes out at the man. We do not see him; we only hear the blow and the stricken sound that comes from him, the protest . . . "no . . . n. . . ." She strikes again. We see only the child's face . . . the widened, shock blank eyes. Then superimposed on the child's face we see the grown up Marnie, the same expression, the same blank horror. We see what they see. The chest and shoulders of the Sailor, his white undershirt, whiter now than ever in contrast to the great splash of red that stains it . . . the white and red . . . the camera moves hard into it, filling the whole screen with the red of blood narrowly edged with white. It is the red and white of Marnie's obsession. The storm crescendos and Marnie . . . our Marnie screams . . . a long, full-throated, hair raising scream.

In Stefano's original treatment and Hunter's script, Marnie returns to find her Baltimore home full of neighbors: her mother has just died. A love scene then takes place between Mark and Marnie, only to be interrupted by the arrival of the police, who have come to arrest her. Hitchcock dropped the scene because he felt there would be an inevitable cliché, with Mark saying to Marnie, "I'll be waiting for you when you come out."[12] During the construction of the screenplay, Hitchcock said he was bothered by the long time period between Marnie getting her job at Rutland's and committing the robbery. Between the two events, the main narrative was Mark amorously pursuing Marnie, which he felt was not enough to sustain interest.

Hitchcock and Allen watched for inspiration the French film *Les Dimanches de ville d'Avray* (Sundays in Cybele) (1962), directed by Serge Bourguignon. Pierre (Hary Kruger) kills a child on a routine bombing mission in Vietnam and subsequently suffers from delayed stress and partial amnesia. Returning to France, he lives like a recluse until he meets a young girl (Patricia Gozzi) who has been left by her father at boarding school. Posing as her father, Pierre contrives to meet the girl every Sunday, to play with her and perhaps recover his memory. The innocent friendship is misinterpreted by nearly everyone, even people who know Pierre well. Later, the film became a classic of French cinema.

A second-draft screenplay was submitted by Allen on August 19. Hitchcock's copy shows many adjustments in his penciled handwriting. Marnie's mother's "trouble" is changed to "the accident"; when Marnie spills ink on her white blouse, the screen is once again briefly suffused with a red glow. Her visit to the automobile show is deleted, as is a dream sequence in which she is likened to Sophie, the pacing jaguarundi in the cage. At the end of Mark's line "That paper deals with the instincts of predators, what you might call the criminal class of the animal world," Hitchcock adds, "where the ladies figure very largely as predators." After the flashback when Marnie screams, Hitchcock wrote, "[As] the screen becomes flooded with red over her face. As the red fades we pull away, back to normality. We are back in the Baltimore living room, as it has always been."

One attribute that Mark and Marnie share is an upbringing that casts them as outsiders. This is most evident in the three short honeymoon scenes that Hitchcock and Allen included to illustrate the passing of time. In the first scene, Mark and Marnie are having dinner. Mark says Marnie will bring some "bezazz" to Wyckwyn as he noticed his father "putting out his silk shirts." In the original shooting script, Mark goes on to elaborate: "I don't think bezazz was the particular specialty of my mother. . . . That's right cement and gravel, Chicago. Nice girl I'm told . . . but more in the line of barns than bezazz. Of course I never really knew her. She died in a hunting accident when I was six weeks old. I was the only boy in my crowd whose mother was buried in her boots."[13]

The last of the three short scenes culminates in the explicit dialogue of "a beautiful flower . . . coral colored with little green tipped blossoms, rather like a hyacinth . . . the flower is not a flower at all but made of . . . fattid bugs. They escape the eyes of hungry birds by living and dying in the shape of a flower." Here, halfway through the script is the crux of the film. Marnie herself has been living a disguise to escape from a predatory society, which includes the sexual advances of men. A line from Mark was dropped that elaborates on the theme of human isolation: "Even the flower the bugs imitate is singular . . . as singular as I am, Marnie, as singular as you." The fattid bug scene according to Allen was of great generic importance, and it should play as fully as possible, at the expense of the other scenes if necessary—hence the elimination of Mark's mother earlier in the dialogue. Allen said she wanted to convey "that in any aspect of beauty there may be extremely ugly elements, but the overall thing is beautiful. Marnie had terrible problems, but [Mark] saw her as a beautiful thing."

Allen returned to New York on September 11 and two weeks later submitted a final script of 224 pages. On October 5, Hitchcock flew to New York to discuss script revisions. He was specifically concerned that somewhere in the film they portrayed Marnie's internal struggle regarding her feelings for Mark. Allen rewrote the whole first visit to mother, and Hitchcock changed the little girl's name from Tommy Jean to Jessie and the mother's to Bernice. A revised final screenplay was handed in on October 9. Twenty-five copies were run off for Hitchcock and his production staff for comments. Tippi Hedren reasonably asked why Marnie tried to drown herself in the ship's pool instead of the sea. She was answered in a telegram from Allen to Hitchcock on November 19: "Regarding swimming pool line she can say, 'The idea was to kill myself not feed the damned fish.' Then she tries to conceal her horror but she is shivering." Hedren also asked why Marnie took the job at Rutland's when the company was such an important client of Strutt's. Mark is made to answer this question during the car ride after he has unmasked Marnie.

## THE AUTHOR'S INPUT

On December 10, 1963, Hitchcock wrote to Graham to express the many changes in the script:

> A new character has been introduced and she is the sister of Mark's dead wife. She is a girl in her very early twenties, and has quite "staked out" Mark for herself. It is she who discovers the existence of Mr. Strutt and is responsible for inviting him to a party at the Rutlands'. Thus, we don't have a coincidence in Strutt turning up. There are many other details that I cannot go into now, and if you'd like, you can look over the script. But, you must be patient with me, the changes haven't been made for the sake of change, there is a reason for all of them. For example, Mark's character has been strengthened considerably by giving him the knowledge, at the beginning, that Marnie is a thief and, as he is intrigued by the idea, this becomes almost a fetish with him. In other words, he becomes a hunter. And, as he feels he has her tamed, lo and behold, she robs him.

Graham generously wrote back on December 18, 1963:

> In fact, I'm not frightfully fussy about keeping to the letter of a book. I feel when a film is made the book has to be unpicked almost to the original idea and then rebuilt in the new medium, maybe using a lot of the book material but only if it contributes in the best way to the re-telling. For this reason I can see that a sister for Mark's first wife may be an advantage: a film story needs more support, more obvious motivation than the same thing in novel form. I think the only thing I am rather anxious about is the spirit of the thing. To me, Marnie and Mark have got to go to war in earnest. . . . Perhaps the anxiety arises a little from your choice of Sean Connery—a first rate actor quite apart from his looks and perfectly capable of anything he is asked to do—but the two James Bond films do tend to type him a little.

When Graham received the script, his concerns were allayed. He wrote to Hitchcock on January 9, 1964:

> I must say I found it a very exciting script to read, and I think over-all it is a quite remarkably excellent one. The mainstream of the story is preserved, it

grips from the very start, and, so far as I can see, there is a steadily mounting interest and tension right to the end.

Certainly there have been plenty of changes from the book, but for most of them I can see good reason. My one main fear, mentioned in the my last letter, certainly has not been realised! Marnie is even tougher than in the book. I can see Sean Connery perfectly in the part he has to play, and I pray for Tippi Hedren, who could come right out at the top with such a part.

I have practically only one qualm, which surfaced slowly through the last quarter of an hour of reading; this was that the script makes Marnie just that bit too tough right to the finish for the sudden happy ending to be acceptable. I wonder if this qualm has any validity. I judge only by the bare script, when the camera can do so much and do it so subtly.

Pursuing this for a moment, in the book while there was little or no relenting so far as Marnie was concerned in her attitude towards sex, there were various indications that she found herself, unable to hate all the rest that Mark stood for. In the film there only remains the scene at the party before she meets Strutt—vital and excellent—and her sudden inability to steal the money from Mark's safe. While I see very well the reasons for not having Mark involved in the hunting accident, I think this is a major loss. When they are both lying there in need of her, Marnie's choice of her hated husband in preference to her beloved Forio is pivotal if one is going to see her as a troubled human being on whom constant kindness is subconsciously beginning to leave its mark.

If she has to shoot Forio, is it not a mistake that any look of satisfaction would come over her face when she's done it? (I know this is meant as a psychological link-up with her having killed the sailor.) Similarly just after this on page 180 she says things "sweetly, reasonable" and "reasonably, pleasantly" and 181 she wears a cunning expression, all of which seems to indicate a state of mind bordering on insanity, where I would have thought bitter distress would have been ample reason for her to be dangerous with the gun.

I would not presume to make any of this comment—since your scriptwriter's view of *Marnie* is by this stage as valid as mine—were it not that the end presupposes a sudden cure, and the more insane she looks the harder this will be to swallow. You and I know, and maybe audiences don't, that to uncover the cause of a repressed psychological trauma is only the first big step towards a cure—there may be a long and trying struggle after—but the more reasonable we could make it all, I think, the better.

Throw this away if it's useless; it may be. You're a wiser man than I am.

I wonder if even the slightest addition at the end might help. Might Mark and Marnie perhaps go downstairs at the very end and get into the car to drive away[?] He puts his arm round her again, offering her protection and sympathy, and she has the same old revulsion and starts away—then half checks herself, stares at him unsmiling through her tears. She says: "Give me a little time, Mark, please. Just a little more time. I'm—so lost." And he, quietly accepting that he has won, nods at her gently and says: "I can wait, my love. Now I can wait."

Graham signed off, saying "Anyway, it's a darned good script, and I wish you all the luck in the world with it."

At the beginning of 1964, Hitchcock was involved in an arbitration with the Writer's Guild of America (WGA) over the authorship of the *Marnie* script. Peggy Robertson, on Hitchcock's instructions, spoke to the WGA on January 6, 1964, categorically insisting that Jay Presson Allen never read Evan Hunter's screenplay and, in fact, had never seen it. A copy was sent to Hunter to compare with his own. His agent, Scott Meredith, wrote to Peggy Robertson on January 14, refusing to send a countersigned release and saying there were far too many major points of similarity and that "the structure of Mrs. Allen's screenplay was too dependent upon Evan's." Subsequently, screen credit for Hunter was requested. Allen had, in fact, read the ten-page synopsis of Hunter's script and inherited many plot devices from it. Hitchcock's office refused to acknowledge this in its reply: "In the event that Evan Hunter is given screen credit by the Writer's Guild, we will make an extra card for Jay Presson Allen to read as follows: Mr. Hitchcock wishes to thank Miss Jay Presson Allen for her cooperation on this picture." The dispute was subsequently dropped, and Allen received sole credit for the screenplay. (In 2000, this author asked Evan Hunter if he was bothered by this and he said he wasn't.)

## CONCLUSION

*Marnie* was the film Hitchcock intended to make after *Psycho.* Together with Joseph Stefano, he hoped to explore a frank sexuality and introduce some disturbing elements like fetishism and sadomasochism into the screenplay. Mark derives cruel pleasure from Marnie's painful entrapment and shows obvious enjoyment when he catches her failed robbery attempt at the safe. Such elements have no equivalent in the original novel, as Winston Graham stated that Mark wanted to go to bed with Marnie because he loved her and the fact that she was a thief was a deterrent, not an inducement.

Evan Hunter subscribed to Graham's view, and his perceived qualms about the rape undoubtedly irked Hitchcock. Hunter had been allowed the freedom to write in New York, and his salary was by far the largest chunk of the writing budget. He was paid $127,579, while Allen earned $24,879, which together with Stefano's fee and Winston Graham's brought the total sum to $226,459. As a novelist, Hunter infused the script with many good narrative ideas, such as the dynamics of the robbery and the flashback, but his refusal to write the rape scene undermined the director's main interest for making the film.

Jay Presson Allen's sensibilities were more in keeping with Hitchcock's. She never thought of the act as rape and was convinced that the character of Mark could be redeemed by the star's charisma, although it wasn't until the script was completed that Sean Connery was cast. In the shooting script, Allen remarks, "The remainder of this scene must be played to reveal Mark, the pragmatist, the man whose patience and sensitivity are equal even to this challenge. The casualness with which he plays this scene is only to conceal the depth of concern and sympathy he is capable of feeling."

Allen's screenplay was initially criticized for facile psychoanalyzing and film dialogue that is more redundant than enlightening. The repetitive speech, however, is perfectly in keeping with Marnie's compulsive behavior, her constant struggle to find her own identity, and the notable failure of language to help define the complexities of human sexuality. Significantly, the Rutland firm is changed from being printers in the novel to that of publishers, and throughout the narrative, Mark's inflexion highlights the defining human trait of speech. The limitations of language is made apparent when Mark confronts Mrs. Edgar about her daughter's past, erroneously saying that he had read the transcripts and knows the whole story, when he is actually ignorant of what actually transpired. After the film was released, one critic, Kaja Silverman, cited *Marnie* as a film that is obsessed with the woman's voice, a voice that is normally repressed in traditional Hollywood film narrative. When Mark brings Marnie home to Baltimore, Silverman observes that Marnie's "voice often seems to circumvent her consciousness altogether. At these times she seeks not so much the language of the unconscious as the language of unconsciousness."[14]

A further insight that Allen brought to the screenplay was her own affinity for writing scenes about children. With *Marnie*, Allen subtly created an infantile woman, haunted by phobias, and one who has a problematic relationship with her mother. Allen's powers of adaptation are also present in her screenplay for *The Prime of Miss Jean Brodie,* in which she similarly created a sympathetic and multifaceted woman. As it turned out, *Marnie* was the first and last realized collaboration between Hitchcock and Allen. Although she worked on two drafts of *Mary Rose* and talked about adapting a John Buchan novel, Allen had a small child to look after and returned to New York and the theater. She would, however, continue to remain in contact with Hitchcock until his death. Both Allen and Winston Graham's input will be expanded upon in Chapter 9.

## NOTES

1. Alfred Hitchcock, American Film Institute seminar, 1972.

2. Unpublished portion of the Hitchcock-Truffaut 1962 interview, Alfred Hitchcock Collection, Margaret Herrick Library.

3. François Truffaut, *Hitchcock* (New York: Simon & Schuster, 1967), 304.

4. Truffaut, *Hitchcock*, 304.

5. Personal interview with Evan Hunter in Connecticut on August 31, 1998.

6. Unpublished portion of the Hitchcock-Truffaut 1962 interview, 242–43.

7. Peter Evans, "Take One: Six Years Since She Made a Film—And the Old Image Won't Be Good for Business," *Daily Express*, March 27, 1962.

8. Unpublished Hitchcock-Truffaut 1962 interview, 128.

9. Patrick McGilligan, *Backstory 3* (Berkeley: University of California Press, 1992), 21.

10. Personal interview with Jay Presson Allen in New York, October 17, 1999. All other quotes originate from this interview.

11. Jay Presson Allen, *Marnie*, first draft (August 7, 1963), 154–55.

12. Truffaut, *Hitchcock*, 306.

13. Jay Presson Allen, *Marnie*, second draft (August 19, 1963), 140.

14. Kaja Silverman, *The Acoustic Mirror* (Bloomington: Indiana University Press, 1988), 65.

*Chapter Three*

# Preproduction

Many times before filming started, we had gone through the character, feeling by feeling, reaction by reaction . . . with me especially, because Hitch was not only my director but also my drama coach, and I could have had no one better than Alfred Hitchcock.

—Tippi Hedren

While Hitchcock was working with his writers, he was simultaneously involved in the intricate preparations for filming with other members of the production team. When moving to Universal's lot, he brought with him his own creative personnel whom he had built up over the years. This talented and diverse group of people became informally known as the Hitchcock "crew." In addition to his personal assistant Peggy Robertson and secretary Suzanne Gauthier, the crew included Hilton Green, the production manager; Robert Boyle, the art designer; Edith Head, the costume designer; George Tomasini, the editor; and Bernard Herrmann, the composer. Hitchcock disliked working with strangers but preferred to work with the same people—talented, professional individuals, expert in their craft, who acknowledged the collaborative art of filmmaking.

## THE CREW

*Marnie* was the first and only Hitchcock film to be produced under Geoffrey Stanley, Inc., which was incorporated on September 26, 1961. Hitchcock was the president; Herman Citron, the vice president; Samuel Taylor, the secretary-treasurer; and Robert Winokur, the assistant secretary. Geoffrey and Stanley were the names of Hitchcock's white Sealyham terriers that he cherished and featured in his cameo during the opening sequence of *The Birds*. On December 13, 1962, a letter was sent from Hitchcock's office to the Motion Picture Association of America (MPAA), with a signed employment agreement. Hitchcock wished the title of *Marnie* to be registered with the MPAA as being produced by Geoffrey Stanley Inc., instead of Alfred J. Hitchcock Productions, Inc. It was necessary for Geoffrey Stanley to join the title registration service for this purpose.

Hilton Green first became associated with Hitchcock through the television show *Alfred Hitchcock Presents*. Assistant directors at the time were assigned by the production office, and Green was appointed for the second episode, which Hitchcock directed. "He came in to look at the sets, on that particular show," recalls Green.

> He spoke to the cameraman, who was Jack Russell, but he never communicated with me, even though I was the first assistant director. So I thought, well, it's good experience to have on your credits, to assist Alfred Hitchcock, but I'll never work with him again; obviously he didn't like me. Then the next show he was going to direct, the office called me and said that I was going to be the assistant. I said, "You've got to be wrong," but the office said, "Well, he requested you." The next time around everything was directed to me instead of the cameraman. It was like we had always worked together. From that moment on, I worked with Hitchcock on all his television shows.[1]

Green was employed as the unit manager on *Marnie*, and it was his responsibility to break down and schedule the script. By first discussing with Hitchcock how he intended to film, Green then met with the various departments—casting, art, and wardrobe—to determine the budget. "Hitchcock was always very critical of what the movie cost. And after approving a figure, he would hold to those costs," affirms Green. Hitchcock never sat in on the production meetings with the key crew but conferred privately with the heads of the department. "It costs roughly $20,000 a day to shoot a feature film," Hitchcock remarked, "and this is engraved in my mind as deeply as the story itself. There is really no valid reason for pictures to go beyond their projected time unless, through improper preparation, they are started in advance of script-completion."[2]

On November 20, 1963, a week before filming commenced, Green submitted a budget for *Marnie* totaling $2,154,698. This allowed for sixty-five days of first unit filming at Universal Studios, two days on location in Hartford, Connecticut, and twelve days of second unit work. The budget was divided up into $421,488 for the talent, $53,069 for the producer and staff salaries, $66,686 for the camera work, $224,147 for set construction and striking, $74,924 for set dressing, $43,053 for wardrobe, $29,905 for makeup and hairdressing, $49,774 for location work, $67,544 for film stock and processing, $36,408 for editing, and $45,403 for music. The accuracy and professionalism in which the budget was calculated is reflected in the final total submitted on April 11, 1964: $2,135,161, which was $19,537 under budget. Savings were made on titles, talent, and supplemental labor, but there were overages on wardrobe, set construction, sound recording, and camera.

In late September, James Hubert Brown began work as the assistant director on *Marnie*. Brown had started working for Hitchcock during the 1961–62 season of his television series when Hilton Green took a hiatus to help his father-in-law as a stockbroker. Starting out from UCLA, Brown became a second assistant director at the age of twenty-five. "I absolutely loved working with Hitchcock," recalls Brown. "He was like a father, and he treated me like a son. He was very kind, very generous, and he would invite me to lunches and dinners at his home in Bel Air and Santa Cruz. Hitchcock was probably the greatest boost anyone could have in his career, because the fact that he chose me to work with him as his assistant director, and that I worked with him for a couple of years, everyone else in the business thought I was really good. So by association, his reputation rubbed off on me."[3]

Brown was Hitchcock's assistant director on *The Birds* and was familiar with his mentor's working methods. He knew that Hitchcock preferred to shoot on the sound stage where he could retain control, rather than on location where filming was often exposed to the vagaries of the weather. Indeed, even with those few films shot on location such as *To Catch a Thief,* which Hitchcock filmed in the Riviera, the majority of scenes were shot back at the studio, either with process photography or backings. "During filming of *The Birds,* when it was cold and windy in Bodega Bay," recalls Brown, "he sat inside his trailer most of the time. He didn't like being out in the elements, and *Marnie* was designed, in such a way, except for the foxhunt and the racetrack sequence, that there wasn't much he had to leave the studio for, and when we did it was to the Disney ranch just outside Los Angeles, to shoot the scene where Marnie has to kill her horse." Accordingly, Brown scheduled the back projection for the car journeys and Marnie's horse riding toward the end of filming.

Any artistic intentions Hitchcock had for *Marnie*, he kept to himself during the planning stages. "He was a very shy person," says Brown. "I had the pleasure of getting as close to him as anyone else ever had. He talked about his life growing up and some personal things, but when it came to work, he kept most of his feelings pretty much inside. I don't think Hitch would ever have made a picture that he thought wouldn't be successful. He felt obligated to Universal and to himself to make pictures that were successful." Hitchcock, according to his colleagues, was an incredible raconteur and listened to other people's opinions about film, for he was very interested in the audience.

## CASTING

The challenge for Hitchcock in the 1960s was finding leading men with the star charisma and strength of character to act opposite his blonde leading ladies. Cary Grant and James Stewart, who starred in four pictures apiece for Hitchcock, were too old. The director partly blamed the aging appearance of James Stewart for the box office failure of *Vertigo.* Rod Taylor had worked effectively but rather blandly in *The Birds.* For *Marnie,* Hitchcock sought a leading man with the strength and charisma who could embody the complexities of the Mark character and in particular his notion of the man's fetishism. As early as May 1, 1962, the *Hollywood Reporter* noted that "Alfred Hitchcock is goading Rock Hudson for a stroll up that garden path with Tippi Hedren in *Marnie.*" On March 8, Hitchcock met with Rock Hudson and his agent to discuss an involvement in the film. Indeed, an early mock-up advertisement appeared in *Life* magazine in July 1962, bearing the title "I married a frigid female thief" with Rock Hudson in the leading man's role. "Rock Hudson, got to make him act," said Hitchcock to Peter Bogdanovich in early 1963. When Bogdanovich said that it would be a challenge, Hitchcock said, "He was good in *Giant,* I think Hudson needs direction."

Jay Presson Allen suggested Peter Finch for the role of Mark Rutland but recalls Hitchcock's invitation to watch footage of an actor, Sean Connery, who was garnering acclaim as the new James Bond in the film versions of Ian Fleming's novels: "When we watched the reel of this upcoming actor with a broad Scottish accent, Hitch and I looked at one another and said, 'Let's just go for it!'" The very essence of Connery's sexiness and youthfulness was what they were seeking in Mark Rutland, which differed from the pale, sallow nature of the original character in Graham's novel. The suggestion of Connery may have been influenced by Wasserman, to give *Marnie* the commercial appeal enjoyed by the James Bond franchise. "There was no one at that studio who told Mr. Hitchcock what to do, except Wasserman," said Hilton Green. "But I don't think he even told him but discussed who would be in it." Regardless, Hitchcock always selected his cast in the projection room and never instigated auditions or readings.

Sean Connery was born in Edinburgh, Scotland, on August 25, 1930. At 6'2" and 190 pounds, he was the son of an Irish father and a Scottish housewife. At the age of twenty-two, Connery broke into the chorus of the London Company of *South Pacific* by taking a two-day crash course in dancing. He toured with the show for eighteen months. Afterward, Connery took a salary cut and joined a small suburban London repertory company where he had a chance to do new dramatic roles every week. Set on acting, he educated himself with ten recommended books, including *My Life in Art, Ulysses, Jean*

*Christophe*, and *Remembrance of Things Past*. He graduated on to stock, repertory, Shakespeare, and British television movies, the latter starring opposite Claire Bloom in an adaptation of *Anna Karenina* for the BBC. In 1958, 20th Century Fox brought Connery over to Hollywood but underutilized his talents in such films as *Darby O'Gill and the Little People* (1959) and a small role as a mercenary in *Tarzan's Greatest Adventure* (1959).

With nine undistinguished film roles behind him, Connery was still voted by *London Express* readers as the ideal actor to play James Bond in the upcoming Ian Fleming thriller *Dr. No* (1961). Signed by producers Harry Saltzman and Cubby Broccoli, Connery was scheduled to make a new Bond film every fourteen months, which allowed him the opportunity to make at least one other major film each year. Following *Dr. No*, he starred in a second Bond picture, *From Russia with Love* (1963), after which he signed for the male lead opposite Gina Lollobrigida in *Woman of Straw* (1964). He was to report for Bond duty again in *Goldfinger* in the coming spring.

On September 24, after Hitchcock's agent Harry Friedman contacted Richard Hatton, Connery's English agent, the director was advised that Connery would not consider starring in a film without seeing the script first, and his asking salary was $200,000. Connery was already receiving $60,000 per picture plus $200 a week expenses, in addition to 5 percent of the gross on Saltzman's pictures. Later Connery conceded, "For the first time in my life I can ask to read a script, and if you had been in some of the tripe I have, you'd know why."

The next day, Hitchcock watched *Dr. No* in his private screening room with his agent Herman Citron, and a month later he viewed *From Russia with Love.* No doubt both men saw in Connery an actor of considerable range and star charisma. Hitchcock probably also detected a confident sexuality and hint of sadomasochism that he perceived in the role of Mark Rutland. "I wanted him for my picture because the part requires a virile, aggressive man, with a lot of authority," said Hitchcock to *Look* magazine.

On October 14, Broccoli-Saltzman sent a cable to Herman Citron stating that the terms of Connery's contract, as well as the asking salary, would include $1,500 weekly expenses and a round-trip fare for Connery's wife, the Australian actress Diane Cilento, and their baby son (future actor Jason Connery). The termination date for twelve weeks' work was February 7, 1964. Hitchcock replied the same day agreeing to the terms, but he stipulated that the additional request of first billing, 100 percent of the title for Connery, would only occur in the United Kingdom, with the rest of the world to be decided on later. In any event, Connery's credit would not be less than second, equal to that of Tippi Hedren's. It was also impossible to accept the end filming date, though Hitchcock expected to complete Connery's involvement in *Marnie* by the beginning of February.

Broccoli-Saltzman accepted two days later after telephone assurance from Citron that Hitchcock would revise the script so that Connery's role equaled that of Hedren's. Broccoli and Saltzman concluded the formal contract in Hollywood on October 25 and emphasized a November 18 starting date, as Connery was expected to finish on *Woman of Straw* by November 1. The actor's services were loaned out from Danjaq-S.A., the Swiss corporation who produced and arranged the distribution of the Bond films.

Universal Studios issued a news release on October 31:

> The Master of Suspense, Alfred Hitchcock, announced he's getting together with the master of counter spies, James Bond—or at least with the man who plays Bond on the screen, Scotland's Sean Connery. Connery and American actress Tippi Hedren will play the leads in *Marnie,* the film story of a woman who becomes a compulsive thief. Hitchcock said he would start filming the picture at Universal Studios in Hollywood on November 18th after Connery winds up a picture he presently is making with Gina Lollobrigida. It will be Connery's first Hollywood part since he leaped into prominence as Bond in film versions of the Ian Fleming novels. Hitchcock said he was going to present a new Connery—instead of being the much pursued bachelor, he'll play an understanding husband. "It will be a real switch," a Hitchcock representative explained after the announcement. "He may not shoot anybody through the whole picture."

The next day, renowned columnist Hedda Hopper added in the *Los Angeles Times:*

> Alfred Hitchcock, with an eye for the great ones, signed Sean Connery for *Marnie* with Tippi Hedren. Hitchcock refused to sit idly by while Cubby Broccoli and Harry Saltzman stole his thunder with their tongue-in-cheekery production of Ian Fleming's suspense stories in which Sean plays the hero, James Bond. *From Russia with Love* is outgrossing everything, including *Lawrence [of Arabia]* all over England. Fleming has readers by the millions and women flip over the rugged Scotsman Connery. Hitchcock starts shooting this month.

After the announcement was made, Hitchcock ensured that Connery be given a top star dressing room suite as well as a trailer on the set. This also applied to the actors who were to be cast in the roles of Lil Mainwaring, Bernice Edgar, and Mr. Rutland. When Connery arrived in Los Angeles on Friday, November 15 from London, he brought with him just two small suitcases. One was packed with clothes. The other was crammed with his favorite books, including complete works of Keats, collected works of Sean O'Casey (who was one of his heroes), and related authors. Universal Studios offered Connery a chauffeured car to take him to and from the set every day. But Connery, whose father was a truck driver, as he himself had been, eschewed the offer. Instead, he accepted a red Chrysler convertible, which he happily drove himself for the rest of the filming. On checking into his hotel, Connery was greeted with welcoming flowers from Hitchcock, with a card reading: "Welcome to California. . . . Best wishes for a pleasant stay here." There was also a bottle of vodka, scotch, bourbon, and La Ina sherry. A guest card was sent for use at the Lakeside golf club, because Connery was an avid golfer. Later when he chose a house to rent on 2114 Sunset Crest Drive, the actor's principal consideration was that it was located within minutes of a golf course.

Connery reported for makeup and wardrobe tests on *Marnie* the week commencing November 18. Hitchcock respected Connery's work ethic and had lunch with the actor three times that week, once together with Hedren and another time with Wasserman. Connery remarked, "Most of the younger British actors today, like Finney and O'Toole and me, are more organic, down-to-earth actors than previous generations. In America there is much more feel for realism than in Europe, where there is still a conception of an actor as being somehow divorced from real life, and in Britain, where acting is still often associated more with being statuesque and striking poses and declaiming with lyrical voices."[4]

With the two principal protagonists cast, Hitchcock and Allen introduced a third character to form the triangle in the script, which Stefano stated was one of the director's reasons for making *Marnie.* Significantly this character changed from being a man (Terry Holbrook) in Graham's novel to a woman, and Hitchcock was instrumental in her casting. An October 2 memo records that Hitchcock originally suggested Elizabeth Montgomery for the part of Lil Mainwaring, the scheming sister-in-law who competes with Marnie for Mark's affections.

The role, however, went to Diane Baker, a Hollywood-raised girl who had studied acting in Los Angeles and New York. Hitchcock watched two of her TV films, *Route 66* and *The Crudest Sea of All*, in his private viewing theater. Baker remembered Hitchcock offering her the part without having met her. Like Connery, she asked to read the script and was told by her agent that none would be forthcoming and that one just accepted with a Hitchcock film. "Of course, I said yes immediately," says Baker. "A few weeks later I was invited to have breakfast with Hitchcock and his wife Alma, at their beautiful Brentwood home right on the golf course. The three of us sat together in their kitchen. It was a late breakfast, eleven or twelve, on a weekend, I remember. Alma brought out a magazine with a picture of Grace Kelly with slightly darker hair. We did look similar. Suddenly I'm being told I look like Grace Kelly, and they began to talk about how they could make me look more like her."[5]

Hitchcock told Baker that she was very much like his idealized actress, cool and reserved, like Grace Kelly. As Baker observed, "Some of the great masters painted images of women who used the same model over and over; it was an obsession. They were never able to get that woman's image out of their minds. Hitchcock had the same obsession. He used actresses with a classic look, with similar hairstyles and similar qualities. Actually I think it was more a quality." Perhaps Hitchcock, feeling abandoned by Grace Kelly, felt a need to find an actress in each of his films who reminded him of her. She had a quality that he fell in love with that he needed to perpetuate. In the *Marnie* showman's manual that was published to accompany the film's release, Hitchcock endorsed Baker: "She's one of the brightest young creatures on the Hollywood scene . . . and she comes over so impressively because she concentrates all her knowledge and energies on her portrayal."

For the demanding part of Bernice Edgar, Marnie's puritanical love-withholding mother, Jay Presson Allen recommended the stage actress Louise Latham. Allen had been friends with Latham at school in Dallas and directed her in a performance of *The Little Foxes*. Latham had become an actress relatively late, after moving to New York. Her television screen credits included playing a frumpy religious fanatic in an episode of *The Defenders*. She was working in a New York theater when Allen called. "Jay knew that I had experience of gritty, hard-luck women who had fought their way through life," says Latham. "I was brought up on a Texas ranch before moving to New York. She said, 'There's a part which I think is very right for you. We'll fly you to meet Hitch and you can talk about things.'"[6]

Latham was brought over to LA at Universal's expense and accommodated in a hotel suite with the *Marnie* screenplay. "When I finished reading it, I knew I wanted this role," Latham remembers. "The characterization of the mother was beautifully conceived. It was such a challenge because it made you wonder why this terrible relationship occurred and what was the cause of all this pain and anger." Latham began investigating the role by trying to fathom the coldness, fear, isolation, and defensiveness that existed inside Bernice Edgar.

On arriving in LA, Latham had the impression that the city was full of taxis, just like New York. She had trouble getting one and arrived at Universal Studios half an hour late. Latham spied Hitchcock getting into the back of his limousine, heading in the opposite direction. She ran after the car and tapped on the window, calling out who she was. Hitchcock rolled the windows down and said, "You're supposed to be older." Latham replied, "Believe me, I've just aged ten years." He invited her in the car, and Latham cites meeting the great Alfred Hitchcock as one of her favorite incidences in life. As always, he was deliberately and marvelously unhurried in any circumstance. During the twenty-minute car journey, they chatted mostly about Latham's work in New York, and by the end of the car journey, Hitchcock said, "Alright, you've got the part."

*Marnie* was Latham's initiation to Hollywood filmmaking. Her training in the theater allowed her to work out her part in detail and depth, and her energy focus was to know her character thoroughly. Latham was surprised that so much of Hitchcock's interpretation of Bernice Edgar seemed to be left to her choice. "Hitch had decided that I was hired to play the older Bernice, and then asked me how about doing both parts. This involved making me both young and old, and there was a lot of work to do, though at the time Universal had great makeup artists in the industry."

Hitchcock was instrumental in casting even the smallest roles in *Marnie* and interviewed each of the actors he sought for them. One small but pivotal role was Susan Clabon, the assistant from whom Marnie steals the key for access to the safe combination. Hitchcock had watched the actress Mariette Hartley perform in Sam Peckinpah's *Gunsmoke,* though most of her previous experience, like Latham's, had been in the theater. She was invited for an interview in Hitchcock's office on November 7. For Hartley, it was a difficult time in her life, as her father had just died, and Hitchcock scared her. As she recalled, "I was an unknown in this town, but during the interview, he was charming, inquisitive, and brilliant. I laughed and it was a very pleasant interview. Later I became conscious of his perfectionism, but it was very rewarding for me to be in such an atmosphere because of the amount I learned."[7] Two weeks later, Hartley was fitted with the costume from the period, complete with 1960s bubble hairdo, and a salary of $3,000 for her work.

When it came to casting the role of Sidney Strutt, the lascivious businessman who Marnie robs in the opening scene, Hitchcock invited the gifted Broadway actor Martin Gabel. Some dissension arose between Hitchcock and Jay Presson Allen over the casting and subsequent portrayal by Alan Napier, the British character actor, of Mr. Rutland senior. As Allen's husband was from Berryville, Virginia, she knew the inhabitants, and Hitchcock didn't, but in his mind, for the audience to believe in a kind of American aristocracy, they had to be fake British.

## ART DIRECTION

For the production design of *Marnie*, Hitchcock invited Robert Boyle, the art director for *North by Northwest* and *The Birds*, as well as having designed the sets for *Saboteur* and *Shadow of a Doubt*. Born in 1910, Boyle graduated from college in architecture during the depression. He worked for three different architectural firms, but they all folded as soon as he got a job. When Boyle went to see Van Nest Polglase, an art director at RKO at the time, he was asked for representative sketches of his work. Boyle worked through the night to draw what he thought movie sets were like. The next day Van Nest Polglase phoned Paramount, and Boyle gained a job as a sketch artist. He garnered a solid grounding in illustration, continuity sketching, and matte painting. Later Boyle became an assistant art director but mostly worked as a sketch artist. Hitchcock had recently directed some films at Fox, and then he came over to Paramount to film *Saboteur,* and he said what he really needed was a sketch artist. So began Boyle's association with Alfred Hitchcock.[8]

"The art director or production designer from my standpoint starts the project with the script," says Boyle. "You have to identify your characters. Really the art director is a contributing factor, and aids the director in getting what he really wants out of the whole film."[9] As early as February 1963, Boyle had met with Hitchcock and Evan Hunter to discuss the production design of *Marnie*. The opening frame illustrates Hitchcock's precision in storyboarding the visuals in his mind, well in advance of shooting:

> The film is going to open with a girl, back view, going to a railroad station at Hartford, Connecticut. At present, I don't know what time of the day we can shoot it because we don't want it full of crowds because it may cover her up. The essential part is that we follow her back view into the station as she goes to the desk or booking office. . . . We go close enough to her to see the color of her hair, and finally she goes on to the platform down toward the train. . . . And we end up with a close shot on a rather bulky handbag under her arm. So that would constitute the first scene.[10]

In mid-March, Boyle traveled to the East Coast to scout potential locations for the film.

> I prefer to do my own scouting, and I'm sure that most art directors would, because they not only have in mind what they're looking for on the outside but what's on the inside. And a location manager or production manager is liable to be thinking about it in terms of how close it is to the nearest Holiday Inn where he can put the troops up and things like that. In other words, it becomes more of a convenience. I find that they will select locations that are convenient, whereas an art director is probably more apt to think of it in terms of its particular value to the film, the location value of the film. I don't say that all location managers are like that, but that's been my experience—that is more often true—that they will think of it in terms of logistics.[11]

Hitchcock was very conscious that many films had an artificial look because the sets were dressed badly, a result of the dresser's lack of knowledge of the character who lived in a particular room. One way that Hitchcock overcame this was to send a photographer with a color camera to take stills: "Like in my picture called *Vertigo*, Stewart was playing a retired detective who went to law school who lived in San Francisco. So I said go into San Francisco, find out where a retired detective lives and make sure he went to law school and go in and photograph his house. Get all the detail and bring it back and dress the set that way."[12]

Boyle began his research on *Marnie* by first making a set list, which established the film's time and place. For three days beginning August 26, Boyle sat down with Hitchcock and Allen for a conference on the script and the set design. Hitchcock chose to film the Baltimore waterfront street, where Marnie's mother lived, on a soundstage instead of on location. The interior of the Rutland mansion was to be filmed on one stage, where they were also to film the process work for the car journeys and horse riding sequences, and the ship's honeymoon suite was to be filmed on another stage. George Milo was called on to dress the set, choose furniture and carpets, and select ornaments and paintings from the prop room. It was Boyle, however, who supervised the overall painting, finishing, and dressing of the set.

One crucial element in *Marnie*'s mise-en-scène was the color scheme. The change from a somber to a bright mood and then back to somber was very interesting to Hitchcock. One way the director achieved this effect was through color. Boyle stated that most of the colors were subdued, enabling the red to be more prominent in the latter half of the film. The same technique had been employed in *The Birds*, and Boyle used Edvard Munch's painting *The Scream* as a source of inspiration for that film's dark and gloomy look. During Marnie's robbery of the Rutland safe, Hitchcock requested that the interior of Ward's office be light in color and the safe be a light gray, so that Marnie's green coat would show up against both. In the Rutland home, as Boyle indicated, the color yellow was an affirmation of life, not a problem color like red, which indicated disaster and death. "I was very interested in *Marnie* because Hitchcock was exploring this problem about a woman who was a thief. And he was exploring why she would become a thief. He was always interested in the psychological, I'm not sure he was always in command of it, but his interest was great."[13]

Early on in the production design, Hitchcock had indicated to Boyle that the whole flashback sequence was to be filmed in desaturated color, which would convey the impression of memory: "Now the whole of this is where we're going to devise a form of flattery, we're not going to do it like they did in *Freud* by putting on oil diffuse around the edge . . . we're probably going to do sharp cutting. . . . Marnie will be in the same position, see, as she was as the child and when we cut we're going to cut to washed out color. We have full color as the present. The washed out color is the past, but they are intercut."[14]

On September 13, Hitchcock and Boyle traveled to Philadelphia to scout background locations for the film. The next day they visited the Atlantic

City racecourse and decided on the shots that the second unit would film for background plates a week later. Boyle returned to Philadelphia the following month, with James Brown and Pierre "Frenchie" Valin, the photographer. They embarked on a research trip to Baltimore, New York, and the Virginia countryside. Requests had been made from the wardrobe department for color photographs of Philadelphia men wearing lounging suits, sports jackets, and top coats. A special request was made to make a tape recording of the speech of a Philadelphia mainline gentleman reading long speeches from newspapers. Brown chose Governer Cadwalader of the Philadelphia Club, whose way of speaking was considered to be very proper Philadelphia. His voice patterns were later carefully studied by Sean Connery.

Color photographs and research of a publishing firm similar to Rutland's were undertaken in Philadelphia. Hitchcock was adamant that the Rutland office staff not be dressed like Californians. In Baltimore, photographs of street exteriors with stores were captured, as well as the dress of children in the street at that time of the year. Color stills were also taken of the Virginia countryside, which artist Albert Whitlock would later use to copy for the matte shots around Wyckwyn, the Rutland home. Garrod's riding stables, the Red Fox Tavern, the Greyhound bus station, the Lincoln Continental car that Mark drives, and locker keys in New York were also investigated.

James Brown's main task was to organize the foxhunt and choose a location for filming. He contacted Nancy Penn Smith Hannum of the Radnor Hunt Club, who lived in Unionville, Pennsylvania, and hired a couple of riding doubles to stand in for Tippi Hedren and Diane Baker. Brown also looked for a house in the Radnor or Unionville hunt countryside that was to provide the authentic atmosphere and the proper Philadelphia background for the film. After searching the hunt regions, Brown settled on Wyllpen Farm, the West Chester residence of Mr. and Mrs. William B. Wilson, who also belonged to the Radnor Hunt Club. The exterior of Wyllpen Farm was photographed for Wyckwyn, but only the driveway appeared in the final cut. The front of the house was to be shot on the Universal back lot.

Later during production, Brown looked for a ship that would provide the exteriors for the honeymoon sequence, when a frantic Mark searches for his missing bride. In early January 1964, Hilton Green went up alone to lay out the sequence at the American liner, SS *Wilson*, moored in a San Francisco port. Then on Saturday, January 11, Hitchcock, cameraman Robert Burks, and James Brown traveled up to meet Green and overlook the liner, in addition to scouting San Jose railroad stations. Green recalled that evening to be one of the finest he ever spent, for the gentlemen then retired to Hitchcock's mountain home in Santa Cruz, where Alma fixed them a gourmet dinner.

## STORYBOARDING

It is well documented that many of Hitchcock's films were extensively story-boarded before filming commenced. In fact, Hitchcock often boasted that he didn't need to look through the camera because he had worked with his scriptwriters for months in advance of production and plotted every scene beforehand. As many as seven hundred camera setups were sketched before the actors began their work. In *Marnie*, there were a number of complicated set pieces, such as the racetrack and hunt sequences (figures 1 and 2), that required careful storyboarding to integrate the location filming with the studio process work.

Harold Michelson was a storyboard artist who had sketched many scenes for Hitchcock's Paramount pictures, including *Rear Window* and *The Man Who Knew Too Much*. Michelson never met Hitchcock at Paramount because the art department sent all the sketches to the director's office. Circumstances changed when Michelson worked for Universal and was employed on *The Birds*. Hitchcock was impressed enough with the sketches Michelson had drawn to invite him on location in Bodega Bay to carry out further work on the film's complicated bird attacks.

"We all felt that Hitchcock was a complete filmmaker, and I learned a lot from him," says Michelson.

> When you lay out a storyboard and you get a criticism from him, it's very good criticism—he's telling you why. His reasons were always right. I did some stuff which I thought was sensational, but Hitchcock said, "These are really terrific, but I can't use them here." That's when I began to learn that we were doing a symphony, with the high notes and the low notes and he knew where to put them. I've worked for fifty years on hundreds of pictures, but Hitchcock is the one person who impressed me the most. He used to say that the picture was done even before it reached the camera.[15]

Michelson began work on *Marnie* on October 16, 1963, and the main purpose of his storyboards was to communicate to other members of the production team:

> In many cases you have carte blanche up to a point, and then you bring it to the director. Many directors feel threatened by it, but not Hitchcock. When he agrees, he makes hundreds of copies, and the makeup person knows where to go, and the special effects person knows where to go. I like to give all the information I can, like shadows and costume. I would get together with the costume designer, and I'd like to get to know what they would wear so I could put them in my sketch.

## COSTUMING

During the 1960s, many actresses were reveling in a frank sexuality, but Hitchcock's ideal woman remained tastefully dressed and sexually mysterious. She may well have had her origins in Hitchcock's mother, Emma, and her Victorian wardrobe.

Like other of his heroines beginning with the letter M, Marnie is the classical locus for Hitchcock's notions of femininity. Throughout the narrative she boasts thirty-two changes of costume, which far exceeds that of any other Hitchcock heroine. Clothes play a crucial role in the plot of shifting identities, camouflage, gender relations, and class distinction. In the early scenes at her mother's and at Rutland's, Marnie dresses respectably, acknowledging her potential as a spectacle for the male gaze.

Hitchcock's favorite designer was Edith Head, whose career spanned an amazing fifty-eight years at both Paramount and Universal Studios. During her lifetime, Head received more accolades, including eight Oscars, than any other costume designer in history. In the 1920s, Head was working as a language teacher when she applied to a sketch artist advertisement for Howard Greer at Paramount Studios:

> I had just started studying at the Chouinard Art School, and I borrowed a lot of sketches. As a result, I had a fantastic portfolio. I had seascape, landscape, portrait, costume design. I showed them to Greer, and he said, "I have never seen so much talent in one portfolio." I got the job. But the next day didn't go as well, because I wasn't very good at drawing, and my sketches showed it. Fortunately, Greer had a sense of humor, and I stayed on.[16]

Head's initial dishonesty proved fortuitous for Hitchcock, as they shared a happy collaboration through eleven of the director's films. Head was also responsible for creating personal wardrobes for the director's protégés Vera Miles and Tippi Hedren. At this time, Universal had five different floors of men's, women's, and character clothing. All of Head's tailored clothes were made at Western Costume, whose staff were experts in hats, jewelry, and costuming, and normally she would have up to eight weeks to prepare before filming began.

"If you're under contract, as I am, you're sent a script and, whether you like it or not, you do it," Head remarked. "Hitchcock will send me a script, and if I say, 'Hitch, what do you like?' he will reply, 'My dear Edith, just read the script.' That's all. Until you have sketches ready to show him, there's no point in asking him what he likes."[17]

After Head had read the script, she would break it down into a very concise wardrobe plot, in which every actor and actress was defined. Head then showed the sketches to the production designer even before she took them to Hitchcock. "I think that unless clothes are synchronized with a room that is a cool color, or a hot color, or that's going to have a floral pattern, or no pattern at all, it's impossible to do a coherent job of designing. I not only work with the art director, but also with the set decorator. . . . Also I work with the cinematographer."[18]

On October 15, Head met with Hitchcock and Hedren to discuss the sketches that she had designed. Head believed that the fundamentals of clothing in film were to translate the wearer into someone they are not. She described her work as a cross between magic and camouflage. "When you work a great deal with a director, you know [his] likes and dislikes. Hitchcock has a complete phobia about what he calls 'eye-catchers,' like a scene with a woman in bright purple, or a man in an orange shirt. Unless there is a story reason for a color, we keep to muted colors, because he feels they can detract from an important action scene. He uses color actually almost like an artist, like using soft greens and cool colors for certain moods."[19]

Hitchcock and Head's collaboration over color costuming in *Marnie* was affirmed by wardrobe designer Rita Riggs, who was apprenticing with Head at the time.

> Hitchcock's color palette was very carefully thought through for the whole film. Both he and Ms. Head loved subtle palettes, the vicunas, the camels, the grays, and punches of color came in for an effect. I used to sit and ask him about color because color has always fascinated me, and I think I learned palette from him. Each color had a symbolism which is fairly general—you know, the blues are fairly passive, yellow is a happy color, and apricot is a warm, receptive color.[20]

One example of where the script positively defines costume and color occurs when Mark brings the horse Forio home for Marnie: "The front door opens. Marnie comes dashing out. She is dressed for dinner in a yellow full-skirted dress (short). . . . Mark and Lil stand and watch the bright slash of color on Forio's dark back diminish in the distance." Hitchcock said in preproduction, "I think the essential part of that scene is to show that Marnie, in herself, has got warmth, if there were only some way to get rid of all her psychoses."[21] Hedren elaborated by saying, "Yellow apparently means change. At this point Marnie is definitely going through a metamorphosis in her relationship with Mark. Edith Head took into account when designing the costumes what the character was doing and what makes a scene. So for this scene when Marnie will be racing off with Forio, she designed a yellow chiffon cocktail dress which was loose fitting and comfortable to wear—it's a very important moment in the picture."

Hitchcock had in mind one color scheme for Tippi Hedren and another for Diane Baker. On November 14, Hitchcock met with Head and Baker to discuss Lil's wardrobe. Baker elaborated:

> Creating the costumes seemed a collaboration between Hitchcock and Edith Head. When I arrived for my first meeting with Ms. Head, she was incredibly energetic and interested in Hitch's concept. She told me what Hitch wanted Lil to wear, how she should look, and how the clothes must be representative of her character. Then she asked me what clothes I had or had recently worn in a film that best suited me (i.e., flattered me) and then asked me if I minded bringing them in for her to look at, which, of course, I did. So, a couple of her designs for my character actually were inspired by other sources. I think she was under pressure during this period as well.

"It was great for me, because Ms. Head let me do the character people," remembers Rita Riggs.

> She did the fashions. I created the Radnor hunt out here from things they sent me from the East Coast. The learning process was irreplaceable, and I was about twenty years younger than my colleagues, so I was just an upstart with very large eyes and big ears, and listening and learning. My first three films were with Hitchcock, I could have been spoiled forever. There was no film school when I graduated from college and took my degrees. This was my doctorate and I often call it that, the years with Hitchcock and Edith Head. . . . But even during the making of *Marnie* I felt a certain sadness. It was a very manicured form of filmmaking. You could stay in an atmosphere and a group like this for so long, and then you're frozen in time. I also felt film was changing so much in the 1960s. Somehow by the end, I had a feeling I wanted to move on.

## HAIRSTYLES AND MAKEUP

Crucial to Marnie's duplicitous personalities and metamorphosis from demure secretary to mainline society hostess were the hairstyles created for her character. "*Marnie* was a difficult picture to do," recalls hairstylist Virginia Darcy, "because we had so many changes and moods."[22] As early as February 7, 1963, Bill Cramer, Universal's photographer, shot fifty stills on the lot of secretaries, script supervisors, and cashiers to give an impression of what Marnie's hair would be like.

Hairdresser Helen Hunt came to the studios to work with Darcy on various styles and colorings for Tippi Hedren. Darcy had first worked with Hitchcock on *The Man Who Knew Too Much*. The director barely said two words to her during that production, but then he began to trust her and respect her professionalism. "I was very lucky," Darcy says. "Hitch was quite wonderful and really had great feelings for me, and we became very close. Not many people got to know him, but when he gets a liking to you, it's a privilege because he was very generous." Later, Darcy worked as Hedren's hairstylist on *The Birds* and often intervened when she felt that the director was pushing his novice actress beyond her limits of endurance. Hitchcock replied, "I don't realize what I'm doing sometimes; I'm just a person." According to Darcy, Hitchcock had a tendency to forget that his characters were also real people, and he treated them like puppets.

When Grace Kelly was heralded for the part of Marnie, Hitchcock decided to hire Alexandre of Paris to design her hair. Alexandre had initiated the beehive and artichoke styles, and in addition to Princess Grace, he listed Jackie Kennedy, the Duchess of Windsor, and Elizabeth Taylor among his best-known clients. He had also fashioned Hedren's hair during her European promotion of *The Birds* a few months earlier, and Hitchcock was satisfied enough with the results to ask him to sketch and carry out hairstyles from the time Marnie was married.

In October, Peggy Robertson wrote a memo to Guilio Ascarelli of Universal Films in Rome, asking him to "please telephone M. Alexandre (the hair stylist) in Paris and find out from him what he would charge to have his assistant Gwendolyn fly out here and do approximately six hair styles for Tippi from Alexandre's new sketches." Alexandre's assistant arrived at the beginning of November and stayed at the Sportsmen's Lodge, where Hedren's hair was styled during that entire week. Darcy was present at the styling, as was Hitchcock, Edith Head, and Rita Riggs. An amusing incident occurred when Hitchcock, who prided himself of being conversant in French, gave instructions to Gwendolyn. Head, who had taught French and Spanish, then discreetly had to offer the correct instructions after the director's blunders. Often overlooked in later biographical assessments of Hitchcock is his generosity to his collaborators, for he arranged a sightseeing weekend for the French woman in New York before she flew back to Paris.

On November 11, Hitchcock wrote a letter to Alexandre: "I would like to express my appreciation of the hairstyles which you have designed for Miss Tippi Hedren who will star in my forthcoming motion picture *Marnie*. I am extremely pleased with them and know that they will be a great asset to my picture." The list of blonde hairstyle changes included the going away with the Rex hat and subsequent return from the honeymoon; the hair down for the first wedding night, the final wedding night, and the nightmare; an evening style for the ship's dining room and ship's lounge; daytime styles for the boat deck, arrival of Forio, and the Lil and Marnie stable scene; and, finally, a party style for the Hunt reception.

Because many of the hairstyles were time-consuming, they had to be abandoned in favor of simpler designs that Darcy instigated. The one outstanding Alexandre creation in the film occurs during the party when Marnie is confronted by Strutt. Both costume and hairstyle combine to meet the demands of the script:

> At this point, she must be beautiful, simply austerely beautiful. The gown she is wearing tonight (white or black) although eloquently simple, in no way resembles camouflage. The dress should make two comments . . . one on Marnie's instinctive flair for drama (when she can afford it) and two, her courage. Unintended by Marnie, the gown bespeaks another element implicit in the evening, her very imminent date with the firing squad.

"The party dress was a fun costume to do," Riggs recalls. "It was just very elegant. It was before fur was taboo, and Tippi is so linear that you could fit it and it just hung. . . . I have always said Mr. Hitchcock was the prince inside the frog. He really loved beauty so much, and I think that's why he loved the tall, blonde heroine."

The hairstyles, too, were as important as any other element in the film, because Hitchcock wanted an overall look. As Darcy remembers, "Everything was planned ahead of time and laid out during the production meetings, and everyone knew what their jobs were. I learned his ways of how production should be done."

On November 8, Hitchcock met with James Brown and Hilton Green to discuss the makeup employed in the film. For the ride in the Virginia countryside, Hitchcock specified that Marnie's face should be "Clean, with shine." At Wyckwyn, the key to the makeup was a style that was quiet, in good taste, neat, and not overdone. Starting in the morning of the hunt sequence, they were to begin with eye makeup to show distress and increase the tragedy in the eyes from the hunt until the end of the film. Bernice Edgar's makeup was described as being approximately forty-four years old as the mother of the present day. In the flashback scenes, Howard Smit, the makeup artist, attempted to make Louise Latham twenty-four years of age. So successful was he in achieving this that when Latham walked on the set as the young Bernice, the cameraman thought that another actress had been hired for the role.

## STORY CONFERENCES

Copies of Winston Graham's novel had been distributed to all key personnel during preproduction. For Tippi Hedren, reading the novel was very enlightening because the thought processes in Marnie's head highlighted her as a sad, devious, complex, and tragic woman. Hedren had attended conferences with Hitchcock and Jay Presson Allen when they were writing the script. Most of Hitchcock's directions were through such conversations, but with Hedren, Hitchcock took special care to discuss the psychological dynamics of Marnie. On October 22, 23, and 28, Hitchcock taped his story conferences with Hedren, just as he had done during pre-production on *The Birds.* The transcripts from their conversations offer the best insight of what Hitchcock perceived *Marnie* really to be. He described the narrative, mood, tempo, and emotion of the central character with great precision, leading his actress through every scene. Hitchcock was adamant on telling the story visually, through pictures and backgrounds, and did most of the talking, whereas Hedren responded only to affirm or question a point.

Hedren had just become engaged to her agent Noel Marshall, an event that displeased Hitchcock. The director was of the old school of thought, telling Hedren that she, and actors in general, should not get married but remain committed to their craft. Their professional relationship at this stage was courteous; Hedren was bright, and Hitchcock was very solicitous of her. Although Hedren had worked with Claudia Franck when she was filming commercials, she had no drama coach previously to Hitchcock. Consequently, an education that normally would have taken fifteen years, Hedren gained in three: "I sat in on every meeting that had to do with the building of the motion picture whether it was screenwriting, set decoration, clothes, wardrobe. The conversations before I went into a scene had already been done over a period of months, because Hitchcock discussed the whole script, every scene, before I went on the set. The character was being developed as the script developed."

The preproduction conferences clearly indicate the theme of Marnie as a hunted animal, a victim of society. Robert Boyle remarked that Hitchcock was very interested in the relationship between humans and animals, exemplified in *The Birds.* Allen had already adapted the character of Mark Rutland to be a zoologist, who had to abandon his preferred career to save the ailing family business. When Marnie glances at the framed photograph of Sophie, the South American jaguarundi, Mark replies, "I trained her . . . to trust me . . . that's a great deal for a jaguarundi." As Tippi Hedren recalls, "We made the comparison because it was a major step for Marnie to trust anyone." A sequence of Mark catching a bee at the racetrack and showing it to Marnie was also discussed but later dropped in postproduction. "He's a man who catches animals, but he doesn't crush them," observed Hitchcock.[23] When discussing the robbery sequence, Hitchcock said to Hedren, "Remember the other day when I was talking to you about what you were wearing—the walls must be painted accordingly." In other words, Marnie's brown costume provides concealment for her predatory actions. Hitchcock later talks of Marnie "holding her breath" when she sees the cleaning woman; Hedren replies, "Like an animal that hears something in the forest." When Marnie is packing under Mark's interrogation, his threat to beat the hell out of her derives a "quick defensive look from Marnie—throws her head up." Marnie, therefore, is a reluctant animal who Mark, the angry tamer with hints of sadomasochism, is trying to beat into submission.

During the height of the thunderstorm in Rutland's office, Hitchcock planned to show Marnie as a distressed, frightened animal: "We could use a lot of breath, breath held, you know, which will give us tremendous tension. . . . I'd rather it to be in the figure than in the face—the face should freeze." When Mark walks toward the immobilized Marnie at the door, Hitchcock noted, "As he comes towards her you see, the room will be dark, and I'll have it lit in such a way that he's a silhouette, almost a sinister thing coming." In Hitchcock's mind, Mark clearly becomes a surrogate for the sailors in Marnie's nightmares, linking thunderstorms and the color red with male sexual power. Hitchcock continued, "When she scrambles up from the sofa—now for the first time we can use the face. That's why I didn't want to use it before. Now the eyes can be wide, wild, you see—and almost unconsciously his hand moves up to her head to stroke it soothingly, as he would a child."

The greatest psychological strengths of the film lie in the theme, which Hedren describes as "a woman who was never able to be a child. She had to grow up very quickly." There are numerous indications of this analytical framework in both Allen's script and the preproduction conferences. Hitchcock planned to capture Marnie's lost childhood in the scene in which she is usurped by the little girl Jessie, for her mother's affections: "I think we should have an abstract expression on Marnie's face. She is looking at the child's hair being brushed, a natural viewpoint. Then we get the close up of Marnie—her eyes should go down a little, perhaps reflectively, and then back. Then we can dolly in to the brush moving across the screen—so close that the brush fills the screen in its movement up and down, and on its last movement down, the brush doesn't return." Hitchcock then intended to pull back to reveal the young Marnie in the ten-cent store and subsequently teased by other girls for having nits in her hair.

Hitchcock also elaborated on Marnie's speech patterns and tempo of dialogue, which would establish her childish nature: "This is a characteristic of Marnie—that when she reaches a certain emotion, as she does with the horse, she drops down and becomes kind of matter-of-fact. See, she builds up on the slap on the face, builds up on Mr. Pemberton, the slap on the face, and then the sudden change—she's controlled, slightly matter-of-fact." Hedren replied, "Like she doesn't want to admit it happened. Like it never happened—it's over and that's it." Marnie's continual refusal to acknowledge her problematic relationship with her mother is symptomatic of her relations to people and outlook to life in general.

The scenes in which Mark has caught Marnie after the robbery, and the subsequent long car journey, were very important to highlight both the range of rhythm and intonations in Marnie's speech and her evolution as a brilliant actress. Hitchcock observed:

> This is the first time she's ever been caught, so she's got two emotions; she's got the emotions of being trapped and cautious and shall we say crestfallen, but at the same time she wants to sound matter of factly truthful. There's the underneath emotion of having been caught and the more surface emotion of making her lies sound convincing. There is a double thing here you see. . . . Once she gets an idea, she lets it roll out—the tempo changes—she fumbles along a bit. . . . I want to make this very conversational, because it's a very long scene and it will need a lot of vitality in terms of its overall tempo.

A character biography in Allen's final script describes Marnie:

> She has loved only in fantasy. One result is that she has evolved into an excellent actress, able to improvise quite brilliantly in almost any situation. She has assumed, perfected and discarded so many roles, that to act (to lie) is as natural to her as putting one foot before the other. . . . She learned early and well that she is unlovable. Consequently anyone who loves her is contemptible and expendable.

Hitchcock added Mark's comment to the script: "What is the degree? Are you a compulsive thief . . . a pathological liar?" During the free-association game, Marnie's speech lapses into childlike patterns: "Stare and that's what you do," accuses Marnie perceptively. "You stare and blare and say you care but you're unfair; you want to pair!" The scene ends with Marnie's desperate cry, "White! White! White!" She turns her face to the bedstead, once again hoping to escape past demons by becoming part of the furniture. "It's a very sad scene, isn't it?" said Hedren. Hitchcock replied, "Yes, but it comes out of anger, it's a big—it's a helluva scene; if you can bring it off that's one of the best scenes in the picture, because of the tremendous light and shade in it."

Hitchcock and Hedren also worked out the subtle changes in Marnie as a result of Mark's therapeutic influence throughout the film. When Marnie inquires, "What about the Rutlands? What would have happened to your family?" this is the first time she expresses her interest in Mark and underscores the beginning of her gradual, deepening involvement with him. She finds him interesting enough to warrant her curiosity, having found all human beings thus far contemptible. As Hitchcock noted, "She laughs at him. I think she is intrigued by him here. I think she is interested in him. This passage here is really the first time she pays attention to him; otherwise she wouldn't have asked."

Hitchcock's subtle behavioral observations are also noted at the end of the racetrack scene, when Marnie passes the stranger: "When she goes by the man . . . I think actually we will get her in profile with the tiniest turn away from him . . . she'll walk not looking at him, to deliberately turn away from him—kind of burying her head in the sand you know." During the stable scene, when Marnie turns from Mark after their first kiss, Hitchcock planned for only the camera to record her anxiety: "This is the point where I'll probably take the camera in close to her, when you see for the first time that she is really under stress . . . her face is suddenly and strangely rather bewildered and pained."

Whereas Hitchcock intended to exclude Mark any knowledge of the extent of Marnie's neuroses, he planned to offer privileged insights to the audience. This is most demonstrable during the wedding reception, when Marnie's anxiety and presumable terror of the anticipated honeymoon night are noticeable only to the viewer. Hitchcock expanded:

> I think that we should try and photograph, as subtly as we can, the inner person and her outward behavior. And I think the way to do it is when she feels that no one is looking at her, although it's hard to discover what moment she would be left on her own, but her face would lapse into a mood, then brighten up when, say, Mr. Rutland kisses her—so that she isn't constantly in an apparently happy marital mood—that we see her now and again with the shadow over her face— but she has to pull herself up and put on a front. . . . Generally speaking I think that if we show that inside her she is going through the motions and externally it's a kind of forced show of happiness, for the benefit of everyone you know.

As Hedren suggested, "We could leave the smiles out of the eyes."

Later during the party scene, when Mark's efforts are beginning to have a positive effect on Marnie, Hitchcock remarked, "She flushes with pleasure . . . this is real pleasure for her and she does touch his arm. She feels that she looks good—she hears the praise about her riding—she's blossomed and she is the mistress of Wyckwyn."

## CONCLUSION

The excerpts from Hitchcock and Hedren's preproduction conferences affirm the collaborative nature between director and lead actress in working out the psychological dynamics of *Marnie.* Very rarely would Hitchcock discuss the needs of the audience, as he had done during such story analyses for *The Birds*. Hitchcock's striking attention to detail in costuming, hairstyles, makeup, and story conferences illustrate his intention for *Marnie* to be a showcase for one of his most psychologically believable characters. At the same time, Hitchcock was aware of the trade-off for building character instead of suspense, his true métier, and what critics and audiences expected of him.

Coworkers Robert Boyle, Harold Michelson, Virginia Darcy, and Rita Riggs all agree that Hitchcock was the most collaborative director that they had ever worked with. Although given a degree of creative license, they were essentially trying to interpret Hitchcock's vision and personal authorship. Hitchcock's feminine concept, together with his need to construct and control, can then account for the fascination with surface appearances in *Marnie* and the obsessive detail to clothing, haberdashery, and hairstyles. This naturally extends to his propensity for studio-bound work and the sketching out of storyboards, so that every camera setup and framing is detailed prior to filming.

Hitchcock's casting of *Marnie* is extremely cunning and correlates to our culture's construction of gender. As theorist Judith Butler describes, gender identity is the constituted effects of repeated poses, gestures, behaviors, and articulations. Rather than being inherently tied to anatomy, sexual identity is psychically and linguistically based.[24] Instead of casting stars of great range, he chose players who could be employed as icons that reinforce gender attitudes. Tippi Hedren, whose assured walk and aristocratic carriage Hitchcock first detected in her television commercial, personifies female assertiveness and liberation. As a professional model, Hedren's self-awareness of her own body language is apparent in front of the camera, and her resilience and practicality are demonstrable in her offscreen role as a divorced working mother.

Hedren also provides two qualities that are exactly what the script demands. First, she has an animalistic quality, inherent in her own love of animals, a prerequisite for Marnie's role as both hunter and hunted. In later years, Tippi Hedren formed the Roar Foundation at Shambala, a preserve for retired animal performers and specializing in big cats. "I've always loved animals, and I'm very overt about that. It's a birth effect . . . they are a big part of my life, my thoughts and my yearnings are to know more about animals. Maybe there is something about those who have a great affinity with nature, and it could well be that Hitchcock sensed that with me." Second, Hedren's childlike physicality and mannerisms aid in constituting an infantile woman during critical moments of hysteria, such as the shooting of Forio. Significantly, "Tippi" in Swedish translates as "little girl."

Selecting Sean Connery to play opposite his newly created star was a very smart casting choice on Hitchcock's part. In the role of Mark Rutland,

Connery benefits from his already entrenched persona of James Bond, a twentieth-century icon of sardonic masculinity and sexual arrogance. Connery has the male magnetism and charm that appeal to women and an indifference toward them that appeals to men. As Rita Riggs observes, "Sean was so much loved by the crew, both men and women." With Connery, Hitchcock indulged in his fantasies of a virile and aggressive male who resolves the sexuality of a neurotic and repressed woman. Furthermore, the massive male presumption in the character easily lends itself to the sadomasochism and fetishistic aspects, which were Hitchcock's reasoning for making the film. They are initially deemed acceptable by Connery's charisma, but these qualities make Mark Rutland's actions reprehensible and formed the source of an uneasiness and reluctance to accept the film when it was released.

By casting Diane Baker, Hitchcock attempted to create an offscreen triangle, in addition to the onscreen triangle of Mark, Marnie, and Lil. As the production was gearing up for filming, relations were turning sour between Hitchcock and Hedren, who felt that the director was making unreasonable demands over her personal life. Baker remembers:

> It seemed that some of his personal disappointment and anger played out during the making of the film. He was often very cold to Tippi, but he was warm and friendly to me. I was possibly too naive to realize all this at the time, but as the film progressed, I became more aware that Hitch's and Tippi's working relationship was coming to an end. Feelings were raw, tinged with innuendo. I've always been a private person, and Hitch was the first director I worked with who seemed to have a personal and emotional agenda on the set.

That turmoil is an undercurrent during the filming of *Marnie*, as we shall discover.

## NOTES

1. Personal interview with Hilton Green, Pasadena, September 5, 2000.

2. *Marnie* showman's manual, Alfred Hitchcock Collection, Margaret Herrick Library.

3. Personal interview with James Hubert Brown, Angels Camp, September 1, 2000. All other quotes originate from this interview.

4. *Marnie* showman's manual, Alfred Hitchcock Collection, Margaret Herrick Library.

5. Personal interview with Diane Baker, Hollywood, October 2, 2000. All other quotes originate from this interview.

6. Telephone interview with Louise Latham, Santa Barbara, California, September 21, 1998.

7. Telephone interview with Mariette Hartley, Los Angeles, July 1, 2000.

8. Robert Boyle, American Film Institute seminar, 1977.

9. Boyle, American Film Institute seminar, 1977.

10. Story outline for production design, February 4, 1963 (transcript of conversation among Alfred Hitchcock, Robert Boyle, and Evan Hunter), Margaret Herrick Library.

11. Boyle, American Film Institute seminar, 1977.

12. Alfred Hitchcock, American Film Institute seminar, 1972.

13. Personal interview with Robert Boyle, Los Angeles, July 16, 2000. All other quotes, unless stated, originate from this interview.

14. Story outline for production design, February 4, 1963.

15. Personal interview with Harold Michelson, Los Angeles, January 31, 2000. All other quotes originate from this interview.

16. Edith Head, American Film Institute seminar, 1977.

17. Head, American Film Institute seminar, 1977.

18. Head, American Film Institute seminar, 1977.

19. Head, American Film Institute seminar, 1977.

20. Personal interview with Rita Riggs, Los Angeles, January 31, 2000.

21. Hitchcock-Hedren transcript, Alfred Hitchcock Collection, Margaret Herrick Library.

22. Telephone interview with Virginia Darcy, Carpenteria, California, September 21, 2000.

23. Hitchcock-Hedren transcript, Alfred Hitchcock Collection, Margaret Herrick Library. All Hitchcock's quotes in this chapter hereafter originate from this transcript.

24. Judith Butler, *Gender Trouble: Feminism and the Subversion of Identity* (New York: Routledge, 1990).

Figure 1. Storyboard for the Atlantic City Racecourse, which was filmed for process plates and backgrounds. Courtesy of the Margaret Herrick Library, Academy of Motion Picture Arts and Sciences, and the Alfred J. Hitchcock Trust.

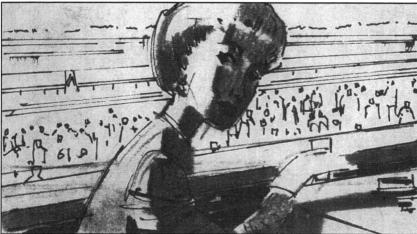

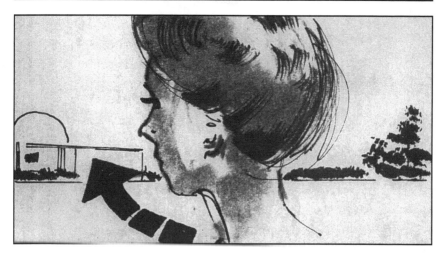

Figure 2. Storyboard for the hunt sequence was used for location filming and studio process work. Courtesy of the Margaret Herrick Library, Academy of Motion Picture Arts and Sciences, and the Alfred J. Hitchcock Trust.

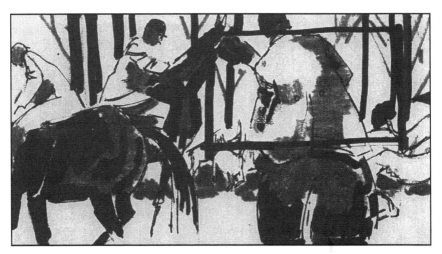

*Chapter Four*

# Filming

Smile as if you have a mouth full of broken china.

—Alfred Hitchcock to an actress on the set of *Marnie*

Hitchcock's preferred cinematographer was Robert Burks, who worked on all of the director's films from *Strangers on a Train* through *Marnie*, with the exception of *Psycho* (which was shot by the television crew). Burks began as a special-effects expert for Warner Brothers and worked on many prestigious pictures from 1944 to 1949. He then became a director of photography for Warner Brothers and later for Paramount, winning an Academy Award for his Technicolor Vista Vision photography for *To Catch a Thief*. His colleagues would praise him as both a gentleman and a fine cameraman. Inevitably Burks knew what Hitchcock wanted from a scene. Many a time Hitchcock asked, "What do you think, Bob?" Burks made his suggestions, and Hitchcock concurred.

Burks started work on *Marnie*, referred to by Universal Studios as Production #9403, on October 28, 1963. He was paid a salary of $1,500 per week, the same amount as for his work on *The Birds*. Burks's camera operator was Leonard South, and Babe Stafford acted as his gaffer. Photographic tests, such as the lightning effects and makeup for the principals, were conducted in the Rutland offices. Tippi Hedren had a 7:00 A.M. makeup call, two hours prior to filming, whereas Sean Connery received a 9:00 A.M. call.

## THE LOCATION SHOOTS

The first film to be shot was at Atlantic City's racetrack, which provided the background and process plates for the scene where Mark takes Marnie to the races. On September 20, a second unit crew traveled up and captured the shots that Hitchcock and Boyle had determined a week earlier. The crew consisted of director William Witney, assistant director James Brown, cameraman Rex Wimpy, camera operator J. Dodds, and matte artist Albert Whitlock. An additional twelve days were spent filming process plates and a few establishing scenes in Virginia and Maryland. The exterior of the Red Fox Tavern where Marnie arrives in the station wagon was filmed in Middleburg, Virginia, in addition to moving background plates of the countryside. In Baltimore, the high-angle shot of the taxi arriving in Mrs. Edgar's street was filmed, and the moving plates for Mark's car journey on Highway 1, with a stop at Howard Johnson's, was captured in West Chester.

Hitchcock assigned James Brown to film the foxhunt in Unionville, Pennsylvania. He had already given Brown the opportunity to choreograph the birthday party and schoolhouse sequences in *The Birds*, so he was aware that his assistant director was competent in working with both animals and a large cast of extras. Armed with a detailed storyboard drawn up by Harold Michelson, Brown returned to the hunt country in Pennsylvania on November 16. Just as the crew was preparing filming for the corning weekend, on Friday, November 22, President John F. Kennedy was assassinated in Dallas. Brown recalls, "Many people who were in the foxhunt were close friends of the Kennedys. Mrs. Hannum, the hunt mistress, called me and said we're going to have to cancel." The hunt was postponed for two weeks, but this turned out to be beneficial from a filming point of view, as only fifty riders participated. The 150 who were planning to take part would not have been nearly as manageable.

The foxhunt was beautifully shot and choreographed. Brown provided everything laid out in the storyboards plus more footage for Hitchcock to choose from. The two young women who had been employed as doubles were marvelous riders, and the horses and Cheshire hounds from Unionville also worked out very well. On November 27, the day before Thanksgiving, the crew filmed at Wyllpen Farm, the exteriors of which would double as Wyckwyn, the Rutland home. Brown hired a helicopter on December 2 to film the back projection shots used in the foxhunt, the shot where Marnie makes a jump and loses her hat, before emerging from the woods pursued by Lil, and the shot where Forio starts to leap over the brick wall.

In January 1964, location filming for Marnie's horse riding at Garrod's occurred on the Golden Oak Disney Ranch just outside Los Angeles. Hedren had worked with the horse that played Forio for three months before production began, developing a great rapport. Jack Carry was the horse trainer and coached Hedren to stop at an X. On January 18, Sean Connery and a crew traveled up to San Francisco, to film aboard the SS *President Wilson*. They filmed Mark's desperate search of the ship for Marnie, and in his rescue of her from the swimming pool, a body double was used.

## ON THE SOUNDSTAGE

Alfred Hitchcock used to say he entered "the area of compromise" only when he walked onto the soundstage, implying that the films he constructed in his head were far more satisfying than the ones he actually had to complete with actors. He also expressed a preference for working with actors who came to him untrained. In his opinion, "Beginners have an enormous advantage over those with experience for the most obvious of reasons, they have nothing to unlearn."[1] Hitchcock was often notoriously quoted as having made the remark that "actors should be treated like cattle." James Brown admits, "I was a little surprised about how little direction he gave to his actors. He left much to the actor's interpretation. He gave a lot of time and thought in casting actors and then letting them bring what they could to the character."

*Marnie* was due to start filming on Monday, November 25, but because of Kennedy's assassination, a national day of mourning was held, and filming commenced the following day. In total the first unit filmed for seventy-seven days, from November 26, 1963, to March 14, 1964, with only a break for Thanksgiving, Christmas Day, and New Year's Day. The Rutland office sequences were the first slated, with Hilton Green acting as the first assistant director until Brown returned from the East Coast. In the first week, the crew filmed the sequences in Ward's office and the outer offices. Hitchcock had an established routine that he liked to adhere to. Green remembers: "Most features used to have a 9:00 A.M. shooting call, but Hitchcock always liked to start at 8:00 A.M., which was a television schedule. You always started earlier, because you had more to do. And he never wanted to work past 6:00 P.M., so we always quit somewhere between 5:00 P.M. and 6:00 P.M. And on Thursday nights the crew had to finish early, because he had a standing dinner date with Mrs. Hitchcock at Chasen's."[2]

During filming, Hitchcock went to bed promptly at 10:00 P.M. He had the habit of waking up at 3:00 A.M., thinking about the picture for an hour, before going back to sleep. He woke up every day precisely at 7:00 A.M.—always without the benefit of an alarm clock. Hitchcock's affinity for routine was reflected in his wardrobe. Every day, he wore exactly the same type of clothes: a dark blue suit, tailored by the same man who had dressed him for years, a dark blue tie, white shirt, black socks, and black shoes. It was an attire that he encouraged his coworkers to adopt, so James Brown and Hilton Green wore a shirt and tie too.

Hitchcock only had coffee for breakfast and read both British and American newspapers before traveling up to Universal City. The crew came early to set up the lights, and the actors arrived for their makeup and wardrobe, so by the time the moves were blocked out, a shot in the can by 8:15 A.M. was a good start to the day. Hitchcock always went back to his office for lunch to watch the dailies. As the Technicolor labs were right on the Universal lot, the challenge was to process the film and synchronize it to the sound, but it was normally achieved with expediency. The crew had their own dailies that they would run at the end of the day. Hitchcock always shot the minimum of film and seldom asked for many takes, and if it worked on the first shot, he'd print it. Brown described the typical procedure before the camera started rolling:

> Hitchcock would tell me what the shot was, and what he wanted and expected. Then the cameraman did his lighting without the principals. I had all of the extras positioned and staged for the party scene, and when Bob Burks was ready to have the first team come in, the actors would come in and take their positions. I would go to Hitch's dressing room and say, "Do you want me to do a rehearsal, or do you want to come and take a look now?" He would say either, "Take a rehearsal, Jim," or "I'll come in." He let me do my own thing in terms of staging the background and the extras. When Bob Burks was ready, he'd either give me a nod or just say, "In five minutes." I would then walk to Hitchcock's portable dressing room on the stage, knock on the door if it was closed, or if it was partially open just poke my head in and say, "We're ready, Hitch."

The schedules were always very tight but possible. As Green affirms, "The times I worked with Mr. Hitchcock, whether as an assistant director or as a production manager, were the best times of my career, though he was really demanding to work with because he expected everyone to be professional and know their job. But as long as you did it, you knew ahead of time what he expected on the schedule, there was never any surprises with him." Rita Riggs added, "Things just ran smoothly, and there was 'please' and 'thank you.' But more important than the amenities, it was the creative juices that happened because of it. The wonderful part about Hitchcock's group was the fact that everyone knew each other, and I think trusted each other, and working was fun because of that. It was a very dignified set."

Hitchcock liked to break for afternoon tea. Hedren remembers, "He liked to hold court. He would hold court on the set; sometimes we would hear the same stories over and over again, but we'd all laugh and listen because of the way he told them. He was a master storyteller, and one of the most interesting things he did in his storytelling was giving more information to the audience than the actors knew."

One fine example of suspense building occurs in Hitchcock's staging of Marnie robbing the Rutland safe. Hitchcock outlined the importance of the robbery scene to Truffaut: "First you have to photograph the mind that steals. A calculating mind."[3] Marnie decides to leave the office door open, facilitating one of the most effective shots in the film. In a long shot, Marnie robs the Rutland safe on the right of screen, while on the left a cleaning woman emerges, threatening her escape route and potential exposure. Hitchcock elaborated on the effectiveness of the long shot:

> In all suspense, you see, the most important thing is to give an audience information. You cannot expect an audience to . . . how shall we say . . . get anxieties, without giving them the information to be anxious about. So, therefore, by presenting on the screen, the girl at the safe and the danger of discovery, you show the two things at the same time, in a long shot. Not the old fashioned way . . . cut from one to another, because that is not as potent to an audience . . . [as] the image of the cleaning woman, and the person robbing the safe. Why is it that the audience is more anxious of the wrong doer than the person they might discover?[4]

Although Hitchcock instigated suspense in his films, in his personal life, it was very different. Alma recalled one evening during the filming of *Marnie* when her husband came home from the studio in an extremely unsettled mood. She asked what were wrong and his reply was, "There's something mysterious going on at the studio, and I haven't been able to put my finger on it. I think some of the people are keeping a little secret from me." When Alma made inquiries, she found out that some members of the production company were planning to throw a surprise party for Hitchcock. Alma put a stop to the plan immediately, recognizing that although the idea was with the best intentions, the results would have been catastrophic. "You see, my husband hates surprises. He can't stand the idea of facing the unexpected, and he becomes downright ill if you keep him in suspense. . . . Before I married Hitch, he used to compose long letters to me. Then he would deliver them personally, because he couldn't stand the suspense of waiting until I got them through the post."[5]

Those who worked with Hitchcock often described the director as being calm and in total control. "If that pool becomes agitated, it churns Hitch up something awful," Alma continued.

> He wants to avoid being churned up and thus live longer. Hitch has a simple formula for eliminating suspense and strain from his life. Everything he does is planned well in advance, to the last microscopic detail. The first day of shooting on many Hollywood sets is usually punctuated with crises, angry complaints about missing equipment or props and last-minute demands for changes in script or lighting. On Hitch's set, however, all is serene. Talk is muted,

everything moves in precision-perfect procession, and even the tea—served during breaks—comes properly hot and on time.

The striving for perfection was a product of Hitchcock's Jesuit upbringing, and he used to say on the set that he was a Jesuit. Though he endured
the strictest education from his teachers, which helped him to be extremely
orderly and organized in his thinking, there was a conflict between his upbringing and the themes he was dealing with in his films. His obsession with
cleanliness culminated in his personal toilet habits. As Diane Baker remembers, "Hitchcock once mentioned in front of a few of us on the set, that he
had a horror of public lavatories. And that he always had to make sure that
there was no one in there, before he felt free enough to go in. In the studio at
Universal, he had his own bungalow, with an office and all the necessities.
He wanted his privacy."

## CAMERAS AND LENSES

Hitchcock worked from a subjective camera and even occasionally referred to
himself as a subjective director. On camera placement he said:

> Well, I think mainly it is a matter of the interest in the composition. . . . I have a
> horror of what I call the passport photograph. Shooting straight in, it's dull, it's
> not interesting and a slight variation on that gives you really, I would say, not
> so much the anxiety to get anything in the way of sharp angles, low or high or
> what have you but merely to avoid the standard level shots.[6]

"His main trick is the subjective treatment," affirms Robert Boyle.

> He goes from the close-up not necessarily to get the reaction of the person,
> although that's part of it, but he wants to get inside the person so he has a subjec-
> tive reason for seeing what the person sees. So a Hitchcock picture looks more
> open, a larger picture than most directors, because he doesn't resort too often
> to over-the-shoulders. He'll go into a close-up, and then you'll see what that
> person sees. It may be a moving point of view. But he uses the point of view as
> a subjective thing, to put the audience within the person. Everybody uses points
> of view, I assume, but I think that Hitchcock, in my experience, understands the
> subjective point of view and uses it better than any director that I know. You
> can quarrel and argue about his content or lack of content, but his use of the
> film language is a very hard thing to argue with or about, because he uses it so
> instinctively.[7]

Most of the time Hitchcock used fixed lenses and rarely a zoom. His favorite
lens was a 50mm, which he said was the lens of his eye. "He used to play
games with me," James Brown recalls.

He'd lay out the shot with Bob Burks and if he was sitting out on the stage and not in his dressing room, he'd pull me over alongside of him and he'd say, "Where are we cutting the girl?" or "What's the size of this two-shot?" So by looking at the distance the camera was from the person that was being photographed, I'd say that I think he was probably cutting about here, and he'd say, "Go look." So I'd look in the camera and come back, and I'd be either right or only an inch or two off. He trained my eye to a 50mm lens, and he gave me a lot of confidence in that you don't have to look through the camera. You can say, "Here's the actress," and to the cameraman, "Put the camera here," and know what you are going to get. He was an absolute genius with the visuals.

On the occasions when Hitchcock employed a zoom lens in *Marnie*, it was to achieve a subjective approach. When Marnie tries to rob the Rutland safe for a second time, her somnolent expression changes to anticipated pleasure, followed by confusion and anxiety, as she is unable to steal the money. Hitchcock described her as "having almost a kind of twisted smile on her face . . . she lays her head back against the safe, you know. I can angle all this—to keep this mood fairly clear."[8] The camera then zooms in and out from the money, crosscutting with Marnie struggling to reach it in a grip of compulsion. Boyle explained the purpose of such a shot: "Hitchcock will push the technical aspect of any shot to any length, if it will satisfy what he feels is that gut feeling of whatever he's trying to do—suspense, terror, and so on. And sometimes he'll push it so far that it doesn't quite make it. The shot becomes a little too strange, a little too far beyond the capabilities of the medium. But he never really worried about that."[9]

One of the most remarkable shots that the director achieved was the *Vertigo* shot, a combination of a dollying in and zooming out. Hitchcock himself confessed:

That effect took thirty years to get. It really did. When I was making *Rebecca*, I had a scene where Joan Fontaine is supposed to faint. I explained to [David] Selznick, I wanted to get the effect of her looking, and everything seem to go far away, and where I got the idea from was—It was at the Royal Chelsea Arts ball in London on New Year's Eve and I remembered at a certain time during the evening, everything seemed to go far away. And I asked for this effect and they said they couldn't do it. I tried it, oh, about five years later, but now with this effect of the vertigo of looking down, can be done. So they tried different effects and finally it was arrived at by a combination of a dolly shot and a zoom lens crossing each other. Dollying and zooming out. Because your sides had to remain constant. So when the head of special effects came to me I said, "How much is it going to cost?" He said, "$50,000 to put a camera high and take it up and zoom it because of the enormous rig." I said, "But there is no one in the set; it's an empty set. You're looking down." I said, "Why don't we make a miniature and lay it on its side. So that your camera and everything is on the stage and do the same effect, comes out the same on the screen." . . . So they did it and cost $19,000.[10]

Hitchcock employed the *Vertigo* shot again at the beginning of the flashback sequence, when Marnie's point of view of her mother's plain green couch dissolves to a memory of their living room many years ago. During a perspective test on the bedroom scene, Hitchcock requested in a memo for it to "have a cubist effect by lighting. Lighting should be abnormal (and) practically black and white but not quite. . . . The lighting of this shot should be in mood with Marnie's face." When Hitchcock discussed the Dali dream sequences in *Spellbound*, he made a useful comparison with Giorgio de Chirico, the Italian painter, which may well have inspired Mrs. Edgar's flashback living room: "Chirico has the same quality, the long shadows, the infinity of distance, and the converging lines of perspective." The track in gives the impression of reclaimed memory.

## PSYCHOLOGICAL DIRECTING

Unlike some directors such as Howard Hawks, Hitchcock did no prerehearsals before his actors arrived on the set. Even then, unless an actor asked a specific question, normally Hitchcock wouldn't do much apart from blocking the moves. Direction was seldom carried out on the stage but during conversations in preproduction. With Tippi Hedren, however, as the story conferences testify, he rehearsed every look and every word prior to filming. With the other actors, he allowed them their own interpretation, but Hedren gained his full attention.

In preparation, Hedren defined her character by reading the script and memorizing all her lines, so that they become a way of speaking for her. Then she thought about the physical mannerisms that Marnie would have and what idiosyncratic behavior she had, such as her walk and facial expressions. The most important element for Hedren was to really know the script, so she never had to try to remember the next line. She reflected on Marnie's relationship to other characters, so that by the time the camera was ready to turn over, Hedren had formulated in her own mind her entire performance. This was important as scenes were never shot in sequence, and it was vital for any actor to know what had preceded it. Many times Hitchcock filmed the rehearsal, and often did so with Hedren, especially in scenes when she was alone.

Hedren acknowledges the importance of being malleable in the hands of any director. Very rarely would she have a difference of opinion with Hitchcock over a scene, because she trusted his judgment completely. Reflecting on *The Birds* and *Marnie* today, however, there are many things that Hedren believes she would do differently or at least discuss with Hitchcock. He was very stylized as a director and fairly mechanical, in that everything was laid out ahead of time. At the end of a day's filming, he frequently wrote notes to Hedren like "Thank you for today," and she gave him a fourteen-carat gold grease pencil because he was always sketching out his camera shots. Hedren elaborates: "When you have so much genius as Hitchcock, but not only the genius but to be able to put forth all these ideas and feelings is pretty amazing. I admired him so much for his craft, for his direction, for his capabilities of manipulating an audience. And what fun he had! He had a great time. He would draw these graphs, and then he would chuckle and say how frightened they'd all be, and then drop them down."

Everyone in the cast and crew expressed an enormous pleasure working with Sean Connery. Long pages of unbroken dialogue were easy for the actor, who as a schoolboy had memorized more than one hundred of Robert Burns's poems. The main directions Hitchcock offered to Connery consisted of advising him to keep his mouth from hanging open when listening to his costars, as well as the insertion of "dog's feet" into his onscreen speeches. "Dog's feet?" asked a puzzled Connery. "Pawses," replied Hitchcock. Hedren describes what a pleasure it was to work with her costar. Connery was an avid golfer and in his free time on the set was always practicing with his club.

Such was Connery's interest in golf that James Brown recalls an incident when the actor wanted to participate in a tournament in Palm Springs, which required him to take Friday off. "I knew there was no way that we were going to be using Sean, but Hitch liked to have his actors on standby. So I kept Sean's dressing room open six inches and the light on like someone was in there, and let Sean go on Thursday night to Palm Springs. I thought, 'Oh, my God, if Hitch decides that he's going to take a shot of Sean, I'm in a lot of trouble.' But he never found out, and I received a beautiful letter from Sean."

One day, during filming of the Rutland office scenes, Hitchcock took Mariette Hartley aside and asked her whether she would like to see how the film was made so far. "He showed me the storyboards. Every single shot of every scene was illustrated," recalls Hartley. "Hitchcock, of course, himself had been a graphic designer. The boards really showed every character, every position; it was astonishing, and I was very deeply affected by what I saw. I did come away feeling that I was in the presence of a genius. No accidents occurred. On some level, that would be his failing, for his sense of control left little room for improvisation."

From Hartley's point of view, it was a very pleasant set, and she often quipped with Hitchcock. Then suddenly he became silent and ceased to talk to the actress for the remainder of her filming period. "I was made to feel that I had overstepped my mark. I woke up in the middle of the night, thinking that I'd be fired," remembers Hartley. "The terror of an actor's ego made me think it was my fault, so I went up to Hitchcock and asked if I had offended him. His reply was, 'Miss Hartley, I think you have problems with men.'" Hartley's recollections echo Hitchcock's sudden indifference to many of his actors and actresses, notably Doris Day in *The Man Who Knew Too Much*. "I sensed he didn't need me anymore; I didn't sense he had a great love for characters," continues Hartley. "They were like chess pieces on the set. Although most actors need to know what triggers their emotions, I think Hitchcock's directions were external—for example, to physically swoon when you see red ink. I wish I could meet him again, because he taught me a tremendous amount in the short time I worked with him."

After the office scenes, filming began on the set of Wyckwyn, the Rutland house. An early scene to be filmed was Mark bringing Marnie home to meet his father and Lil for tea. Diane Baker remembers, "I was shaking like a leaf in rehearsals when I had to pour the tea. All I could think about was, 'I'm being directed by Alfred Hitchcock.' I kept saying to myself, I mustn't shake, or I'll make terrible sounds with the cup rattling against the saucer and this tea will leap out of the cup. I simply have to get through this without rattling the cup of tea.'" On the actual days she worked, Baker recalls that Hitchcock was very kind toward her:

> I felt that he really cared about me, that he trusted me to do my job, he suggested only a few ideas, but mostly relied on my own instincts which gave me the freedom to act. In many ways I think it's a great way to direct. He had enough confidence in his vision to know how to create the right mood on the set, which allowed him to maintain control over his actors. If a director loses control over an actor or actors it can be dangerous or a disaster. If an actor disagrees with a director like Hitchcock, then his performance is at risk, because Hitch had his own vision . . . and we were all a part of that. I worked with Paul Newman just before *Marnie*, and I don't know how he got along with Hitchcock on Torn *Curtain. . . .* Paul is an incredibly intelligent actor; he asks questions and needs to have answers. But I'm sure out of respect for Hitchcock, he found a way to get the answers he needed to create his role.

As an example of Hitchcock's working methods, Baker cites filming the scene where Lil is rummaging among Mark's private papers:

> A male family friend who was head of transportation at Universal came to visit me on the set. Hitch made a comment in front of the crew which upset me, and I reacted spontaneously without thinking. I actually spoke up in my own defense; I stood my ground. Hitchcock was such a powerful presence that very few people dared to speak up. Was he being personal, or was he helping the actor to deepen his character? When I look back I wonder if these "incidents" happened on purpose to make me a better actress, or were they part of his own personal turmoil, as a result of Tippi's imminent departure? Luckily most of the time he

treated me with genuine warmth and sensitivity, but during the filming of one particular scene, he turned his back on me and was very abrupt. I remember during one rehearsal during the take, in the scene on the front porch when Sean and I watch Tippi ride away, while they were readjusting the lights, he caught my eye and then just turned away and talked to someone else. I thought that he was upset with me personally, that I had done something wrong, but he gave me no direction, and later I realized he wanted Lil to be strong-willed and have an element of hurt. He got that from me. He was the master, the Svengali, the one in charge. He was provoking me to act in a certain way . . . though I didn't realize it, at the time.

Similarly, a scene that remains indelible in Hedren's mind is when Mark has caught Marnie after her theft of the Rutland money, and she is packing under his interrogation. Just before filming, Hitchcock walked up to Hedren and said something that made her so mad and irate that for the first time she could hardly remember her lines. The fact that Hitchcock may have done it deliberately didn't occur to Hedren until she had time to reflect on his directing methods.

When it came to the rape scene, which had caused so much controversy during preproduction, Hitchcock adhered to the script directions, which have their genesis in Graham's novel: "I felt I'd let him get on with his lovemaking and be like a cold statue dead to every feeling except hate, and just see what he made of that." When asked whose point of view was being represented in the love scenes of *Marnie*, Hitchcock replied that they were in his point of view: "You know, a woman can be in an embrace with a man and think, 'Oh, my, I wonder what time it is?' while she's kissing him. And the man's mind can be somewhere else. I don't think the actual physical action of a kiss always connotes emotional feeling."[11]

During the party scene, which took a week to complete, Hitchcock taught Baker the most important lesson in film:

> It was about contrast. It's become a law with me almost. That you not start a scene in a serious mood that is to end in shock. The best way is to start with laughter and smiles, so you can travel a greater distance. . . . And at the beginning of the party scene, Hitchcock asked me to be smiling and greeting guests. He said, "The minute you see Strutt walk in, your face will slowly drain from smiling to shock. If you don't do that, and you start on a serious note when you see Strutt, then you border on horror." And he showed me how it would look.

Hitchcock often mentioned the Kuleshov effect, the impact of which depended on the immobility of an actor's face and its neutrality when seen in close-up. By reducing acting to its zero degree, the force of a scene is dependent on the power of montage. Hitchcock makes such a reference to James

Stewart's looks in *Rear Window*[12] and to Paul Newman's in *Torn Curtain*.[13] In *Marnie* an example occurs when Diane Baker's character is eavesdropping through the window on the newlyweds: "Hitch asked me to smooth my face out and think absolutely nothing. To simply look and have no expression. He molded my face with his hands to show nothing. He didn't talk about motivation; he expected you to work it out."

Another instance that remains with Baker is Hitchcock's direction to the actress who plays Strutt's wife: "He told her to 'Smile as if you have a mouth full of broken china.' If you can visualize that, something happens to your face. It's a kind of smile that occurs like you're trying to hold in a mouthful of broken china."

The motifs of Marnie as both a hunted animal and an infantile woman, carefully delineated in the screenplay and the story conferences, were acted out by Hedren under Hitchcock's direction. They become most apparent during the thunderstorm in Mark's office. The storm begins with the flashes of lightning against the white curtain, which induces extreme panic in Marnie. Robert Boyle said that Hitchcock experimented with the white lightning effects to suggest the buried terror in Marnie's subconscious. Pressed against the door, like Melanie Daniels recoiling against the lampshade and fireplace during the bird attack on the Brenner house, Hitchcock asked Hedren to adopt a peculiar stance; her left arm is flipped up against the door, and her right palm is pressed down. During the storm, the honeymoon, and the free-association game, Marnie seeks refuge from her phobias by trying to become part of the fabric of her surroundings. More often or not, she will turn her face toward the wall in an attempt to escape from her problems. This classic childhood response of evading reality, like hiding under the bed, suggests Marnie's retarded development as a result of her trauma. Her immobilization against the Rutland office door during the storm is an extreme reaction to escape from her nightmares. As Hitchcock said in the production design conference, "We may eventually surmise her behavior as paralleling that when she was a child."

The analogy between Marnie and that of a hunted animal is visually apparent during the filming of the honeymoon sequence. Hitchcock suggested, "I think we should play her quite calm, quite unresponsive, just keep the tension in the breathing, the held breath, until—right at the very bottom, when he goes to kiss her—now it breaks!" Marnie's response to Mark's advances recalls the bird attacks on the Brenner house. In both Tippi Hedren draws her legs up and cowers on the sofa. Hedren says that she and Hitchcock did not consciously make the connection but concedes, "It's a very animal thing to do, when cornered and something is about to pounce, and in the car journey, Mark has already said, I've really caught something wild this time.' Mark was overpowering the beast, just like he did with Sophie [the jaguarandi]."

When it came to filming the sequence when Marnie is dressed up like a "cat burglar" as she attempts to flee from Strutt, Hitchcock asked Hedren to pace restlessly like a caged animal: "He said you're trapped, you are like you're in a cage, and that's very definitely what that character would have felt like. She wasn't used to being caught for what she did. As the cliché goes, she had never been busted." Rarely would Hitchcock have two cameras operating, but during the "cat burglar" scene, when Marnie is about to flee from Strutt's arrival at the party, Hitchcock had one camera follow Hedren's movement and another follow Connery's. Moreover, he allowed his actors to improvise, so that wherever they went, the cameras followed, sometimes crossing each other.

Marnie is also visually presented as a little girl during the shooting of Forio, when her mannerisms take on that of a desperate child. The fast tempo and Hitchcock's camera follow the gun in close-up, as if it was the impetus for Marnie's movements. Hitchcock said of the highly poignant moment when Marnie shoots Forio, "Death of a horse—and the expression—long change—like a little baby: 'There. There now.' Hardly hear it."[14] In his conversations for the production design, Hitchcock emphasized that he wanted Marnie to reenact her story rather than simply remember it. When Marnie puts Forio out of his misery, the guilt of her original crime of killing the sailor is purged by the love for her horse. In Hunter's script, the connection between the horse and the sailor is made explicit by Roman, the psychiatrist: "There are very few symbols in psychiatry—but the horse is a classic symbol for father." Marnie's killing of the sailor is compounded by the fact that she never knew her father. In her subconscious she may well have killed him, so she tries to compensate for her crime by lavishing love on Forio and buying her mother gifts. Marnie will repeat the words "There. There now," after remembering her part in the killing of the sailor. In creating this highly emotive scene, Hedren says that she thought back to her own feelings of watching her pet dog die from distemper.

The presence of Lil during the shooting of Forio is a surrogate for Mrs. Edgar, who similarly watches in horror as Marnie kills the sailor. A subsequent scene of Marnie mounting Lil's horse was shot but later dropped in the edit. What is notable from the missing scene is Marnie's childlike parting words to Lil's amazement: "Oh, you walk, Lil; I'm going to keep the gun. I like it." In the subsequent scenes of Marnie climbing the Rutland stairs to steal the safe key, Hitchcock employs high camera angles. He outlined his intentions to Hedren:

> I am going to try and photograph it in a kind of grotesque way. . . . I don't want to lose the crazy mood of going up the stairs. . . . We don't know what she is doing—we don't reveal anything . . . but I'm terribly scared that after the craziness

of the horse: "I like the gun . . . I'm going to keep it"—I don't want to lose any of the mood between there and at the safe. She's still got the gun, you see—the reason being that by the time you go into that trauma in Baltimore, I don't want any normality to intrude anywhere.

Hedren elaborates, "We wanted to show how Marnie was psychologically hurt very badly. She was almost outside of her body, so the effect is that you watch her very closely."

When Marnie returns to try and rob the Rutland safe for a second time, Hitchcock films what the script describes: "The hand freezes . . . literally. It will not advance and she will now allow it to withdraw. And so she stands, like a child playing statue."

Marnie's regression into a child is carried over to the storm at her mother's house. Hitchcock begins the sequence with a high shot of thunder and lightning against the painted backdrop of the ship. In doing so the director makes three statements: "It's a high shot looking down upon the house, like that. You don't see the car. Then the camera pans off down the street. You still don't see the car. We see the angry sky and flashes of lightning. Here we are in Baltimore—the lightning and thunder are on—look—Marnie's terrified. She can't come out of the car." Mark is forced to drag Marnie like a reluctant child. Hitchcock said, "I did it that way to prepare for the trauma to come." The combined effect of all these sequences presents Marnie as a girl who had to grow up very fast because she was psychologically traumatized as a child. This is made explicit by Mark after the flashback: "When a child of any age can't get love, Marnie, it takes what it can get, any way it can get it."

## SCENES WITH MOTHER

On Friday, January 31, 1964, Hitchcock filmed the first scene with Louise Latham as Bernice Edgar. The scene he chose to film was the climactic thunderstorm when Mark brings Marnie home to confront Mrs. Edgar about her daughter's past. "I think Hitch wanted to test me that day," Latham recalls. "We were all caught up in the intensity of the scene. When I was wrestling with Sean, I didn't hear Hitch say, 'Cut,' and I carried on. Sean, who was a warm, wonderful presence, asked me afterward, 'Are you OK?' Some scenes have such resonance and depth, and that was one of them." The crew marveled how wonderful it was to watch Latham at work, but no one was more quietly impressed than Hitchcock. At lunch a few days later, Hitchcock confided to Latham how doubtful he was at first in hiring an actress whom he had never worked with. He even telephoned Jessica Tandy, the actress who played Mitch's possessive mother in *The Birds*, asking her to step in if

Latham did not work out. Hitchcock then said to Latham, "Well, I never had to call her after your first day."

During the rest of that week, Hitchcock filmed the scenes of Marnie crying. The sight of her mother struggling with Mark induces the beginning of Marnie's memory of the incident that has plagued her since childhood: "You let my mama go," she pipes up in a little girl's voice. Hedren's skill is admirable in her ability not only to maintain the intensity but also to portray the childlike image. She says she prepared herself for such an intense scene, just like the shooting of Forio, by recalling a bad experience in her own childhood: "Hitchcock wanted me to go back to being a frightened child. He was so proud of the scene that he invited Lew Wasserman—I thought it was a great honor."

In staging such a dramatic scene as the confrontation, Hitchcock would draw on his own memories and apply them years later. When Latham and Hedren face each other after the reclaimed memory, Hitchcock makes the visual analogy of two fighters who are so exhausted they can only just sit and look at one another. Latham remembers that her ensuing monologue was a wonderful relief, because the barriers were down and although there was still pain, much of the horror had been exorcised. She recalls that Hitchcock never gave much direction to herself or Connery, but to Hedren he told when to blink an eye or smile. In the preproduction conference with Hedren, Hitchcock emphasized the importance of the scene when Marnie tries to get affection by kneeling at her mother's lap but is usurped by Jessie: "I think as Marnie scrambles up—I think if we do that in close up, we'll get her discomfort and embarrassment, having to do this in front of the child . . . I think there is quite a moment there. I'll photograph it on the face." It was during the filming of this sequence that Hitchcock offered one direction to Latham: "He said, 'Remember that you love the child now,' so he wanted me to distance myself even more from Marnie."

When Mrs. Edgar is shown in silhouette at the top of the stairs as rigid and corpselike as Mrs. Bates in *Psycho,* Latham says that Hitchcock had asked her to walk slowly down the stairs: "All of her being was in containing this tight, electric horror. She was a suppressed woman, and my whole drive was playing this desperate woman whose strength was quite extraordinary. But the passion in her life was her child. I thought about the emotions that would drive a person to kill. Everything she did was because she loved that child." Hitchcock's portrayal of Mrs. Edgar as a sinister, silhouetted figure is carried through to her voice: "I'm going to drop Bernice's voice down to a rather sober—not the whining voice of Bernice—but the sinister more menacing kind of voice."[15]

Hitchcock demonstrated great sensitivity during the filming of the flashback sequence between Latham and Bruce Dern, an actor who appeared in

Hitchcock's television series and was hired in the role of the sailor. The set was closed: "It was like a graveyard," Latham remembers. Hitchcock shot a great deal of coverage for the flashback, and makeup artist Howard Smit used a gallon of blood, which was more than he had used for any other production, including westerns he had worked on.

Regarding the couple of weeks Latham spent on the set, she describes Hitchcock as lovely, cerebral, and thoughtful throughout. His relationship with assistant Peggy Robertson was quiet, professional, and very English. Sometimes the emotional intensity was maddening, but Latham believes a person would not have misbehaved on a Hitchcock set for fear of being sent home. The director had a consummate understanding about what he wanted. During long waits between camera setups, he would read an article about wine, perhaps a Californian Bordeaux that was served with lunch that day.

## PROCESS AND BACKDROPS

The back projection for the Atlantic City racetrack, the car journeys, and the horse riding sequences had been scheduled toward the end of filming, to allow time for their organization and for Hitchcock to view the dailies so that he could determine where he needed his close-ups. During preproduction, Hitchcock affirmed his intention to use background plates for Marnie's horse riding: "And then we go to close ups which will mean plates and things, for her close ups, showing her enjoying it, and her hair blowing and it's very important that we establish here one big close up of the hair blowing as she's riding . . . it's a leitmotif that goes through the film."[16]

"Back projection was a system used in many of Hitch's films, mainly because he thought he was in control," says Robert Boyle.

> In *Marnie* we were dependent on back projection in relation to the movement. For the horse riding scenes we used backgrounds shot from a helicopter, but the results were not too satisfactory. But for Hitch it didn't matter. His main concern was the visceral sensation—the feeling aroused was more important to him than the technological perfection.

The sensation Hitchcock intended was also outlined by Evan Hunter: "We wanted to show the real woman Marnie was, with the wind blowing in her hair. We were going for a feeling of being safe."

The art department hoped to utilize blue screen for the background plates, where an actor is filmed against a blue matte. The distinction between foreground and background is less obvious with blue screen than with traditional rear projection, where it is apparent that the actor is standing in front of a screen. However, when test shots were made of Hedren's blonde hair blown by a wind machine, a halo effect was created against the blue screen. The technique had to be abandoned in favor of the more traditional rear projection, where no matte lines are created because the camera is in sync with the projector behind the screen. Both are opening and exposing film at the same time, preventing resultant flickers or even a black screen. The switch to rear projection would cause a great deal-of controversy when the film was later released.

Hitchcock wanted to film Hedren on a real horse on a treadmill for Marnie's riding. He asked Hilton Green to find the largest treadmill in the business and train horses to walk on it. Green was astounded because this had never been attempted before, and the results could be catastrophic for horse and rider. Hitchcock's response was to try it out, so Green borrowed a thirty-foot treadmill from MGM and hired Jack Carry to train one horse to walk on it. A copy of the screenplay was sent to the American Humane Association in Los Angeles. Harold Melniker, the director at the time, wrote back saying it contained animal action that required a representative on the set, not only for the treadmill sequences but also when Forio makes the jump and fails to clear the wall. Melniker advised that "the horse's screams and actual views of the downed, injured horse be held to a minimum. It is suggested also, that excessive yanking of the reins be avoided."

Peggy Robertson sent a memo to Green on December 13 with specific requests for filming the process shots for the hunt sequence:

1. Mr. Hitchcock mentioned he would like to have more than one horse on the treadmill for some of the shots in the hunt sequence.
2. A reminder that we will use the same horse on the treadmill as Tippi has been riding.
3. A reminder that we will have a mechanical horse to standby for the treadmill, as a precautionary measure.
4. The hunt people should be cast very carefully. We do no want any "cheesy" extras.
5. In order to trigger Marnie off for her gallop, we will shoot close-ups of the pink (red) coats and the white britches. We will then zoom into a Big Head of Marnie's reaction to this red and white, and she will turn.

When Hedren was astride the treadmill horse, Green attempted to attach a safety harness in case the horse slipped and fell. However, this didn't work out, so Hedren had to ride without a harness. Much to everyone's relief filming progressed smoothly. Certain shots, such as the close-up of Marnie on Forio jumping, could not be achieved with a real horse inside the studio, so Hitchcock asked Green to investigate a mechanical horse owned by Walt

Disney, which he had heard was very authentic. Green met Disney and borrowed the mechanical horse, which was later used for extremely close shots
of Hedren and also for Baker when she is riding in the hunt.

For the Atlantic City racetrack, Hitchcock asked Robert Boyle to create
a small section of the paddock and stalls where Connery and Hedren were
to perform in front of the back projection filmed on location. In Boyle's
opinion, sunlight scenes on a soundstage were not effective, because the
only source of light, the sun, couldn't be duplicated. Like the sand dune
sequence in *The Birds,* the racetrack turned out to be the most artificial and
least effective process photography in the film, because of the problem of
re-creating natural light. In both the riding and racetrack sequences, Hitchcock and his collaborators strived for realism but were undermined by the
technology available.

Hitchcock frequently used back projection, with varying degrees of success, for the car journeys of his characters:

> That's a decision that you have to make quite a bit. For this reason, it depends if
> you are shooting a long dialogue and you go outside and your shoot is outside in
> an open car in the street, you've got to dub that whole scene because of your ex-
> ternal sounds. Now you've got to do that or you can do the best back projection
> you can get, and it can be well done, and it can be badly done, at least then you
> can let the players have the comfort of being able to play the scene naturally and
> spontaneously. . . . They'd be distracted by traffic, the guy driving the car; there
> have been lots of pictures made that way with the camera strapped on the front
> and the windshield taken off, but you do run the risk of having to re-dub the
> whole thing, so when you're dubbing a whole long dialogue, you know, you're
> not going to get the necessary emotion into the scene. That's the risk you run.[17]

The scene where Mark and Marnie are in the car after work on Saturday was
reshot using process instead of blue screen. During the filming of the automobile scenes, Hitchcock fell asleep. When James Brown asked, "Hitch, is that
a print?" Hitchcock woke up and said, "OK, let's do it again." So the actors
were forced to do another take.

When preparing for the filming of the dockyard street where Marnie's
mother lives, Hitchcock remained adamant to use a studio with a painted
backdrop of a ship, despite his collaborators having scouted locations in Baltimore. Hitchcock himself described the symbolism he intended during the
story outline for the production design:

> It's one of those streets where they have all those steps . . . you know, the white-
> wash steps. This again is a tremendous contrast, because you see, we've practi-
> cally shown we've done all this cinematically. We told the mystery of this girl in
> a series of images of pictures and settings and backgrounds. That's why they're

all very important because they do make statements all the time. . . . Well, it's like the north of England street . . . rows of houses and chimneys . . . at the end of the street—we could see masts of ships because this is very important later on.

"Hitchcock had an image of a tremendous ship from London or someplace where he lived at the end of the street, and I know the feeling. As a matter of fact, we even saw it in Baltimore," says Boyle. "But we did a miniature ship which was mostly cut-out, and then we did cut-out, reduced perspective on the sides, and we should have done it in real materials, but we did it with flat cut-out board. Then it was raining, as I remember, and the rain got on it and made it all slick so that nothing looked right. Anyway, the whole thing was a disaster, and it looked terrible. And it was designed for two heights, one at street level and one higher. And the higher one you had to naturally raise the backing. Which we did. We did all those things."[18]

Why the painted backdrop of the ship appeared less realistic than originally intended in the film was explained by James Brown:

Bob Boyle had designed a painted backdrop for a high camera shot, about twenty to thirty feet above street level. Boyle had it lined up that way and painted it that way. The crew arrived at 7:00 A.M. in the morning and both Boyle and Bob Burks put the camera up about thirty feet in the air on a platform, because that was the way it had been designed for a high shot looking down. When Hitch came on the set that day, he decided to have the camera at street level and that put things on a different perspective. It distorted the entire backdrop and the forced perspective that Boyle had built into the set. Why Hitch did that, I don't know.

Boyle recalls that Burks was not satisfied with the backdrop and asked Hitchcock to reconsider:

Well, Hitch thought it was fine. He never minded technical flaws. . . . I went to Hitch afterward and said, "Hitch, I've never asked you to do this before, but I would like to have this retaken." I said, "I think we can fix it." I'd already talked to the cameraman, Bob Burks, and he admitted that he had lit the sides of the street too much. And we both were at fault. And we stayed up all that night after seeing the [dailies] trying to figure out some way that we could repair the damage. But Hitchcock wouldn't reshoot it. He would reshoot it if Tippi Hedren's hair or dress was awry, but not that.[19]

"It didn't matter to Hitch if it didn't look realistic; what was important was that it was realistic to him. That's the impression he wanted to create," Hilton Green stated. Hitchcock was adamant in retaining a painted backdrop despite alternative suggestions from his collaborators. Jay Presson Allen similarly said, "It wasn't for a lack of money, because Universal would have given

Hitch every cent." Hitchcock's decision to keep the painted backdrop would cause a furor from the critics when the film was released.

## TROUBLED RELATIONS

The greatest controversy surrounding the production of *Marnie* lies in Hitchcock's working relations with Tippi Hedren, who was planning to marry her agent Noel Marshall after filming. The following words from Hedren describe their dichotomous relationship:

> Hitch loved the mysterious. He liked to see women wearing sunglasses, wearing hats, so that you don't see everything that you're going to get. And that was what he may have found very mysterious about me, because I never talked about my private life. Never! It used to drive him crazy. He was almost obsessed with me, and it's very difficult to be the object of someone's obsession. I never talked about it for twenty years, because I didn't want people to think about it in the wrong light. I felt such empathy for Hitch. To have such strong feelings and to have them not returned is very difficult.

According to Jay Presson Allen:

> He was an old Turk. He liked to be surrounded by women, he liked to control them, he liked to work with them—you know, it's not that unusual. But he did have a Pygmalion complex about Tippi. It was an old man's cri de Coeur. Hitchcock had a crush on her. . . . He was enormously manipulative—that's what he did for a living, that's what directors do . . . but he wasn't a misogynist. He was crazy about women; he tried to get rid of their husbands, not them. . . . Although I think Hitchcock's camera was sympathetic to women, I don't believe he necessarily understood them all that well. He was a very complex man. He always liked women who were assertive. But at the same time, I think there was no question in his mind that he thought in subtle ways he could control their assertiveness.

Hedren maintained a dignified discretion despite the turbulent undercurrents during filming. When she spoke to Allen on one occasion about the tension, the screenwriter advised her to finish the film and then get on with her life and be happy. Virginia Darcy also tried to intervene, telling Hitchcock not to be possessive: "Hitch was a romantic, and he got the romance in his life through his films. *Marnie* was a very difficult job for him and it took its toll. He put himself in the leading man's role and was possessive of his leading ladies. Tippi felt rightly that she was not his property, but he'd say, 'You are, I have a contract.' She didn't know his ways. Tippi was from New York, and the modeling scene there is very different to Hollywood."

Diane Baker describes the competitive triangle Hitchcock tried to create between himself and his two actresses:

> It was difficult being in the middle between Hitch and Tippi. Here the leading actress was leaving a contract. As far as a falling out, there was definitely a change in their relationship. Hitch enjoyed his long lunches with the best red wine; he was a connoisseur of both good wine and good food. Of course, I never ate much lunch normally, but I was invited along with several others to join him in his bungalow where these extraordinary lunches were catered, but I couldn't drink during the filming and never will. The conversations were stimulating, often with the creative team. But Tippi was never there, which made me uncomfortable. I felt he was ignoring Tippi and bringing me in to replace her. I was thrilled on the one hand to be included in this special world, but I was afraid of falling under his control. Once when Tippi was nearby, Hitch was talking to me, with respect and warmth, then he would say something unkind about her which was meant to hurt her. I was determined not to engage in this backbiting.

The actress found herself retaliating in the only way she knew how. Baker confronted the director: "'Mr. Hitchcock, if you are saying these things about Tippi, I'm wondering what you're saying behind my back.' To which Hitchcock replied, 'Oh, I would never say anything against you. I would never do that to you.' One of the studio people took me to lunch one day, knew that I was disturbed, and whatever I said during that lunch was reported back to Hitchcock, and he knew that I was upset. The tension did get so great, one day just before Christmas I was sick."

Universal Studios first began to play watchdog over Hitchcock during the production of *The Birds*. Although Hitchcock's agent and longstanding friend Lew Wasserman had been elevated to being the head of Universal, this didn't stop Hitchcock from making sarcastic comments about "the front office," even when that office was Wasserman's. As Jay Presson Allen surmises, "Wasserman had been Hitch's agent; now he was his boss. That's a very big shift in authority, and I think Hitch resented it—I know he did. Nevertheless, it was a fact of life." Wasserman employed Edd Henry, one of the Universal executives, to act as his liason during the production of *Marnie*. Henry was snidely referred to as "Dr. No" because he said no to most requests.

Hitchcock's attempts to control Hedren's life during work and after hours resulted in a row. The catalyst arrived when publicity manager David Golding sent a memo to Peggy Robertson on January 21, 1964: "To recapitulate, Tippi Hedren will be receiving the award as the Most Promising New Star which is based on the poll by the *Photoplay* readers. They would like her in New York in the early afternoon of February 5th. The actual taping will take place at 6:30 P.M. and Tippi will be on throughout the show which goes on to 11:30 P.M. In addition, *Photoplay* has taken over the Playbill restaurant where they will make the actual presentation for newspaper and newsreel coverage. Furthermore, NBC plans a special promotion on Tippi's appearance three weeks in advance." On January 30, 1964, Golding sent a further memo to Hitchcock:

> According to your production aides Sean Connery will have six to eight free days between now and his scheduled last date on February 28th. However during all this period, Tippi Hedren will be working each day. From the looks of things, Tippi would have little or no time during any shooting day to be pulled away for pub-ad shots, even at a gallery set up on the sound stage. Thus even if we can get Sean to come in during some of his free days, this would not automatically ensure our getting the required two-shots. This poses a time element dilemma that possibly only you can solve by setting aside on the production slate a specified time in which we can obtain the required material. As things shape up now Tippi does have a half-day off on February 27th, but this in my opinion is putting things off almost to the end and by that time the entire picture might change. Again, going by the present schedule, which is highly subject to change, Sean Connery's free days are February 11th, 12th, 13th, 18th, 25th, 26th, 27th, 28th. We asked Tippi if, should no other time be available, she would consent to come in on a Saturday for such shots. She said that under ordinary circumstances she would gladly do so. However, now she needs all the strength she can summon, is bone tired, and just had a debilitating session with the flu bug, and therefore doesn't feel she could do so. I wanted you to be aware of the situation and hope there is some way that we can solve this problem which is confronting us.

Peggy Robertson brought the memo to Hitchcock's attention, saying that the foreign press had nominated Hedren as a "Star of Tomorrow." Other nominees were Leslie Parrish, Elke Sommer, Joey Heatherton, Ursula Andress, and Maggie Smith. The awards ceremony would take place on February 5 in the Empress Room of the Ambassador Hotel in New York. Louis Blaine, Universal's publicity officer in New York, felt it was a rat race and there were too many people present to give much individual attention. However, he noted that Hedren's appearance may have some bearing on the finals for the Golden Globe Awards in March.

Hitchcock felt it was impractical for Hedren to fly to New York midweek to accept the award, given the tight filming schedule for the cast and crew, compounded by Connery's impending departure at the end of February. He advised that Leslie Parrish could accept the scroll on her behalf. Hedren believed it was the culmination of Hitchcock's excessive control over her personal life. "If they had a row, it wasn't on the set—it was after work, in her dressing room, or in his office," says James Brown. "I had worked with Tippi all through *The Birds* and *Marnie* and we became close friends. I knew when she was upset just by her body language, and I knew when Hitch was upset because he let me know. So there were times when their relationship was not as friendly as it could have been. I was a kind of go-between. Hitch would say, 'Tell the Girl,' Tippi would say, 'Tell Hitch,' and so there was maybe a week or two when they really weren't communicating."

Brown affirmed that Hitchcock was losing interest toward the end of the filming of *Marnie* and that his lack of enthusiasm may have been triggered by the falling out with Hedren or the simple fact that he was tired. "I think it was age and he was losing his edge. We spent a lot of time and energy on *The Birds*, and by the end of *Marnie* he was getting bored. Sometimes he wouldn't come out of his trailer for a short scene, but he never completely abandoned ship; as a result, the filming was not up to his usual standard."

Diane Baker, too, was feeling the strain. The actress was hired to act in a film in Israel in early February called *The Sands of Berosheboe* with Tom Bell. Although being an observer on the set for most of the time during the filming of *Marnie*, Baker had only one more scene to film herself—the hunt sequence where she is riding the mechanical horse in front of back projection.

I did appeal to the assistant director, Jim Brown, and Hitch knew that I had to be in Israel to start rehearsals for filming, but he kept me until the end of filming. I've often wondered if this was an aspect of control or a production necessity. Jim Brown kept looking at the shooting board and saying you've been shifted constantly. He said he told Mr. Hitchcock, yet this scene was being moved back. I had a commitment to be in Israel. It would have been nice and kind to finish the film and get on with my life. It's important to put some of these earlier thoughts into perspective. I grew up as a kind of maverick all my life. I was the only one in my immediate family who earned a living at eighteen, moved into an apartment and was living on my own. I had just finished a 20th Century Fox contract for five years and had enough of a time fighting up for myself over there. Being suddenly free, I was excited about new possibilities. Then Universal offered me a contract, and I turned it down, for these very reasons. I didn't like being under anyone's thumb; I didn't like the idea of being the next Grace Kelly, or anyone else but myself. I told Hitchcock this clearly one day before we finished the film. Tippi was strong and I admired her for that. I got to know Tippi later, and she is a great person. And I would like to acknowledge how much I learned about moviemaking from [Hitchcock]. He was a consummate filmmaker and gave me wonderful insights into acting. Alma, too, was always there, behind the scenes one could feel her presence—a remarkable woman.

## WRAPPING UP

Hitchcock's manipulation of Hedren and Baker was very different than his working relationship with Sean Connery. For two Saturdays after Christmas, Hitchcock entertained Connery and his wife Diane Cilento by taking them to the races. On another occasion, Connery and the Hitchcocks dined at Jack's restaurant in San Francisco, and on Valentine's Day, Cilento watched a rough cut of *Marnie* with Alma, followed by lunch with their husbands. On Friday, February 28, 1964, Hitchcock hosted an evening party at the studio commissary to mark Connery's departure from Stage 28, after three months of filming. As well as the fifty-nine cast and crew members, fourteen office workers, and selected Universal staff, representatives of the press were invited, including Art Seidenbaum and Hedda Hopper.

A collection was taken up to buy Connery a $741 watch from Ruser's Jewelry Store in Beverly Hills and charged to the *Marnie* account. On the back were engraved the words, "To Sean from his fellow-workers on *Marnie*." The card that accompanied it read:

> Greetings. We, the undersigned, on the Friday, the Twenty Eighth day of February, in the year of Our Lord One Thousand Nine Hundred and Sixty Four, hereby present, as a token of our esteem, the accompanying chronometer, which is to adorn the prima palmae pars of our delightful colleague and earnest co-worker, Sean Connery. It is fitting that the prima palmae pars should correctly accommodate the chronometer, because the fitting has not actually been ascertained. Nevertheless and consequent upon a cursory examination of the prima palmae pars, an approximation was estimated in the earnest hope that such approximation would readily accommodate the token of esteem bestowed upon you. Given to you on this Twenty Eighth day of February, in the Jewish Year of Five Thousand Six Hundred Seventy Eight.

Connery took off the watch that he was wearing and put the new one on. "I had a great time with Hitchcock," he recalls. "He tells you on the set what moves he wants. . . . He used to tell me funny stories before a take quite often, but he never dwelt upon the psychology of the character. . . . His humor was pretty schoolboyish." Once Hitchcock said to Connery, "If I'm paying you as much as I am and you don't know what you're doing, then I deserve what I get in the way of performance."

Following Connery's return to England, the first unit filmed more scenes between Marnie and her mother. The movie house sequence, where Marnie robs the box office takings, was eliminated, allowing studio filming to finish early on Friday, March 13. The crew drank the two dozen bottles of champagne that Connery had bought them, and Hedren contributed hors d'oeuvres. On March 20, Robertson wrote to Connery on the set of *Goldfinger*. "Everyone was delighted with your thoughtfulness and they all send you their love and thanks . . . it was a good end of the picture party."

Principal photography on *Marnie* came to an end on Saturday, March 14, 1964, with what constitutes the first scene in the film. Hitchcock flew from Los Angeles to San Francisco, where he was then driven to San Jose Southern Pacific railroad station. Bob Burks and Leonard South traveled on a separate flight. They filmed the famous opening shot of Marnie walking away from a tracking camera, carrying a bulging yellow handbag full of stolen cash. Hitchcock had remarked to Hedren in the preproduction conference, "The question is should it be a brisk walk, should it be a furtive walk, should it be a casual stroll? I'm torn between a brisk walk—that would indicate that's she going somewhere. I think in a way it ought to be a casual stroll, a nonchalant stroll, don't you?"

Hitchcock also discussed this scene with Jay Presson Allen at great length: "It's unreal in a sense, but I have deliberately shown no other people around—not a soul. And this is because I want the audience not to be confused by any other matters except this one figure of the girl with the yellow bag . . . so I chose 3:30 in the afternoon when nobody was around. That's the reason I did it, you see. So, I think the casual walk will do it for us."[20] In the story conference for the production design, Hitchcock asserted, "I feel that we ought to cheat like they do in the Italian films and have nobody around if we can. Because otherwise we don't draw enough attention to the girl." Hitchcock was so successful in making the comparison in this respect that Archer Winsten in the *New York Post* later observed, "It reminds one somewhat of Fellini's abstract train depot in *$8^1/_2$*." The director wanted the yellow purse to stand out, and if it wasn't strong enough, he had planned to jump cut back to the purse at the end of the shot. As Boyle affirms, "Hitchcock worked in depth, whereas many directors today don't understand image size in relation to the emotional impact on screen. He liked to show people receding from life or a particular incident, images of leaving, and a corridor always gave that sense as the actor could recede or come toward camera."

The second draft of the *Marnie* screenplay of August 19, 1963, reads: "Somehow, in the gray limboistic loneliness of the station, only that handbag seems to have an aura of vitality." Rita Riggs described the costume that Marnie is wearing as "Brunette disguise, dark tweed suit, swing pleated skirt, black walking shoes, black kid gloves, bright yellow handbag large enough to carry a 'considerable sum of money'—and that was a quote from him."

## RETAKES

The process of retakes had begun in earnest in mid-December 1963, when Robertson sent a memo to Green requesting to retake scene 131, the insert of the red ink spilling onto Marnie's white sleeve. "This time we will shoot down and see the bottle of red ink spill onto the sleeve," Hitchcock instructed. Green conceded that Hitchcock was very particular with scenes or shots where a specific story point had to be made. If a shot was not achieved to the director's satisfaction, the crew would have to reshoot it over and over. The most famous example that Green recalls is the shot in *Psycho*, when Lila Crane hits the naked light bulb in the basement, causing it to swing across Mother's eyes. For Hitchcock, those key shots had to be perfect. Green remembers seeing the director angry only twice: when the cameraman Jack Russell repeatedly failed to get the shot of the swinging light bulb, and on the set of one of Hitchcock's television shows, with a prop man who had a lackadaisical attitude toward serving meals, which Hitchcock was very particular about.

Another retake was requested of the close shot of Mark in Ward's office as he reacts to Marnie at the safe. In the story conferences, Hitchcock had talked about dollying to Marnie's hair or doing "easy tricks" by overlaying Strutt's voice: "But it may be that the building of his looks from the very beginning may be sufficient to put it over without being obvious or on the nose, as you'd say." Hitchcock was intent to photograph Mark's viewpoint of Marnie and his expression in such a way as to carry Strutt's words over. Connery, however, was able to convey Mark's irony and skepticism of Marnie, with tremendous skill.

Allen was adamant that the scene in Ward's office should definitely establish to Mark who Marnie is. Hitchcock wanted him to be more uncertain:

> For example, you see, from his POV, Scene 102—Marnie comes around his desk to the right of the picture—the wall safe is in the center of the wall—and for a moment we put Marnie right in front of the wall safe, as though it were a frame of a picture around her—then cut back to Mark, and we cut Scene 104 (Marnie framed by the safe). Off screen we hear Ward's voice: "Sit down . . . sit down, Mrs. Taylor." See what happens—Marnie moves away from the safe, and we see her lower herself into a chair out of the picture, and the camera stays on the safe, just for a brief moment. Then we go right back to Mark. He looks down into the direction of the seated Marnie. He gives a very slow, faint smile.[21]

An additional scene, 134A, was also shot, with Mark in Ward's outer office corridor, looking down toward the glass door with the women's washroom on camera left, after Marnie has run in to wash off the red ink. On December 27, Hitchcock asked for further retakes of the red ink dropping onto Marnie's blouse and her subsequent washing off the red ink. Allen said that Hitchcock and herself worked out the red suffusions very carefully to induce terror in the viewer, in addition to the audience experiencing Marnie's subjective state. After the spilling of the red ink, Hitchcock counterpoints Marnie's verbal dismissal of the event by inserting a shot of her hand vigorously rubbing at the stain on her blouse. The combined effect is that no matter how hard Marnie scrubs away at the red ink, like the memory of her childhood trauma, the stain is indelible. As Hitchcock noted, "During this scene she is working very hard on the stain—but the language and the voice is completely counterpoint to the hand action." There is no clearer evidence that Marnie's compulsive actions are instinctual and beyond her control.

On January 9, 1964, Hitchcock sent a memo to Albert Whitlock with a revised list of six mattes, for the Baltimore street, the Rutland exterior, the stable, the Wyckwyn wedding, the hunt, and the change in Baltimore. An additional matte shot for scene 402A of Marnie crossing from the house to the stables was made, but dropped in the edit. On January 10, scenes in the ship's cabin were retaken, because Sean Connery's arm tattoo had been detected by the camera. In the retake, the tattoo was covered with makeup. The scene where Lil eavesdrops out of the window was first shot on location but was retaken in the studio with a pane of glass with an old backing behind it. On January 30, an extra shot was requested from Hitchcock and Allen, when Mark and Marnie return from their honeymoon. Just outside the bedroom Marnie hangs back. Mark takes her arm and steers her into the room: "'Come on, Marnie. It's not a house of correction, you know.' He pilots her into the room." The next day, the big close-up shot of Mark's eyes looking down toward Marnie after she had been placed on the bed was requested. The intention was to cut in as Marnie's head hits the pillow. On March 10, scene 52A of Bernice standing in the doorway was asked to be retaken, because she appeared too bright. Hitchcock instructed, "There should be no light on her face and softer light behind her." Finally, scene 52, the close shot of Bernice standing in the doorway, was also retaken as there was too much light on the side of her face, and the shadows were too black.

## CONCLUSION

The production history of *Marnie* emphasizes Hitchcock's total involvement as a subjective director. As Robert Boyle acknowledges:

> The scene also dictated how it would be subjective. It didn't necessarily mean the old thing of a close shot and what the close shot sees. But if the scene is working, even a long shot can be subjective. Because it is expressing what the character is feeling—that's what he was interested in. Getting the feeling. Putting you the audience into the character. And by whatever means. It might be the standard viewpoint shot which is a close shot and what that person sees. But he didn't always work that way. Once he got you involved in the scene,

sometimes a great long shot, a vista could reveal what a character felt. He was mostly interested in feelings.

Hitchcock consistently talked about the roller coaster as his main endeavor, hence his propensity to draw graphs that charted the audience's emotions throughout the film. His desire to create an emotional response was the impetus for the expressionistic devices, such as the red suffusions, the painted backdrops, and the zoom lens, derived from his early days working in German cinema. This preference for working on the soundstage instead of on location and for using matte shots and process photography was considered anachronistic at a time when films, such as *Lawrence of Arabia* (1962), were being shot in foreign locations using long lenses. Television also provided an outlet for films, so audiences were becoming increasingly sophisticated and demanding of a more cinematic experience than studio-bound films could provide.

Hitchcock was a man who relished order and control above all else, but during the filming of *Marnie*, he lost that control. Many on the set expressed concern for Hitchcock's heavy drinking, which caused his weight to rise dramatically, suggesting that he might have a heart attack at any moment. Norman Lloyd, producer of the television show *Alfred Hitchcock Presents*, discloses in his memoirs that at one point during the production, Hitchcock asked him to step in and complete filming, should he become incapacitated.[22] Events never reached that point, but Hitchcock's condition was no doubt exacerbated by his own emotional turmoil.

The director had made a considerable investment in Tippi Hedren. His appropriation of her is not unusual in the film and television industry where artists spend a great deal of time and creative energy together and professional conduct is mistaken for personal interest. This is not a defense of Hitchcock's actions but merely a rationalization of events that have been overblown by the media. Hedren had every right to maintain her assertiveness and individuality, and she conducted herself professionally by never talking about her personal life. What is evident from the production history is that whatever transpired between Hitchcock and Hedren did not adversely affect the completion of the film or its intrinsic design. Later, after filming was complete, Hitchcock approved the arrival on the set of a representative to give Hedren the Photoplay Award, which he had denied her attending due to the tight filming schedule.

After *Marnie*, Hedren says she told Hitchcock, "I can't work with you anymore. I have to get out of my contract and I will get out.' When that happened, everything changed." Hitchcock's response was "I'll ruin you," and according to Hedren he tried very hard to do that by discouraging others from using her: "For two years after *Marnie* I never worked, just sat around withdrawing my $500 a week because he wouldn't release me from my contract. When I look back at *Marnie* today and I watch particular scenes, I think about what was going on in my personal life at the time. But they were all my choices. I have my own morals and standards of living, and breaking free was what I needed to do, even though there was a lot of hurt involved because Hitch was so controlling. Especially when you take a grown woman and have such a demanding effect on her life."

Hitchcock and Hedren were still on speaking terms, however. On June 30, they met to discuss Hedren's forthcoming promotional tour for *Marnie* in the United States, and on August 19 and December 16 they had lunch. When Hedren was finally released from her contract, her next film was *A Countess from Hong Kong*, which Charlie Chaplin directed in London in 1966. During filming, Hedren met with Hitchcock and Alma, and they had tea at the Ritz.

Sean Connery's association with Alfred Hitchcock, although much briefer than Hedren's, in the long run proved to be beneficial. After working with Hitchcock on *Marnie*, Connery returned to England to make *Goldfinger*, which is considered to be the best in the James Bond series. Connery's performance exudes a sexual confidence, which no doubt benefited from his association with Hitchcock. In a *Rolling Stone* interview in 1983, Connery remarked:

> I know that Hitch was intrigued by that blond Grace Kelly type of woman, but I find it kind of sad to be looking for something like that against somebody as special as Hitch was. I'm not mad about that sort of Sherlock Holmes bit, you know. . . . It's funny, but the film buffs at UCLA are constantly dissecting *Marnie* these days to see how it was done. . . . I adored and enjoyed working with Hitchcock tremendously. He never lost his patience or composure on the set. And he never looked through the viewfinder because he had every frame of the movie in his head from the first day of shooting. . . . Hitchcock certainly wasn't an emotional basket case. He always had a most active mind, and he survived to eighty—pretty good for a man who never did any exercise, always weighed over two hundred fifty pounds, and had a fair whack of booze.

## NOTES

1. *Marnie* showman's manual, Alfred Hitchcock Collection, Margaret Herrick Library.

2. Personal interview with Hilton Green, Pasadena, California, September 5, 2000.

3. Unpublished portion of the Hitchcock-Truffaut 1962 interview.

4. Huw Weldon, BBC *Monitor* interview, 1964.

5. Mrs. Alfred Hitchcock as told to Martin Abramson, "My Husband Alfred Hitchcock Hates Suspense," *Coronet* (August 1964): 12–17.

6. Alfred Hitchcock, American Film Institute seminar, 1972.

7. Robert Boyle, American Film Institute seminar, 1977.

8. Hitchcock-Hedren transcript, Alfred Hitchcock Collection, Margaret Herrick Library.

9. Boyle, American Film Institute seminar, 1977.

10. Hitchcock, American Film Institute seminar, 1972.

11. Peter Bogdanovich, *Who the Devil Made It?* (New York: Ballantine, 1997), 538.

12. François Truffaut, *Hitchcock* (New York: Simon & Schuster, 1967), 265.

13. Truffaut, *Hitchcock*, 390.

14. Hitchcock-Hedren transcript.

15. Hitchcock-Hedren transcript.

16. Story outline for production design, February 4, 1963 (transcript of conversation among Alfred Hitchcock, Robert Boyle, and Evan Hunter), Margaret Herrick Library.

17. Hitchcock, American Film Institute seminar, 1972.

18. Boyle, American Film Institute seminar, 1977.

19. Boyle, American Film Institute seminar, 1977.

20. Hitchcock-Hedren transcript.

21. Hitchcock-Hedren transcript.

22. Norman Lloyd interviewed by Francine Parker, *Stages: Norman Lloyd* (Metuchen, N.J.: Scarecrow, 1990), 187.

*Chapter Five*

# Postproduction

Hitchcock finishes a film 60 percent, and I complete the rest for him.

—Bernard Herrmann

Hitchcock's working methods of intense planning and careful storyboarding allowed his editors to work alongside him while the film was still being shot. Such was his meticulous preparation that Hitchcock even storyboarded scenes in *Marnie* that were then photographed and inserted into the edit, prior to them actually being filmed.

His editor, George Tomasini, joined the creative team on *Rear Window* and thereafter worked on every Hitchcock film until *Marnie*, with the exception of *The Trouble with Harry*. A large, jovial man, Tomasini was married to the silent film star Mary Brian. He began work on November 18, 1963, at the same time principal photography started. Bud Hoffman, an assistant editor on Universal's payroll, had begun assembling the test rolls three weeks earlier. Sequences of the film were assembled together throughout filming, and every weekday between 12:00 and 2:00 P.M., Hitchcock worked with Tomasini in the projection room.

## FIRST SCREENINGS

During production, Hitchcock's greatest critic and confidant was his wife Alma, who was influential in everything her husband did. "I know he relied on Alma," recalls Robert Boyle. "It was partly reliance, partly fear; she was the fulcrum around his life, no matter what his fantasies were." Hitchcock enjoyed the company of women more than he did the company of men, and he was very dependent on his wife. Alma loved and appreciated him and tried to protect him in a maternal way. Hitchcock once said to Joseph Stefano, "Her feelings about things are what make the sunrise for me." Whereas criticism by others was evaluated by what they knew, Alma's criticism was the word.

Alma was present during the time Jay Presson Allen was writing the script, but she did not attend the writing sessions. Alma and Jay liked each other and socialized a great deal, but Hitchcock tended to be rather possessive of his wife. She was more knowledgeable and sophisticated than Hitchcock, and her contributions are apparent in the script notes. Of the car show sequence, which was subsequently dropped, Alma wrote, "How long did Mark wait at the motor show—he could easily have missed her. I don't particularly like any of this sequence—it doesn't seem to do anything—I know it's the 'red' recurrence, but unless Mark sees this there seems no scene to me." In another incident when Marnie shoots Sophie, the jaguarundi, after Forio's death, Alma observed, "It takes away from the shooting of Forio," so this scene, too, was dropped. One of the most valuable contributions Alma made to the script occurs during the foxhunt. Alma inquired, "Do huntsmen wear red coats? If they do, or even if one man does—it could cause Marnie to lose control of Forio."

Having been a successful editor before her marriage, Alma made substantial notes during the cutting of a Hitchcock film. On December 19, 1963, a memo records that it was Alma who suggested that Jack Carry, the horse trainer, watch the shots of the doubles for Marnie and Lil, so that he could match their method of riding on the treadmill. Hedren and Baker were also asked to study the film. In the red ink sequence, Alma requested a new scene with Mark outside the washroom, to register his puzzlement arising from Marnie's panic. Hitchcock concurred, for he wrote a memo to himself the next day: "When Jay gets back, discuss with her a new scene to follow the washroom red ink scene, which would be 134A, a scene with Mark, possibly Artie Nelson regarding the red ink." Then on January 24, 1964, Alma suggested to lose Susan's superfluous line after Marnie is asked to come in and work on Saturday: "You ever notice how in the movies it's always the cool, ladylike type who turns out to be the sex pot?"

Alma's skill and experience as an editor is also apparent in the sequence when Mark and Marnie depart from Wyckwyn for their honeymoon. Alma suggested that the cut from Lil listening to Cousin Bob should be followed by a cut to the departing car and then back to a close-up of Lil. The insertion of the point of view makes for an extremely poignant moment, as the viewer briefly identifies with Lil in that any possible future with Mark is being taken away from her. For the scenes inside the Wyckwyn hall, Alma suggested that the audience see Lil go to the library door and listen; the sound of Marnie dialing on the telephone should be played over Lil at the door, and after the telephone conversation, Lil should then be shown going back upstairs.

A running point of contention was a scene between Marnie and Lil in the stables, which takes place the morning after Marnie's nightmare at Wyckwyn. When Marnie expresses her reservation about the impending foxhunt, Lil replies in astonishment, "Really? Killing is my very favorite thing! There's absolutely nothing as relaxing as a good hot blood bath!" Lil goes on to register that Marnie is nothing like her deceased sister Stella, Mark's first wife: "When Stell was dying she asked me to take care of him . . . she left him to me." She then attempts to buy Marnie off, adding, "And I mean to have him. This business with you, whatever it is . . . this little intermission . . . when the curtain goes up on the last act . . . the leading lady . . . c'est moi. Dig?"

The scene had been filmed shortly before Christmas but was never popular with Alma. Of scene 426, on page 176 of the script, Alma wrote:

> I do not like this scene at all. I do not think it gets over what you think it does:
> A. If Marnie were smart, she'd have used Lil as an "out" with Mark, wouldn't she?
> B. Or she'd hit her. Lil is so objectionable.
> C. Unless there is a suggestion here that behind everything Marnie *could* or *does* love Mark (barring the physical contact of course), I am frankly not interested whether Lil wants Mark or not.

The element of theatricality in the dialogue arises from Jay Presson Allen's own association with the theater. Allen had definitely refused to rewrite Lil's dialogue but later agreed with the Hitchcocks that the scene should be dropped. Another scene that was cut was Marnie mounting Lil's horse after shooting Forio. On seeing the finished film, Diane Baker felt that the dropping of both scenes resulted in a clipped feeling to Lil: "There seemed to be a missing dot to the sentence of my character."

While Hitchcock and his crew had been filming over the Christmas period, Jay Presson Allen had been vacationing at the Mount Kenya Safari Club with her husband and daughter. Allen returned to Los Angeles on Monday, January 27, 1964, to begin script consultations for *Mary Rose*. The next day, Allen watched a rough cut of *Marnie* with Hitchcock and Tomasini, noting eight points:

1. First office scene (Rutland's)—when Mark is standing at Ward's door with Ward and Miss Blakeley, there should be a shot of Marnie from Mark's RO.V. [Point of view]
2. After Mark enters Ward's office, it would be nice to have him reopen door, stick his head out to take another look at Marnie, and close door.

This should trigger the girl's shrug and come before Ward's summoning of Marnie. This will show up Ward's lack of humor and clarity.

3. Mark's "take" after his look at Marnie and safe is too quick and too pat. True, he should at this point make the connection with Strutt, but his acceptance of the connection is too immediate. The takes of him that follow—four I believe—seem weak and unfocused to me. The fact that he is smiling rather benignly throughout this sequence waters down the suspense considerably. I think his uncertainty about Marnie should not come before her line, ". . . good, hard demanding work." I had rather see fewer shots of him—I believe one longer, more defined shot would be more effective. Also, I hate to lose the feeling at this point that Mark most likely represents a considerable threat to Marnie's career. Any smile of his at this point should contain a sinister element. Mark's last close-up is splendid.

4. Is it possible to cut Susan's line about ". . . the cool, ladylike type turns out to be the sex pot"? It seems out of sequence and doesn't come off.

5. There should be a wild line from Lil under Mark's and Marnie's entrance into library after honeymoon. It could be confined to a simple exclamation, i.e., "What on earth are . . . Mark?"

6. In the second office scene, Rutland's, where Mark watches Marnie through the partition, we should also have a shot of the safe from Mark's P.O.V.

7. When Marnie is washing the ink from her blouse and saying her final line, "What a lot of excitement over nothing . . ." the camera should be on her rather cheerful face as her hands continue their compulsive scrubbing at the stain.

8. Exterior Mark's bedroom—return from honeymoon—After she shuts the door in his face, the line "You don't have to lock the door, Marnie. Believe me." Should be reinstated at whatever costs and his smile—all of it—should be cut.

After filming was complete, Allen returned for another viewing on March 23, together with Lew Wasserman, his wife, Edd Henry, and the Hitchcocks. After the screening the group retired to Perino's for dinner. Wasserman's notes of the following day suggested eliminating the flashback sequence of the three girls berating a young Marnie for having nits in her hair. He also advised using the shorter version of the opening platform scene. Interestingly, Allen wanted the kiss after the thunderstorm to be dropped in the edit, but Hitchcock retained it, because for him the effect was "like awakening from a nightmare, and then she eases away from him."[1]

As Hitchcock's early career was as a graphic designer, he was very involved in the font used in the credits for his films. Previously, he had employed the graphic designer Saul Bass to create the elaborate, spiraling titles of *Vertigo*, the haphazard trajectories of *North by Northwest*, and the stark, black-and-white vertical and horizontal bars of *Psycho*. The opening credits for *The Birds* foreshadowed the horror to come, with the eerie shadows of the black crows against a stark white background, creating a vortex of compressed violence. With his romance, *Marnie*, however, Hitchcock was in need of something more traditional.

In a letter to Max Reinhardt of Bodley Head Limited, London, dated January 23, 1964, Hitchcock elaborated: "In my constant search for fresh ideas for motion picture titles I find I get involved in all kinds of trick ideas. . . . I think for the picture *Marnie* I am going to do an about-face and have a series of main titles at the beginning of the picture." Hitchcock went on to ask who were the best classic printers in London. The job eventually went to Stellar Press in Hertfordshire, which designed the title credits for £300. Two title cards were made for the actors: one with Tippi Hedren taking precedence over Sean Connery in the American prints; another with Sean Connery receiving top billing for the United Kingdom prints, as agreed in his contract.

## MUSIC AND DUBBING

Bernard Herrmann was born in 1911 in New York and studied with Albert Stoessel, Philip James, and Percy Grainger before making his professional debut as a conductor at the age of twenty. In 1934, he joined the Columbia Broadcasting System as a composer and conductor, and later he was appointed chief conductor of the CBS Symphony Orchestra, giving countless radio performances of little-known and neglected works, including many American premieres. By the time the CBS orchestra was disbanded in the mid-1950s, Herrmann was a distinguished composer for motion pictures. He had made his film debut in 1940 with Orson Welles's *Citizen Kane*, now recognized as one of the masterpieces of world cinema. He himself cited *Ivan the Terrible* by Prokofiev and *Karamazov* by Karl Rathaus as the greatest film scores ever written.

"Cinema is a great opportunity to write a remarkable kind of music in the sense that it is music of the theater," remarked Herrmann in an interview.[2] "At the same time, it is music that becomes part of a whole new artistic phenomenon which is known as cinema, which is a combination of all the arts—and music is cinema. . . . [C]inema is an illusion, and it is the combination of the camera, photography, music, and of course, the word that creates the illusion of what is known as cinema. It is something that the audience partakes of and makes, and the audience need not know about music or photography—only that they are affected by it."

Herrmann's association with Alfred Hitchcock began in 1954 when he wrote the jaunty score for *The Trouble with Harry*. For the next ten years Herrmann scored every Hitchcock film, adding immeasurably to the resonance and success of *Vertigo*, *North by Northwest*, and *Psycho*. In 1962, he acted as the sound consultant for *The Birds*. Hitchcock himself was not a musically sensitive man, but according to Herrmann, he had "the great sensitivity to leave me alone when I am composing." Three of the films that Herrmann scored, *Citizen Kane*, *The Magnificent Ambersons*, and *Vertigo*, consistently rank among international critics' top ten lists. The composer remarked that with the exception of Orson Welles, none of the directors he worked with knew anything about music, even how to communicate on a simple level with a composer. "Hitchcock left it completely to me."

"Benny was like many people who are very intelligent. He reacted to people on the basis of their intelligence," says longtime friend Annette Kaufman, whose husband was a member of Herrmann's orchestra. "He was very informed in music and poetry and was based on an idea that music was poetic. He didn't like senseless music that was sometimes written. Benny was a very sensitive person, and he had a great deal of conviction for what he knew, and he resented when people who didn't know anything about music told him what to do."[3]

With the burgeoning of youth culture in the 1950s, the MCA talent agency, once the Music Corporation of America, was at the forefront to tap into a new and potentially lucrative audience. MCA not only controlled Universal Studios but also owned Revue Television Studios and had a record company associated with them. Lew Wasserman most likely urged Hitchcock to reconsider his style to appeal to the youth market, starting with a more marketable pop theme that would sell many records. The director had already enjoyed some success with Doris Day's song, "Que Sera Sera" in *The Man Who Knew Too Much*. A hit tune for *Marnie* would most likely bolster what Wasserman perceived to be a largely uncommercial venture. MCA had made Hitchcock a rich man, and he felt obligated to them. On December 10, 1963, Suzanne Gauthier sent a memo to Harry Garfield at Universal, saying that "Mr. Hitchcock would like to know, as soon as possible, the composers of the theme songs from *Union 76*, *Glendale Federal Savings and Loans*, *and Tareyton cigarettes*."

Herrmann, like Hitchcock did not readily adhere to others' wishes. He later remarked, "The vain hopes of the director with poor taste is that music will make money for the film with a theme song or a title tune. . . . They're not getting hit records, and they're not getting instant composers. They just get a lot more garbage. And it is not worth discussing in a serious discussion about film music. After all, if we're going to discuss the novel, we don't talk about comic books, do we?"[4]

With these conflicting objectives in mind, and fueled with his own resolution to write a symphonic score, Herrmann began work on *Marnie* on January 6, 1964, for a fee of $17,500. At the time, he was married to his second wife, Lucy Anderson, an attractive and vivacious blonde. However, the fiery, irascible composer was not an easy man to live with, and by the time *Marnie* was scored, their marriage was in difficulty and divorce procedures began in March. "I think he was very creative, and very talented, extremely sensitive and emotional as a person," recalls Anderson. "The studio was anxious to have a popular song, a hit song. They were stressing Hitchcock at the time, and he didn't seem to be able to refuse them."[5]

Herrmann stated that he could never work from a script when scoring a Hitchcock film because it was the director's timing that created the suspense. The suspense sound that Herrmann utilizes is a harmonic device—the persistent use of the seventh chord. This device permeates the scores of *Vertigo*, *North by Northwest*, *Psycho*, and *Marnie*. It is this feeling of restlessness and dissatisfaction, a craving for resolution, that Herrmann exploits as a means of creating musical suspense. Musicologist Percy Scholes, speaking of the effect of the seventh chord in some works by Bach, suggests, "All the mere triads give a feeling of satisfaction in themselves: they were concords. This 'chord of the seventh' gives a feeling of restlessness: the ear is dissatisfied until it had passed to the next chord and the seventh itself has moved to the note below. This chord of the seventh, then is a discord—not necessarily, observe, a chord of harsh effect, but a chord that demands following in a certain way, i.e., resolution."[6] Delaying the resolution is one of the most important strategies exploited by Herrmann to create suspense in a Hitchcock film.

In the musical prelude that plays over the main titles, the seventh chords form the harmony of the romantic theme associated with Marnie throughout the film. The sevenths remain constant, but the triads within them waver between major and minor, while the melody oscillates around the seventh. From the outset, Herrmann establishes Marnie's conflicts and ambiguities within her theme music. Another example of the effective use of the seventh chord can be heard at the end of the failed robbery attempt, where Marnie's inability to steal is intercut with subjective zoom shots of the money. The cue ends on a seventh chord, the dissonance is poised like a question, creating expectation in the listener. Herrmann frequently used dissonant intervals or chords at the end of a cue to create the feeling of anticipation.[7]

Chromaticism was another effective strategy employed by Herrmann to create musical suspense, and it underscores Marnie's reaction to the color red. The turbulent music that opens the credits cue is an *agitato* played loudly by a full orchestra. It abruptly begins with a brass and woodwind trill introducing a rapid arpeggio figure that rises like a shriek.

The power of chromaticism derives from blocking the motion to the normal diatonic tones, while at the same time, the progressive persistency of the opening trills creates ambiguity and tension. Marnie's reaction to red is clarified at the end when the chromatic music accompanies the release of the repressed memory, namely the killing of the sailor. For maximum effect, Herrmann employs both the seventh chords and chromaticism simultaneously to engender suspense.

*Marnie* is one of the most conventional of Herrmann's scores, employing a symphony orchestra with prominent strings, in addition to wind instruments like French horns, flutes, and clarinets. Lacking are the exotic percussion instruments and Wagnerian references of *Vertigo.* The range of tambours is less broad, and when present they are specifically arranged within the score. The whole effect is to give *Marnie* the feeling of chamber music, creating an intimate sound, with a more immediate and incisive presence. The score is very sequential and repetitive, with an intense lyricism unusual for Herrmann. The romantic score is very effective during the film's quieter moments, for the composer's greatest talent was creating mood. For example, during Marnie's horse riding, the music reaches a romantic peak, as detailed in Allen's script: "At this point, the music should rise to a thematic crescendo—very romantic, melodic, full of nostalgia, warmth, expressive of the real Marnie whom we have never seen until this moment. This is the Marnie theme. Suddenly the music cuts off, as though the ecstasy were immediately past."

One of Herrmann's favorite sequences was the hunt. In his biography of the composer, Steven C. Smith observes, "Herrmann opens the sequence on a note of rousing cheer, with a lively riding theme for strings answered by the call of huntsman's horn. Herrmann's gallop becomes a relentlessly driving, nightmarish variant of [Marnie's] theme, building momentum until horse and rider tumble over a brick wall."[8] The sequence leading up to Forio's death illustrates Hitchcock's mastery of composite montage and rapid cutting. According to Robert Boyle, Hitchcock was always experimenting with quick montage, exemplified in *Psycho*'s shower murder and *Marnie*'s horse accident.

Like the song the children sing in *The Birds*, when the crows gather behind Melanie at the jungle gym, *Marnie* has a song that was volunteered by the scriptwriter. After the theatrics of the storm when Marnie remembers her childhood trauma, the local street urchins sing, "Mother, Mother, I am ill. Send for the doctor over the hill. Call for the doctor, call for the nurse, call for the lady with the alligator purse." In *The Birds*, Evan Hunter suggested the song because his children liked to sing it. Jay Presson Allen chose Marnie's song because she thought it to be funny and amusing.

Music editor Dick Harris had begun work with Herrmann on February 3, but to meet the finish date, another editor, Donald K. Harris, was contracted on

March 23 for two weeks. Herrmann completed his work on *Marnie* on April 3, and Harris finished work on May 1. The studio still wanted a commercial score that could be marketed as a pop song. Wasserman persuaded Hitchcock to hire Nat King Cole to record lyrics for a *Marnie* theme song. The record was released on June 29 in both the United States and Britain. As a promotional push, Hitchcock requested that Bernard Herrmann be given publicity for having scored the music. Universal's Harry Garfield also recommended that $2,000 be allocated to promote and publicize Nat King Cole's lyrics. Since Garfield had managed to obtain the artist's services free of charge, he felt that Universal should enter into a joint promotional campaign with the record companies: "I think this extra effort among the disc jockeys and the music dealers could be a helpful factor in our exploitation activities in connection with *Marnie*." Hitchcock approved of the expenditure, and the advertising slogan read, "Nat the King sings the beautiful lyrics of the tune inspired by the brilliant Alfred Hitchcock production for the Capitol Records label."

When it was time to dub the film, sound recordist Walden Watson asked that the same crew for *Psycho* and *The Birds*, headed by Bob Hoyt, be employed on *Marnie*. On March 18, Hitchcock distributed six copies of detailed dubbing notes via Peggy Robertson. For the opening sequence on the train platform, the director requested, "We should have no sound on this scene except the sound of Marnie's heels as they tap away into the distance. Once she has stopped and set her bag down, we should just hear the whistle (query horn) of the approaching diesel train." The motif of passing trains runs throughout the sound track, suggesting the journey element in the film's design. Inside Mrs. Edgar's house, Hitchcock stated, "By the time Marnie goes upstairs to sleep, we should be in complete silence so that the tapping on the window can be distinctly heard."

Hitchcock had already experimented with no music and just an electronic sound track for *The Birds*. With Marnie's robbery of Rutland's, Hitchcock again exploited the effectiveness of just silence punctuated by sound effects:

Now this will be a long track—with all the off stage noises, which are the sounds of people going home. And the way I'll get the off-stage track to work—it will be full of voices that will get less and less, but even when the wash room is empty, there'll still be faint sounds of doors shutting and distant "good night, good night." After that shot has gone on for a short while, [Marnie's] ready at any time for someone to come in . . . to go nonchalant. . . . Various voices should continue until the final "Goodnights" are heard outside and then we have a long silence. The rest of the scene should be silent and even the mopping down should barely be heard.

However, when we come to the night watchman his voice should be made very loud in contrast to the cleaning woman's quiet response.

For the foxhunt, Hitchcock requested all the necessary sounds of the horses' hooves and the baying of hounds, which should reach their greatest intensity when Marnie watches the killing of the fox: "In other words, we should get as much horror into the sounds for its effect upon her. The rest would be the gallop of the horse away and the distant gallop of Lil following. When we reach the wall we should put in a crash and the sounds of the falling horse. Note: We should be very judicious about the whinnying of the injured Forio. There should be quite a stillness after Forio is shot."

On March 4, Hitchcock made a note to loop all of Tippi Hedren's dialogue in the first Baltimore house sequence, scenes 33 through 55. Hitchcock was present at the recording to give the reading of the lines. On March 16, he also requested, "We will have to get a scream for Marnie in Scene 512, when she reacts to the blood. This should be recorded by a girl, other than Tippi Hedren (who cannot give the requisite scream). The timbre of this girl's voice, should of course, be similar." Allen suggested that when Marnie screams "No!" after Mark rips off her nightgown, Hedren's voice should also be dubbed with a real scream. In the American prints, the scream was replaced with a more highly charged scream, but not in the British prints. At the end of March, Hitchcock sent George Tomasini a memo with additional dubbing notes: "Make sure the sailor (Bruce Dern) in the flashback, speaks the following: "What's the matter? Why you crazy . . . You'll get yourself hit back." He also suggested to pull up the children's song over Marnie's dialogue when she first visits her mother.

## CENSORSHIP

Hitchcock had been engaged in long running battles with film censors in the past, notably over suggestive dialogue in *Rear Window* and *Psycho*'s shower murder. According to Hilton Green, the director was always trying to push the margins of what was deemed acceptable on celluloid. *Marnie*'s rape and sadomasochism were elements likely to be difficult to approve.

On September 24, 1963, a copy of the screenplay was sent to the Motion Picture Association of America in Hollywood, part of the Hays Office that regulated a code of ethics for motion pictures distributed in the United States. The comments that came back on October 7 from administrator Geoffrey Shurlock stated that the screenplay basically seemed acceptable under the requirements of the Production Code. However, they requested dropping Strutt's expression "little bitch" (in the script this was changed to "little witch"). Shurlock also urged that the sounds of a toilet flushing be eliminated in the washroom. Mark's line of dialogue to Marnie on their honeymoon,

". . . or onto your back across an office desk with some angry old bull of a businessman taking what he figured was coming to him," was deemed unacceptable, as was the expression "crissake."

Although Hitchcock and Allen had never delineated Mark's actions as rape, Shurlock's office thought differently: "As presently described, this marriage consummation scene seems unacceptable. Mark's actions could almost be described as an action of rape. His stripping Marnie nude could not be approved and the subsequent action when she is placed on the bed and he apparently starts to make love to her also is unacceptably suggestive." A final request in accordance with the code requirements was that the American Humane Association be consulted in all scenes where animals were used.

Peggy Robertson wrote back on November 1, submitting the final shooting script for *Marnie*: "I think you will find that we have dealt with the comments made in your letter of October 7, after you have read the first screenplay. We have sent a copy of the first screenplay to Harold Melniker of the American Humane Association and a copy of the final shooting script was sent for his comments." Shurlock wrote back a month later, saying that while they could approve use of the words *hell* and *damn* in moderation, the expression *goddam* was unacceptable. With regard to the rape scene, Shurlock wrote, "The acceptability of this sequence depended on the discretion with which it is presented on screen. We will be unable to approve any scenes of nudity. This would apply to the long shot described on this page. Also, the action should not go on long enough to suggest that the close-up of Marnie amounts to photographing a woman engaged in intercourse." He signed off saying that the final judgment would be based on the finished picture.

On March 30, *Marnie* was screened for the Shurlock office at 10:00 A.M. in Hitchcock's projection room. The film was approved in its entirety, and Hitchcock had won another battle, by depicting rape in a mainstream Hollywood film. The Humane Association also approved viewing of *Marnie* on April 30, certifying that it was in accordance with the requirements of humanitarian interests and was acceptable in its conduct and portrayal of animals.

By June, with the music scored and postproduction completed, prints of *Marnie* were being distributed within the United States and overseas. Although, 350 prints had already been sent out to the various exchanges, fifty-five of which went overseas, Universal Studios was anxious over some dialogue. At the end of the film, Mrs. Edgar confesses to bartering her virginity: "And I wanted Billy's basketball sweater. I was fifteen. And Billy said if I'd let him, I could have the sweater. So I let him. . . . I still got that old sweater. And I got you, Marnie." On June 10, Hitchcock agreed to drop the tawdry reference to Marnie's conception, and George Tomasini was asked to come in the next day and make the cuts from the studio copy. In its final cut,

*Marnie* ran at 129 minutes, and the onus now was on the publicity department to exploit the unusual nature of the film.

## CONCLUSION

The postproduction files for *Marnie* corroborate Hitchcock's substantial involvement in a film that was meticulously edited while still being shot. Previously overlooked in assessments is Alma Hitchcock's significant contribution to key scenes that influenced the tone and overall shape of the final film. Hitchcock was reliant on both Alma's and Jay Presson Allen's comments, as well as George Tomasini's expertise. After *Marnie*, Hitchcock lost Tomasini's collaboration, as the editor suffered a fatal heart attack in November 1964 at the age of fifty-five. He also lost his favorite cinematographer, Robert Burks, who died in a house fire.

The services' of another valued member of the Hitchcock crew, Bernard Herrmann, also came to an end. Upon release, the *Marnie* score was castigated by Universal for being lazy and derivative, with origins in the prelude for *The Seventh Voyage of Sinbad*, composed six years earlier. Herrmann was deemed to be recycling his old scores, a criticism compounded when his next work, *A Joy in the Morning*, a mediocre MGM film starring Richard Chamberlain, was likened to be too thematically similar to the *Marnie* score. The backlash against Herrmann was no doubt an attempt by Universal to persuade Hitchcock to drop him for contemporary artists like The Beatles, who had scored the title song for *A Hard Day's Night* (1964). Poet Philip Larkin made the famous remark that the sixties only really began in 1963 with The Beatles' first album.

During this time of social change and the explosion of youth culture, Universal's charge of derivativeness was aimed at the homogenous concept of Herrmann's work. Indeed, Herrmann's style did simplify in the 1960s, as he subscribed to the axiom that listeners only listened with half an ear. It wasn't beneficial to be too elaborately composed. *Marnie*'s instrumentation was later utilized in Truffaut's *The Bride Wore Black* (1969).

Hitchcock still had faith in Herrmann, for he asked the composer to score the music for his fiftieth feature, *Torn Curtain*. On November 4, 1965, Hitchcock sent a telegram to Herrmann's London home:

Let me say I am very anxious for you to do the music on *Torn Curtain*. I was extremely disappointed when I heard the score of *Joy in the Morning*; not only did I find it conforming to the old pattern but extremely reminiscent of the *Marnie* music. In fact the theme was almost the same. Unfortunately for we artists, we do not have the freedom that we would like to have because we are catering to an audience and that is why you get your money and I get mine. This audience is very different from the one to which we used to cater. It is young, vigorous and demanding. It is this fact that has been recognized by almost all of the European filmmakers where they have sought to introduce a beat and a rhythm that is more in tune with the requirements of the aforesaid audience.

Herrmann wrote back the next day promising to comply; however, when Hitchcock arrived for the recording session, he heard music that was typically Herrmann. A bitter argument ensued, and Hitchcock dismissed Herrmann from the project. The final words Herrmann said to Hitchcock were "You know I'm not a pop tune writer and I never have been. Hitch, you can't out jump your shadow."[9] The incident brought their eleven-year collaboration—and friendship—to an end. Hitchcock wanted the music to be more mainstream, but Herrmann would never write a commercial score.

## NOTES

1. Hitchcock-Hedren transcripts, Alfred Hitchcock Collection, Margaret Herrick Library.

2. Irwin Bazelon, *Knowing the Score: Notes on Film Music* (New York: Van No strand, 1975).

3. Personal interview with Mrs. Annette Kaufman, Los Angeles, November 18, 2000.

4. Bazelon, *Knowing the Score*.

5. Personal interview with Lucy Anderson, Los Angeles, November 25, 2000.

6. Percy Alfred Scholes, *The Oxford Companion to Music* (Oxford: Oxford University Press, 1970).

7. Bazelon, *Knowing the Score*.

8. Steven C. Smith, *A Heart at Fire's Center: The Life and Music of Bernard Herrmann* (Berkeley: University of California Press, 1991).

9. Personal interview with Lucy Anderson.

## Chapter Six

# Marketing

Actors come and go, but the name of the director should stay clearly in the mind of audiences.

—Alfred Hitchcock

Like many celebrated artists, Hitchcock was reluctant to discuss the thematic content of his work in any depth, preferring to offer interviewers familiar technical anecdotes about the challenge of filming various scenes. Yet he clearly relished appreciation from his peers and considered self-promotion to be one of the keys to his professional success. Recent assessments suggest that in the early 1960s, Hitchcock was attempting to alter his image from that of master entertainer to serious artist.[1] Beginning with *The Birds*, his most prestigious and expensive marketing campaign, Hitchcock was involved with prominent members of the film community and institutions such as New York's Museum of Modern Art. The director debuted *The Birds* to the world's press on the opening night of the 1963 Cannes Film Festival. Critics and audiences, however, were baffled by the film's lack of resolution and self-conscious European style.

Hitchcock himself compared his output to that of a great painter whose works share a distinctive style: "If you take Paul Klee, well, Klee does a certain type of work."[2] With *Marnie*, Hitchcock planned to expand on his efforts to promote himself as a serious artist, and his reputation was about to be given a boost from an unexpected quarter.

## THE FRENCH DIRECTOR

As early as 1956, Hitchcock had received requests for his memoirs from many reputable publishing firms such as Faber and Faber, Opera Mundi in Paris, Random House, Doubleday, the British Film Institute, and various literary agencies in Los Angeles and New York. His response was always the same: a polite decline, saying that he felt more material was needed. "After all, I still am only the boy director and I hope I have a long way to go."[3] In France, the team of the film journal *Cahiers du Cinéma*, François Truffaut, Eric Rohmer, Jean-Luc Godard, and Claude Chabrol, became friends because of their admiration for Hitchcock. They believed that his films had a vertiginous depth and that every cut and angle was clearly chosen. In this way, Hitchcock demonstrated what directing was, and the French embraced this idea because they, too, wanted to be the authors of a film.

In the winter of 1954, Truffaut, along with Chabrol, went to interview Hitchcock at the Studio St. Maurice, where he was engaged in postsync for *To Catch a Thief*. In the excitement of watching a loop of the film, they accidentally stumbled into the frozen pond of the studio yard, so the interview was delayed until later that evening. Truffaut continued to meet Hitchcock on his subsequent trips to the United States, and during this period, he became a filmmaker himself, with three pictures to his credit. His latest, *Jules et Jim*, was shown in New York.

On June 2, 1962, during the filming of *The Birds* and preproduction on *Marnie*, Truffaut wrote to Hitchcock from Les Films du Carrosse, Société de Production Cinématographique:

> During my conversations with the foreign press, and particularly in New York, I have noted that on the whole, there is too often a superficial approach to your achievements. On the other hand, the propaganda we initiated in the *Cahiers du Cinema*, while effective in France, carried no weight in America, because the arguments were over-intellectual. However, now that I am a film maker, my admiration has, if anything increased, strengthened by additional bases for appreciation. I've seen each of your pictures five or six times, now observing them primarily from the angle of construction. Some directors have a love for the cinema, but what you have is a love of the film. And that is what I should like to explore with you.

Truffaut went on to request an interview to be recorded over a week, amounting to some fifty hours of transcription. The material was intended for a book to be published in New York and Paris simultaneously, with Helen Scott, the press director of the French Film Office in New York, acting as an interpreter. On June 11, Hitchcock cabled a reply: "Your letter made me cry and how grateful I am to receive such a tribute from you. I am at present still shooting *The Birds* and this will continue until July 15th; after that I have to start editing the picture which will take some weeks. I think I should wait until shooting on *The Birds* is finished so that I can get in touch with you again with the idea, perhaps of our meeting around the end of August."

The director kept to his promise, and Truffaut and Scott flew to California to begin work on August 13, Hitchcock's sixty-third birthday. Every day during that week, Hitchcock collected Truffaut and Scott from the Beverly Hills Hotel at 8 A.M. and took them to his office in Universal City Studios, where they talked until six at night. They only stopped for lunch and had the same meal every day: steak, fried potatoes, and ice cream. All of Hitchcock's films were discussed—why he had decided to make each one, the actors he hired, the scenario construction and the technical problems of filming. From the third day onward, Hitchcock's sensitivity emerged and he became self-critical. He described scenes in which he thought he had filmed something that was foolish, pretentious, or careless. Truffaut was moved by the contrast between the public man, so sure of himself and so cynical, and what seemed to be a very vulnerable and emotional man.

The following year, on July 13, 1963, with *Marnie* in preproduction, Truffaut wrote to Peggy Robertson saying that he had finished writing the book interview with Hitchcock in French and hoped that it would be published the following spring. Scott in New York was translating the English language version and would submit it to the director for his approval. Hitchcock also gave authorization for *Cahiers du Cinema* to publish the chapter concerning *The Birds* to coincide with the French release of the film in September. As it happened, delays in both translation and obtaining stills and permission from the various studios that owned the films resulted in the book not being published until 1967.

By the end of 1963, when Hitchcock was filming *Marnie*, he instructed the director of publicity at Universal to solicit and disseminate a tribute from Truffaut, dated December 16, elaborating on Hitchcock as one of the greatest:

> The idea for a book first came to me when, in discussions with American journalists and, mainly, with the New York critics, I became aware that they had a false and quite superficial idea about Mr. Hitchcock and his contributions to the cinema. Mr. Hitchcock has been, for a long time, the contemporary director whom I admire the most. To me he seems the most complete, the most artistic, the most efficient.
>
> 1. He is instinctive. In the fifty films he has made he has presented a selective universe which belongs to him alone. He has in his head dreams, obsessions and preoccupations which are not those of the masses, but which he successfully transmits to the screen, and then offers to the public. He practices a cinema

which acts physically on the spectator. All creative artists dream of accomplishing such a goal.

2. By definition an artist is a man apart from society. To succeed he must not integrate himself with society. But he must impose his originality. In other words, an artist must make himself accepted by society without renouncing his artistic dreams. Alfred Hitchcock is the filmmaker who has best resolved the problem of communicating with the public.

In effect, like the short subjects of Norman MacLaren, in Canada, or of Trnka, in Czechoslovakia, all of Mr. Hitchcock's films have been experimental in aspect. . . . What is his speciality? I think it is in creating, in each film, a sort of realistic dream, based not only on the framework of nightmare, but on the everyday reality of life. . . . Alfred Hitchcock has understood that the cinema, which is one of the entertainment branches, is an art of sustained impression, like music. And, like music, it is subject to laws of progression and rhythm which, for example, have nothing in common with the laws of writing a novel. Many films resemble novels. Those of Alfred Hitchcock resemble a symphonic concert.

At Hitchcock's request, copies of the tribute were sent to key journalists, such as Art Seidenbaum of the *Los Angeles Times*, as a basis for an interview that Hitchcock conducted on the set in January 1964. On April 29, Peggy Robertson sent a memo to Edd Henry: "Mr. Hitchcock suggested today that the Truffaut article, a copy of which I sent you on April 27th, might be sent to the New York critics—he mentioned Murray Schumach." Hitchcock identified Schumach, a critic for the *New York Times*, as someone who had consistently praised him over the years and who might have an influence on other critics. When the English translation of a previous article by Truffaut, published ten years earlier, appeared in the highbrow journal *Film Culture*, this, too, was distributed among the press.

Hitchcock met Truffaut in New York on April 23, 1964, and allowed the Frenchman to view *Marnie*. After the screening, the two spent a few hours filling in the gaps in the book. Later that year, Hitchcock had finished reading the manuscript and wrote to Truffaut on October 22, "I think you have done a wonderful job. Some times I feel a little self-conscious when I read such things about my work, as expounded by you. . . . Of course, at last, having had comparatively lesser known stars in the last three pictures, I have now consented to please the whim of the 'front office' and use two well known players." Hitchcock's last reference was to the hiring of Paul Newman and Julie Andrews in his next film, *Torn Curtain*, for $750,000 each, a fee that he greatly resented.

Truffaut paid a further tribute to Hitchcock in an interview conducted by the *New Yorker* on October 31. The thirty-two-year-old director was in New York for a few days during the opening of his new film, *The Soft Skin*. The interview was forwarded to Hitchcock by Helen Scott: I know you'd rather see the completed manuscript, but here's something to keep you entertained in the meantime. It really is very nearly ready and I'm not sure whether he wrote to you. . . . Truffaut took the unfriendly reception of the New York critics to his latest picture in his stride, since he had been fortified by the Cannes experience I need hardly tell you how often we think of you. You can see for yourself that the interviewers who turned up to do a piece on Truffaut, came away with an article on Hitchcock. In answer to why he was writing a book on Hitchcock, Truffaut replied:

> Because I have long been sure that he is the greatest director of films in the world . . . and with every passing day I am surer than ever. Each week for the past few years, I have been going to see at least two of his pictures. *Vertigo* I see at least every two months. . . . The more I see of Hitchcock's pictures, the less desire I have to see other pictures other than his. And I learned what I needed to know—all the things I had sensed but had never clearly formulated. For instance, the principle, extremely important, that an emotion must be created on the screen and then must be sustained—on the technical level as well as on the scenario level. Many can create an emotion on the screen, but very few know how to sustain it.[4]

Because of their respective schedules, Hitchcock and Truffaut did not meet again to conclude the *Marnie* chapter until July 1966 in London. In a letter dated October 21, 1966, Truffaut wrote:

> Our book, *Le Cinema selon Alfred Hitchcock*, will be published around November 20th, approximately at the same time as *Torn Curtain* opens in Paris. The publisher, Robert Laffont, wanted to set up a cocktail reception to mark the double event, but it's my feeling that without your presence, it would be of no great interest. This being so, I have an alternative proposal, which I hereby submit for your approval: Rather than send copies of the book to the film press, as is customarily done, I would invite them to pick up their copies in person at a special Hitchcock program, to be held at the Cinematheque of the Palais de Chaillot. There, prior to a cocktail party, which apparently is a "must," the program will consist of a sixty-minute montage of excerpts from your films. With your permission, I shall work up the montage myself.

The clip that Truffaut elected to show from *Marnie* that night was the free-association scene between Mark and Marnie after her nightmare.

## STUDIO PUBLICITY

Within the studio system, a unit publicist is assigned to a production from the start until the end of filming and is responsible for creating materials and stories that are of interest to the press, both television and magazine. The challenge for any unit publicist is to get a star's or director's name in print. Hitchcock had the prestige for this to be easily achieved, for he was more of a celebrity than most of his actors. Harold Mendelsohn was a unit publicist at Universal Studios for twenty years, working for directors like Dunne, Hathaway, Ford, and Chaplin. Although he only worked on one Hitchcock film, *Marnie*, Mendelsohn affirms, "Of all the directors, Hitchcock was without question, the most thoroughly prepared on the set. He had everything blueprinted."[5] The set was quiet and organized and Hitchcock reacted to everyone professionally, never raising his voice.

As the unit publicist, Mendelsohn was in daily contact with *Marnie*'s stars, and 90 percent of his work was achieved at the typewriter. "Sean Connery had a tremendous personality," Mendelsohn remembers, "and it didn't take him long after his arrival, to get people in Hollywood interested in him. He impressed everyone he met and was exact and professional. I found him very refreshing, he was just himself and wasn't pumped up with a false impression. Like most British actors, for him acting was a business, and he took it in his stride. Tippi also was very warm and wonderful, as both a person and an actress. She came in, did her work and was nice to everyone on the set. The press was interested in a new actress to a starring role and Tippi warmed to it."

On November 11, 1963, Hitchcock met with Mendelsohn and David Golding, the publicity director for *Marnie*. Golding had been stationed in Rome during World War II, as the managing editor of the Mediterranean edition of *Stars and Stripes*, reporting news from the front line. Before becoming a publicity director at Universal Studios, Golding was the vice president for promotions and publicity at 20th Century Fox. After *Marnie*'s release, he was promoted to the position of publicity director for Universal's London office. Mendelsohn recalls that Golding was very talented and industrious, but his aggressive approach was one that would bring him into conflict with Hitchcock.

During the time *Marnie* was made, the publicity office at Universal Pictures received eighteen to twenty-five copies of a movie script for distribution to all publicity and advertising personnel. However, Golding specified a list of people who must get a script, including the publicity department in both the Los Angeles and New York office, the advertising department on Universal's lot, and Ed Fisher of National Press. On October 10, he sent a memo to Hitchcock suggesting subjects for discussion in their next meeting:

> I have noted the reference to the *Marnie* theme in the script. I don't have to tell you what the *Spellbound* theme meant for the exploitation of your picture. As a matter of fact, I believe it was the first time that a musical theme was used to

such an advantage as it was in *Spellbound*. The *Marnie* theme could likewise work for us very effectively and I would like to get your thoughts on this. . . . A campaign on Tippi Hedren. I haven't met her yet and I would like the girls who help me in magazine planning, Gail Gifford and Betty Mitchell, to get to know her too. What is needed are some guidelines from you so that we can establish a working relationship that meets with your approval.

A further memo dated October 14 proposed to capitalize on the filming of the hunt sequence:

> In addition to the unique photographic possibilities that the filming of the fox hunt presents, I think we have an opportunity here to get some national publicity from the event. In so much as you will probably photograph this at some hunt club, I think we should attempt to get some of the leading socialites in that area to be the extras and play themselves. Some of the country's leading blue bloods reside in that part of the country and if they worked in a scene in the motion picture, I think we could get some unusual features on this.

David Golding also tried an experiment by contacting the general manager of Associated Press Worldwide, which serviced more than five thousand newspapers overseas. The outlet seemed to want motion picture industry news, and Golding stated he would continue to utilize their outlets by disseminating news about *Marnie*'s production. On November 8, he sent a memo to Hitchcock claiming news of his success and his commitment to continue using the service. Three weeks later, Hitchcock met with Bob Thomas of Associated Press, in an interview that the director had already scripted.

The campaign for Tippi Hedren began in earnest with a headlined article, "Tippi Hedren: Can Hollywood Still Make a Star?" in *Parade* magazine, published on December 8. Hitchcock elaborated on his plans for casting his protégé in *Marnie*:

> It's going to be tough . . . but what I plan to do is to promote Tippi in big pictures, films of quality that compel attention. The thing to do is cloak Tippi with a veil of mystery, keep her out of the gossip columns. . . . I want Tippi to get a publicity build up away from the movie pages, and I want it to be gradual and dignified. We're getting her a new wardrobe. Alexandre, the hair stylist from Paris, has flown his assistant over here to redo her hair. I'm trying to teach her a new taste in art and literature, because she's going to play a great variety of roles for me. I honestly think she's got what the public wants—subtle and wholesome sex. She's a female volcano whose lava is about to erupt.

Hitchcock concluded by confiding in his plans for Hedren to perform in two or three of his films, so that a favorable word-of-mouth campaign was started. He wanted to build up a young actress of beauty, dignity, and mystery, a gracious high-style lady, someone like a young Grace Kelly or Myrna Loy. He was convinced that this was the type of star the film going public wanted, rather than the type of blonde personified by Marilyn Monroe.

During the production of *Marnie*, Harold Mendelsohn entertained as many of the top press as the set could accommodate. Penelope Gilliat of the *London Observer* and Ernest Betts of *People* interviewed Hitchcock on November 1. Normally, the unit publicist's task was to steer the interview in the direction in which it should evolve. But Hitchcock, a master of self-publicity himself, knew exactly what he wanted to say and gave a perfect story. On December 10, Jennie Dohnt of *Live Review*, Belgium, Henry Gris of *United Press International*, and Bud Gray of the *London Sunday News* interviewed Hitchcock, Hedren, and Connery. In the new year, two more foreign journalists arrived: Frederick Porges, who represented *Berliner Morgenpost*, *Freudin/ Film-Revue* of Berlin, *Film-Journal* of Karlsruhe, *Film Suisse* of Zurich, and *National Zeitung* of Basel; and José Jasd, who represented *Mi Film* in Caracas, *Pantalla* in Mexico, *Ondas* in Madrid, and *Imagenes* in Barcelona. Brief interviews were also arranged with Yani Begakis of Tokyo's *Screen* magazine, Kosta Alexander of *Athens Press*, Roy Cummins from *BBC Radio Times*, and Maurice Woodruff of the *British Evening News*.

Still needed were photographs and portraits of Tippi Hedren and Sean Connery, some of which were to include the horse, Forio. The photographs were to be taken in between camera setups during the busy filming schedule. Golding had written a memo on January 30 expressing his anxiety that there was little time left for further publicity shots of Connery, whose finish date was February 28. A photography shoot was laid out for Hedren at John Engstead's studios on February 6. During the session, the actress wore the white evening dress and Alexandre hairstyle from the party sequence, and at the end of the day, pictures of Hedren in her riding habit were taken, with her hair down and the wild look in her eyes as she appears in the Wyckwyn hall after the death of Forio. On February 19, production was finally able to capture the two shots of Hedren and Connery.

At the beginning of March, Hitchcock drafted a curious letter to David Lipton, the head of publicity at Universal Studios:

> I am terribly sorry to have to write you a letter like this. I do not want Dave Golding to have anything to do with our picture henceforth. Would you please give him specific instructions to have nothing to do, in any shape or form, with our picture, *Marnie*, either in contact with artists making commitments for interviews, or making commitments for journalists to come on the picture, in the form of accommodations for travel or hotels. My reason for writing you is that I am not happy at all with the "aggressive," and wrongfully aggressive, behavior patterns of Mr. Golding. If you wish a more elaborate explanation

from me I will be very happy to meet you and expand. I hope you will not ask me to meet you.

The letter was never sent. It is quite probable that Golding's persistence, efficiency, and constant memos irked Hitchcock, who never liked to be told what to do.

Harold Mendelsohn believes Hitchcock's assessment of Golding to be unfair: "Hitchcock liked to have his own way on everything he did. But what David Golding had to do was basic salesmanship. Unless you have an aggressive approach, you don't get very far in publicity. Many people in production resented and misunderstood the work of the publicity department. Not only did films need to be made, but they had to be marketed also." Indeed, a film's publicist was one of the last groups within the film industry to receive a recognized on-screen credit. There's no denying Golding's talents however, because during his time as head of the Universal London bureau, Golding achieved color front covers on two magazines, *Look* and *Life*, for the Charlie Chaplin film, *A Countess from Hong Kong*.

## EUROPEAN TRIP

During 1963, Hitchcock discovered that the French government was planning to award him the Legion of Honor. On December 27, he wrote to Guilio Ascarelli of Universal International Films in Rome: "In connection with the coming campaign on *Marnie*, do you think a good public relations publicity could be found in the fact that I am supposed to be given the Legion of Honor? Perhaps you might ask Andre Malraux what's been holding it up all this time!" He wrote again on February 18, 1964: "I expect to be in Paris Wednesday, May 6th. During the three days in Paris, would you like to make some publicity arrangements in connection with *Marnie*?" Ascarelli wrote back on February 26:

> Upon receipt of your letter at the beginning of January, I immediately contacted Mr. Favre le Bret (you met him in Cannes—he is the Festival Director and Secretary of the Paris Opera House). Mr. Le Bret told me he was going to write immediately to the French Consul in Los Angeles in order to get the matter started. In fact, he indicated that the proposal of the Legion of Honor to a foreigner must originate from the French Ambassador of the respective country (Mr. Alphand) who in turn will make the recommendation to the French Foreign Minister (Mr. Couve d Mourville). Mr. Le Bret is a great admirer of yours, as I am sure Mr. Alphand is too, but it is an involved procedure that always requires a great deal of time. As you will be in Europe, I think it is most important for the publicity of *Marnie* that you have press interviews in several major cities, namely, Paris,

Vienna, Munich, Frankfurt and Milan. In view of the fact that Italy is an extremely important market which you have not visited for some time, it would be most advisable that you meet the press in Milan, which is just a little over one hour by car from Como. . . . Your visit to Milan would take place just while the Cannes Festival is on (April 29th to May 13th) and we should therefore have an additional angle for the press. As a suggestion, a visit that we could arrange for you to the famous Milan Prison San Vittore. This would be a very good angle for the press if you do not object to it, and from a public relations point of view it would be in a way amusing and logical that you visit such a jail. Kindly let me know if you agree with this—if not, we will develop another angle, possibly connected with *Marnie*. Both in Paris and Milan, in my opinion, we should not have a regular press conference because as you well know, it does not bring the proper results but on the contrary, individual interviews with a few selected important newspapermen in order to get important exclusive stories.

Hitchcock wrote back saying he would leave the arrangements to Ascarelli but that he wouldn't be able to go to Milan. He requested that any pressman be brought to Lake Como, Vill d'Este, where he and Alma would be staying. Ascarelli assured Hitchcock in his reply that everywhere along their European tour he would have the top journalists from the most important dailies and weeklies for the advance publicity of *Marnie*. Press conferences were scheduled in Vienna, Munich, and Frankfurt, with individual interviews in Paris on their return. On April 3, Hitchcock sent a letter to Charles Young of the Rank Organization, who was in charge of all advertising, distribution, and exploitation of *Marnie* in the United Kingdom, inviting him to Paris for lunch to discuss the marketing campaign.

However, only four days later, Hitchcock had a change of plan. He cabled both Ascarelli and Young: "I am very sorry to inform you that the plans for our European visit are undergoing a change and this change has to do with dates and times when we will be at various places. In view of this uncertainty, I am afraid I am going to have to ask you to cancel all proposed press interviews as previously outlined between Wednesday, May 6th and Thursday June 11th. If perhaps, the opportunity arises for me to make myself available, I will let you know with good advance notice."

At the beginning of May, Hitchcock and Alma traveled from New York to Le Havre aboard the SS *France*. Hitchcock's green 1964 Lincoln Continental automobile was also shipped to France, although it was scratched in transit. An English-speaking chauffeur took the Hitchcocks to Paris, where they spent three days beginning May 6. They continued on to Geneva, Trieste, Dubrovnik, Sarajevo, Belgrade, Vienna, Munich, Frankfurt, and Luxembourg, before arriving in London for eight days on June 11.

While Hitchcock was in Europe, Charles Young sent an urgent letter regarding publicity for *Marnie* in England. The letter was never received, so on

May 15 the text of the letter was dictated over the phone to Hitchcock's office. Young requested that Hitchcock appear on two BBC television programs during his London visit from June 11 to 19. The first was an exclusive twenty-minute interview by the BBC's *Monitor*, a prestigious program devoted to the arts. The second program, *Juke Box Jury*, was a popular entertainment series with an audience of twelve million. It consisted of a panel of four personalities commenting on the latest pop tunes released. Hitchcock's comments on *Juke Box Jury* would be strictly about records, while the *Monitor* interview would be about news and Hitchcock's work. Young stated, "From their own point of view both programmes are important as they cover two completely different age groups thus getting to the entire movie-going public." Hitchcock subsequently agreed to appear on both.

Hitchcock's intention for *Marnie* to reach as broad an audience as possible is also reflected in his compliance with different print media. On May 18, Juan Cobos, a journalist for *Film Ideal* based in Madrid, wrote to Hitchcock requesting color slides from *Marnie*. The magazine was preparing a whole issue devoted to Hitchcock's work, having voted *The Birds* as one of the best five films of the previous year: "Among our critics your films are big hits. We have seen your modern films at least seven or eight times each of them. Every week we look for any of your films in the cinemas and we know *Vertigo, The Wrong Man, The Man Who Knew Too Much, The Birds, Spellbound, Sabotage, North by Northwest*, almost by heart." On May 21, Peggy Robertson contacted Hitchcock at the Metropole Hotel in Belgrade, Yugoslavia, stating that Ruth Harbet, a journalist for *Good Housekeeping* magazine, wished a screening of *Marnie* on May 25 so that it could be the possible picture of the month in the August issue. Hitchcock simply replied, "*Good Housekeeping* O.K. Hitch." He also received a cable from Edd Henry with news that exhibitor showings of *Marnie* in New York and other major cities were excellent and that it was anticipated to outgross *The Birds*. A preview was also shown at the Director's Guild on June 1 for the magazine reviewers and elicited favorable reactions. Hitchcock cabled Edd Henry on June 8 from Paris, advising that *Marnie* had received an X certificate (over eighteen-year-olds only) in England, and therefore it was wise to avoid an early release when children would still be off school. A special screening of *Marnie* was set up at the Academy Awards' Shrine Theater on June 22 for disc jockeys, Capitol Records dealers, book and department stores representatives, and radio, television, and promotion groups.

On the return journey back to the United States, Hitchcock was in good spirits and sent the following telegram from the middle of the Atlantic to his office: "Attention Robertson, Henry 6/22/64. Position Latitude 46 20 degrees West. Longitude 41 50 North Noon from Porthole. No idea where we are.

Advise Robertson. Retain Longitude. Decrease Latitude. Advise Hedren. Increase Upper Latitude. Retain Longitude. Advise Perry. Increase Longitude between . . . ? Confusion all this prompts immediate dive overboard. Hitch."

When Hitchcock arrived back in Los Angeles, he met with Tippi Hedren on June 30 to discuss a forthcoming promotional tour of *Marnie* in the United States. Between July 6 and July 24, Hedren visited New York, Cleveland, St. Louis, Kansas City, Minneapolis, Detroit, Philadelphia, and Washington, D.C. She brought with her the $40,000 wardrobe for the film, as well as clothes from her New York publicity premiere of *The Birds*. The previous year, Hedren had attended the Cannes Film Festival and the London premiere of *The Birds*.

John Behr, the publicity controller for the Rank Organization theater division, wrote a letter to Hitchcock regarding *Marnie*'s forthcoming release in England. First he conveyed his involvement in a movie magazine that sold about 210,000 copies per month in theaters. He requested color slides of Hedren that he would publish in the magazine to coincide with the West End premiere: "I hope you will be coming over so that we can renew our acquaintance. Is Tippi likely to make the journey again? I hope so because of two reasons. First (perhaps I'm sentimental) she is the nicest and best American I've ever been associated with; and secondly—we would like to do a picture story on her in *Showtime* for the release of the picture. Please give her my love and let me hear from you as a matter of urgency."

Hitchcock, however, chose to confine Hedren's promotional appearances to the United States. He outlined his reasons in a letter to Charles Rank in London:

> Fred Thomas, some time ago, made a request for Tippi Hedren's presence in England for a tour of the provincial cities. Naturally, of course, I would like to help him, and I am sure that Miss Hedren would be extremely pleased to help publicize both herself and the picture in foreign territories. However, I am adopting a particular policy regarding publicity for Tippi in the United States and it is this: As much as I would like to get both the picture and Tippi as much advance publicity as possible, I feel that her performance in the picture is so impressive that I'm going to have her interviewed only by journalists who have seen her performance in the film. Such a policy as this, I feel, will yield much greater results than just merely interviews prior to an unseen picture, or her unseen performance. Naturally, all the foregoing would apply to any interviews that she may have in London. As you realize, it is not necessary to wait for the picture to come out, it only applies to journalists who have seen the picture, even if only a day or two before opening, that these interviews could take place.
>
> However, there is an additional factor to which I should draw your attention, Charles, and that is this: We can only assume that all the foregoing would be possible if Tippi were free, but it is possible that she may be occupied in the

shooting of another picture in which case, of course, she would be tied up and not able to come, so would you please explain all this to Fred Thomas and make him aware of the whole situation. Should the preoccupation of another picture prevent her from coming over, then perhaps we could have what we call here a conference call, or two, with some of the press over the Transatlantic phone lines.

## THE TRAILERS

During the 1960s, Hitchcock's growing fame as the host of *Alfred Hitchcock Presents* contributed to the shift in advertising campaigns from the stars to the director. The man responsible for writing the trailers to a succession of Hitchcock films was James Allardice, a top television comedy writer and Emmy winner who was first brought to the director's attention by MCA. For ten years beginning in 1955, Allardice wrote the droll monologues that began and ended Hitchcock's television shows. Never once did Hitchcock refuse to do a particular skit, even if it involved dressing up in women's clothes or hamming it up next to a lion. "He wanted the world to love him," Joseph Stefano says. "Stars were loved and he wanted to be loved." Hitchcock's manufactured persona of a bufoonish character reached every home that had a television set. When Allardice died in 1965, Norman Lloyd felt that Hitchcock didn't want to go on with the series any longer because Allardice was irreplaceable.

Hitchcock asked Allardice to first read the script before meeting him for lunch on January 23, 1964, to discuss writing the main trailer for *Marnie*. Two weeks later, Allardice brought in a two-and-a-half-page draft:

> How do you do. I am Alfred Hitchcock and I would like to tell you about my latest motion picture, *Marnie*, which will be coming to this theater soon. *Marnie* is a very difficult picture to classify. It is not *Psycho*. Nor do we have a horde of birds flapping about and pecking at people willy-nilly. We do have two very interesting human specimens—A man and a woman. One might call *Marnie* a sex mystery—that is, if one uses words like that. But it is more than that. I believe the best way to tell you about the picture is to show you a few scenes. This is Mark. A thoughtful man . . . dark and brooding. In a sense, Mark is a hunter. And this is what he is hunting. One wonders how two such different people could cross paths—it was certainly not Marnie's idea.

Three specially shot scenes were requested for the *Marnie* trailer. The first was a long shot of Mark coming down the Wyckwyn stairs, walking into a waist shot. The second was a long shot of the blonde Marnie coming down the stairs of the Baltimore home and similarly walking into a waist shot. The third was a shot of the blonde Marnie at the open safe that contains the

Rutland money. Because of Connery's departure, his scene was filmed on February 28, while the rest of the trailer was recorded on March 12.

Allardice also wrote trailer scripts for theatrical, television, and radio spots, as well as promos for *Alfred Hitchcock Presents*. The *Marnie* sixty-second radio spot began:

> Attention all employers. This is Alfred Hitchcock warning you to be on the look-out for an attractive sometimes blonde, sometimes black-haired, sometimes red-headed young lady named Marnie. She is usually found applying for a job. But you will never see her at her true occupation. Actually, Marnie is a kind of cleaning woman. She cleans out safes. Empties strong boxes. Collects old money. Eventually Marnie meets a man who finds her out. But being a thief is only the symptom of Marnie's true secret. You must probe deep if you wish to solve the mystery of Marnie. You must also go to your local theater—for that's where you will find the real Marnie.[6]

The thirty-second radio spot read: "I wouldn't trust Marnie any further than I could throw Alfred Hitchcock. I realize this is a terrible thing to say about a lady. But then—Marnie is no lady. Personally, I wouldn't have a thing to do with her. However, if you would, you'll find her at your favorite theater." *Marnie*'s ten-second radio spot announced, "I wish to report a robbery. At your favorite theater. It was Marnie again. Hurry before she leaves town." For five days in August, 397 radio spots on ten stations across the country heralded the arrival of Alfred Hitchcock's *Marnie* in movie theaters.

Television also proved to be an effective means of publicity. Between August 2 and 6, a *Marnie* television campaign took place during forty-eight spots on five stations. Durations were from ten to sixty seconds throughout the day. The cost was $7,450.

When Hitchcock returned from Europe, he stopped in New York on June 26 to record a one-hour, closed-circuit press interview at NBC Studios as part of the film's publicity campaign. Allardice wrote the two-minute opening remarks, which began, "I have only recently finished editing my latest feature picture, *Marnie*, which will be released in a few weeks. It is a rather difficult picture to classify. *Marnie* is not *Psycho* and it is definitely not *The Birds*. One might call it a psychological chase—a search for the hidden motives which make Marnie the woman she is."

## PRINT ADVERTISING

The official press kit for *Marnie* and the showman's manual for theater owners were issued to journalists and critics shortly before the film's release in June 1964. Both emphasize Hitchcock as a significant artist:

The familiar legend—"An Alfred Hitchcock Picture"—carries a significance understood over all the world. He is one of the few directors whose name evokes a specific image in the filmgoer's mind. The prestigious Museum of Modern Art in New York recently presented a cycle of the milestone productions which have come forth from his creative genius. In France, where the cinema is accorded undisputed status as a true art form, he is hailed with reverential esteem. No less an authority than François Truffaut describes him as "the doyen of the Nouvelle Vague"—an accolade which elicited a typical Hitchcockian rejoinder: "Oh, dear, I hate to be the doyen of anything; it makes me sound so much older than I feel." Hitchcock's goal, from the beginning, was nakedly clear—avoid the cliché. In pursuit of this elusive objective he has given filmgoers some of the most imaginative entertainment ever captured on film. He is constantly trying for new effects, meeting new challenges, deepening his view of the cosmos.[7]

One review of *Marnie* in the showman's manual reads:

> Hitchcock's suspenseful sex mystery *Marnie* emerges as powerful film drama: Alfred Hitchcock's *Marnie* finds him at the dazzling peak of his protean talents Blending suspense and drama with an unusual love story the Technicolor film, a Universal release is evocative of the Hitchcock mastery exhibited in such previous triumphs as *Spellbound*, *Notorious* and *Rebecca*. Rarely has the elusive art of the cinema reached such heights as are marshaled in the tautly limned story fashioned for the screen by Broadway playwright Jay Presson Allen from the novel by Winston Graham.[8]

In describing the backgrounds of individual cast members, the press releases emphasized their experience in the more celebrated medium of theater rather than film. For example, *Marnie* allowed Sean Connery "a far broader histrionic stage on which to display the skills he meticulously nurtured. . . . For years he was in British repertory, considered the world's finest, and he also has done most of Shakespeare. In fact, Shakespeare is his first love, even though, for most of his performances, at the Oxford Theatre, in England, he works for minimum scale of $75 a week."[9] Similarly, the biography for Martin Gabel claimed him as "one of Broadway's most gifted men, functioning alternately as producer, writer and actor." Louise Latham was described as "a product of the renowned Margo Jones repertory company in Dallas. She makes her screen debut in the film after having starred in numerous footlight productions."

In the permissiveness of the 1960s, *Marnie* was promoted in the film posters as a "sex mystery" with "sex and suspense!" Teasers for *Marnie* were specifically designed to exploit the unusual aspects and nature of the film: "Only Alfred Hitchcock could have created a woman, so mysterious, so fascinating, so dangerous as Marnie. She was a cheat, a liar but more woman than any man could resist!" *Marnie* was billed as a sex story, a mystery, a detective story, a romance, a story of a thief, a love story, and more. Theater owners were encouraged to promote the film with a "Prettiest Secretary" competition, a safe lobby contest, in beauty parlors, and through Olympia typewriters that appeared in the film. Signs proclaimed, "No one will be admitted during the last ten minutes as the dramatic riddle of *Marnie* unfolds," just as they had been instigated for *Psycho*.

On March 31, 1964, John Attenborough, the deputy chairman of Hodder and Stoughton Ltd., which was planning the paperback edition of *Marnie*, wrote to Hitchcock having heard from Max Reinhardt that filming was complete. He expressed that they had not yet received any stills for the paperback edition they were planning, any wording suggestions, or any advertising appropriation of the film through the paperback. Attenborough stated that the tie-in between a book and a film had been accomplished effectively during the last few months in England, with both *The Carpetbaggers* and *The Group:* "In each case, the book acted, so to speak, as a pilot fish for the film. If you are interested, we for our part would be delighted to co-operate with you. . . . But it takes time to produce and launch a paperback if we are to cooperate to the maximum extent. So if you can reply helpfully to the three points in this letter, I shall be enormously grateful."[10] Hitchcock passed the letter on to Charles Young asking him if "you might like to deal with this."

In Britain, the advertising trade publication *Adam* had selected the English teaser ad for *Marnie* as the "Advertisement of the Month." A silhouette shot of the portly director framed the words "Alfred Hitchcock's Back with his latest suspense thriller *Marnie* Cert X." The Rank Organization on behalf of Universal International Films was responsible for the ad. The magazine stated:

> This is a classic example of the way in which clarity of thought about exactly what an advertisement is intended to do can produce the kind of vivid concentration of the reader's attention that is often described as a brilliant idea, but is really a brilliant solution to a problem. The distinction is important, if only because management tends to demand ideas from creative people, much as petrol is demanded from filling-station attendants. . . The concentration of attention, here, is achieved by sole use of a visual entity that has branded itself on millions of minds via the TV screens, and by containing the brilliant, punning, news-worthy message beginning "Hitchcock's Back," inside those broad, bowed shoulders.

The review went on to say, "It is guaranteed that all readers of all the papers in which this six inch single appeared and who (a) see the Hitchcock TV films (b) saw *Psycho*, will have the liveliest anticipation of seeing X-certificated *Marnie*."

## THE RELEASE

When *Marnie* was released in the United Kingdom, two weeks before its American debut, Sean Connery was given top billing, because of the British public's affinity with James Bond. At the Odeon Leicester Square, in London, *Marnie* opened on July 8, 1964, and earned £8,036 in its first week, some £2,500 below *The Birds* the previous year. It netted a total run of $60,000 over forty-three days. The year's greatest money-making picture in Britain was *Goldfinger*, and *Marnie* ranked twelfth. No doubt Hitchcock's film was helped by the presence of Sean Connery; a Motion Picture Herald annual box office poll of cinema managers ranked the Scotsman as the star who drew in the largest crowds.

In the United States, *Marnie* first opened in New York at the Palace and perimeter theaters, on July 22, 1964. In the first week, the total box office for the two venues was $192,857; $89,371 was earned during the second. Other Universal films on release at the time were the Doris Day romantic comedies, *That Touch of Mink* and *Lover Come Back*, which outgrossed *Marnie* during the first opening weekend.

*Marnie* opened in twenty-eight theaters throughout the Los Angeles area on August 5, for $20,555, with a Saturday peak gross of $46,693, but by its second week, figures had declined rapidly to under $10,000. The film was shown in theaters across the United States until November 18, though *The Birds* enjoyed a longer run. In the United States, *Marnie* didn't even make the top thirty films of the year, netting a profit of just $3.3 million in domestic rentals for Universal in Canada and the United States. In comparison, *Goldfinger* earned $23 million for Eon/United Artists. (The figures are the sum returned to the distributors as their share of the box office gross.)

On September 25, 1964, Hitchcock heard better news of *Marnie*'s fortunes in Europe from Universal's New York office: "Just received following cable from Calvo Italy. 'Delighted communicate *Marnie* national release. Yesterday Rome 54% above *Birds*; Milan 89%; Turin 47%; Naples 10%; Florence 28%. Same story all over. Reviews Rome, Milan, satisfactory. Details following." *Marnie* performed better in all four cities in the second week than the first week and earned $62,541, compared to $58,599 for *The Birds* in the same period. By the third week throughout four key cities in Italy, *Marnie* was still outgrossing *The Birds* by some $5,000.

## CONCLUSION

In a speech made to the Screen Producer's Guild of America in 1965, Hitchcock remarked that he remained a prisoner of his old image and that inside a fat man was a thin man trying desperately to get out. Both Stefano and Truffaut speak of Hitchcock as a sensitive and vulnerable man who was easily hurt by criticism. In particular, he was upset with the New York reviewers who claimed that his films of the fifties lacked logic and characterization. With *Marnie*, Hitchcock made a concerted effort to transform himself from popular entertainer to serious artist.

The self-interested campaigning by François Truffaut, who himself wanted to be regarded as a film auteur in the same way that he perceived Hitchcock, was instrumental in *Marnie*'s marketing campaign. Hitchcock actively encouraged Truffaut's adulation and requested that copies of the French director's tribute be sent to key New York critics prior to *Marnie*'s release. When asked by interviewer Huw Weldon whether he was gratified by the praise from the avant-garde film critics in France, who had practically canonized him, Hitchcock replied, "I think so. One should be flattered by that; of course there are constant divisions among the devotees." His decision, however, to appear on the prestigious BBC *Monitor* arts program was to have a lasting impact on the British reviewers. How successful his marketing campaign strategies were will be discussed in the next chapter.

## NOTES

1. Robert Kapsis, *Hitchcock: The Making of a Reputation* (Chicago: University of Chicago Press, 1992).

2. Alfred Hitchcock–James Allardice conference, April 2, 1963, Alfred Hitchcock Collection, Margaret Herrick Library.

3. Alfred Hitchcock letter to Walter Ross, New York, dated October 1, 1962, Alfred Hitchcock Collection, Margaret Herrick Library.

4. François Truffaut, *The New Yorker*, October 31, 1964, 45–46.

5. Telephone interview with Harold Mendelsohn, Los Angeles, on September 1, 2000. All other quotes originate from this interview.

6. Drafts of trailer scripts by James Allardice, Alfred Hitchcock Collection, Margaret Herrick Library.

7. Marnie Showman's Manual, Alfred Hitchcock Collection, Margaret Herrick Library.

8. Marnie Showman's Manual.

9. Marnie Showman's Manual.

10. Correspondence regarding tie-in editions of paperback book, Alfred Hitchcock Collection, Margaret Herrick Library.

*Chapter Seven*

# Critical Reception

Of course, at least we're able to blame it on the French. I think Hitch would have loved all this. I think he would have adored it, but I think it would have made him giggle.

—Jay Presson Allen

Perceptions about a film can alter throughout time, reflecting changes in audience tastes and the cultural forces that determine how a film is received. The history of Hitchcock criticism parallels the evolution of film theory. Since its initial release in 1964, *Marnie* has been influenced by the auteur theory, the development of feminism arising from the work of the French psychoanalyst Jacques Lacan, and the continual growth of Hitchcock scholarship, which includes controversial biographical legends of the director. Hitchcock himself treated critics with skepticism. "I think they are very human," he remarked in an interview. "They're subject to all kinds of human foibles and I think they mean very well. I won't stress the word *mean*; I said they mean very well. They have their job to do and I have my job to do."[1] This chapter examines why *Marnie* was initially dismissed by the journalist critics and how its reputation only improved when it was embraced by scholars, at a time when the auteur theory and feminism became dominant in academic film studies.

## THE REVIEWS

On June 9, 1964, the *Motion Picture Daily*, the national newspaper of the entertainment industry, began the reviews promisingly:

In *Marnie*, the redoubtable Alfred Hitchcock has turned again to the psychological mystery genre—a type of film he had left to others in recent years. . . .

143

Thanks to the craft of Hitchcock, the picture hypnotically arouses suspense and builds beautifully to the explosive climax. His work here, as always, offers a study in the art of film direction. The use of color photography is particularly effective. Exhibitors can usually count on Hitchcock for a winner, and *Marnie* is no exception.

A review in *Film Daily* on the same day offered similar appraisal: "A suspense mystery done in Hitchcock style. Nerve tingling. Good box office prospects. Smart cast."

When *Marnie* opened midweek in England on July 8, the British film reviewers voiced their perception of Hitchcock's growing pretentiousness. In their estimation, Hitchcock was a director who made entertaining thrillers, and the milestone of his success was his early British period, not the later American films. Their annoyance was ignited by Hitchcock's interview that had just aired on the BBC intellectual *Monitor* arts program, in addition to persistent praise from the French critics. "Whatever has happened to Alfred Hitchcock?" asked the reviewer of the *Evening News* on July 9. "Has he been paddling too long in the shallow water of TV films, or has high-brow praise in *Les Cahiers du Cinema* gone to his head?"

Unwittingly, a new book titled *Cinema Eye, Cinema Ear*, a study of six contemporary directors, including a chapter on Hitchcock, added to the debate. The author was John Russell Taylor, who later wrote the official Hitchcock biography. John Coleman of the *New Statesman* began his review by quoting Taylor:

> What ever will come next from this most inventive, unpredictable of filmmakers is anyone's guess. . . . Unfortunately Mr. Taylor goes on to spit in fortune's face, "it" turns out to be *Marnie*. . . . An otherwise unrevealing Wheldon interview with the Master last *Monitor* found him—I thought—unusually pontifical, as if he himself were rather in thrall to the startling image of him projected by a few influential French critics (this activity substantially began with the Rohmer-Chabrol book in 1957). What exercises me on this occasion, to the point of seeing red in a simpler fashion than Marnie's, is that a considerable entertainer's talent appears to be wasting itself by courting seriousness: the result, as in much of *The Birds*, is oddly unpleasant.[2]

Philip Oakes echoed the assessment two days later in the July 12, 1964, *Sunday Telegraph*: "Hitchcock has rarely been drawn to detail ('I don't care what plans the spies are after,' he declared in a *Monitor* interview) but *Marnie* is over expository, and under inspired." "Hitchcock without Thrills," complained Patrick Gibbs in the *Daily Telegraph* on July 10, 1964: "Amazingly from Hitchcock, somewhat monotonous. Scenes are well made, often nicely colored, always competently acted, yet without a single surprise or deepening of the interest, the film proceeding deliberately without variation of pace as if marching to a metronome. . . . The film, then, is to be judged as an experiment, worth making, perhaps, but certainly not worth repeating: not at least, unless Hitchcock realizes the fallacy he has fallen into (which Proust considered fatal to fiction) of thinking the springs of behavior more interesting than the behavior itself." A review in the *Times* was kinder:

> It is easy to see why the plot outline should have taken Mr. Hitchcock's fancy. It is essentially *Spellbound* turned inside out, with this time a male psychiatrist (amateur) fighting to save the female patient he loves, and once more a traumatic experience in childhood to be uncovered in the final settling of accounts All in all a field day for enthusiasts, in fact, and over two hours of very glossy entertainment for anyone else. . . . The surroundings in which the action takes place are, unexpectedly again after the hep-ness of Mr. Hitchcock's recent work, almost prewar in their bland acceptance of studio-built exteriors—the set of the street in which Marnie's mother lives is like something Trauner might have cooked up for Carne in the good old days—and Mr. Bernard Herrmann's surging, emotional score and the straightforward, classify printed credits all convey the same reassuring image.

The remaining reviews appearing over the weekend, offered better insights from the female critics. Penelope Gilliat wrote in the *Observer* on July 12:

> Never has he taken more pleasure in physical handicaps and the mannerisms of hysteria. Cinema literature now is full of modish theses about "l'univers hitchcockien" which try to present him as a moralist with a world-view of ringing themes like the exchange of guilt; John Russell Taylor has an amiable go at this fad in his shrewd new book, *Cinema Eye, Cinema Ear*. What seems to be much more present in Hitchcock's work than moral awareness, is his fascination with physical humiliations and feminine sexual panic.

Pauline Richardson in the *New Daily* on July 13 perceptively argued:

> I would say *Marnie* isn't so much successful as a thriller, but as a tender and unconventional love story. It's really about Sean Connery's love for the criminal girl and his attempts to solve and save her. On this level, it makes compelling viewing. I think Hitchcock has a possible winner here, but it's not as a thriller that *Marnie* will make its mark! Still, it's the prerogative of Hitchcock to come forward with what is different and unexpected, and in this way, he's remarkably true to his own tradition.

Geoffrey Watkins, the press officer for the Rank Organization responsible for distributing the film in England, sent the reviews over to Edd Henry at Universal Studios on July 13, as an early foreshadowing of journalistic reaction. At the end of the year, the annual *Film Review* journal summed up the major consensus of the English critics: "*Marnie*, unfortunately, seemed to be well below the best Hitchcock standard. It is perhaps significant that the further Hitchcock gets away from his true métier, the thriller, the less impressive he is."

In the United States, *Marnie* opened in New York on July 23, at the RKO Palace and seventeen other theaters. The previous year, the city's Museum of Modern Art played host to a premier screening of *The Birds*, in addition to a major retrospective of Hitchcock's work. When *Marnie* was released, Hitchcock's marketing campaign to promote himself as a serious artist had a negative impact with the New York critics. The majority derided the expressionistic techniques Hitchcock employed, criticized the lack of suspense, and dismissed the naive Freudian assumptions. On July 23, Eugene Archer wrote in the *New York Times:*

> Alfred Hitchcock's *Marnie* is at once a fascinating study of a sexual relationship and the master's most disappointing film in years. . . . The villain once again is Mama, but this time the director is making a comment on the Yankee Puritan hangover and the twisted society it leaves in its wake. . . . Curiously he has also settled for an inexplicably amateurish script, which reduces this potent material to instant psychiatry—complete with a flashback "explanation scene" harking back to vintage Joan Crawford and enough character exposition to stagger the most dedicated genealogist. . . . A strong suspicion arises that Mr. Hitchcock is taking himself too seriously—perhaps the result of listening to too many esoteric admirers. Granted that it's still Hitchcock—and that's a lot—dispensing with the best in acting, writing and even technique is sheer indulgence. When a director decides he's so gifted that all he needs is himself, he'd better watch out.

Many critics believed that the tautness that distinguished Hitchcock's earlier works, demonstrable in *The 39 Steps*, *Rear Window*, and *North by Northwest*, was lacking in *Marnie*. Judith Crist of the *New York Herald Tribune* concurred:

> Somewhere along the plodding plot line of *Marnie*, Tippi Hedren says to Sean Connery "You Freud—Me Jane"—and there you have the 110 minutes of Alfred Hitchcock's new—or rather most recent—film. New it isn't in form or content. Mr. Hitchcock himself made this kind of movie nigh on to twenty years ago and made it a lot better. In the interim we've been so belabored on movie and television screens by five per cent psychiatry wrap-up in true romance and-or the annals of crime, that *Marnie* can only strike us as pathetically old fashioned and dismally naive.

Andrew Sarris echoed the assessment in the *Village Voice*: "*Marnie* is a failure by any standards except the most esoteric." Only one positive review stood out, Archer Winsten's in the *New York Post*:

The new Hitchcock picture, *Marnie*, provides three or four unexpected pleasures along with the familiar patterns of crime and the long-suspected Damoclean sword. First, and best, this one has a human warmth and sympathy that makes it Hitch's most appealing since *Rear Window*. . . . Second, Tippi Hedren . . . makes the longest and quickest stride forward to acting grace yet recorded on film. She's really good now and she needs not the slightest apology of being in merely her second film. Third, Sean Connery adds the tiny touches of charm and humor that his masculine force needed to make him a permanently popular movie star. With all that working for it, and Hitchcock pulling the strings of a Freudian festival of delayed horror, stubborn criminality in a beautiful girl, and irresistible helpfulness in a forceful man, the picture becomes a superior item.

Hitchcock's promotional efforts achieved better results when *Marnie* was released in Los Angeles on August 5. The next day, the *Los Angeles Times* motion picture editor, Phillip K. Scheuer, applauded Hitchcock's experimentation:

Like *Vertigo*, *Psycho* and *The Birds*, Alfred Hitchcock's *Marnie* takes place in a twilight world, one in which even the colors (an unnatural predominance of reds and blues) and the sounds (strangely subdued when Marnie is hearing them) apparently have significance. As a story it seems naggingly improbable and, as drama, a nightmare from which the spectator constantly pulls away, struggling to wake up in a less disordered universe. No question, though, that it is at least fitfully effective. Nearly all of us, I believe were sorrowed when the tongue-in-cheek Hitchcock gave up the chase to enter his new phase—the exploration of the dark recesses of the mind and spirit. But as his astonishing career falls into perspective, he may yet be acclaimed for having taken the step. Psychiatrists probably love him for it already.

Abe Greenberg, in the *Tribune/Advertiser*, disagreed:

Hitch confounds himself in *Marnie*: Alfred Hitchcock's a "wise guy," literally and figuratively, but he's slipped his hitch by sacrificing suspense for psychiatric study in his newest chiller-diller, *Marnie*, a Universal picture . . . by seeking to achieve an outstanding character portrayal for his star . . . and, in so doing, lost the famed Hitchcock suspense touch. . . . Sean Connery's talent is wasted in an innocuous role although this gifted Scotsman is as smooth and competent a performer as we've seen in many a moon.

One of the year's most contemptuous reviews appeared in the international film quarterly *Sight and Sound*:

Hitchcock's sham-Freud gambles in the field of audience gullibility, apparently left the Master himself feeling that it's hardly worth the bother anymore. The often crude Thirties technique . . . is a perfect match for the picture's social attitudes . . . which tells you that whatever [Marnie's] forced to go through . . . she'll eventually find other riches, new riches, in the bed instead of on a horse. The rest, alas, is decided solely by technique, intermittently diverting, mainly familiar, and altogether subordinate to Hitchcock's brinkmanship and—well, yes—contempt for the whole lot of us.

## AUTEUR THEORY

In the middle of the twentieth century, revaluation of Hitchcock's films began with the French new wave cinema—specifically, in the pages of the journal *Cahiers du Cinéma*. From the start of its publication in 1951, *Cahiers* relied on postwar critical ideas that Andre Bazin developed, with principal subjects being neorealism, Hollywood stylistics, and French directors like Jean Renoir and Robert Bresson. *Cahiers* fulfilled the function of an intellectual review, quickly becoming the most influential film journal in the world, remaining unchallenged until the 1970s.

Eric Rohmer and Claude Chabrol's first book-length study of Hitchcock's films, *Hitchcock*, published in 1957, characterized the director as specifically a Catholic artist, obsessed with predestination and original sin, whose narrative was based on a transference of guilt, the motif of the double, and a tone of moral pessimism. Together with François Truffaut, they promoted the auteur theory, which stated that certain directors were the true authors of a film, and their work could be seen collectively as an oeuvre, distinguished by defining traits and styles. This was a modernist attempt to take film seriously by establishing traditional themes accorded to the other art forms, as the British literary critic F. R. Leavis had sought a generation earlier with English literature.

The most influential film journal in Britain in the early 1960s was *Movie*, which had its genesis from film articles in the student journal *Oxford Opinion*. As undergraduates, Ian Cameron, Victor Perkins, and Mark Shivas adopted *Cahiers'* taste in directors but were more inclined to technically analyze a film. They displayed an unprecedented attention to a film's thematic range and formal texture, in a style that borrowed from Cambridge practical criticism. Ian Cameron and Richard Jeffrey's analysis of the first shot of *Marnie* demonstrates how the film achieves a coherence of theme, subject narrative, and style:

It is a shot of enormous complexity. From one point of view it is a single shot montage of bulging handbag, Marnie and empty station, telling us quite clearly that she is traveling some distance at an unusual hour with this bag and its contents. The end of the shot has the chilly symmetry of a street or corridor, seen down its length, an image used in *The Birds* (for example, where Mrs. Brenner starts down the corridor towards Dan Fawcett's bedroom) and more in *Marnie* where it fits more closely into the design. Its function is often to make us wonder what we may find at the other end.[3]

Robin Wood was the first to publish a full-length book on Hitchcock in the English language, *Hitchcock's Films* (1965). Although the growing acceptance of film studies was implicit in the analysis of such academic disciplines, Hitchcock at the time was not considered to be a significant artist. Wood sought to redress the balance, arguing that the highpoint of Hitchcock's films was not the British period previously favored by his English contemporaries, but rather the films of the fifties and sixties. He viewed *Marnie* as coming at the end of an unbroken string of masterpieces, beginning with *Vertigo* in 1958, the latter described as "one of the four or five most beautiful films the cinema has yet given us." In a letter to Hitchcock dated March 7, 1965, Wood called his book a "labour of love" and said that few twentieth-century artists had given him such intense and lasting pleasure from their work.

Much of Wood's evaluation of *Marnie* was in response to the British journalist's criticism of the artificial devices and simplistic psychology. Wood began by defending the Baltimore street set:

The back-drop of the ship needs to be considered as part of the set it dominates: the street in which Mrs. Edgar lives. Unbroken rows of tall ugly brick houses which give us a sense of imprisonment, claustrophobia, all possibility of freedom and openness shut out; at the end, the ship looming up ominously, as if blocking the exit. When we first see the image it is not precisely explicable, but it conveys admirably—if our responses are open, and free from preconceptions about "realism"—the intolerable constriction of Marnie's life. Only at the end, when the crucial role played by a sailor in the arresting of her development becomes clear, does the huge, blocking ship take on a more precise symbolism. Perhaps something of the same effect—though it could scarcely have looked so ominous—could have been achieved with a real ship and a real street; but this would have sacrificed the most important aspect of all: the constrictedness of Marnie's life belongs essentially to the world of unreality, the trap she is caught in is irrational and her prison will be finally shattered by true memory; at the end, the storm over, the sky a clear blue (as it never has been behind the ship before), she and Mark drive away past the ship, turning off where we had not previously been aware of the existence of a road.[4]

Instead of focusing on the metaphysical relationship between men and God, as Chabrol and Rohmer had previously, Wood concentrated on the sexual and emotional problems of men and women. *Marnie*'s rape scene, for Wood, offered "one of the purest treatments of sexual intercourse the cinema has given us: pure in its feeling for sexual tenderness. Yet what we see is virtually a rape. To the man it is an expression of tenderness, solicitude, responsibility; to the woman, an experience so desolating that after it she attempts suicide. Our response depends on our being made to share the responses of both characters at once."[5]

Furthermore, Wood advocated a therapeutic theme throughout Hitchcock's major works, "whereby a character is cured of some weakness or obsession by indulging in it and living through the consequences." He insisted on Hitchcock's "extension of this therapy to the spectator, by means of encouraging the audience to identify," so that always it is our own impulses that are involved.[6] Later proponents of the auteurist view similarly emphasized that Hitchcock's technical skills were aimed at "destroying the separation between the film and it's audience," in an effort "to bring his audience from the detachment of irresponsible spectators to the involvement of implicated participants."[7]

Although academic film critics immediately recognized Wood's book as a founding text in the explication of Hitchcock's films, its publication was met with resistance by the director's detractors. In her review of the book in *Sight and Sound*, Penelope Houston wrote:

> It's the section on *Marnie*, however, which is the most obviously strained . . . the trouble with these devices, to my mind, is they simply don't work on the screen in the way they are coaxed into working in Mr. Wood's analysis. Far from finding the zoom lens shot "direct," I find it distracting: not a help to identification with Marnie, but a positive obstacle. And the back projection is not "dream-like" (as, for instance, are the shots of the cars moving along real San Francisco streets in *Vertigo*) but just the old studio rocking-horse.[8]

Later, Wood admitted that he made an error in trying to defend the artifice in *Marnie*, not because the devices were indefensible but because his arguments provided critics with the opportunity to evade the major issues he was trying to withhold in the film—namely, the significance of Marnie and Mark's relationship, the characteristic Hitchcockian preoccupation with different sorts of order (valid and invalid), and the positive moral values embodied in Mark himself. Implicit in this neglect was a disregard for the subtle nuances of character building that Hitchcock and Hedren had circumscribed in preproduction and instigated during filming. Wood acknowledged his position at the time was ignorant of both ideology and feminism.

## FEMINIST PERSPECTIVES

Since the 1970s, a large amount of feminist film criticism reflects the growing sophistication of how film images are assembled and interpreted. In film journals such as *Cahiers du Cinéma* and *Screen*, the auteur analysis was superceded by a psychoanalytic theory, together with a developing feminist criticism, which itself was an extension of the women's movement, beginning in the United States in the late 1960s. Though these debates developed within film theory specifically, their implications were felt more widely within a cultural milieu that was experiencing great unease about representations of gender and the oppression of women in society. Hitchcock's films (and *Marnie* has special prominence here) became central to the formulation and practice of feminist film theory, as sociological pieces with emphasis on the role of women at work and their constraints within a marriage.

While feminist critics in the United States continued to regard film as a vehicle for personal change, several women in England began to develop other theoretical models, grounded in French studies of psychoanalysis, particularly by Jacques Lacan and Jacques Derrida. Lacan developed a Freudian analysis of the structures of sexuality, using the now-available sciences of linguistics and semiotics. He opposed the view of the self as having an identity, emphasizing the individual's division and coherence. For Lacan, the self defines itself in culture through a series of unifying attempts that are illusory and external, and representations that offer the images it may become.

Foremost among the English theorists' work was Laura Mulvey's article "Visual Pleasure and Narrative Cinema," which was first presented as a paper in the French department at the University of Wisconsin in spring 1973, before appearing in *Screen* in the summer of 1975. Mulvey detailed the way in which men consciously and unconsciously control the production and reception of film, creating images that satisfy their needs and unconscious desires. Drawing on the work of Freud and Lacan, Mulvey examined the ways in which cinema used the image of women to dissipate male castration fears by forms of voyeurism, which contained sadistic and fetishist aspects. By emphasizing the predominance of "the gaze" in narrative cinema, Mulvey described how on screen, men are the bearers of the look, while women are the objects of the gaze. By implication, therefore, women spectators could only have a masochistic relation to this form of cinema. The scopophilic instinct as Mulvey describes is the pleasure in looking at another person as an erotic object:

> In Hitchcock, by contrast, the male hero, does see precisely what the audience sees. However, in the films I shall discuss here, he takes fascination with an image through scopophilic eroticism as the subject of the film. Moreover, in these cases the hero portrays the contradictions and tensions experienced by the spectator. In *Vertigo*, in particular but also in *Marnie* and *Rear Window*, the look is central to the plot, oscillating between voyeurism and fetishistic fascination. His heroes are exemplary of the symbolic order and the law—a policeman

(*Vertigo*), a dominant male possessing money and power (*Marnie*)—but their erotic drives lead them into compromised situations. . . . Marnie, too, performs for Mark Rutland's gaze and masquerades as the perfect to-be-looked-at-image. He, too, is on the side of the law, until, drawn in by the obsession with her guilt, her secret, he longs to see her in the act of committing a crime, make her confess, and thus save her. So he, too, becomes complicit as he acts out the implications of his power. He controls money and words, he can have his cake and eat it.[9]

Mulvey's paper became a founding document for psychoanalytical feminist film theory, detailing how the gaze was organized by social structures that surround images and determine how they are represented. Her interpretation instigated a series of debates on the act of looking as a cultural, rather than physiological phenomenon, and it had repercussions in art practice as a whole.

Another major influence on feminist criticism of Hitchcock at this time was the work of Raymond Bellour in the film journal *Camera Obscura*, which first appeared in 1976, with the declared purpose of working on cinematic representation and the signifying function of women within this system. Bellour's textual analysis of films, deriving from French literary critical theory, investigated how meaning was produced in classical narrative and clarified the mapping of sexual differences. In his essays on *Psycho* and *Marnie*, Bellour argued that the functioning of the classical fiction film depended on structures of perversion, voyeurism, and fetishism.

With *Marnie*, Bellour extended Mulvey's notion of voyeurism to that of the film camera itself. In a detailed analysis of the film's opening sequences, he theorized how Marnie is inscribed in the film via Hitchcock's male surrogates—namely Strutt, Rutland, and Garrod. Critical to Bellour's reading was Hitchcock's early cameo appearance, which established the director as the "enunciator" of Marnie's story: "A new level of intensity is reached in the system of signature. Before Hitchcock positioned himself diegetically and symbolically so as to figure in the logic of fantasy. But in *Marnie*, he assumes a specific position in the cinematographic apparatus, whereby he asserts himself as enunciator by representing himself in the scene and on such an axis that he comes to embody both the look and the camera."[10] According to critic Sandy Flitterman, the point in Bellour's essay most crucial to understanding how women function as the object of male desire is the moment when Marnie looks in the mirror: "Marnie's preoccupation with her own image makes her an object of desire for the male spectator, for the source of the camera-wish-Hitchcock, and for the male characters. For the woman spectator, it can only stimulate the identificatory desire to be the image."[11]

More recently, feminist theorists such as Tania Modleski contend that the female spectator is not merely passive but has her own equivalent of male desire. By extrapolating from the Freudian premise of an essential bisexuality in both men and women, Modleski argues that the female spectator's involvement is not masochistic, but instead experiences visual pleasure in watching the women on the screen that are her own sex. The female's bisexuality reminds men of the feminine aspects of themselves, both of which challenge male dominance and patriarchy. Violence toward women in Hitchcock's films, then, results from a male hostility toward this threat of bisexuality, and the director's work is an expression of cultural attitudes and practices existing to some degree outside his control.

In 1982, Modleski published an article on Hitchcock's first American film, *Rebecca.* Such a film facilitates a limited expression of female desire and traces a female oedipal trajectory, rather than following the male oedipal journey, which Raymond Bellour sees as the course for all Hollywood narrative. In the process they reveal some of the difficulties for women in becoming socialized in patriarchy. For Modleski, the strong fascination and identification with femininity revealed in Hitchcock's films subvert the claims to mastery and authority not only of the male characters but of Hitchcock himself. Subsequently, his work is characterized by a thorough going ambivalence about femininity, which can then account for the conflicting critical interpretations his films have generated and the woman's position within them:

> As the figure of Norman Bates suggests, what both male and female spectators are likely to see in the mirror of Hitchcock's films are images of ambiguous sexuality that threaten to destabilize the gender identity of protagonists and viewers alike. . . . Although in *Psycho* the mother/son relationship is paramount, I will argue that in films from *Rebecca* on it is more often the mother/daughter relationship that evokes this threat to identity and constitutes the main "problem" of the films. Marnie's main "problem"—as far as patriarchy is concerned—is an excessive attachment to her mother that prevents her from achieving a "normal," properly "feminine" sexual relationship with a man.[12]

The mother/daughter relationship for Modleski therefore is one of the chief factors contributing to the bisexuality of women.

Other critics also adopted Jacque Lacan's theory of ethics with the more recent discussions of feminine subjectivity and bisexuality. Through a close reading of eight of Hitchcock's films—*The Lady Vanishes*, *Spellbound*, *Rebecca*, *Notorious*, *Vertigo*, *Marnie*, *Rear Window*, and *The Birds*—Robert Samuels argued that just as Freud posited a fundamental bisexuality for each individual, "we can affirm a form of universal bi-texuality that is repressed through different modes of representation yet returns in unconscious aspects

of textuality (dreams, word play, jokes and symbolism)."[13] The heteroge-
neous nature of Hitchcock's films presents multiple forms of sexual identification and desire, although most often they have been interpreted through the
male gaze. Characters in the Hitchcockian universe are inherently bisexual;
Marnie's own sexuality is imbalanced between self-abjection and an affirmation of a repressed bisexual desire.

In her essay "The Queer Voice in *Marnie*," Lucretia Knapp redirects attention to lesbian moments in the film that have been considered insignificant
by other theorists.[14] Specifically, she cites exchanges between Marnie and Lil
as key moments in the film's identificatory lesbian desire. Knapp suggests
that instead of a male fetish in the film, as posited by Bellour and Hitchcock
himself, there is a female fetish—specifically, a lesbian fetish that uses objects such as the purse as a focus for the homoerotic gaze. Hitchcock's films
provide a rich source of paradoxes and ambiguities in which gender identity
is questioned and explored, and they are of central importance as they disrupt
social norms with homophobic fears. *Marnie* especially evokes a repressive
culture, in which the protagonist is an outsider who challenges patriarchy by
robbing it, lending it a feminist discourse that has found empathy for nonhet-
erosexuals.

Shameem Kabir, in her book *Daughters of Desire: Lesbian Representations in Film*, refers to being enamoured of *Marnie:*

> With the imagings of women, I often preferred to experience desire for them
> rather than as them, as my identifications with the masculine position made me
> complicit with the values and operations of objectification. With the imagings
> of men, I saw their vulnerabilities despite their apparent power. I saw their
> emotional engagements as a testimony to their relational capacities even though
> these often took an exclusively sexual trajectory. I saw these men were attempt-
> ing to resist the more commonplace enculturations of masculine behaviors. But
> they too were capable of rape. I am thinking of *Gone with the Wind*, as well as
> the suggested and equivalent rapes in *A Streetcar Named Desire* and *Marnie*.
> No matter how delicately implied or thankfully left off screen, these rapes
> confirmed that an assertion of masculinity can sometimes be an expression of
> aggression against the woman.[15]

Film critic Molly Haskell charts the celluloid treatment of women in her engaging book *From Reverence to Rape*. *Marnie* is the film in which Hitchcock
sides with his blonde and is

> one of his most disturbing and, from a woman's point of view, most important
> films. Almost a parody of the woman on her way up the professional ladder,
> Tippi Hedren's Marnie changes her job as well as her wigs regularly, plays up
> to her employers and steals from their safes. . . . The flimsiness of the happy

ending in *Marnie* indicates not so much that certain perversities are too deep for resolution, but that perversity is the very soul of attraction; that the images we construct and fall in love with are at least as important and "real" as reality.[16]

By placing a female at the center of the film narrative, Hitchcock ventures from the defined roles traditionally assigned to women in classical Hollywood cinema. Throughout the film, Marnie constitutes a threat to the male ego and poses a castration complex, which the film and Mark Rutland seek to redress. Marnie robs male employers of not only their money but, by her very resourcefulness and efficiency, their sexual identity, too. She is a particularly elusive and dangerous female predator who must be caught and tamed so that male patriarchy may be restored. Her involvement in the narrative with money, false identities, keys, and guns are objects of power for the male prerogative; therefore, she must be punished, raped, and rendered submissive within the business world and confined to the ultimate entrapment for women—marriage.

In the 1960s, Robin Wood's book set out to address the question "Why should we take Hitchcock seriously?" However, in the 1980s, as a response to the growing amount of feminist criticism that dominated Hitchcock scholarship, he asks, "Can Hitchcock be saved for feminism?"[17] Some feminist readings have unambiguously interpreted Marnie's last remark, "I don't want to go to jail; I'd rather stay with you," as evidence that marriage to Mark will be a form of legal entrapment.[18] As Wood points out, however, the chain of events leading to Marnie's memory recovery shows that it is Mark who crucially has been the one to precipitate it in a directorial role, and he does so deliberately by tapping on the wall. Mark knows he can't control Marnie's experience once it begins. He has come to accept that Marnie's cure requires that he acknowledges the limits of his control over her: "Perhaps the film's finest psychoanalytical perception is the sense that ultimately Marnie is responsible for her own cure—that she is herself consistently struggling (on some subconscious level) towards the retrieval of the memory that so terrifies her. One might say that Marnie cures herself, using Mark as her instrument."[19]

Moreover, Wood cites the principle of dual identification, which operates consistently in Hitchcock's greatest works (*Notorious*, *Vertigo*, and *Marnie*): the superficial trajectory of the male gaze as detailed by Mulvey and Bellour, but the far greater identification with the woman's position.[20] After the flashback, the final shooting script notes, "From this point on, Marnie should present a different face to us. She is now in the gentle wash of the shallows, after having battled deep, dragging waters for most of her conscious life. For possibly the first time since she was five years old, she can look objectively at another human being. She looks at her mother and she looks at Mark." Hitchcock's camera during these final scenes demonstrates an astonishing sensitivity and affinity with the subjectivity of women. His camera's intimacy with women is no less essential to his artistic identity than his camera's apparent identification with the male gaze. This is exemplified in the last image of Mrs. Edgar, whose final remark, "Goodbye, sugar pop," is spoken to no one in particular as Mark and Marnie have already left the scene. In response to Marnie's "I don't want to go to jail; I'd rather stay with you," Mark replies, "Had you, love?" Mark is being ironic as he has been through most of the film, and his irony underscores, rather than denies or undermines, his sincerity. (His original line was to read, "Then we're making progress, Marnie; we're making progress.") This change in him suggests the possibility, but not certainty, of him and Marnie having a real future together.

## BIOGRAPHICAL ASSESSMENTS

The most famous book on Hitchcock, of course, is the director's series of interviews with Truffaut, the motivations of which were outlined in the previous chapter. *Hitchcock* was published in 1967 and given consequence by Truffaut's growing stature as a film artist. American film critic Andrew Sarris noted, "Truffaut's *Hitchcock* may leave the impression that there is no sympathetic criticism of Hitchcock in the English language. Robin Wood, Peter Bogdanovich and Ian Cameron have covered much of Truffaut's terrain . . . but no mere critic is likely to match the influence of the director of *Jules et Jim*."[21] Although the academic critics under the influence of the auteur theory helped elevate Hitchcock's status, the journalistic critics still refused to acknowledge him as a director worthy of serious merit. Furthermore, publication of Truffaut's book was bracketed by the release of two films considered the weakest among Hitchcock's late works, *Torn Curtain* (1966) and *Topaz* (1969). Neither was well received, bringing the argument that Hitchcock was a serious artist to an impasse.

More central to the book were deficiencies in Truffaut's approach and his propensity to focus on technical cinematic issues and philosophical themes, such as a Catholic sense of guilt, at the expense of the psychology. Leo Braudy's 1968 review maintained that Truffaut was "so doggedly technical, so intent on style as opposed to meaning" as to miss "how Hitchcock in his best films manipulates the deepest reactions of his audience."[22] Furthermore, Braudy insisted that Truffaut missed hint after hint offered by Hitchcock of his deeper purposes: "While Hitchcock vainly implies the emotional and psychological relevance of his details, Truffaut concentrates on an intellectualized appreciation of the fine finish and professional gloss."[23]

The revised edition of *Hitchcock*, published after Truffaut's death in 1984, also traced the director's declining years. Truffaut described *Marnie* as belonging to the category of a "great flawed film,"[24] which is a project weakened by errors in production during writing, casting, or filming and an overall anomaly between the original intention and the final execution. This notion can apply only to the works of a great director, one who has demonstrated previous artistic perfection. For the connoisseur, a great, flawed film like *Marnie* may be preferred to Hitchcock's more canonized works, as it vividly reveals the directors preoccupations and engages the audience's emotions. Accordingly, *Marnie*'s status, especially in the United States and France, has grown to be a cult film rather than a fully acknowledged masterpiece. Truffaut attributed Hitchcock's decline to the failure of *Marnie*:

> I am convinced that Hitchcock was never the same after *Marnie*, and that its failure cost him a considerable amount of his self-confidence. This was not so much due to the financial failure of the film (he had had others), but rather to the failure of his professional and personal relationship with Tippi Hedren, whom he had discovered through a television commercial. In casting Tippi Hedren in two of his films, he entertained the notion of transforming her into another Grace Kelly.[25]

According to Truffaut, this was part of a larger difficulty Hitchcock had after the loss of his favorite male stars (Cary Grant and James Stewart) and female stars (Ingrid Bergman and Grace Kelly). He had a crisis of confidence in the aftermath of *Marnie* that led him unwisely to part company with his most important collaborators, such as the composer Bernard Herrmann.

A determining influence in the historical reception of *Marnie* has been Hitchcock's biographical legend. In 1983, Donald Spoto published his controversial biography, *The Dark Side of Genius: The Life of Alfred Hitchcock*. The director is presented as a man in the grip of uncontrollable impulses, whose pathological urges included misogyny, sadism, and sexual fantasies. These impulses came to a crux during the filming of *Marnie* when he tried to transform Tippi Hedren into a major star and the incarnation of his romantic and artistic visions. When she forcefully rejected him, Hitchcock, according to Spoto, lost all interest in the project, allowed careless backdrop and process work, and had a minimal input in the film's postproduction and marketing.[26]

Spoto quotes from two sources: interviews with Tippi Hedren and Jay Presson Allen, conducted shortly after Hitchcock's death. The presentation of facts is suggestively biased, and much of the production history, dates, and assumptions that Spoto cites are challenged in this book. The *Marnie* files held at the Academy of Motion Pictures, which forms the cornerstone of this research, were not available to Spoto, as Patricia Hitchcock refused to cooperate. Furthermore, several key participants, including Diane Baker, are notably absent. The most serious of Spoto's claims is a "cavalier dismissal" on Hitchcock's part following the Hedren rebuff, which can account for the film's "technical blunders" such as the painted ship backdrop and the rear projection. Since these elements were inherent in the overall design of the film and detailed during preproduction, Spoto's accusations are unfounded.

*The Dark Side of Genius* is indicative of a current trend to interpret popular biography for a film's critical analysis. Indeed, Spoto's account of *Marnie*'s production can be defined as the single most influential text, which has affected subsequent analysis of the film by journalistic media in the last thirty years. Spoto ignores the cultural and sociological factors that influence an artist's vision. Hitchcock's motivations are described as the result of a deep-rooted neurosis, and indeed the popular assumption is that he translated those impulses that caused him personal difficulty into his films.

Hitchcock has often been wrongly accused of misogyny, a propensity arising from a graphic depiction of violence against women in his films. Jay Presson Allen, one woman who was very close to him, fervently denies the accusation. Indeed, the production history, and the recollections of many women who worked with Hitchcock, suggests that his feelings toward women were ambivalent. Hitchcock never depicted rape and violence in a way that might be thought to encourage such acts against women. By focusing on Marnie's distress and horror while she is being raped, Hitchcock notes the devastating consequences the act has on her, culminating in her attempted suicide.

The erroneous notion of Hitchcock as a misogynist is now commonplace, as a result of Spoto's biography. The 1996 publication of *The Oxford History of World Cinema* remarks, "In his later films violence towards women increases, and Hitchcock's tendency for narrative and camera to control, investigate, and immobilize his female characters becomes overwhelming. *The Birds* (1963) and *Marnie* (1964) were uneasily received. Later films did even worse, and Hitchcock never regained his popularity with film audiences." Tippi Hedren has recently been praised by Camille Paglia in the British Film Institute handbook on *The Birds*, and in *A Biographical Dictionary of Film*, David Thomson says, "Hitchcock who drew out all the brittle insecurity in her Melanie Daniels in the first: that might simply be a performance nursed by a great director. But *Marnie* is an actress's triumph as well as a director's, and the way in which Tippi Hedren mutters 'There . . . there now' when she shoots her horse is typical of the insight and pathos she brings to the sexually inhibited thief."

## CONCLUSION

*Marnie* is an enormously complex film that has generated various interpretations during different historical periods, and its critical reception reflects something of the history of film theory and Hitchcock scholarship over the past fifty years. In 1964, the journalistic denunciation of *Marnie* was a result of Hitchcock's attempts to elevate his status from that of popular entertainer to serious artist.

Hitchcock's romantic thrillers of the fifties became the benchmarks for judging whether *Marnie* was a good film. Audiences expected a Hitchcock film with wit and suspense, but *Marnie*'s dark sadomasochistic streak and perverse romance puzzled viewers. "It Creaks—But the Cruelty Fascinates," Alexander Walker perceptively wrote in the *Evening Standard.*[27]

> Hitchcock has never filmed a more cruel scene than Connery, unaware of Marnie's frigidity, probing into the past relations he thinks she has had with men. His marriage proposal is made to sound like a blackmail threat. And even when he finds out the truth he refuses to be balked of his prey. . . . *Marnie* will please connoisseurs. But I can't think it'll be widely popular. It is too cruel. . . . And what are you to do when the only love interest in the film is the gratification that Marnie gets opening a safe door and fondling the dollar bills?

In the 1970s, academic criticism under the influence of the auteur theory dominated film studies, and feminist evaluation of Hitchcock's films also enhanced the director's reputation. Robin Wood's own cultural values and academic priorities came to significantly shape the outcome of *Marnie*'s interpretation during this period. In response to the journalistic critics, Wood defended Hitchcock's use of artificial devices such as the back projection in the horse riding sequences, claiming they were aptly expressionistic. Much of Wood's critical analysis of *Marnie* has found meaning lying outside, as David Bordwell says, "the conscious control of the individual who produces the utterance." Wood himself cites his favorite aphorism: "Never trust the artist, trust the tale."[28]

However, Wood's polemical agenda led him astray, as he himself later admitted. By defending the artifice, Wood provided his opponents with a means of evading the major issues that he wished to uphold—namely, the significance of Marnie's and Mark's relationship and the characteristic Hitchcockian preoccupation with different sorts of order, both valid and invalid. In later analyses, Wood acknowledged the inner tensions and contradictions which focused on the character of Mark. The biggest obstacle for many audiences was unequivocally accepting Mark as a hero. His massive male presumption contributes toward the film's stifling sense of claustrophobia and the pervading feeling of uneasiness.

The indeterminate qualities of Mark can be attributed to the multi-vocality of the *Marnie* text. Graham's straightforward stationer was infused with a fetishistic instinct by Hitchcock and given zoological and psychological credentials by Allen. Mark's preferred career had to be abandoned to save the ailing family business, which is portrayed as a patriarchal world, banal and listless, with motivations inadequate to satisfy its employees. Marnie's belief in "nothing," with the significant exception of horses (i.e., nature), is symptomatic of a culture that represses femininity and the growth of the environment. Later, after she is caught and being driven back to Rutland's, Marnie acknowledges that Mark is different from other men, which is part of her reason for liking him. There are indeed feminine strains in Mark's character, a man associated with nature, who captures animals to observe and understand them, as he did with Sophie, the jaguarundi. However, his honeymoon rape of Marnie could be perceived as an indoctrinated rejection and fear of his own feminine side, which Robin Wood sees as the source of violence to women in a culture that encourages patriarchal capitalism.[29] Mark's self-awareness of his own motivations and limitations is acknowledged at the end of the film, when he has learned as much about himself as about Marnie.

## NOTES

1. Huw Weldon, BBC *Monitor* interview, 1964.

2. John Coleman, review of *Marnie*, *New Statesman*, July 10, 1964, 62–63.

3. Ian Cameron and Richard Jeffrey, "The Universal Hitchcock," *Movie*, no. 12 (1965): 21–24.

4. Robin Wood, *Hitchcock's Films Revisited* (New York: Columbia University Press, 1989), 174.

5. Wood, *Hitchcock's Films Revisited*, 189.

6. Wood, *Hitchcock's Films Revisited*, 71–72.

7. Leo Braudy, "Hitchcock, Truffaut and the Irresponsible Audience," *Film Quarterly* 21, no. 4 (1968): 22–24.

8. Penelope Houston, book review of *Hitchcock's Films*, *Sight & Sound* 35, no. 1 (1965): 49.

9. Laura Mulvey, *Visual and Other Pleasures* (Bloomington: Indiana University Press, 1989), 14–26.

10. Raymond Bellour, "Hitchcock, the Enunciator," *Camera Obscura*, no. 2 (1977): 66–91.

11. Sandy Flitterman, "Woman, Desire and the Look: Feminism and the Enunciative Apparatus in Cinema," *Ciné-Tracts* 2 (1978): 63–68.

12. Tania Modleski, *The Women Who Knew Too Much* (New York: Routledge, 1988).

13. Robert Samuels, *Hitchcock's Bi-Texuality: Lacan, Feminism, and Queer Theory* (Albany: State University of New York Press, 1998).

14. Lucretia Knapp, "The Queer Voice in Marnie," *Cinema Journal* 32, no 4 (1993): 6–23.

15. Shameem Kabir, *Daughters of Desire: Lesbian Representations in Film* (London: Cassell & Washington, 1998).

16. Molly Haskell, *From Reverence to Rape: The Treatment of Women in the Movies* (Chicago: University of Chicago Press, 1987).

17. Wood, *Hitchcock's Films Revisited*, 371.

18. Michele Piso, "Mark's Marnie," in *A Hitchcock Reader*, ed. Marshall Deutelbaum and Leland Poague (Ames: Iowa State University Press, 1986), 288–303.

19. Robin Wood, "Looking at *The Birds* and *Marnie* through the *Rear Window*," *Cineaction* 50 (1999): 85.

20. Robin Wood, "Why We Should (Still) Take Hitchcock Seriously," *Cineaction* 31 (1993): 44–49.

21. Andrew Sarris, "*Jules and Jim* meets *Psycho*: A Review of Hitchcock, by François Truffaut," *Washington Post*, January 14, 1968.

22. Braudy, "Irresponsible Audience," 21.

23. Braudy, "Irresponsible Audience," 22.

24. François Truffaut, *Hitchcock* (New York: Simon & Schuster, 1985), 107.

25. Truffaut, *Hitchcock*, 327.

26. Donald Spoto, *The Dark Side of Genius: The Life of Alfred Hitchcock* (Boston: Little, Brown, 1983), 471–79.

27. Alexander Walker, review of *Marnie*, *Evening Standard*, July 9, 1964.

28. Wood, *Hitchcock's Films Revisited*, 171.

29. Wood, "Looking at *The Birds* and *Marnie*," 84–85.

## Chapter Eight

# Artistic Interpretation

*Neue Sachlichkeit* with psychology—one which goes so far in its perversity to attempt to naturalize a rape scene.

—Artist Stan Douglas on the mise-en-scène in *Marnie*

Hitchcock was a man who was inspired by art. He was an admirer of Paul Klee, Georges Rouault, Raoul Dufy, Maurice de Vlaminck, and Auguste Rodin, owning a number of their works.[1] He once said: "I compare myself to an abstract painter. My favourite painter is Klee."[2] Paul Klee was a Swiss painter, watercolorist, and etcher who was one of the most original masters of modern art. He created works known for their fantastic dream images, wit, and imagination. Another artist, Salvador Dali, famously collaborated on the dream sequence for *Spellbound* (1945), and many of Hitchcock's films such as *Saboteur* (1942) and *North by Northwest* (1959) resonate with surrealist images. Like the Italian painter George De Chirico, whom he quoted, Hitchcock portrayed a distorted universe filled with human anxiety and fears.

By the end of the twentieth century, cinema was described as the paradigmatic art form, and Hitchcock, the medium's defining artist.[3] Other artists have recognized both the cinematic medium and Hitchcock's films as a powerful stylistic presence in their work. Dali, Duchamp, and Cornell all experimented with film, and in the last twenty years, contemporary painters and photographers have been inspired by cinema with increasing frequency.

The development of feminist film theory within academia paved the way for the revaluation of Hitchcock's films and signaled attention to causal factors operating within his body of work. Hitchcock was inspired by centuries of symbolic, romantic, and surreal images that he utilized in his films. Parallels can be drawn within the Hitchcockian universe and how painters, photographers, and illustrators from the last 100 years have responded to the same cultural inspirations. Hitchcock also influenced a generation of contemporary artists. Many, such as David Salle and Cindy Sherman, have ventured into film directing, a natural result of film being multimodal, reliant on other art forms such as painting, writing, and music. The cross fertilization has invoked Hitchcock's work in film, art, theater, and new media.

## FILM INFLUENCE

Hitchcock's ability to create a dream state existing somewhere between reality and fiction has influenced international directors in the realm of both commercial and art house cinema. A number of François Truffaut's films in the late sixties echo *Marnie* stylistically and thematically. The idea of a woman's revenge against male patriarchy forms the locus of *The Bride Wore Black* (1969), which Truffaut likened to a fairy tale. He derived the idea from a book he had read when he was fourteen years old, about a woman who kills the five men responsible for the accidental shooting of her husband on their wedding day: "It was a story about fatality, about men who had done something in their youth, and this bride had the mission of vengeance to carry it out," remarked Truffaut.[4] Jeanne Moreau plays the widow, Julie Kohler, who murders the five men. Midway through the film, a flashback reveals that the victims were formerly friends, who had accidentally shot a young man emerging from a church where he had just been married. "I told Jeanne Moreau not to be tragic, to play it like a skilled worker with a job to do, conscientious and obstinate." The character of Julie Kohler is enslaved to the idea of revenge; just like when Marnie steals, she is in the grip of compulsive behavior.

In Truffaut's film *Mississippi Mermaid* (1967), Louis Mahe (Jean-Paul Belmondo) is a plantation owner on Reunion Island. At the beginning of the film, he is waiting at the port for Julie Roussel (Catherine Deneuve), his wife-to-be. He has never met her since they have only communicated through the marriage ads of a newspaper. The woman who arrives bears little resemblance to Julie's photograph, but Louis is enchanted, finding her even more beautiful, and the two marry. Although Julie acts suspiciously during their marriage, they are basically happy until she runs away with his money. It turns out that she is not Julie but an imposter named Marion. Louis follows her to France and, acknowledging that he loves her, shoots the detective on her trail. They hide in a cabin, but then he realizes she is poisoning him. After a change of heart, Marion tries to keep Louis alive, and the two walk away together in the snow.

The plot of *Mississippi Mermaid* evokes *Marnie*, in creating a heroine with a frigid and neurotic sexuality who steals from her husband. When Louis finds Marion, she becomes incapable of sex, but after he shoots the detective, she wants to make love to him with her clothes on.

Like *Marnie*, *Mississippi Mermaid* was a commercial failure when it was released. In both films, Hitchcock and Truffaut pushed the disruption of tone and genre to an extreme in a daring artistic experiment. Another drawback was the expectations of big-name casting; audiences were hoping for a more conventional romance than what was offered. In *Mississippi Mermaid* the mysterious woman is in control of the narrative, whereas the man's fate is in her hands.[5]

Another director of the French new wave, Claude Chabrol, breaks down the critical barrier between art and popular cinema. *Le Boucher* (1969) is one of Chabrol's most popular works. The film charts the tragic romance between a schoolteacher and a butcher with conflicting values. The schoolteacher, Mademoiselle Helene (Stephane Audran), represents education and civilization. The butcher, Popaul (Jean Yanne), personifies sex, death, and violence. Helene cannot kiss Popaul until it is too late, and she is only able to do so when she knows that Popaul is dying. Her sexual frigidity recalls that of Marnie's. She also tries to bury the past by taking on a new job and has blackouts at critical moments, and the image of Popaul at the schoolroom window recalls the sailors who plague Marnie's nightmares.

The highly expressive mise-en-scène in *Marnie*, with its red suffusions, painted backdrops, and conspicuous rear projection, contributes to a dream-like state that exists between reality and theatricality. Other directors have adopted this technique of how realistic elements are enmeshed with formal devices that signal attention to the artificial and the contrived. Nagisa Oshima, a major postwar director of Japanese cinema, is generally regarded as one of the most important after Kurosawa. His early films represent the Japanese New Wave at its zenith. He was an innovator in the strategies of film style, producing provocative works that confront issues of sexuality, power, domination, and identity. His film *Shonen*, a.k.a. *Boy* (1969), is regarded as one of his most humanistic. When first released, many critics, like those who berated *Marnie*, called *Boy* a retrograde step for the director, while others were receptive to the youthful protagonist and linear structure. The film evokes empathy for a young Japanese boy (Tetsuo Abe) in Kyoto in 1932. Fumio Watanabe plays the father and Akiki Koyama the stepmother, caught in a family trap of crime, ritual abuse, and imaginary escape.[6]

The color scheme in *Boy*, like *Marnie*, selects red as the focal point, creating exaggerated repetition and displacement across the frame. In *Marnie*, the red suffusions form a structural progression culminating in the repressed memory of the sailor's bloody shirt. As red is always depicted against white in Marnie's tensions, it also represents loss of virginity and childhood innocence. Oshima similarly uses red in psychoanalytical terms across a number of objects in *Boy:* a baseball hat, the stepmother's suit, a boot, and blood. By virtue of their color association, these objects are connected with the loss of the boy's real mother.

Hitchcock's affinity to women's fiction and melodrama in *Marnie* are ties adopted by Rainer Werner Fassbinder, one of New German Cinema's most talented exponents. In a short-lived fifteen-year career, Fassbinder directed thirty-six feature-length films and was particularly inspired by American gangster and women's pictures. In Fassbinder's estimation, American cinema was the only one he could take seriously, because it reached an audience in the same way as the prewar German cinema had once done. His admiration for the German-American director Douglas Sirk, Raoul Walsh, and Hitchcock was based on their ability to direct films within the capitalistic and industrialized studio system, all the while subtly subverting the conformist ideologies that Hollywood traditionally reinforced.

Fassbinder's agenda was to make, if not exactly a German-Hollywood film, then one "very much like Hollywood," a film that is "as entertaining as Hollywood, and yet that says something about reality," in the manner that Sirk and Hitchcock managed to achieve. "The best thing I can think of would be to create a union between something as beautiful and wonderful as Hollywood films and a criticism of the status quo," Fassbinder said in 1974. "That's my dream, to make such a German film—beautiful and extravagant and fantastic, and nevertheless able to go against the existing order," such as Hitchcock's *Suspicion* (1941), "the most drastic film against the bourgeois institution of marriage I know."[7] His view of *Marnie* was that it was boldly experimental: "I just couldn't make a film like Hitchcock's *Marnie* as *Marnie* is told, because I don't have the courage for such naïvete, simply to make such a film and then at the end to give such an explanation. I don't have that something which is a natural part of courage, but maybe some day I will have it, and then I'll be just like Hollywood."[8]

Like Hitchcock, Fassbinder preferred shooting techniques inspired by German expressionist films of the 1920s, such as deep focus shots, and high contrast lighting that often left a large part of the frame and individual faces in shadow. Fassbinder defended his lighting style in *Berlin Alexanderplatz* (1980), pointing out its similarities to the paintings of Rembrandt and Hitchcock's films. The story was basically the longest narrative film ever made, fifteen half-hour episodes exploring the character of Franx Biberkopf, as well as the Alexanderplatz area of Berlin he inhabited.

Another experimental filmmaker, Warren Sonbert, similarly explored themes of desire and mortality. He often introduced screenings of *Marnie* in

New York at the Collective for Living Cinema in the early 1980s, praising the film's bold coherence. Sonbert had a passion for music and was an ardent opera buff. He believed that the divergent rhythms of sound and film hindered each other, so he made silent films for twenty years. Like Hitchcock, Sonbert was very influenced by Russian montage and saw film as a language, in which the connection between two shots produced the intent of the third shot. His films were full of visual puns and metaphors that juxtaposed color with movement, and they were rich with anthropological observation and personal details. A Guggenheim exhibition amplified the sympathy between the film, art, poetry, and music that were the fulcrum for Sonbert's artistic development during the sixties and seventies. Sirk and Hitchcock were favorite directors because they undermined plot and mainstream sexual conventions, as he once wrote, "[t]he hollow cupidity and superficiality of middle class ideals." Sonbert's film *A Woman's Touch* was an homage to *Marnie*, exploring similar themes of female entrapment and escape.

Martin Scorsese is one director who has been inspired by Hitchcock's use of associational montage, in the revelation of character and plot to an audience. Hitchcock established a motif of hands and feet for the opening scenes of *Marnie*, and Scorsese uses the same technique for the thriller aspects of *After Hours* (1985). He admits that Hitchcock was an important influence:

> *After Hours* is to some extent a parody of Hitchcock's style. Over the years his films have become more emotionally meaningful for me. By the time I realized he was moving the camera, it was over and I had felt the effect of the movement emotionally and intellectually. So if you take the scene in *After Hours* when Paul is running with the invitation in his hand—there's a shot of a hand with the ground below—basically this refers back to the moment in *Marnie* where she's holding the gun and going to shoot the horse. When I first saw *Marnie*, that shot remained in my mind and I kept going back to watch the whole two hours just to see it again. I loved the feeling of it, and then I realized that it was also Bernard Herrmann's music—the story and the acting—all these came together over the years and the whole combination was overwhelming.[9]

In 1968, at a screening in Paris of *The Bride Wore Black* and *Marnie*, Scorsese was excited about the prospect of four hours of Herrmann's music: "I had become aware of Bernard Herrmann's scores when I was eleven or twelve. I loved them . . . He did the Hitchcock pictures, especially *Marnie* and *Vertigo*; *Psycho* is the traditional one to mention, but the *Marnie* score is even more interesting." When it came to scoring his film *Taxi Driver*, Scorsese was faced with the challenge that his central character Travis Bickle (Robert de Niro) was an isolated character who did not listen to anything. In Scorsese's mind, the only composer who could capture this was Bernard Herrmann, and subsequently *Taxi Driver* was the last score Herrmann devised before his death in 1975. At the Eighth Annual Film Preservation Festival in 2000, Scorsese introduced *Marnie* as a

> companion piece to *Vertigo* in its complex treatment of obsessive love and its understanding of the human psyche. . . . As you see Hitchcock's treatment of Mark and Marnie's ambiguous and constantly shifting relationship is highly nuanced and very moving. Hitchcock created unforgettable screen kisses in *Notorious* and *Rear Window*, but there is a kissing scene in *Marnie* which is the most impressive of all because the director uses it so cleverly to advance the psychological aspects of the story. It takes place during a violent thunderstorm. A terrified Hedren falls trance like into Sean Connery's arms. Hitchcock's camera moves into an extreme close up and Connery attempts to kiss her. His mouth finds her forehead, travels down her cheek until it passionately meets her lips and she re-emerges all to the surging accompaniment of Bernard Herrmann's lush music. Not only is this moment highly sensual, it also marks the beginning of the healing process for Hedren's character.

The sexual problems of a married couple and the terrors of intimacy also form the central narrative pulse of Stanley Kubrick's last film, *Eyes Wide Shut* (1999). The story on which it is based, *Traumnovelle* (translated as *Rhapsody: A Dream Novel*), was one that intrigued Kubrick for many years. Like *Marnie*, *Eyes Wide Shut* was panned on its release. Critics faulted the film for being slow, overlong, pretentious, artificial, and lacking in resolution. It featured two of the most popular stars of the time, Tom Cruise and his then-wife Nicole Kidman, as an upper-class New York married couple, Bill and Alice Hartford. After a party one night and high on marijuana, Alice confesses to Bill that she has a recurring fantasy of being seduced by a naval officer and dreams of taking part in an orgy to spite her husband. Her confession awakens a dormant, castratory fear in Bill, and the film's preoccupation deals with his attempt to find his own sexual identity and overcome the threat of impotency.

*Eyes Wide Shut* is fundamentally a critique of male sexual anxiety. Bill Hartford is a man so troubled by his wife's desires that he embarks on his own sexual adventures. He in effect becomes a walking surrogate for the wheelchair-bound L. B. Jefferies (James Stewart) of *Rear Window*. The people whom Bill encounters on the streets of New York are embodiments of his own sexual fantasies, in the same way that the occupants living in the apartments across a Greenwich Village courtyard represent the states of marriage or singleness that are open to Jefferies. In the course of his wanderings, Bill meets a prostitute whom he later discovers has AIDS; a nymphomaniac daughter who is regularly bartered to Japanese businessmen by her father; and a gay hotel clerk whose open flirtations to Bill are both comedic and pathetic. Significantly, Bill is taunted by a gang of male youths and called a "fag" from San Francisco. Indeed, there is an underlying current within *Eyes*

*Wide Shut* that Bill's meanderings are drawn by a latent homosexuality, rendering him an outlaw in patriarchal society, an argument of which has also been posited for *Marnie*.

Bill is unable to consummate any of his wish fulfillments, and being passive in his spectatorship, he has no control over them. His dreams can turn into nightmares at any moment, hellishly realized during the orgy scene at the mansion where he is singled out for interrogation. *Eyes Wide Shut*, like *Marnie*, employs a highly artificial mise-en-scène to create this otherworldly effect. There is an unnatural predominance of reds and yellows in the mansions and lavish interiors of New York apartments.

Kubrick, like Hitchcock, was reluctant to work outside a soundstage because he relished the control that the studio afforded. Just as the Baltimore street set in *Marnie* insists on its symbolic representation, the studio mockups of New York streets in *Eyes Wide Shut* are flagrantly artificial and are intercut with second unit photography of real streets. The scenes in which Bill drifts almost like a sleepwalker through these artificial streets recalls both Monica Vitti wandering dazedly through Antonioni's *Red Desert* and Tippi Hedren in *Marnie*.

*Eyes Wide Shut* ends with a sequence in a toy shop. Bill and Alice are together with their daughter, evoking a reassuring image of family togetherness and a superficial sense of closure. The ending recalls that of Mark Rutland as he strives to awaken Marnie from her nightmares and join him in matrimony. Alice's last words are similarly an appeal to Bill to return to the real world of marital sexuality and forget his fantasies: "And you know there is something very important that we need to do as soon as possible," she says. "What's that?" Bill asks. "Fuck," she replies. The tentative ending of *Eyes Wide Shut*, like *Marnie*, suggests the possibility, and only that, of a successful heterosexual union. In their lack of resolution, both films offer a prelude to the curing of a dysfunctional sexuality, by bleakly charting the upheavals caused by the shifting relationships between men and women.[10]

## ART INSPIRATION

The continual fascination of Alfred Hitchcock's films lies within the universality of his themes, the explicit use of Freudian analytical concepts, and the centrality of the look. Sigmund Freud, beginning with *Interpretation of Dreams*, examined the need for therapy on the state of modern man, and the impact of his neurotic tendencies on art and philosophy. When Hitchcock started as a director in England, Freud's ideas were being embraced in Paris by Andre Breton and a group of poets who developed into the surrealist group, an international movement dedicated to the revolutionary use of psychoanalysis as an attack on bourgeois reality. Hitchcock's interest in the modern style of surrealism reflects his own obsession with man's imbalance and his interest in appropriating a therapeutic discourse in his films. Hitchcock himself acknowledged:

> And surrealism? Wasn't it born as much from the work of Poe as from that of Lautréamont? This literary school certainly had a great influence on cinema, especially around 1925–1930, when surrealism was transposed onto the screen by Bunuel with *L'Age d'or* and *Un Chien andalou*, by René Clair with *Entr'acte*, by Jean Epsein with *Fall of the House of Usher*, and by your French academician Jean Cocteau with *Blood of the Poet*. An influence that I experienced myself, if only in the dream sequences and the sequences of the unreal in a certain number of my films.[11]

The Salvador Dali dream sequence in *Spellbound*, the nightmare sequence in *Vertigo* by contemporary painter John Ferren, and Saul Bass's opening credits in *Vertigo*, *North by Northwest*, and *Psycho* indicate the close affinity Hitchcock had with surrealism and modern art.

The desire to see oneself seeing unites cinema and art within the motif of the look. The extremely visual style of Hitchcock's films, with psychoanalytic or voyeuristic themes, such as *Rear Window*, *Vertigo*, *Psycho*, and *Marnie*, have influenced filmmakers such as Brian De Palma, David Lynch, and David Cronenberg. Contemporary artists like the fact that Hitchcock's films are centered around "the look."

That same prestige extends far beyond the frontiers of film. The motif of the look in Hitchcock's films has been inspirational to a generation of artists, ranging from Annette Messager's *Chimeres* series to Judith Barry's *In the Shadow of the City . . . Vamp ry*. Many of the photo artists associated with *Screen* magazine in the 1970s, such as Victor Burgin and Eve Lomax, were influenced by Hitchcock. Evoking Lacan, and the radical relevance of his work to theories of representation, Burgin remarked, "There is no essential self which precedes the social construction of the self through the agency of representations."[12] This investigation into the modern mind becomes in turn the subject of the artist's work on Hitchcock, who focused on the director as a nexus of cultural traumas, with his more psychoanalytic films becoming the official canon.

In 2000, the Montreal Museum of Fine Arts mounted a major exhibition drawing parallels between Hitchcock's creative development and the artistic and philosophical trends spanning the twentieth century. "Hitchcock and Art: Fatal Coincidences," as the exhibition was titled, illustrated how the major currents of painting from classicism to modernism ran through Hitchcock's films.[13] Over two hundred works of art were featured including major works from Dante Gabriel Rossetti's *Proserpine* to De Chirico's *Hector and Andromache*. There were also works by Böcklin, Redon, Khnopff, Spilliaert, Vuillard, Max Ernst, and Edward Hopper. The exhibition was conceived in 1990 when the exhibition's two co-chief curators, Guy Cogeval and Dominique Païni, were both working at the Louvre. Cogeval later became the director of the Montreal Museum of Fine Arts and Païni, the director of the Ciné-mathèque Française in Paris. By designing the exhibition as a sort of three-way "split screen," they provided both movie fans and art lovers an insight into Hitchcock's films, his imagination, and hidden connections with nineteenth- and twentieth-century art and literature.

The exhibition was a celebration of Hitchcock's personal creative expression, delving into the symbolic and surreal works of art that inspired him and works inspired by him. Raphael Delorme's painting entitled *Woman and Steamship* (1928), shown in the exhibition, depicts a naked woman carrying two valises in front of a huge liner, an image that prefigures Hitchcock's *Marnie*. As Païni remarks: "Hitchcock is probably the only film director whose life and work show the influence of all of the major twentieth-century art trends—classicism, symbolism, mannerism and modernism. Hitchcock's work encompasses it all. Besides, he was a true art lover and regularly visited the National Gallery of Art in Washington when he was preparing his films."[14]

The fusion of new media, electronic and digital technologies, was the impetus behind "Notorious: Alfred Hitchcock and Contemporary Art."[15] This exhibition originated at the Museum of Modern Art in Oxford as a showcase to celebrate the centenary of Hitchcock's birth. One reviewer described how "Notorious highlights the way that Hitchcock's imaginative universe and its structures have caught the modern art imagination more than any other filmmaker's—as the exhibition note says, there has never been a comparable exhibition on art and Orson Welles or John Ford (although I suspect that there may have been a few on art and Disney)."[16]

"Notorious" abounds with references to *Vertigo*, *Psycho*, *Marnie*, and *Rear Window*. The exhibition brought together the works of fourteen artists, ranging from dramatic contemporary video portraits, to large installations that envelop the viewer in a sensual play of sound and images. On display was Douglas Gordon's twenty-four-hour *Psycho*, a scene from *Vertigo* into which David Reed digitally inserted one of his own paintings, and Cindy Sherman's famous photographic remake of herself as a Hitchcock heroine. The six Phoenix tapes by two Germans, Christoph Giradet and Matthias Muller, formed an inventory of Hitchcock motifs across his career—a miniencyclopedia edited to music with staircases, stranglings, signatures, guns, kisses, and mothers.

Prominent in the exhibition was *Subject to a Film:* Marnie, a six-minute black-and-white video remake of the robbery sequence by Canadian artist Stan Douglas. Born in Vancouver in 1960, Douglas studied at the Emily Carr College of Art, and since 1981, he has exhibited in Canada, the United States, and throughout Europe. The Pompidou in Paris launched a major retrospective of his work, and he is a regular name at the Whitney Biennial. Douglas is considered one of the foremost video artists of today, whose work combines traditional cinematic techniques with new technologies to produce images often suggestive of repressed memories and forgotten histories. His work is layered with the artist's observations on social alienation and psychological states. He also wrote a publication among others titled *Shades of Masochism: Samuel Beckett's Teleplays.*

Douglas said that he was first attracted to *Marnie* by its perversity: "When I first saw the film, I perceived it as a failed work. At the time, I was not aware of the theoretical controversy surrounding it, such as the shot by shot analysis by Raymond Bellour or the patriarchal reading by Kaja Silverman."[17] For Douglas, the pivotal moment in the film is the robbery, which is set up so that Marnie will be caught by Mark. The robbery turns out to be Marnie's last free act in the film, and although she makes one attempt to flee the Rutland home, even after she has been cured, she may very well be waiting for the ideal moment to escape.

Douglas restages the moments just before Marnie robs the office safe. The office is modern-day, with computers substituting for typewriters. What is first assumed to be a single tracking shot turns out to be nine shots and a trick dissolve, so that it is all on a loop. Douglas's piece evokes the seamless repetition, without beginning or end, of the infinite retake. The thief never gets to leave the scene of the crime but instead is trapped in the endless loop of the installation. The effect underscores Marnie's inability to escape her mental illness while simultaneously calling attention to the watchful gaze of the spectator. In creating the circular nature for his film, Douglas remarked, "I was interested in the interface between the working and private life. The moment when one is neither on company time or one's own time. All of the action depicted might, in fact, be the protagonist's fantasy, it is the spatialization of a moment."

As an artist himself, Douglas was impressed by the sets and painted backdrops in *Marnie* that create an artificial, constructed environment. He describes the coldness of *Marnie*'s mise-en-scène as "*Neue Sachlichkeit* with psychology"—one that goes so far in its perversity to attempt to naturalize a rape scene. *Die Neue Sachlichkeit* (The New Objectivity) was an expressionist movement founded in Germany in the aftermath of World War I by Otto Dix and George Grosz. Other artists associated with the movement included Max Beckmann and Christian Schad. When Hitchcock was working in Berlin in 1925, Gustav Hartlaub presented an exhibition at the Mannheim Stadtische Kunsthalle titled "Neue Schlichkeit: Deutsche Malerei seit dem Expressionismus."

In *Neue Sachlichkeit* painting, objects and firm outlines are preferred, in contrast to the more flimsy physiques in expressionist painting. One example can be found in Christian Schad's *Half Nude* (1929), in which the female portrait offers a wealth of closely observed detail: pillow creases, hair under the model's arms, and the veins in the model's breast. *Neue Sachlichkeit* is characterized by a realistic style combined with a cynical, socially critical stance. The focus is on the reality and details of simple objects and direct and precise shapes. A concentration on everyday objects and banal, unpretentious subjects betrays no aversion to what is ugly. Patterns are geometric and controlled, and colors are rational-emotional. *Neue Sachlichkeit* offers a visual sobriety and acuity, as well as an unsentimental, largely emotionless way of seeing. The pictorial structure at Rutland's is often static, suggesting a positively airless, glassy space, and a general preference for the stagnant over the dynamic. The sense of claustrophobia is expressed in the concentration on objects, colors, gestures, and patterns of behavior and relationships. In *Marnie* they are offset by the red suffusions that echo the heroine's realistic movement, creating a tension between a symbolic and pure somatic energy.

Another artist inspired by *Marnie* is Sean O'Connor, a writer and director with credits on the BBC soap operas *The Archers* and *Eastenders*. After graduating in English from University College London, he worked as a theater director in a number of productions throughout England. His adaptation of *Vertigo* opened at the Chester Gateway theater and later played at Windsor and Guildford. In 2001, O'Connor staged the world premiere of *Marnie* at the Haymarket theater in Basingstoke. The play cleverly utilized a cast of only five adults and one child, with Sophie Shaw in the role of Marnie and Peter Lindford playing Mark Rutland. O'Connor first saw Hitchcock's film as a boy, and the disturbing elements remained in his mind. Later, he bought a first edition of Winston Graham's novel in London and read and liked the story, finding the postwar period interesting and the issues raised intriguing.

"*Marnie* is a typical kitchen-sink story of the gritty, realist 'angry' school that burst on the British literary scene in the late 1950s and early 60s," says O'Connor.[18] "Like Joe Lampton in *Room at the Top* or Arthur Seaton in *Saturday Night and Sunday Morning*, Marnie feels trapped by her class and background. But she also feels an extra sense of confinement—she's a woman. She (literally) tries to steal her way out of her class." Like Graham, O'Connor professes to being a feminist and acknowledges the prejudices against women in our society.

O'Connor felt that Hitchcock had blunted much of the social resonance of the story by transferring the setting to the broader expanses of Philadelphia and by affording the film lavish Technicolor production values with rising star Sean Connery. In his theatrical adaptation, O'Connor restores the original story to the gritty realism of postwar Britain in 1960 and the provincial towns of Birmingham, Plymouth, Sheffield, and Swindon. The war haunts the narrative throughout and exposes a fractured society as a result of it.

"Graham's novel presents a country recovering from the effects of the war," remarks O'Connor.

> All the characters in some way have been shaped by their wartime experiences. In many ways, they represent the immediate post-war generation, still stifled by the memories of rationing and utility. This was the fag end of the fifties, with Britain smarting from the recent crisis in Suez. National decline was a national debate. With the last curtsies from the last debutantes presented to the Queen in 1958, and now an end to National Service, the country was on the cusp of change. The Lady Chatterley trial of 1960 helped to usher in such change but also reaffirmed a society driven by class.

For O'Connor, what happens to Marnie during the war is symbolic of the effects on a whole country. The story raises the question if Britain can ever recover from its social and political wartime past in the same way that an individual can overcome traumatic events in his or her lifetime. Marnie is an iconic figure struggling with her hinterland, and only by retreating to those dark days of the mid-1940s can she confront her psychosis. The story has relevance for modern audiences, because Marnie embodies quintessential British hang-ups about sex, class, and money. For a woman without money, it is nigh impossible to rise above her social standing.

It took O'Connor a while for the play to be realized, as many people were uneasy about the subject matter. One theater owner said *Marnie* couldn't be shown, because it depicted marital rape, despite the fact that murders are regularly reenacted on stage.

In many ways, theater lends itself to the psychodrama of Graham's novel better than film. O'Connor skillfully melds the past seamlessly with the present. At the beginning of the second act, Marnie defiantly sits in the foreground with Roman the psychiatrist, while the ghost of her ten-year-old self dances with her mother in the background, to the tune of "Que Sera Sera." The child is then handed over to dance with Mark Rutland, presenting a sight at once moving and disturbing. Later, during the hunt sequence, it becomes very apparent that the hunted animal is Marnie.

Originally, as in the novel, Terry Holbrook was to betray Marnie at the end by handing her over to the police, suggesting that the story is narrated from prison. But toward the end of rehearsals, O'Connor altered the ending, because he firmly believed the story was about Marnie trying to find herself and acknowledging her past, rather than another character determining her fate. O'Connor leaves it up to the audience to decide what happens to Marnie, and the final image of a lonely future cut off from all humanity, as she walks off hand in hand with her child self, is very moving.

The stage background effectively evokes the repressive nature of Marnie's life. A vast tiled lavatory or washroom with six mirrors around allows the audience to see two or even three sides of the actors at a time. The mirrors suggest that no matter how many sides we see of other people, a feeling of inscrutability remains. In the middle of the set, the seventh wall has collapsed into a mound of rubble left after an air raid, and train tracks lead into the distance, a metaphor for the past that has blasted Marnie's present. The washroom conveys Marnie's obsessive need to clean herself after each robbery and her sterile, listless life.

The play opened in the New Year to favorable reviews. On January 25, 2001, a reviewer for the *Times* wrote, "[O'Connor] solves the scenic complexities of *Marnie* with skill and elegance—he is also the director—on a tiled and mirrored set by Matthew Wright."[19] The *Guardian* added, "Marnie's tragedy is played out not merely as psychodrama but as a gritty parable of repressiveness in which sex, class, money and even vowel sounds are major motivators."[20] The play's release allowed a new generation to respond to *Marnie*, at a time when half of all marriages end in divorce, and every person embarking on a new relationship is encumbered by unresolved issues from their past.

## CONCLUSION

During Hitchcock's centenary, a panel of top directors, including Martin Scorsese, Atom Egoyan, and Bruce Robinson, assembled by the British Film Institute's *Sight & Sound* magazine, voted for the ten greatest Hitchcock works. They chose (1) *Psycho*, (2) *Vertigo*, (3) *Notorious*, (4) *The Birds*, (5) *North by Northwest*, (6) *Shadow of a Doubt*, (7) *Foreign Correspondent*, (8) *Frenzy*, (9) *The Lady Vanishes*, and (10) *Marnie*. A film that was universally scorned when first released, *Marnie* had now become a time capsule for gender representations and psychoanalytical ideas for key traumas and events. The film may well be Hitchcock's testament in which his signature is left on every shot. The fact that these images linger long after we have seen the film, and that they have been influential to a vast array of other artists, is testimony to Hitchcock's power as a filmmaker. What makes his work so enduringly and eminently accessible is the presentation of fundamentally significant human issues in an entertaining and provoking manner. Hitchcock's films have captured the realm of popular imagination, suffused our culture, and continue to remain an engaging critique of male and female sexual relationships.

## NOTES

1. Telephone interview with Patricia Hitchcock, Santa Barbara, California, July 11, 2000.

2. Thomas Samuels, *Encountering Directors* (New York: Putnam's, 1972), 239.

3. Richard Allen and S. Ishi Gonzalés, *Alfred Hitchcock Centenary Essays* (London: British Film Institute, 1999), 1.

4. Sanche de Gramont, "Life Style of Homo Cinemmaticus," *New York Times*, June 15, 1969.

5. Annette Insdorf, *François Truffaut* (Cambridge: Cambridge University Press, 1994), 39–67.

6. Maureen Turim, *The Films of Nagisa Oshima: Images of a Japanese Iconoclast* (Berkeley: California University Press, 1998).

7. Wallace Steadman Watson, *Understanding Rainer Werner Fassbinder* (Columbia: University of South Carolina Press, 1996), 105–9.

8. Wilfried Wiegand, "Interview with Rainer Werner Fassbinder," in *Fassbinder* (New York: Tandam, 1981), 90.

9. David Thompson and Ian Christie, *Scorsese on Scorsese* (London: Faber & Faber, 1989), 101.

10. Robert Kolker, *A Cinema of Loneliness* (New York: Oxford University Press, 1999), 170–73.

11. Alfred Hitchcock, "Why I Am Afraid of the Dark," originally published in French in *Arts, Letters, Spectacles 777* (June 1960). Reprinted in *Hitchcock on Hitchcock*, ed. Sidney Gottlieb (Berkeley: University of California Press, 1995), 144.

12. Victor Burgin, "The Absence of Presence," in *The End of Art Theory: Criticism and Postmodernity* (Atlantic Highlands, N.J.: Humanities Press International, 1986), 41.

13. Dominique Païni and Guy Cogeval, *Hitchcock and Art: Fatal Coincidences* (Montreal Museum of Fine Arts, 2000).

14. Montreal Museum of Fine Arts interview with Dominic Païni for "Hitchcock and Art: Fatal Coincidences" 2000 exhibit.

15. Kerry Brougher, Michael Tarantino, and Astrid Bowron, *Notorious: Alfred Hitchcock and Contemporary Art* (Oxford: Museum of Modern Art, 1999).

16. Jonathan Romney, "A Hitch in Time," *New Statesman*, July 19, 1999, 36.

17. Telephone interview with Stan Douglas, Vancouver, British Columbia, October 5, 2000. All quotes originate from this interview.

18. Telephone interview with Sean O'Connor, Chester, England, February 10, 2001. All quotes originate from this interview.

19. Jeremy Kingston, "Review of Marnie," *Times*, January 25, 2001, 14.

20. Lyn Gardener, "Review of Marnie," *Guardian*, January 24, 2001, 18.

The English author Winston Graham in 1961, the year *Marnie* was published. He describes himself as "an instinctive feminist." Photo copyright Winston Graham.

*Psycho* screenwriter Joseph Stefano was in analysis himself when he wrote the original treatment for *Marnie*. Photo copyright Joseph Stefano.

Novelist Evan Hunter, screenwriter for *The Birds*, spent a year working on *Marnie* before he was abruptly fired from the project because of his reluctance to write the controversial rape scene. Photo copyright Evan Hunter.

Playwright and screenwriter Jay Presson Allen. *Marnie* was her first screenplay, a contributing factor to a film she describes as having "many flaws." Photo copyright Jay Presson Allen.

Alfred Hitchcock signs the contract for *Marnie* with Universal head Milton Rackmill. Behind them is the infamous painted backdrop that Hitchcock approved. Copyright © 2002 by Universal City Studios, Inc. Courtesy of Universal Studios Publishing Rights. All rights reserved.

The Baltimore street set initially caused much derision and embarrassment for art director Robert Boyle. It was later applauded by the auteur critics for apt expressionism, reflecting back to Hitchcock's own childhood memory of the London dockyards. Copyright © 2002 by Universal City Studios, Inc. Courtesy of Universal Studios Publishing Rights. All rights reserved.

Edith Head's costumes for Tippi Hedren transformed Marnie from demure secretary to elegant society hostess. Photos courtesy of Rita Riggs.

Diane Baker's clothes reflected old money in both her riding outfits and evening gowns. Photos courtesy of Rita Riggs.

The Rutland office scenes were the first to be filmed. Hitchcock offered two directions to Sean Connery: Pause after a sentence, and keep your mouth closed when listening to fellow actors. Photo courtesy of the Museum of Modern Art Film Stills Archive.

Hitchcock directs Hedren and Connery during the thunderstorm in Mark's office. Seated next to the director is his favorite cinematographer Robert Burks. Photo courtesy of the Museum of Modern Art Film Stills Archive.

Two images of Louise Latham. Top: With Alfred Hitchcock as the young Bernice Edgar prior to filming the flashback. Bottom: As the older Mrs. Edgar with Hitchcock and Sean Connery. Photos copyright Louise Latham.

Hitchcock with his first assistant director, James H. Brown (right), and second assistant director, Pat Casey (left), as they wait for the process photography to be set up and rewound. "I think he got a little bored with the project towards the end," affirms Brown. Photo courtesy of James H. Brown.

The *Marnie* crew presents Alfred Hitchcock with a Christmas gift and sketches of the Rutland safe and the Wykwyn staircase. Front row, left to right: Harold Michaelson, Hilton Green, Robert Boyle, Alfred Hitchcock, Tippi Hedren, and James H. Brown. Photo courtesy of James H. Brown.

Diane Baker and Alan Napier, who played Mark's father, in a scene that was dropped in postproduction. Baker felt that her character was unresolved in the final cut. Copyright © 2002 by Universal City Studios, Inc. Courtesy of Universal Studios Publishing Rights. All rights reserved.

Marnie, astride Forio, upbraids Lil in the stable scene that was disliked by Alma Hitchcock and consequently dopped postproduction. Copyright © 2002 by Universal City Studios, Inc. Courtesy of Universal Studios Publishing Rights. All rights reserved.

Equestrian imagery in *Marnie*. Tippi Hedren and Diane Baker on location at the Disney Ranch outside Los Angeles, for filming the conclusion of the hunt sequence. Copyright © 2002 by Universal City Studios, Inc. Courtesy of Universal Studios Publishing Rights. All rights reserved.

Tippi Hedren and an extra ride horses on treadmills in front of studio back projection during filming of the hunt sequence. Photo courtesy of Museum of Modern Art Film Stills Archive.

Solicitude or sadomasochism? Conflicting interpretations surround Mark's relationship to Marnie. Photo courtesy of Museum of Modern Art Film Stills Archive.

Freudian imagery in *Marnie*. "The horse represents the father," said Hitchcock in a rare instance of thematic analysis. Copyright © 2002 by Universal City Studios, Inc. Courtesy of Universal Studios Publishing Rights. All rights reserved.

Sean Connery, Diane Baker, Tippi Hedren, and a colleague enjoy a joke and a tea break during filming on Universal's back lot. Copyright © 2002 by Universal City Studios, Inc. Courtesy of Universal Studios Publishing Rights. All rights reserved.

Sean Connery was given a watch at the wrap party by the *Marnie* crew as a token of his professionalism. Assistant director James H. Brown is seated next to him. Photo courtesy of James H. Brown.

Hitchcock with his screenwriter Jay Presson Allen. The two had a fabulous rapport, and Allen would later interpret his dreams, while he would encourage her to direct. Photo copyright Jay Presson Allen.

Hitchcock invited Allen to write a first draft of *Mary Rose*, but the project was shelved by Lew Wasserman, who also harbored doubts about *Marnie*. Photo copyright Jay Presson Allen.

Two posters as part of the marketing campaign. Top: The original Italian release in 1964. Bottom: The British re-release in 1972 gave Sean Connery top billing according to his contract. Copyright © 2002 by Universal City Studios, Inc. Courtesy of Universal Studios Publishing Rights. All rights reserved.

Tippi Hedren in Cleveland on a ten-day promotional tour of *Marnie* in the United States. On display is the original poster for the American release. Copyright © 2002 by Universal City Studios, Inc. Courtesy of Universal Studios Publishing Rights. All rights reserved.

Hitchcock and his wife, Alma, returning from their European vacation on board SS *France*. Copyright © 2002 by Universal City Studios, Inc. Courtesy of Universal Studios Publishing Rights. All rights reserved.

June 18th, 1962

Dear Hitch –

It was heart-breaking for me to have to leave the picture – I was so excited about doing it and particularly about working with you again –

When we meet I would like to explain to you myself all of the reasons which is difficult to do by letter or through a third party. It is unfortunate that it had to happen this way and I am deeply sorry — Thank you dear Hitch – for being so understanding and helpful — I hate disappointing you — I also hate the fact that there are probably many other "cattle" who could play the part equally as well — Despite that I hope to remain one of your "sacred cows" —

with deep affection –
Grace —

Top: Handwritten letter from Grace Kelly to Alfred Hitchcock explaining why she turned down the lead role in *Marnie*. Bottom: Hitchcock's reply to Grace Kelly after she declined the role. Copyright Alfred Hitchcock Collection, Academy of Motion Picture Arts and Sciences.

DRAFT

June 26, 1962

Dear Grace,

Yes, it was sad, wasn't it. I was looking forward so much to the fun and pleasure of our doing a picture again.

Without a doubt, I think you made, not only the best decision, but the only decision, to put the project aside at this time.

After all, it was only a movie. Alma joins me in sending our most fondest and affectionate thoughts for you.

P.S. I have enclosed a small tape recording which I have made especially for Rainier. Please ask him to play it privately. It is not for all ears.

## Chapter Nine

# A Woman's Voice

I think he wanted a woman's voice on *Marnie*, which is why he hired me.

—Jay Presson Allen

*Marnie* has been described as a film obsessed with the woman's voice, and fifty years after its release, that voice still creates controversy, making it one of Hitchcock's most widely misunderstood and maligned films. The recent biographical assessments and dramatization in the media have accused Hitchcock of misogyny and sadism and *Marnie* is more often than not cited as evidence for both, especially in its depiction of marital rape and female entrapment. In particular there is an uneasiness about the character of Mark Rutland and the film's supposed simplistic assumption that a woman can be cured of her frigidity through marital rape.

This chapter examines the two determining influences in the evolution of the *Marnie* story and screenplay, which may account for these conflicting interpretations. Firstly, the empathy with the woman's position of Winston Graham, who described himself as an "instinctive feminist," and secondly the female perspective of screenwriter Jay Presson Allen, who was hired by Hitchcock because he thought she'd bring a "woman's voice" to the picture.

When Graham and Allen were interviewed between 1998 and 2001 for the first edition of this book, they were friendly, supportive, but still essentially private about specific aspects of their personality and family background and how that may have shaped the *Marnie* text. The biographical information they volunteered was circumspect and unrevealing, and it was not until after their deaths, Graham's in 2003 and Allen's in 2006, that parallels could be directly related to the *Marnie* text. Graham's autobiography *Memoirs of a Private Man* was published posthumously in 2003, and the very title suggests an author who was reluctant to give interviews during his lifetime and who shied away from publicity. Graham will always be remembered for the twelve Poldark novels he wrote, with his novel *Marnie* coming second, chiefly because of Hitchcock's adaptation.

After Jay Presson Allen died in 2006, her daughter, Brooke Allen, bequeathed her mother's files, and those of her father's, film and theater producer Lewis Allen, to the Harry Ransom Center, University of Texas at Austin. These files cover a period from 1960 to 1990, including the years when *Marnie* and *Mary Rose* were written. While it would seem that both Graham and Allen did indeed sympathize with the Marnie character, new biographical information on both author and screenwriter suggest neither were "feminists" in the true sense of the word. This data is indeed revealing; it adds to and interprets the characters in both source novel and screenplay, accounting for the conflicting interpretations and multivocality of the *Marnie* text.


## WINSTON GRAHAM


When questioned about his position about the abjection of women in society, Winston Graham described himself as an "instinctive feminist." The roots of his feminism can be traced back to his childhood, early in the twentieth century. Graham was born in Victoria Park, Manchester, in 1908, six years before the start of the First World War. He already had a brother, Cecil, who was ten years older. Graham's mother, Anne Mawdsley, wanted him to be a girl, so she mollycoddled him as a child. He wrote in his autobiography, "Many years later it dawned on me, looking back over the evidence, that my mother badly wanted a girl when I was born, and although she mostly disguised her feelings she would dearly have loved to dress me up in buttons and bows."[1]

Because of the age difference between his brother Cecil and himself, Graham was in effect brought up as an only child. When it turned out that he was "delicate" of health, unlike his older brother, his mother used that as an excuse to channel her mixed feelings on wanting him to be a girl by lavishing him with excessive attention and spoiling him, even to the point of delaying his schooling until he was seven. This may account for Graham's feminine roots and empathy with the woman's position.

"The image my father liked to present of himself was that of a frail child," says son Andrew Graham.[2] But the reality was Graham was in relatively good health for most of his life and indeed lived until the age of ninety-five. His son believes that he cleverly used his appearance and claims of fragility so that not only was he spoiled by his mother, but later in life, he often pretended to be weak so women would look after him or conduct chores on his behalf.[3]

Graham's mother, Anne, also had the reputation of being delicate. Before she married Graham's father, her mother told him that they could never have children, saying that Anne was too delicate. In reality she lived to the age of eighty and produced two sons, whose longevity exceeded hers.

The Graham family never adopted a scientific approach to medicine and remained fearful of ill health. Just before Graham's fourteenth birthday, he became seriously ill with pneumonia; his mother also contracted double pneumonia and nearly died. Graham remembers being sent to the cinema one night when she was gravely ill.[4] When Graham was sixteen, he contracted pneumonia again, and his own life too was in jeopardy. He also had a weak heart and, when enlisting for service, was turned down by the air force, army, and navy for medical reasons. "When it came time for me to register I chose what I thought the least uncivilized of the three services, which was the navy," remembers Graham. But he failed the medical and was passed from the navy to the army. The army too turned him down, so he applied for the coastguard service and was accepted in 1940.

Although the character of Marnie is the product of an overtly religious up-bringing at the hands of her mother, Graham's family was not religious. As he mentions in his memoirs, "Were we God-fearing? Not really. My mother kept steadily, if quietly to her beliefs all her life, but her father was very much a free-thinker and associated with atheists and agnostics."[5] Graham shied away from overt religion and would only go to church twice a year with his mother. But he used his knowledge to create the character of Mrs. Elmer, Marnie's zealously religious mother in the novel. The girl Christine, his childrens' babysitter, also believed in her faith. "It came from Christine, because her mother was religious at the time," said Graham. "I transferred my sympathies to her, and anything religious came from the person that I was writing about."

As already mentioned in chapter 1, after Graham's father died, his mother supported him in his writing career. "When my father died I was nineteen and my mother knew there was only one thing I wanted to do in life, and as she could just afford to support me if I lived at home, she offered to do so," says Graham. "I never earned a living any other way." His mother was depicted as being frail and of ill health, but in reality she was a very strong character, a proper Victorian lady, who told him frightening stories as a child. "She loved to make your flesh creep—and God, did she not make mine! It was not of ghosts of which she spoke but of ill-health." She spoke about her cousin Ernest who contracted pneumonia and was dead within a week, and of other relatives who similarly died young, scaring the young Winston with tales of illness and disease.

Andrew Graham believes that his father's fear of ill health, compounded by his own mother's, enabled him to write about Marnie's fear of sex. A grave fear of bad health and dying is therefore equated with a great fear of sex. In the free-association scene, when Mark offers the word "death," Marnie's reply is "me." On the origins of the character Marnie, Andrew Graham says that while Christine the babysitter and the other women in the newspaper articles undoubtedly helped his father start the process of creating *Marnie*, "the ideas that come from them are just the start and not more than that. My father believed passionately that characters have to come alive and live in the author's imagination if they are to have conviction. Further, I suspect that my father did not have a huge problem in working on Marnie's introspection. My father's elder brother was ten years older and so my father was brought up almost as an only child. What is more his mother 'molly-coddled' him and gave him a fear of ill-health and I think he used this to find his way into Marnie's fears about sex."[6]

Graham himself acknowledged, "I'm a novelist and I like to create characters sympathetically, and I don't really use characters to make a point of my own." The characters in *Marnie* were those he identified with, such as Marnie's view of sex equated with his fear of illness. He was definitely writing from Marnie's point of view during the rape scene, as he was writing in the first person. "All the time you were seeing Mark more or less through her eyeline," said Graham. "That's one of the problems in writing from the first person." The reader was seeing Mark Rutland from the neurotic standpoint of Marnie. And Graham firmly believed that Mark was a straightforward stationer with none of the fetishism and hang-ups that Hitchcock gave him.

Among the other characters in the story, for example, Graham described the character of Terry Holbrook as a necessary one, "Where I thought about him, I think I got him from a man I knew in London, and he was exactly as I described him in the book, fond of pretty women and fond of enjoying himself, and the sort of person who would make up to Marnie." Graham said that he was always more interested in other people than himself when writing characters, though there was something of himself in every character he created else they would not come alive.

"I'm absolutely fascinated with human beings, even when they are horrible. I'm fascinated and that takes priority over everything else," said Graham. He wasn't familiar, for example, with the world of fox hunting or the upper-class milieu of the Rutlands. "I'm fairly genteel but never had anything to do with fox hunting. I've never chased a fox in my life or killed an animal if I could help it." What is evident is that Graham never created a character based solely on his own imagination but always tried to find something within him to help him formulate that character.

Graham also had a couple of chips on his shoulder. Because he had come from a non-intellectual background and had never gone to university, he felt both class-conscious and that he had missed out on a proper education. His background was not as desirable as he may have liked—he described his family as "semi genteel, middle-middle class, rather modest and retiring but with an underlying sense of position,"[7] as his maternal grandfather was a wholesale grocer in Manchester. But with that experience he was able to infuse Marnie's hang-ups about social class and her elevation from the slums of Plymouth to the gentrified world of the Rutlands. In later life, Graham may have compensated his earlier upbringing, for example, by going to exclusive gentlemen's clubs, such as the Savile Club and Blacks, and cultivating a genteel lifestyle in London.

By 1939, Graham was thirty-one years old and very eligible for work. When he became successful as a writer, he liked to describe himself as the "most successful unknown author in Britain." It was a part of an image he liked to project and cultivate, and there was some underlying truth to the role he played. He wrote his first Poldark novel, *Ross Poldark*, in 1945, which quickly became a Book Society Recommendation. This was followed by *Demelza* in 1946. Up until 1948, when the Poldark novels became a success, Graham was writing a succession of novels but making little money. Living in Cornwall, he would write books to order, for example he wrote *Cordelia* in 1949 for the book of the month club, and gained good income from its American sales. It sold well in 1949, but until the Poldark series no-one knew who Graham was as an author. Soon three-quarters of his income would come from the American sales of his books. Later, when *Marnie* hit the headlines in 1962, Graham remarked to the press, "I was the most successful unknown novelist in England."

Despite the considerable sales of the Poldark novels, Graham still questioned his success as a literary author. In his mind, he didn't sell very well; as an author he was neither the intellectual type nor did he write blockbusters. He wrote in his memoirs, "I am, I suppose, what is generally called a popular novelist."[8] But in Andrew Graham's estimation, the books on Cornwall are far better than their Daphne du Maurier equivalents such as *Jamaica Inn* (1936) on smuggling. Unlike du Maurier, who came from a more upper class background—her father was Gerald du Maurier, an actor and theatre manager, and her grandfather George du Maurier, the cartoonist for *Punch* magazine—Graham was more middle-class. Whereas Daphne du Maurier's writings are solidly upper-middle-class, Graham—coming from a lower-class background—was able to write an authentic glimpse of what life must have been really like in the Cornwall of the late eighteenth and early nineteenth centuries. In his first four Poldark novels, he writes evocatively of resilient tin miners, rough squires, and famished laborers, all struggling to survive in the harsh Cornish landscape. It was with this class consciousness that Graham was also able to write *Marnie*.

"I automatically became part of Marnie," said Winston Graham. "With any luck, I saw she did have a happy ending. I tried to imply at the end of the book that she had now come around and felt about Mark." Foremost a storyteller, a skill which he developed from childhood, Graham was a novelist rather than an intellectual. He was always putting some of himself in the story. Graham described himself as "very young—younger than my years—in spite of having been a professional writer so long; and I was too romantic. My approach to women was too romantic—it still is—but it was by then a part of my nature and was too inbred to be changed."

The director Sandy Mackendrick, who Graham met at the Savile Club, who would go on to make the hit film *The Sweet Smell of Success* (1957), once said to Graham, "Do you know, Winston, your characters are always particularly good, attractive, intelligent, they are real people, real women, with real emotion. But they are all what I might call white ladies, people who embody the right side of life. Have you ever thought of writing a book about a grey lady, one who is maybe a transgressor of some sort?" This Graham says, may have contributed to the genesis of *Marnie*.

Despite Winston Graham's claims to be a feminist, albeit an instinctive one, his son Andrew believes that his father wouldn't understand what being a genuine feminist really was. "He may have been sympathetic to a feminine view of the world. But in terms of his women having rights, few of his characters did, apart from Demelza Carne (the servant girl in the Poldark novels), who was feisty," says Andrew Graham. Graham himself said, "I may be an instinctive feminist, not that I believe in holding banners or anything, because a number of feminists I've met have been perfectly awful."

Also Graham had no view of women running companies, and being a member of Blacks, the gentleman's club in Soho, could be perceived to have an antiquated view of same-sex establishments. He didn't believe that women should go to work, and indeed he didn't want his wife Jean to do so. His daughter-in-law, Peggotty Graham, who has read most of his books, has the opinion that his portrayal of women is unconvincing. "He had a very old fashioned view of women," said Peggotty. "He was no more of an instinctive feminist for someone of his time. I wouldn't have thought he understood what feminism was. Maybe outwardly he thought he was an instinctive feminist, but inwardly he wasn't. I agree with Andrew's [Graham] view; he liked to think he was a feminist, but he wasn't. He liked women, and wasn't a misogynist or anything like that. But he didn't want his wife to work, although they did run a bed and breakfast when they first moved to Perranporth."[9]

Winston Graham may have been sympathetic toward women, but he can not have had direct experience with their objectification in patriarchal society. Although he may have used his own fears of illness to equate with Marnie's fear of sex, could he ever be truly sympathetic or understanding of the prejudices faced by women when he himself had no direct comparison? Indeed he started writing *Marnie* in the first person and then switched because the identification of "He kissed me" seemed awkward from a male point of view. If Graham wasn't a feminist in the true sense of the word, that could explain the conflicting interpretations in the *Marnie* text, and the identification with the Mark Rutland character. As a man, it's debatable whether he could really know what it was like to be a woman faced with sexual harassment or unwanted attention in a patriarchal society.

## JAY PRESSON ALLEN

When Hitchcock hired Jay Presson Allen to take over from Evan Hunter, he wanted a woman's voice to infuse the screenplay. Jacqueline Presson was born to parents Albert Jack Presson and May "Bill" Presson from San Angelo, Texas. Allen's mother's side of the family was German, and came to America in the nineteenth century, while her father's side came from England. They settled in Texas in the years after the American Civil War, mainly because the wide-open space afforded opportunities for ranching.

As a child, Allen and her family moved to San Angelo, where her father ran a department store named Barnes & Co. Her mother later took a job working in the haberdashery section of the store. Allen enjoyed a good upbringing in a frontier town and her parents gave her lots of freedom. It was a safe environment to run free and she had a wonderful childhood. The family were animal lovers and raised cats as pets. Allen also kept creatures like harmless snakes and horned toads in jars, and would later develop these instincts about animal behavior in her work, especially in *Marnie*, making Mark Rutland a zoologist and infusing the narrative with studies of instinctual behavior about two very interesting human specimens.

When Allen was young, her parents all but adopted one of her younger cousins, a pretty, doll-like girl named Janet Stanlind, daughter of an aunt from her mother's side of the family. She had curly golden hair and looked like she was from the Shirley Temple era. "I can imagine my grandmother fussing over her and my mother seething," says daughter Brooke Allen. This she believes forms the basis of the little girl Jessie being fussed over by Marnie's mother Bernice (originally named Jessie in Jay's first-draft screenplay). Art came to imitate life as Jay's mother lavished attention over Janet Stanlind, the pretty doll-like niece, and Jay raged over the fuss being made. "The character of Bernice, as interpreted by [Louise Latham], always struck me as a rather subtle swipe at Jay's mother," says Brooke. "So much of Jay's life was in *Marnie*, and it's so obvious when you watch the movie."[10] Although the character of Marnie's mother was nothing like Allen's own mother, she did sound exactly like her, and the patterns of speech and tone of her voice were very similar to hers.

Jay Allen, like Marnie, was an only child, and as a young girl, she would spend all day every Saturday and Sunday in the local movie house, until she had to be dragged out at seven o'clock in the evening. Favorite films included Van Dyke's *The Thin Man* (1934), but she was comprehensive in her taste for all movie genres, and enjoyed screwball comedies, musicals, and thrillers. William Powell, Myrna Loy, Cary Grant, and Katharine Hepburn were some of Allen's favorite film stars and she wanted to become an actress from an early age.

Edward Harte was a close friend of Allen's in public school in San Angelo. He later became the board chair of the National Audubon Society, was an ardent conservationist, and played an important role in preserving vast tracts of open space and stretches of seashore in the state. He was also co-founder of the Harte-Hanks Newspapers in Texas. His daughter Julia became Allen's goddaughter, and Brooke was his goddaughter. But it was when Allen started at Mrs. Hockaday's preparatory school for young ladies in Dallas that she would meet another lifelong friend, who would also play a part in the *Marnie* story.

Louise "Nonnie" Latham grew up in frontier country, and like Allen was from a Texan ranch. She came from San Saba, close to Allen's own home-town, and she too was an only child. "I created diversions like Jay, and always had a vivid imagination in the era of ranching country," remembers Latham in 2012. Allen and Latham immediately liked each other. "Some people are just attracted to each other and we became good friends," remembers Latham. "Jay and I were out-of-towners in that prep school and we bonded together." Latham also remembers how clever Allen was and she was always top of her class. "I remember we had a particularly tough English teacher and Jay was the smartest person in the room," remembers Latham. Both of them enjoyed films and plays, and the two of them relished going to performances together. "I remember coming back from the movies one evening and we were still nattering about what we had just seen," says Latham.

Both Allen and Latham wanted to become actresses and go to the big city, New York, and work in the theater. Going to college wasn't necessarily the thing to do at that time, so they both skipped college, and at the age of eighteen went to New York. Here they joined a theater touring company, which actresses often did to break into show business. But Allen was not happy in the long run being an actress, and thought she may have taken the easy way out. "Within ten days I realized it was a terrible mistake," she said. "The lifestyle was a shock to me, and I was totally unfitted for the work. I loved rehearsing, but I hated performing."[11] Instead she turned her hand to writing and enjoyed success with dramatic television shows such as *Playhouse 90* for CBS and *Philco Playhouse* for NBC.

Just like Marnie's eagerness to escape from her poverty-stricken background in Baltimore and her mother's slum home, Allen may have had a "real eagerness to get out of the stultifying small town, just like Marnie, and see the world." So Allen used that aspect of her life to relate to Marnie, who wanted to experience the finer things. In New York, Allen and Latham kept in touch off and on and would sometimes run into each other. "I stayed in New York to train as an actress and work on projects," says Latham. It's not surprising then that Allen would turn to her childhood friend when Hitchcock was looking for someone to play the part of Bernice Edgar. She had to be gritty, tough, and real. Even though Latham came from an upper-class background compared to the character of Bernice, Allen knew that she had knowledge of hard-luck women and knew how to play them. She would also later acquire or maybe reacquire the same Southern accent for her role in the film.

It was while in New York that Allen met her first husband. "I married the first grown man who asked me," she remembers.[12] She moved to California during the Second World War and lived in a small academic town called Claremont. She also landed roles in a couple of B movies for Republic Pictures, and wrote her first novel, *Spring Riot*, published in 1948. The story was autobiographical and about her experience in the movie business, and she used it to write her way out of her first marriage. Later Hitchcock read the book, saw that Allen had a knack for dialogue, and got in touch with her. Allen herself was a voracious reader, but scorned academics and intellectuals.

"There was that period after World War II and coming out of the fifties where women were supposed to be in the kitchen or doing their nails," she remembered. "There was a sense of psychological and even physical weakness about women—and therefore executives and directors maybe felt it would not be suitable to grind a woman writer down the way they would another man. It's not a business for sensitive souls. I think the minute they figured you weren't going to cry, you were on track."[13]

When Allen returned to New York, she wrote a play, *Stars in a Person's Backyard*, which never made it to the stage. She had no better luck with her next effort, a comedy called *The First Wife*, in her attempts to produce the show on Broadway. But the rights were purchased by producer Hal Wallis, who turned the comedy into the 1963 film *Wives and Lovers*, with Edward Anhalt writing the screenplay. Allen's play was optioned by theater producer Bob Whitehead, who she had sought out because he had produced a play called *Member of the Wedding*, which she loved. Most importantly, it was through Whitehead that Jay met her second husband, Lewis Maitland Allen, at a party in 1954. She approached him and he immediately enjoyed her bossy, dominatrix side. They went on a date to a stage club and both fell asleep during the first act—from that moment on, they knew they had something in common.

Born in 1922, Lewis Allen grew up in Berryville, Virginia, where his well-to-do family had a long line of descendants. Allen's father was a doctor, and head of the hospital in Winchester, and his brother Howard Allen lived in nearby Middleburg (as of 2013, he still lives there, age 93). In 1945, Allen graduated from the University of Virginia in Charlottesville, where he majored in history, and went to New York, where he became a theater producer.

When Jay Presson went with Lewis to meet the well-to-do Allen family in Virginia, it was like the scene from *Marnie* when Mark brings Marnie home to meet Rutland senior. In fact the scenes where Marnie visits Wyckwyn, the Rutland home, are exactly what Jay went through when she first met Allen's family, an experience she liked to describe in great detail and with much laughter later—the Texan girl visiting the American aristocrats. Just like Lil interrogates Marnie over afternoon tea, a great aunt put Jay through her paces. But Jay was able to hold her own and she and the aunt became great friends for the rest of their lives. So the scenes of Marnie going to meet the Pennsylvania gentry are straight out of Jay's own autobiography.

There were also strong similarities between Mark Rutland and the Rutlands and Lewis Allen and his family. "My father was, as Jay describes Mark, 'an extremely well-bred man from a Virginian family who had a dark streak. He was also a very good man,'" says daughter Brooke. Lewis Allen was a kind man, and never raised his voice. But his dark streak came more from having a cynical view of the world, which is rather like that of Mark Rutland when he says to Marnie, "Nothing ever happens to a family that traditionally marries at least one heiress every other generation."

"Lewis was heaven," remembers Gabrielle Kelly, who worked as an assistant to Jay Presson Allen and Sidney Lumet in their Warner Brothers Company "Screenplay Productions." "He was the perfect foil for Jay, always very gracious, polite, and very much the Southern gentleman. He was funny, wry and brilliant." The Allens lived in Central Park West and Lewis had an office on 1 West Seventy-second street. He went on to produce the stage play *Annie*, which opened in 1977 and ran for six years. Allen won a Tony award for it and for two other plays he produced: Herb Gardner's *I'm Not Rappaport* (1986) and Terrence McNally's *Master Class* (1996). He also produced several films, including François Truffaut's *Farenheit 451* (1966) and both the 1963 and 1990 versions of *Lord of the Flies*.

With much in common, Lewis and Jay married in 1955 and their only child Brooke was born in 1956. They moved to the countryside, where Lewis wrote and Jay raised Brooke spending two and a half "absolutely wonderful years in the country" doing absolutely nothing but looking after her young daughter. Lewis and Jay were also both Democrats; "Yellow dog Democrats—never voted for Republican," says Brooke. Jay Allen uses this similarity in lines that were dropped from the *Marnie* screenplay, when Mark's father says that Mark went to Columbia University, whereupon Lil adds that he is "a registered Democrat."

When Jay returned to work, producer and friend Bob Whitehead encouraged her to write more plays, which she did; she wrote *The First Wife* and *The Prime of Miss Jean Brodie*. After Hitchcock picked up a pre-production copy of the latter play, he invited Jay to his Santa Cruz home to talk about *Marnie*. On Wednesday, May 29, 1963, Allen flew from New York to San Francisco and was driven to Santa Cruz. Hitchcock immediately liked Jay and most importantly the two just clicked. "Her brain was so fascinating, so quick and so aware, it enchanted Hitchcock—and she was good looking," said Louise Latham. Allen stayed for a couple of days at Hitchcock's house and then returned to New York on May 31. She then traveled to LA a couple of days later to begin story conferences on *Marnie*. A fourth-floor poolside suite was reserved for her at the Sportsmen's Lodge on 12825 Ventura Boulevard for six weeks from June 3, 1963, throughout which she was very busy writing *Marnie*. Allen also disliked the solitude of writing, finding it nerve wracking—she called writing a very lonely business and a divorcement from life. When starting on a script, Allen would write all day, until she was tired, sleep a little, and then write some more. But much of the time she found it excruciating and not enjoyable. "You're always in a rush," remarked the friendly receptionist at the hotel. "Ms. Allen, what do you do which makes you always in a hurry?" She probably didn't tell him she was working for the great Alfred Hitchcock.

That first week in LA, Allen stayed from June 3 to June 9, then went back home for five days. Hitchcock had a three month and one year subscription of the *London Observer* delivered to Allen and Peggy Robertson so that they could keep up with international news. On July 20, Allen went shopping in Beverly Hills to buy a present for her daughter Brooke's seventh birthday. There isn't anything particularly unusual about this except for the fact that the shopping trip resulted in a very amusing letter that is preserved among the archives held at the Hitchcock collection. Allen recounts her experiences to Hitchcock and his daughter Pat, and the witty letter demonstrates both her talent and her great ear and fondness for dialogue:

> This report, written in haste and hysteria, is addressed to anybody out there who has not yet succumbed and surrendered to the craziness of LA. This goes for

those of you who are as far north as Santa Barbara, even. Because, don't kid yourselves! It's not just Hollywood. . . . At home, in my own circle, I am considered a lazy, rather easy-going type; am acknowledged to have a fairly good sense of humour and a quick, superficial grasp of events. But I am categorized mentally as pretty light weight, I have accepted this judgement. It is, in that arena, a fair one. I am a little shaky to find that my rooms at the Sportsmen's Lodge are unquestionably a veritable olympus of intellectual fement, me. The pitiful truth is that these people are like collies. This whole city this vast reservoir of vacuity is for the birds . . . the ones that is coming. Get out before it's too late.

She signed the report "The Jaybird." Allen, always one to see the amusing side of life, and with the funny references to Hitchcock's previous film *The Birds*, had a quick-witted sense of humor and was soon adored by Hitchcock and his family. Very often she would stay with them rather than in the hotel. On Sunday, July 21, Allen returned to San Angelo, Texas, for one week to visit her parents. There they celebrated Brooke's seventh birthday together the following day with Lewis. Then Allen returned to work with Hitchcock on July 29. On August 8, Hitchcock signed his first will with Allen as a witness. Another memo on August 13 from Peggy Robertson to Price Waterhouse accounting shows that according to a contract dated June 27, 1963, $9,000 would be delivered to Jay upon delivery of the first-draft screenplay and that her checks would be paid to the William Morris Agency. By the end of September the first draft was complete.

Allen liked to write strong male characters as well as female ones; she did have a tendency to create compelling leading men, beginning with Mark Rutland in her first screenplay. "I think I have a particular strength with male characters," said Allen. "Male characters are easier to write. They're simpler. I think women are generally more psychologically complicated. You have to put a little more effort into writing a woman." In *Prince of the City* she created a complex role for Treat Williams as a narcotics detective investigating corruption in his department. "*Prince of the City* was about psychic violence," says Allen.[14] The character of Daniel Ciello (Treat Williams) was based on Robert Leuci, an NYPD narcotics detective, who became an advisor for Allen when she was working on the screenplay.

"She didn't pull any punches," remembers Bob Leuci in 2012 about working with Allen. "She quickly understood the complexities of the world of narcotics, and she was someone who had a clear view of her world and the world around her."[15] Leuci also said that Allen was very democratic and very liberal in her politics.

Some later reviewers would make a link between the character of Mark Rutland and John F. Kennedy. As already noted, JFK was the president of the United States when Allen was writing *Marnie* in the summer of 1963, and he was assassinated in Dallas on the very day that the film was to begin shooting. Did Jay Allen have Mark Rutland in mind when she wrote JFK? "I doubt she was inspired by JFK or any politician," says daughter Brooke. "She laughed about Kennedy being a womanizer, so I discount the theory that she was influenced by him." Jay and Lewis, however, did know Teddy Kennedy and were friends, as they often spent time together on Martha's Vineyard, where the Allens had a summer home since 1952.

Jay Allen's patrician taste and upper-class background also helped with the costuming in *Marnie*. She knew about Philadelphia mainline society, how they dressed and their social customs, even to the point of advising Edith Head, the costume designer, where to buy Lil's clothes, which needed to reflect "old money." On September 26, Allen wrote to Edith Head, suggesting that "The place to buy Lil's clothes is the 'Women's Haberdashery' which has two shops here on Madison Avenue and a branch in Philadelphia, where I believe, they started. These are semi custom, upper moderate priced clothes. They are very clean, undetailed, rather epicene day clothes—countryish. They carry sweaters, slacks, bags, everything for the girl who isn't quite a woman which is not to imply that they are dull or Peck & Peckish. The lines are excellent and very flattering to slender figures. As to Lil's evening dress, we are in great luck this season with the separates. I should think she would wear quite a good looking blouse and skirt in the old Lauren Bacall tradition. These are available in every good store in town, both here and on the coast. It was such a pleasure talking to you and so comforting to me—whose clothes prejudices can best be described as violent—to know that you are doing *Marnie*'s wardrobe." Jay herself loved to walk up and down Madison Avenue and had very elegant taste, which colleagues would remark upon. Her apartment was also very tastefully decorated with contemporary and luxurious furnishings.

By early October, a third-draft script of *Marnie* had been written. From October 5–11, Hitchcock went to New York for script conferences. Brooke Allen remembers meeting Hitchcock: "I was seven years old at the time, my parents didn't take me to California very often, but I do remember dining with Hitchcock. He was wonderful with children. All the direction he used was good with children because he was used to dealing with actors. He was lovely and wrote in my books, and would give me ghost and mystery stories." When asked about how he was with his own three granddaughters, Jay Allen also agreed, "He was very good with children."

When *Marnie* started rolling for the cameras, Jay Allen and her family took a two-month vacation in Africa. Brooke was taken out of school to join her mother and father on an exciting family adventure. They had never been to Africa before and traveled all over Egypt, Ethiopia, and Kenya. The three spent Christmas 1963 at the Mount Kenya Safari Club, where Jay wrote a letter to Hitchcock, who was in the midst of filming. "It was an exciting holiday," remembers Brooke. "It was very dramatic and I have vague memories." Later Allen would write *The Tsavo Story* in the 1970s, about conservationist Daphne Sheldrick, and from that story developed a friendship.

The Allens traveled back to the United States via London in early 1964 and Jay started writing an adaptation of J. M. Barrie's *Mary Rose* for Hitchcock. On Tuesday, January 14, 1964, Jay wrote to Hitchcock from the Dorchester Park Lane hotel in London: "I am absolutely beset with curiosity about *Marnie*. I saw *From Russia with Love* and detected faint signs of acting talent in the Connery and got all excited again." The second James Bond movie had been released in the UK in October 1963—it reached number 1 at the UK box office—before it was released in the United States in April 1964.

Allen then flew on Monday, January 27, to LA for further script consultations on *Marnie*. By this time Hitchcock and his crew were three-quarters of the way through filming and some of the biggest scenes were still to come, including Marnie's mother and the flashbacks. It was during this week that Tippi Hedren had her big row with Hitchcock over attending the Photoplay award. On one occasion, Hedren came to speak to Allen about the tensions on the set and Allen advised her to "finish the picture, get on with your life, and be happy." Her good friend Louise Latham had also just started in the role of Bernice Edgar and was to begin filming that week.

After the week's script revisions, on Monday, February 3, Allen flew to Brownwood, Texas, to see her father, Albert Jack Presson, for approximately two weeks. While Hitchcock was finishing *Marnie*, Allen then returned to New York to continue writing *Mary Rose*. On February 23, 1964, she wrote a letter to Hitch. "I do love you, you pathologically greedy-compulsively generous old thing. . . . You are a lousy correspondent and never even send a mildly dirty postcard flying my way. You know I am consumed with curiosity about the flick and the folks involved. I am 3,000 miles away damn it!" It was evident that Allen, the facile writer, was the better correspondent, whereas the taciturn Hitchcock was preoccupied in finishing *Marnie*.

After filming was finally completed, on March 23, Jay flew from New York to LA and stayed at the Beverly Hills hotel for four days to view *Marnie* with the Hitchcocks. She made copious editing notes and, very rare for a writer, was allowed to have her say. This aptly demonstrates how close their relationship was, as Hitchcock allowed her, along with Alma, to have input in the editing process. Jay's comments on March 24, 1964:

1. Shipboard prerape Marnie's "No" when Mark strips her clothes off should be looped with a real scream. Her line, "I Can't I Can't I Can't," should be looped with the highest scream that she can give at this point.

2. Tippi's reading of the line, "I supposed I would become a society hostess" is much too straight. It sounds serious and ridiculous. It should be read with humor and sarcasm.
3. Fattid bug sequence.
4. The kiss in the storm in the sequence in Mark's office should be cut (although I think it would be useful in the trailer).
5. Return to Wykwyn after the honeymoon—cut Mark's smile when the door is closed in his face.
6. Cut the stable scene between Marnie and Lil.
7. Cut mounting the horse after Marnie shoots Forio and go straight to bringing her into Wykwyn hallway.
8. In the last Bernice sequence after the flashback, is there an alternate take or another angle of Mark maneuvering Marnie to the seat opposite her mother? The actual movement from the stair to the seat seems very mechanical. I feel it would be better to have close ups here, particularly since he's saying "You're all right."
9. In the tea-party sequence, extend Mr. Rutland's speech "Shouldn't think you'd find old Mark very interesting. Doesn't hunt, doesn't even ride, sheer affectation."
10. Would still like to see more of Cousin Bob for fun and sense.

Allen's notes, like Alma, agreed that the stable scene between Marnie and Lil should be cut because it did nothing to advance the story. However her suggestion to cut the kiss in Mark's office after the thunderstorm was not adhered to by Hitchcock. Allen's first two editing comments acknowledge Hedren's inability to register vocal terror or sarcasm, highlighting what Allen perceived as her limited range as an actress. In the case of the scream, Hedren's voice had to be dubbed with a more highly charged scream.

Allen obviously contributed enormously to the *Marnie* screenplay. She and Hitchcock departed radically from the structure of Winston Graham's novel, discarding the Terry Holbrook character and adding Lil, increasing the part of Mark Rutland to accommodate Sean Connery's star billing (as per his agent's request), making the character a zoologist, and infusing the screenplay with the themes of hunter and hunted animal.

Given that Allen wasn't a feminist, what attributes did she then bring to the *Marnie* screenplay? Certainly her familiarity with Virginia and Pennsylvania mainline society was very autobiographical in the screenplay, including Marnie's sudden initiation into a rarefied world reflecting her own with Lewis Allen's family. Though Allen's background was an upper-class one, whereas Marnie's was lower-class Baltimore slum. Allen and Marnie were both from the South, and Allen also liked working on productions that included children. "My parents used to wonder, laughingly, why they were always involved with children when dealing with showbiz children and their parents is not always easy or rewarding," remembers Brooke. "My father produced the original *Annie* on Broadway. He also produced the original *Lord of the Flies* in 1961. Jay was very much involved with this film; it was shot on Vieques and the boys lived in a sort of tented camp with various young men who were supposed to keep them in line but were always quitting as the boys were so naughty. My mother and another wife had the unenviable task of periodically going to the mainland to round up more suckers for the job."

"I love writing children. Because they're fun," acknowledged Allen. "It's almost impossible to write a dull kid. Writing children?—that's an only-child syndrome. I'm an only child, I have an only child. Only children think a lot about their childhood, and it maintains interest. In any case, I find itty-bitty babies the most riveting things on earth. They are little learning machines, and there's a kind of violence in their madness to take everything in. Children are fascinating. It's exciting to be around them. Exhausting but exciting."

Aside from identifying with Marnie, did Jay bring a feminist slant to the story? And if so, what was Jay's relationship like with other women? In 1979, Gabrielle Kelly was a young graduate, who started working for Allen as her assistant. Kelly was born in Ireland, and following a career in book publishing in New York, she worked with director Sidney Lumet and Allen on films such as *Just Tell Me What You Want* (1980), *Prince of the City* (1981), and *Deathtrap* (1982).

"She was formidable, inspiring to a young woman starting out in the business and terrifying," says Kelly about working with Allen. "Staggeringly intelligent, very Texan, great fun and had great taste. I remember when I went for my job interview, Jay had some small strips of paint on the table labeled with different names. She took away the labels and asked me to identify the paint colors by name. No one has ever done that to me before or since during an interview."[16]

Allen's Park Avenue apartment was very tastefully decorated, as was the blue note paper with her name printed at the top. "I once said to her, 'You have a great name,'" says Kelly. "She said, 'Of course, you don't think it happened by accident, do you?'" Her name made everyone think she was a man, and they were always surprised when they met her in person, which gave Allen the advantage. "I remember she said to me, 'Don't cry, this isn't a woman's world in business, people will hold it against you, if you must cry go to the bathroom," remembers Kelly. "She also said I have no time to tell you anything." Allen expected Kelly to learn fast and on the job. With her you had to keep up or get out.

She was always chiding Lewis, too, but loved him dearly. Kelly also remembers that Allen was very close to Hitchcock, and that they were real friends, she'd write him funny notes. "She'd say to me, 'Get Hitch on the phone, will you?' So I would call him and keep him entertained until Jay was ready if she was tied up on another call. She always wanted to talk to him though, they were kindred spirits."

During the 1970s, Allen worked with some of the biggest female stars in the entertainment industry, including Ali MacGraw, Liza Minnelli, and Barbra Streisand. Screenplays by Allen won Oscars for Maggie Smith in *The Prime of Miss Jean Brodie* (1969), creating a sympathetic portrait of a three-dimensional woman, and for Liza Minnelli in *Cabaret* (1972), one of American cinema's greatest roles for women, in her portrayal of a bohemian club performer. These works made Allen one of the five most important screenwriters working in the United States. Noted for her powers of adaptation, Allen's work has been compared to the female creations of Bergman and Antonioni of the same period.

Allen was also able to separate personality from talent. She worked with Barbra Streisand for the 1975 film *Funny Lady*, which was a follow up to *Funny Girl*. "Streisand liked Jay, and when she came into the office, it was a huge deal, she was such a big star," remembers Gabrielle Kelly, while acknowledging her formidable personality. Allen later worked with director Sidney Lumet in the film adaptation of her novel, *Just Tell Me What You Want* (1980), as she had always wanted to work with him. When Lumet cast Ali MacGraw in the part of Bones, she had just ended a six-year marriage to Steve McQueen. A Wellesley graduate, MacGraw had impeccable taste and style, which Allen both admired and shared. "Jay was crazy about Ali as a woman who was from East Coast blue stock," says Kelly. "She really adored her. Ali was very similar to Jay, both intelligent and with great taste."

"My mother was great friends with Ali MacGraw," affirms daughter Brooke. "She thought that [in *Just Tell Me What You Want*] it might be Ali's best performance. She was a good comedian in it, and had personality and talent. She loved Ali, who's a really smart woman and lovely." In an interview MacGraw reciprocated the feelings: "I met [Jay] for another project that didn't materialize and I loved her. She was smart and funny and had great, great taste and education. She was someone I came to be very crazy about."[17] MacGraw also says that she was privileged to work with a woman with the "a level of experience and clout and wild sense of humor," which Jay had.

In the same way that Hitchcock said "All actors are cattle," Jay Allen once said that "I've never met an actor with an IQ more than 90." She was ferociously intelligent, devastatingly articulate and witty and 98 percent of people who interacted with Allen weren't up to her intellect, as they were constantly being humiliated in her presence. Someone like Hitch, who was on her intellectual level, was a tremendous joy and relief, which is why they became such good friends. "We laughed a lot," said Allen. Together they would play jokes on Lew Wasserman when he came to see them in Hitchcock's office.

Allen would pretend to type in the corner while Hitch spun a tale about how well the screenplay was progressing, when in reality the two of them had been playing.

However, Allen's intelligence may have been intimidating for some people. "She could scare the life out of you and humiliate you in two seconds flat," says Bob Leuci on his time with Allen on *Prince of the City*. "But she could identify with all POVs; that was one of her greatest talents. She was the most impressive lady I've ever met."

Sean Connery remarked in a BBC interview that he thought Jay put Tippi Hedren off a bit in preparing and playing the role.[18] Allen could have strong feelings for her female co-stars, as evidenced with MacGraw, but unfortunately she didn't have that same connection with Hedren. As she herself acknowledged, she may not have guided Hedren in making her character appear more vulnerable. Allen was never sympathetic toward the actress during conversations with this author and was fiercely protective of Hitchcock. She would say, "I never thought Tippi was vulnerable. She had a very brittle, edgy quality, which would have been quite marvelous in many things, and she certainly pulled it off in *The Birds*, but if you're playing someone who's a thief and a liar, you need a woman who's deeply vulnerable."

She also dismissed the rumors of Hitchcock's obsession over Hedren. To *Newsday* she said, "He was certainly having an old man's cri de coeur over Tippi, but the rest of the story is completely untrue. I was there every minute, and nothing like that happened."[19] And of Hedren she said, "[Hitchcock] was having trouble with Tippi and it stands to reason that he would give her an uneasy moment." But this was also coming from the writer who didn't see Mark Rutland's action as rape, unlike her predecessor Evan Hunter, and she even publicly criticized him for it. "I'm very fond of Evan, but I think he was psychologically a little niave. There's a vast audience of women out there who fantasize the idea of rape, as has been proved over and over and over again."[20]

Allen's reaction to Hedren may be of no surprise to those who knew her well. Her daughter Brooke said, "She probably thought that Tippi was over twenty-one and could take care of herself." She avowedly jeered feminists, never thought Hitchcock's behavior was harassment, and shared his sense of humor. This is evident in their mutual practical jokes at Lew Wasserman's expense. Allen would have lunch with Hitchcock and Wasserman three times a week. "The thing Hitch loved to do to discomfort Lew was to have me go into this little cubicle which I didn't use as an office and sit there and pretend to be writing and Hitch would be in there with me when Lew arrived to pick us up for lunch." The gag for Hitchcock was to see how long he could make Wasserman sit in that office, feeling discomfort every minute of it. Not very long was the answer.

Years later, Allen remained displeased with her first screenplay. When asked what she brought to *Marnie*, laughingly she said "Ignorance!" and "Ineptitude!" But *Marnie* remains the most fully autobiographical of Allen's scripts—maybe that's why she didn't like it? She was also a perfectionist and much about her earlier work did not come up to her standards as she gained experience. But there was so much more of Allen in *Marnie*, "the full 360 of her," as her daughter says, than in her other screenplays. First novels and first scripts are often very autobiographical, and maybe she didn't like *Marnie* because it revealed too much about herself. Allen also said that "My films play better on television because they are edited down," as being a playwright she tended to write long. "I remember once being at my mother's house in the 1970s and she said, 'Oh, *Marnie*'s on.'" I said, let's skip it. But we ended up watching it, and they had cut down the running time, maybe excising about thirty minutes off the running length, and I thought it played much better."

"I think my mother was genuinely dissatisfied with the quality of the script, but knew that it was an incredible opportunity to work with Hitchcock and have a big budget," says Brooke. "She didn't have a whole lot of experience in movies at the time." Brooke concluded that her mother's greatest achievement was *Cabaret* (1972), whereas Lewis's was *Fahrenheit 451* (1967).

## CONCLUSION

Winston Graham and Jay Presson Allen both brought tremendous amounts of their own personalities and influences to the *Marnie* text. Graham's fear of illness and ill health became equated with Marnie's fear of sex; and Jay Presson's initiation into the upper-class world of the Allens parallels that of Marnie's into the Rutlands. Being a woman, Allen had more direct experience with the psychological and physical pressures on women in the workplace than Graham. She also had knowledge of being discriminated against as a female in the movie business, and in the 1970s was only one of two screenwriters who had more than two films produced. But Allen was able to use any experience of discrimination and her own toughness to her benefit. She identified with Mark Rutland—through comparisons with her husband Lewis—which allowed her to be strongly sympathetic to the male point of view. This was also of benefit to Hitchcock, who was interested in the fetish aspect of Mark Rutland, and saw in Jay Allen a fellow genius. However, like Allen, Hitchcock was dissatisfied with the end result.

"I think the thing that didn't really come off in the picture was the fetish," said Hitchcock. "I wonder if it was clear to audiences. He wanted to go to bed with a thief, that was the essence of his fascination and determination with this good looking girl who was an expert thief. When she turns up in his office, his sights are set immediately. It's almost as if he would have liked to have had her sexually right during a robbery, by the safe, like necrophilia. He's damned unhealthy as a character."

Both Mark and Marnie are in need of cure. As Robin Wood famously said, "Marnie cures herself, using Mark as her instrument." When asked by Peter Bogdanovich, "Did they cure each other?" Hitchcock's reply was, "I feel eventually when they got the background of the girl, that gradually the fetish would die away and be taken over by a genuine relationship. The ambiguity was how long would it take to cure. She wasn't completely cured, in time he would wear her down. He might have gone to bed with her in the future with dollar bills stuck all over the bed and the floor."

## NOTES

1. Winston Graham, *Memoirs of a Private Man* (London: Macmillan, 2003), 17.

2. Interview with Andrew Graham, Corfu, August 25, 2012.

3. Interview with Andrew Graham, Corfu, August 25, 2012.

4. Graham, *Memoirs of a Private Man*, 31.

5. Graham, *Memoirs of a Private Man*, 11.

6. Interview with Andrew Graham, Oxford, England, March 8, 2012

7. Graham, *Memoirs of a Private Man*, 35.

8. Graham, *Memoirs of a Private Man*, 3.

9. Interview with Peggotty Graham, February 13, 2013, Oxford, England.

10. Interview with Brooke Allen, July 7, 2012, Connecticut.

11. Bob Thomas, "Ladies Win the Oscars (With Jay Allen's Help)," *Toledo Blade*, October 19, 1975.

12. Patrick McGilligan, "Backstory: Jay Presson Allen," 1986.

13. Jay Presson Allen, "She Made It," The Paley Center for Media.

14. Lynn Hoogenbook, "Jay Presson Allen Eschews Car Chases," *Prescott Courier*, July 1, 1988.

15. Interview with Bob Leuci, Rhode Island, January 27, 2013.

16. Interview with Gabrielle Kelly, Los Angeles, December 17, 2012.

17. Alonso Duralde, Ali MacGraw on "Just Tell Me What You Want," December 22, 2010.

18. Sean Connery to Barry Norman, *Film*, BBC documentary.

19. Randall Short, "Jay Presson Allen," *New York Newsday*, March 22, 1990.

20. Jay Presson Allen, in conversation with Richard Allen, Hitchcock Centennial, NYU, October 1999.

# Chapter Ten

# *Mary Rose*

A Ghost Story by Alfred Hitchcock, that'll get 'em.

—Alfred Hitchcock

The year 2014 not only marks fifty years since Alfred Hitchcock and Jay Presson Allen wrote a screenplay for *Mary Rose*, but also the one hundredth anniversary of the start of the First World War. Set in the aftermath of the war, *Mary Rose* is a portrait of a world changed, featuring characters deeply affected by loss. Hitchcock had a lifelong interest in plays, and an obsession with *Mary Rose*. When his official biographer John Russell Taylor asked Hitchcock if there was anything he regretted not having done, his answer was, "*Mary Rose*, which I really wanted to do, but they didn't want to let me. Do you know, it's written specifically into my present contract that I cannot do *Mary Rose*?"[1]

In the 1960s he commissioned a screenplay by Jay Presson Allen that opened up the play, making it more cinematic, but keeping much of the same dialogue. In his series of interviews with François Truffaut, Hitchcock also spoke nostalgically about Barrie's stage drama and joked that it must have been written into his contract with Universal Pictures that he could make any movie under $3 million, so long as it wasn't *Mary Rose*. Why did the play about a ghost hold such a magic spell on him? What was it that he saw in the play that made him want to adapt it into a film for the rest of his professional life? And how is *Mary Rose* connected to Hitchcock's masterpieces *Vertigo* and *Marnie*, two of his most intensely personal films? The seeds can be found in J. M. Barrie's adaptation, which is about longing, regret, and yearning.

## THE PLAYWRIGHT J. M. BARRIE

The Scottish playwright James Matthew Barrie was born in Kirremuir, Scotland, in 1860, the ninth child of David Barrie, a weaver, and Margaret Ogilvy. He had an older brother named David who was adored by his mother, but he was killed on the eve of his fourteenth birthday in a skating accident. The whole family was deeply affected. Barrie's mother would dress him up in his brother's clothes and he was mindful that he was a replacement son. Barrie was six at the time and the attempt for him to become a replacement for the lost son led to Barrie's own arrested development, sexually and psychologically. In 1894 Barrie married the actress Mary Ansell, but the marriage remained unconsummated, and two years later his own mother died. Loss figured early in Barrie's life and may have shaped his attitude to love and relationships—the pain of loss, interrupted childhood, disruptive motherhood, and speculative regret.

J. M. Barrie, of course, would be forever known for *Peter Pan*, or *The Boy Who Wouldn't Grow Up* (1904), an adventure story with the overwhelming longing of the central character to remain a child forever. The lives of the du Mauriers were also entwined with J. M. Barrie's. Daphne's father, Gerald du Maurier, was Barrie's favorite actor, and he fell in love with her mother, Muriel, when they starred as the romantic leads in a Barrie play. Gerald's sister Sylvia was the mother of the five "Lost Boys" that inspired Peter Pan. In adult life, Barrie's closest friends were Arthur and Sylvia Llewelyn Davies, both of whom died young, leaving Barrie as guardian of their five sons, George, John, Peter, Michael, and Nico—the "Lost Boys" upon whom, according to Barrie, he based his most famous play *Peter Pan*.

In the First World War, one of the boys, George, of whom Barrie was particularly fond, was killed in action. This may have shaped Barrie's sense of loss even more than the death of his brother David. Later his close friend, *Peter Pan* producer Charles Frohman, reportedly declined a lifeboat on the torpedoed liner *Lusitania*, repeating a line from *Peter Pan*: "To die would be an awfully big adventure." Barrie also befriended Robert Falcon Scott, who would die leading an expedition to the South Pole; one of the last letters found in Scott's tent in the frozen Antarctic was addressed to Barrie. So Barrie's early life was surrounded by a tragic sense of loss.

The seeds for *Mary Rose* appeared in the author's 1902 novel *The Little White Bird*, which also contained the first version of the story of *Peter Pan*. "*Mary Rose* runs like a leitmotif in Barrie's life," says biographer Andrew Birkin. "It reoccurs in one shape or form, cropping up in different guises. It comes into the *Little White Bird* in 1902."[2] The novel's narrator puts forward an idea that has long fascinated Barrie: "The only ghosts, I believe, who creep into this world, are dead young mothers, returned to see how their children fare . . . what is saddest about ghosts is that they may not know their child. They expect him to be just as he was when they left him, and they are easily bewildered, and search for him from room to room, and hate the unknown boy he has become. Poor, passionate souls, they may even do him an injury."

Barrie was long fascinated with islands and as a child often visited the Outer Hebrides in Scotland. Like Barrie's earlier *Peter Pan*, *Mary Rose* deals with an enchanted island that serves as "a safe place" for lost children. The germ of the idea for *Mary Rose* also appears in one of Barrie's notebooks from 1905, as "a sort of Rip Van Winkle." And in a letter written in 1911 to the British writer Arthur Quiller-Couch, Barrie makes reference to the play's structure: "I have often thought of it in three acts and see the first two all right. The third seems to amount to this. No one should ever come back however much they were loved."

In the summer of 1912, Barrie rented a housed called Amhuinnsuidh in the Outer Hebrides. He drew inspiration from Celtic mythology as these islands are full of folk tales and superstitious beliefs, including a Kilmeny legend of a girl taken away and returned by fairies. There are many phrases in these folk tales that would inspire a writer, for example "The sea likes to be visited." In a 1912 notebook, Barrie had jotted down "The island that likes to be visited." A related legend, which he also used in *The Little White Bird*, is about mother ghosts who return to their former homes to see how their children have fared. In a dedication to the five boys, in the published version of *Peter Pan*, he refers to Amhnuinnsuidh as "the place where we caught *Mary Rose*."[3]

Barrie's notebooks have shown that in a sense *Mary Rose* was caught in 1912, but there would be at least one more inspiration for the play—a Norwegian story, on the same theme, told by a Dr. Fridtjof Nansen, before this part of the play took final form. During that summer of 1912, Nico Llewelyn-Davies, one of the Lost Boys, remembers visiting Mary Rose's Island with Barrie, in Loch Voshimid, Outer Hebrides. It was here that Barrie conceived the story about a girl who disappears on a Scottish island, only to reappear years later, un-aged like Peter Pan. The real Mary Rose's Island is far smaller than the one described by Barrie in the play. "It is a little rocky place. There's no size to it at all," remembers Nico. "[Barrie] and I were sitting on the mainland about thirty yards away when he suddenly crystallized the idea which had been in the back of his mind for some time."

Nico would later describe the island as the closest thing to his heart. "We went up there in 1912, and then fifty years to the day in 1962 I went back there again, and I've been back there every year. . . . I remember sitting there with Uncle Jim (Barrie) for the first time, but I've got a picture of Mary Rose island and I know the whole place backwards. It's my mecca, my number 1 place and hasn't changed at all." Nico would later say *Mary Rose* was his favorite play for 1001 reasons.[4] His particular love for *Mary Rose* derives from having been with Barrie in the summer of 1912 when he pointed out the island. Nico was also around for most of the rehearsals later, and felt very involved with the stage production of *Mary Rose*. The fact that his beloved brother Michael was drowned shortly thereafter must also have had an influence.

When Barrie told Nico about *Mary Rose* in 1912, though, the story is likely to have been rudimentary in his mind. "There's something very sentimental and whimsical about Barrie's work," says Birkin. Barrie may also have drawn inspiration from a Norwegian story which is purportedly true. A friend of Barrie's named Admiral Mark Kerr believes it's based on a true story and in 1937, he wrote an article to the *Sunday Times* to say so:

Early in 1919 I had luncheon with Barrie in his flat. He asked my opinion on the following story, as he knew that I had for some years been investigating the effect of ether vibrations which convey sight and sound, and also their connection with mesmerism. He said: A great friend of mine, a Scotsman, who has fishing rights in Norway, and a man on whose word I thoroughly rely, told me the following story. His 12 year old daughter disappeared on the tenth day on a small island after he left her sketching there every day while he was fishing. The police searched and eventually the man decided to return to Scotland (after a 10 day absence). The day before they were to leave, he walked to the river, not to fish but to see the island once more. When he got there he saw the little girl sketching in the usual place. He jumped into his boat, and her first words when they met showed that she did not know she had been away. "Have you finished your fishing, daddy?" He replied, "Yes dear, we must get back now." When he got to the hotel he rushed upstairs, told his wife, and instructed her not to say anything about the ten days absence. They then took her home, and later visited two brain specialists, who both gave the same advice, not to say one word about the ten days she had been away, but to continue the conversations about fishing, the island, and so keep them in the child's memory until she was eighteen years old. They were then to ask her if she had any recollection of what had happened. When the child was eighteen they found that her mind was an absolute blank concerning this period, and she remembered absolutely nothing.

Barrie asked me what I thought. I told him that some people must have stolen the child, not realizing what money could do in such a sparsely inhabited country, and when they found the police were combing their district, they mesmerized the girl, told her to forget the ten days, and then put her back on the island. Barrie replied, "That is the only reasonable explanation I have ever heard." Three months later I was having tea with him and remarked that it was time he wrote another good play, and he replied: "I cannot get an idea for one, and I shall not write one unless I do think of something original and good."[5]

Yet another interpretation is that *Mary Rose* is an allegory about Mary Ansell, Barrie's first wife, whom he divorced after she had an affair. He may have chosen the name "Mary" for a particular reason. His wife wanted a second chance, and she had taken a house near his. Barrie could not use his wife's surname and so he may have approximated it as he could by calling her after the flower of England. After all, he was Scottish and she was English. Rosemary has also been used as a symbol for remembrance during weddings, war commemorations, memorials, and funerals in Europe and Australia. Mourners would throw it into graves as a symbol of remembrance for the dead. In Shakespeare's *Hamlet*, Ophelia says, "There's rosemary, that's for remembrance" (Hamlet, iv. 5).

In his preface to the 1913 edition of R. M. Ballantyne's *The Coral Island*, Barrie included the words, "To be born is to be wrecked on an island." What did he mean by these words? In early drafts of *Mary Rose* the island was identified with *Peter Pan*'s Neverland, but it became more sinister as he wrote the play, becoming a site for good and evil. Harry the son says to Mary Rose, "it was as if there were two kinds of dogs hunting you—the good and the bad."[6]

It seems a combination of stories and events influenced the development of *Mary Rose*. The trip to Mary Rose Island in 1912, the Norwegian story, and the death of George Llewelyn Davis in 1915. Barrie began writing *Mary Rose* in the summer of 1919. The play begins with Harry, a young Australian soldier, who visits a Sussex Manor House that is for sale. Harry talks to the keeper of the house, Mrs. Otery, and explains that he used to live there as a child, pointing out details he remembers. After Harry inquires about ghost stories, at the end of the first scene, he has a spooky encounter with the unseen ghost. And then we go back in time in a flashback structure to when the house was new. Mary Rose Morland is to marry at the age of 18. Her parents recount a strange story to her fiancé, Simon Blake. Mary Rose mysteriously disappeared at the age of eleven while on holiday with her parents on an uninhabited island in Scotland's Outer Hebrides. She returns after many days, in exactly the same place she disappeared, knowing nothing of where she has been. Simon laughs the story off, but Mary Rose's mother warns him about her, saying she is a little different from other girls. She says, "I have sometimes thought that our girl is curiously young for her age." Act 2 opens four years later. Mary Rose bears a child, but on a belated honeymoon with Simon to the same island, she vanishes again. This time she is gone for many years. Act 3 returns to the Morland's house, twenty five years later. Mary Rose returns when her parents are old and her son, Harry, is fully grown. But she herself remains the same, in appearance and manner, as the innocent young woman who disappeared all those years ago, seemingly unmarked by the passage of time.

Barrie had a recurring theme about mothers in his work. One of the original titles for *Peter Pan* was "The Boy Who Hated His Mother" and it was conceived as a revenge play. In Barrie's notes for the play, it's mentioned that actress and mother Dorothea Baird should play Captain Hook rather than Gerald du Maurier. In the end she portrayed Mrs. Darling in the original 1904 production of *Peter Pan*. What's interesting is that Peter isn't the villain, it's the mother.

"You know how just a touch of frost can stop the growth of a plant yet leave it blooming?" asks her mother as she muses about Mary Rose's ethereal and permanently child like nature. The touch of frost refers to Mary Rose's inability to mature and grow old. First when she was eleven years old, going unaccountably absent for twenty days during a family holiday in a place that is shunned by the superstitious locals and nicknamed the "Island That Likes to Be Visited." She disappears a second time when she revisits the island with her husband and a baby boy, but this time her absence from this world and her own responsibilities lasts a quarter of a century.

## OPENING NIGHT

The title character of Mary Rose was first played by the British actress Fay Compton. Born in London in 1894, she grew up in a stage family—her father was actor and manager Edward Compton. In her reminiscences "Rosemary: Some Remembrances," Compton implies that Barrie wrote the play specifically for her: "I was wondering about her, wondering if it could really be true that Barrie was going to write a story especially for me, wherein I should find a heroine with whose creation on the stage he could entrust me . . . the chance of interpreting that fragrant, delicate, intangible, appealing creature was yours if you dared to take it."[7]

Fay Compton had appeared in many of Barrie's works onstage in London, and by 1920 her blossoming film career included roles in *Odd Man Out*, *Laughter in Paradise*, *Othello*, and *The Haunting*. Barrie may have thought about Compton when writing the play as being perfect in the lead role, and believed she possessed the ethereal qualities to make the role work. As Compton said in "Rosemary," "During the rehearsals we all felt the spell of her; she weaved an enchantment of forgetfulness, brushing away from our minds, the world of today, taking us back to the seventies, to her orchard and her pretty home, not allowing us to remember the streets and traffic of the 1920s or the reality of a stage, an auditorium and an audience."[8]

The Theatre Royal in Haymarket was built in 1720, making it one of the oldest theaters in London. In the 1910s it staged some of its most fascinating productions, including Somerset Maugham's first venture in playwriting, *Lady Frederick*, Maeterlinck's *The Blue Bird*, and Ibesen's *Ghosts*. *Mary Rose* was first performed at the Haymarket on April 22, 1920, with the last performance, the 398th, on February 26, 1921. The cast included Fay Compton as Mary Rose, Jean Cadell as Mrs. Otery, Norman Forbes as Mr. Morland, Mary Jerrold as Mrs. Morland, Arthur Whilby as Mr. Amy, Robert Loraine as Simon Blake (later played by Leon Quartermaine), and Harry and Ernest Thesiger as Cameron the Gillie. Every evening performance started at 8:30 pm, and there were three matinees weekly, every Wednesday, Thursday, and Saturday at 2:30 pm. The action of the play, which covers a period of thirty years, passes between a small manor house in Sussex and an island in the Outer Hebrides.

> All of this room's past which can be taken away has gone. Such light as there is comes from the only window, which is at the back and is incompletely shrouded in sacking. For a moment, there is a mellow light, and if a photograph could be taken quickly we might find a disturbing smile on the room's face, perhaps like the Mona Lisa's, which came, surely, of her knowing what only the dead should know.

These are the opening stage directions for *Mary Rose*. As Peter Hollindale notes in his introduction to the Oxford World Classics edition of *Peter Pan and Other Plays*, when Barrie wrote *Mary Rose* immediately after the First World War, "his own awareness of a tragic tension between time and timelessness had become a nation's."[9] Time and timelessness are prominent themes in *Mary Rose*. When the play opened only eighteen months after the end of the First World War, there was hardly anyone in the audience who had not lost a loved one. As soon as the curtain opened, one of the two characters onstage was Harry, a returning soldier. *Mary Rose* may also be based on mothers who lost their sons during the war, in which over 700,000 British servicemen were killed, and the audience's immediate identification with the play was almost certainly due to the tragic relevance of losing a child.

One member in the audience that opening night of *Mary Rose* was Alfred Hitchcock. Hitchcock's father, William, loved the theater and passed that interest to his son.[10] As a child, Hitchcock was very much an observer, sitting quietly in a corner, watching. From the age of sixteen, he would read trade papers like film journals, and by the age of nineteen, Hitchcock would often go to the theater. He said, "I had great enthusiasm for the theater and for films. I would go to the theater first night alone."

Watching the play, Hitchcock was spellbound by Fay Compton, the art direction, the lighting, the performances, and the music. At the time, Norman O'Neill had been the musical director of the Haymarket theater for many years, and he wrote the beautiful, haunting music for *Mary Rose*, which inspired not only the performers but Hitchcock too. As Fay Compton said of O'Neill's music, "I have a tremendous debt of gratitude to that music I can never hope to repay." The lighting effects, by Charles la Trobe, "created an atmosphere of ghostliness no amount of intricate mechanical contrivances could hope to better."[11] An opening review of *The Times* stated,

> Sir James Barrie has used here once again the idea whose sadness underlies his masterpiece, *Peter Pan*, the idea of one lover growing old while the other remains young. *Mary Rose* is indeed full of beautiful ideas. It would not be Barrie's otherwise. But there is something wrong with it. It has not the true magic. In his best work, Barrie is a master at handling sentiment, he is a great humourist, but the real thing which makes him the genius he is is an unnameable something which dives deep down into our inmost being, takes hold with uncertainty of a nerve whose existence we hardly realized before and tugs. In *Mary Rose* the unnameable something has lost its certainty; it fumbles for the little nerve and just fails to find it. . . . Miss Fay Compton as Mary Rose is delightful, she improves with each part she undertakes. In the scene on the island she makes us realize what happiness Mary Rose must have brought into her husband's life so keenly that we can scarcely bear to contemplate his terrible loss. In the last scene—the ghost scene—she is sweet and appealing.

In summary, for *The Times* reviewer, considering the great expectations that a Barrie first-night aroused, the key note of the evening was disappointment, tempered to a very great extent, however, by pleasure.

Fay Compton's performance was universally praised by reviewers. Ivor Brown in the *Observer* commented on Compton's "actress-power of sending what she means speeding out from her, like light from a lamp, as if she had no need of movement or speech for expression."[12] He went on to comment, "What if this were not a ghost, but a still living woman, left behind by a past that was past? It hardly bears thinking of; and yet something very dark lurks in the background and it may be that Barrie shrank from it." The theme of the lost child (like Marnie) had great resonance for audience members in 1920, who had just witnessed the loss of a generation of young men. It's also of note that at the time an epidemic of sleeping sickness was drawing to a close.

As Michael Meyer writes in his biography of August Strindberg, *Mary Rose*, like Strindberg's *Easter*, requires a "very special kind of actress," and if the right actress isn't available, these plays are "better left undone."[13] *Tatler* magazine observed in their review of the play, "Seldom has there been a play which has aroused more speculation or more interest."[14] Barrie biographer Patrick Chalmers observed that Barrie's "lovely and spiritual conception was staged in the ugly and uneasy period that followed immediately upon" the armistice, bringing "joy and peace and a tear or two to thousands, weary of the War and the War's aftermath, during the years of its run." As Joseph McBride notes: "Audiences took from the play a mystical answer to Rudyard Kipling's cry of national bereavement, 'But who shall return us the children?'"

Haunting still photographs of the play show Mary Rose's ghost enjoying what in life she said would be the "loveliest time of all" the moment when her son is a man and takes her on his knee. But as a ghost she is unable to savor the full bliss of her experience, as she does not recognize her baby Harry in the grown-up solider. Although she has found what she is looking for, she does not realize that her quest is over. Her tragic sense of loss echoes those mothers mourning for the sons who disappeared overseas and were killed in action, and for those who did come back, but were scarred by war.

*Mary Rose* eventually came to an end at the Haymarket theater after almost 400 performances, which was J. M. Barrie's longest running play. It would have gone on much longer in normal times "and still be playing to a big profit if cost was as it used to be before the war."[15] But it was eventually revived again in 1926, with Fay Compton once more in the title role. *Mary Rose* was seen on Broadway very briefly in 1951 and revived again in 2007. Charles Isherwood in his review wrote, "The play is in many ways a more mature and mournful reworking of themes Barrie explored in the tale of the boy who refused to grow up. Time is seen as a quiet despoiler of happiness and innocence, and the idea of another world unblemished by its passing has an irresistible seduction."[16]

## HITCHCOCK ADAPTS

Hitchcock was so enraptured by the play that he retained many elements in his memory, especially the music, production design, and lighting. He was also so enthralled by Fay Compton's performance, he cast her as Countess Helga von Stahl in his only musical 1933 film, *Waltzes from Vienna*. Later, when he was preparing to produce *Mary Rose* in the early 1960s, he inquired about Compton's availability (probably to play Mary Rose's mother.)

The music remained hauntingly in Hitchcock's mind. Thirty-seven years later, during the production of *Vertigo*, Hitchcock had sought out from England the play's original score and sound effects by Norman O'Neill, and the idea was to give the music to his composer, Bernard Herrmann, for inspiration. Hitchcock was especially struck by "the Call" connected with Mary Rose's disappearance, an effect produced by bagpipes and "wordless voices" sounded from a musical saw, as Joseph McBride observes. Hitchcock remembered the music like celestial voices, like Debussy's *Sirenes*.

The search for the long-lost music began in earnest. On May 9, 1957, Hitchcock's production manager Herb Coleman for *From among the Dead* (the working title for *Vertigo*) wrote to Kay Selby at Paramount British Productions Ltd. at the Plaza Theatre, Jermyn Street.

> Dear Kay,
>     In April 1920, at the Haymarket Theatre in London, JM Barrie's play "Mary Rose" was presented, and in the play, there was used very effectively a background sound effect, probably a record, off stage, of eerie music, angels singing and low moaning wind. The music was written and conducted by Norman O'Neill. Hitch is most anxious to obtain a recording of this—the original, if possible, to be used as a guide for the composer here for his new picture, "From Among the Dead." He thinks you might be able to locate someone who had something to do with the play, if not you might find the record by advertising. Failing in this, he would like you to have a tape recording made from the original score using the same number of musicians and voices and wind effect as in the original under the supervision of the person you will find who was with the original company. Sorry to have to always hand you the tough ones, but can think of no one who could do as well.

Frank Caffey also wrote to Mr. Russell Holman at the Paramount New York Office on May 10, 1957, saying "would you kindly communicate with London, asking them to move as rapidly as possible in connection with this request." On May 17, 1957, Sally Nicholls from the British Paramount Productions replied to Herb Coleman:

> This is a personal plea to you regarding the records which have gone from Mr. Holman to Mr. Hitchcock, via Frank Caffey's organization. The second hand gramaphone exchanges here were raked to no avail. Fay Compton (the original Mary Rose) at the Haymarket 1920 couldn't help. The remainder of the cast have passed on. Nor have the BBC been much help in respect of this music which was used in a sound broadcast many years ago.
>     However, Schotts, the music publishers, had a couple of these very old records, saying that they were scratched and ghastly but that they would hire us for a half a guinea for a three week period the two records "The Prelude" and "The Call," on one condition that they were returned after three weeks. I gave them this guarantee—or otherwise we wouldn't have obtained the records. So, please, Herbie see that the records are returned, in good packing, in around the stated period. These are the only known records in existence and Schotts hired them out to repertory theatre when the background music for *Mary Rose* is required. If their records get lost or broken, it appears that's the lost.

The records would have been returned to Larry Bachmann's office at the Plaza Theatre in London. A memo from David J. Grimes to Russell Holman on May 17, 1957, noted that Norman O'Neill died two or three years earlier, but that his wife was still alive. The music was still in copyright and they would seek clearance from Mrs. O'Neill.

## WRITING THE SCREENPLAY

When it came time to make *Marnie* in 1963, Hitchcock often told screenwriter Jay Presson Allen of his dreams, which she would interpret. During these sessions, the subject of the dream-like *Mary Rose* was brought up as a possible play for them to adapt. Because Hitchcock and Allen got along so well, it seemed natural that she'd be the one to bring his beloved *Mary Rose* to the screen. In August 1964, Hitchcock would be sixty-five years of age, retirement age in the United Kingdom, and he had longed to bring Barrie's play to the screen for the whole of his professional life. He thought of casting Tippi Hedren in the lead role, after the filming of *Marnie* was complete.

On August 26, 1963, during the preparation for *Marnie*, Hitchcock discussed with Peggy Robertson at his house hiring Fay Compton for a part in *Mary Rose*, and asked her to find out about her availability and salary. A later memo was sent from Robertson to Hitchcock about Fay Compton dated October 1, 1963; "Miss Compton is going into a play on September 30 on the road. We will know after the opening if it succeeds in which case she will continue with it. Miss Compton's salary is £500 per week for a London motion picture and $100 a week for the New York stage, Miss Compton's agent is Ronnie Waters."

Meanwhile Hitchcock set about acquiring the story rights from Paramount. The Studio was the owner of the silent rights for plays in the estate of J. M. Barrie, including *Mary Rose*. It had owned the rights to the play prior to 1953, having considered a stage production in 1944, but that was abandoned. In 1947, there was some question as to whether they owned the talking picture rights to the play and it was inadvisable to expend any sums at that time for their acquisition.

Paramount's rights to *Mary Rose* expired in June 1962 and it was a prime opportunity for Hitchcock to buy them. He instructed his agent Herman Citron to offer $2,500 for the play, which at that time was a bargain. At the same time Hitchcock was also planning to travel to Scotland to research filming locations for the island. On August 16, 1963, he sent a memo to agent Herman Citron; "If while I am away in England you acquire the rights to *Mary Rose* and or *The Three Hostages*, would you please register these titles as soon as possible with the Motion Picture Association of America Inc." Another letter on August 20 stated, "Further to my letter of August 16, an alternate title to

*Mary Rose* is 'The Island That Likes to Be Visited.' So if we do acquire *Mary Rose*, would you also have this alternate title registered with the MPAA."

Hitchcock traveled with Alma to the Outer Hebrides to visit Mary Rose island. They were accompanied by Nico Llewelyn Davies, the youngest of the Lost Boys, who was sixty years old at the time. Only three years earlier, Nico's older brother Peter, who was considered the inspiration for *Peter Pan*, committed suicide by throwing himself in front of a train. Years later Nico wrote a letter to Andrew Birkin saying how unpleasant he thought Hitchcock was. But how did Hitchcock get in touch with Nico in the first place? He may have done so through Peter Davies, publishers of Denis MacKail's 1942 biography *The Story of J.M.B.* Davies was a notable publisher, which was eventually bought by Heinemann. Hitchcock most likely contacted Peter Davies, who introduced him to Nico.

A memo on August 23, 1963, stated that an agreement had been reached with Herman Citron that Paramount would issue a quit-claim on the property *Mary Rose* to such person designated by Citron, upon receipt of a consideration of $2,500 payable to Paramount Pictures Corporation. By March 1964, just as filming of *Marnie* was completed, the deal was consummated. Hitchcock's attorneys Taylor and Winokur wrote to Gertrude Rosenstein at Paramount Pictures, "I may be premature and somewhat optimistic, but I am hopeful that we may get the *Mary Rose* agreement signed later this month. We are waiting the signed documents including the consent to the quitclaim from Paramount to Geoffrey Stanley." Paramount sold the rights to Geoffrey Stanley, Inc. and the proceeds of the sale were credited to studio overhead.

By this time, Jay Presson Allen had submitted a second-draft script of *Mary Rose* on February 15, 1964. Albert Whitlock was also asked to draw up some preliminary sketches: "Yes, and I'll tell you, the most impressive thing about it is it was a good script . . . and it wasn't anything like Barrie's story. . . . And I did a lot of sketches, again a very moody thing, and I said to him, because he was always very strong on the selling point, 'What's the selling point, Hitch?' He said, not 'Hitchcock's *Mary Rose*,' but 'A Ghost Story by Alfred Hitchcock,' and then '*Mary Rose*.' He was going to have a new presentation on the titles. He said, 'That'll get 'em.'"

The challenge for the production team was how to show the ghostly *Mary Rose* to a modern day audience. As Albert Whitlock remembers, "There were only going to be matte shots, as far as I know, and getting the girl to disappear. I mean really, it was a piece of mysticism, wasn't it? She came back years later when everybody else has grown old and she's young. And it fascinated him. The idea that somebody could come back again . . . young. I mean, again, it's one of his phobias. He hated getting old. Just the idea fascinated him of a young girl coming back and confronting her husband who is twenty years older than she is."

During this time in late 1963 and early 1964, Hitchcock was promoting *Mary Rose* as his next project to the press. On November 26, 1963, *The Times* of London reported, "After *Marnie* a story about a compulsive thief in his own style and tradition, which he is now directing, he will make J. M. Barrie's *Mary Rose*, but under the title *The Island That Wants to Be Visited*. He fears, however, that his sponsors may want concrete evidence of where the island was and what are its tourist attractions."[17]

When in May 1964, Hitchcock traveled to Europe, he sent a cable from Austria to an associate at the end of the month: "I have a script ready for a short scheduled feature of Sir James Barrie's play *Mary Rose* which I intended shooting before Christmas stop. Then I have a commitment start on the script of John Buchan's *Three Hostages* which is a bigger picture than *North by Northwest*."

When Hitchcock was in London in June 1964, he said to *The Times*, "'I see it essentially as a horror story.' To hear him describing effects he had in mind for the latter, like having the semi-phantom Mary Rose lit from inside, so that she casts a ghostly glow instead of a shadow on the walls, and in the death scene letting her husband feel her brow when she goes into a trance and find his hand covered in blue powder ('I don't know exactly what it signifies, but I like the idea'), one is left in no doubt that he starts his films very much from the visual end of things."[18]

Hitchcock returned to LA at the end of June. But *Mary Rose* was never filmed. Why? The reasons are manifold, involving the falling-out with Tippi Hedren, the critical and commercial failure of *Marnie*, Hitchcock's own personal and career crisis, and Lew Wasserman's concerns about audience expectations of him at the time. Universal vetoed the project, worried that a melancholy and sentimental film about a ghost would further diminish the box office value of the Hitchcock brand.

Tippi Hedren acknowledges that *Mary Rose* would have been their next project had things not deteriorated on *Marnie*. "He gave me the play to read," Hedren recalls. "Oh, I loved it. My daughter owned it for a while. What's difficult was how do you show a woman as a ghost? How do you do that visually? That became the reason it wasn't done with or without me. Now, of course, they could do it very easily."

Albert Whitlock enquired to Hitchcock what happened to *Mary Rose*: "I used to ask him what happened with the front office and their acceptance of the idea, and he said, 'They believe it isn't what the audiences expect of me. Not the kind of picture they expect of me.' And I said, well here we are. *The Birds* wasn't exactly the kind of picture that was expected from him, but they let him make that. But that was it. They wouldn't let him make it. And he didn't want to put his own money into it."

Jay Presson Allen was disappointed that Hitchcock wasn't able to make the film, plus he was drinking excessively and this alienated her from him, as she had a small child to look after. She didn't want to be in that kind of environment so she returned to New York. Throughout the 1960s, Hitchcock continued to talk about *Mary Rose* to interviewers, trying to find a commercial angle to make the film. On August 16, 1966, as part of his promotion for his fiftieth feature, *Torn Curtain*, Hitchcock said to Peter Bogdanovich: "*Mary Rose* is on the stop for the time being. I'm looking for a science fiction reason for that story, which will probably turn Barrie in his grave anyway." *The Twilight Zone* was airing on television and the popularity of science fiction with viewers was something Hitchcock was hoping to capitalize on.

That same year, Hitchcock was interviewed by François Truffaut, updating his series of interviews for his soon-to-be-released book *Hitchcock*. Again the director described *Mary Rose* as "a little like a science-fiction story. I still haven't definitely dropped the idea of making it. A few years back it might have seemed that the story would be too irrational for the public. But since then the public's been exposed to these twilight-zone stories, especially on television."[19]

Hitchcock also went on to describe how he would create the ghostly presence: "If I were to make the film, I would put the girl in a dark-gray dress and I would put a neon tube of light inside, around the bottom of the dress, so that the light would only hit the heroine. Whenever she moved, there would be no shadow on the wall, only a blue light. You'd have to create the impression of photographing a presence rather than a body. At times she would appear very small in the image, at times very big. She wouldn't be a solid lump, you see, but rather like a sensation. In this way you lose the feeling of real space and time. You should be feeling that you are in the presence of an ephemeral thing, you see." "It's a lovely subject," commented Truffaut. "Also a sad one." Hitchcock's reply was, "Yes, very sad. Because the real theme is: If the dead were to come back, what would you do with them?"

In the 1970s, Hitchcock became reacquainted with John Russell Taylor, who had interviewed him previously in London and in Cannes. Eventually Taylor would write *Hitch*, the official biography of Hitchcock, in 1978. When asked about why *Mary Rose* never materialized, Taylor's reply was,

> He had a script as I understand and he had all these ideas about her, her clothes will always be lit from the inside, there was an unearthly glow about her. People don't realize there are strong elements of a horror movie. Don't you think it's absolutely horrifying, the idea of a young man sitting there with his mother on his lap, as a young woman? It seems to me an absolutely horrifying thing. He

tended to infuse an element of that into it. He told various people that the studio took one look at the script and barred him from making it, so there is some truth in it; he was considering it, maybe if things hadn't gone wrong on *Marnie*, that was his next. There was also the question of Tippi's popularity or otherwise with the public. Wasserman was very commercially minded, because he was also Hitch's agent.

A memo on June 13, 1972, from Jim Weinberg to Peggy Robertson, showed that Hitchcock owned unlimited rights to *Mary Rose* until 1987. Now at the age of seventy-two, he was in poor health, and despite the success of *Frenzy*, he knew that it was only a matter of time before he had to quit making movies. When interviewer Charles Thomas Samuels asked Hitchcock in 1972 if he had any scripts he was hoping to adapt, the reply was "I own one now: J. M. Barrie's *Mary Rose*, but at present, it doesn't seem to have any commercial potential." That was the real problem with the script—it was uncommercial. But the drive to adapt *Mary Rose* was about to be picked up from another source.

## *MARY ROSE* RESURRECTED

It was 1972, and exactly eight years had passed since Jay Presson Allen wrote the script for *Mary Rose*. The American actress Mia Farrow, star of Roman Polanski's *Rosemary's Baby* (1968), was starring in her first British appearance on stage at the Shaw Theatre in London. The production was *Mary Rose*, and a five-week run was due to start on July 12, with co-star Ralph Bates, Carmel McSharry, Lee Fox, Oliver Ford-Davies, Roy Sampson, and Ann Way. The director was Braham Murray and the composer was John Tavener.

Mia Farrow generally received good reviews for her performance. Irving Wardle in the *London Times* praised Farrow's "great eyes and wraith-like appearance," which emphasized the title character's strangeness.[20] Jay and Lewis Allen agreed when they saw the play while visiting London and thought it would be very timely to once again try to adapt the screenplay, considering the stage play was such a success. Hitchcock owned the story rights, so the first task was to try to acquire them from him, which would not be easy.

Two years later, on October 24, 1974, Lewis Allen wrote to Hitchcock: "Knowing how you keep up with everything, I am sure you must already have thought of it and rejected it. As you no doubt know, Mia Farrow played in *Mary Rose* in London and had, I understand, a considerable success. It occurred to us that she might be a possibility for a film version should you ever want to pick it up again." At this point, Allen first asked to buy *Mary Rose*, ten years after the first script was written. A month later, on November

25, Lewis wrote to Peter Witt, Mia Farrow's agent: "I am writing to you about Mia Farrow, whom I presume you still represent. I wanted to find out if she would be interested in doing a motion picture version of *Mary Rose* with screenplay by Jay. You may or may not know that several years ago Jay wrote a screenplay of *Mary Rose* for Hitchcock, which he planned to do as Hitchcock's Ghost Story. He put off doing it until his contract with Universal expired, but now, in part I think because of his own and his wife's health, has given up the idea of trying to do it."

Lewis also tried to garner the interest of Alan Ladd at Twentieth Century Fox. On January 28, 1975, he wrote: "Dear Laddie, Enclosed is the screenplay by Jay of *Mary Rose*. Jay will of course commit to doing a rewrite. This is a very early screenplay of hers, and she feels it needs opening up considerably more." The Allens were keen for Mia Farrow, perfect as the child woman, or the woman who doesn't age, to play Mary Rose. Farrow's career continued to blossom as she had just played Daisy in *The Great Gatsby* (1974) opposite Robert Redford.

On February 13, 1975, Lewis Allen wrote to Mia Farrow informing her, "Because of commitments, Jay won't be able to rewrite *Mary Rose* until the summer. This means that we certainly would not be able to do the show until the fall. Jay's novel has been sold to Warner Bros. and that it appears that Mike Nichols will be directing it." The novel that Lewis was referring to was *Just Tell Me What You Want*, which would later be adapted into the film directed by Sidney Lumet.

That same day, on February 13, Allen also wrote to Mike Nichols, director of *The Graduate* (1967): "I am enclosing a screenplay adapted by Jay from the play *Mary Rose*. Mia Farrow, who did the play quite successfully in London, would love to play it and it seemed to Jay and me that it would make a fine special for ABC."

Whilst Lewis Allen was assiduously trying to gain interest, and assign a director and lead to *Mary Rose*, there was concern about the screenplay itself. Jay felt that the script was too long and wrote some notes for a possible rewrite. The talky, lengthy screenplay that Jay had written for Hitchcock was not without its faults. It was in need of updating, as the verbose dialogue that Jay was fond of was also part of the problem with the *Marnie* screenplay. In contemplating a rewrite, Jay summarized:

The action of the story spans 43 years (1896–1939) a period during which England underwent many changes. It would be good to see some of these changes take place in the background of the story. To do this it would help if the Morland house were set in either of two places. 1) It is a large house, set in its own grounds in either Richmond or Wimbledon or any other affluent upper middle-class suburb of London. It would still be remote enough for Mrs. Otery to be alone and terrified, but we would have the opportunity of seeing Kenneth as a small boy going for walks with a nanny or maid, and meeting local figures—the policeman, the postman, the newsboy etc. For instance in May of 1900, the siege of Mafeking ended and England went mad. It was also the same year that cars started to be seen on the roads. 2) The house is the 'big house' of a small village, slightly apart from it. A small village, post office, store, a pub or two. Everyone knows everyone and there are no secrets. Of the two locations, I prefer the first. I would also like to open the story up within the household and to include the servants. Not on the level of 'Upstairs, Downstairs' since the Morlands belong to quite a different social and economic class to the Bellamys. But there could, for instance, be a scene where Kenneth, as a small boy, at lunch with his grandparents (now in their 60s) slips away from table during a boring political conversation (or not so boring—Winston Churchill in a top hat directing troops during the battle of Sidney Street) and goes downstairs to the kitchen where Cook is telling the housemaid's fortune in tea leaves.

I think there should be a couple of scenes where the outside world reacts to Mary Rose's disappearance. Everyone must assume that she has run off with a man. One assumes that Kenneth goes off to boarding school at the age of seven or eight. Does he tell the other boys that his mother is dead? Maybe he pretends that nothing has happened and that she is safe at home, but can never make it to Sports Day. What do the servants say? Perhaps there is a scene where they are discussing it and Kenneth overhears them. As a contrast to Kenneth as a little boy, I would like to know a little more about him before his scene with Mrs. Otery. Maybe one could do this by, after the titles over the island shots, going to Kenneth in London. The sensitive little boy who is going to touch us by waving good-bye to his mother (before Mary Rose disappears) is now a tough American officer, has fought in two bloody World Wars. We could see him as this very American man in London (maybe we should change the date of these scenes to 1941 after Pearl Harbor) during the war. Then, already knowing who he is and what kind of a man he is, we take him to the house where he can play his scene with Mrs. Otery. Then, in the flashback we can see him being brought up by grandparents and servants. Without making Mary Rose any more grown up, I would like to make her love for Simon, and his for her, a little more passionate. I think this would make his rejection of his son after her disappearance a little more understandable. Since Mr. Amy is the local vicar, we might have an after church Sunday morning scene.

On November 15, 1974, Hitchcock's agent Herman Citron replied to Lewis Allen's query about story rights: "Since Mr Hitchcock is not planning to do *Mary Rose* as a film, I thought I would make you aware of this information and if you are interested in acquiring the property from him it is available subject to whatever costs are involved." By January 8, 1975, Citron replied, saying that Hitchcock would accept $100,000 for his rights to *Mary Rose*. He wasn't about to give the rights away for a small sum, even between friends.

Allen wrote back saying that he was going to arrive in California on January 20 and would call Citron to discuss it. One hundred thousand dollars for the rights was a lot of money then, and Allen's first concern was raising the cash to buy them.

Two months later, Allen still was unable to raise the funds for *Mary Rose*. He wrote a letter to Citron on March 10, 1975: "Mrs. Allen and I feel that we will regretfully have to pass for the moment at least, on buying back *Mary Rose*. She feels that the script will need a substantial rewrite to make it a feature, and she is unable, because of other commitments, to consider such a rewrite until probably the end of the year." By August of the same year, Allen was still pressing for a purchase. He asked Citron if Hitchcock would accept $50,000 cash and the remaining $50,000 to be deferred in first position. Later that month, on August 19, Allen received word that Hitchcock was willing to accept Allen's terms. According to her original contract, Jay Presson Allen was still owed $13,500 from the work on her screenplay, after the first exhibition of *Mary Rose.*

Even though the Allens hadn't secured funding, the quest to attach a cast to *Mary Rose* that would attract big money investors continued. Lewis and Jay met Mia Farrow during the summer of 1975 at Martha's Vineyard, where the Allens had owned a home since 1952. On August 8, Lewis wrote to Farrow, "It was very nice meeting you at the Vineyard and talking about our production of *Mary Rose*." Allen said he had also located Roman Polanski and was sending him a copy of the screenplay. As well as directing *Rosemary's Baby* (1968), Polanski had also directed *Macbeth* (1971) with another Hitchcock actor, Jon Finch, and was seen as the ideal director, as he combined gothic with assured performances. Two weeks later, on August 22, 1975, Allen wrote to Farrow saying that he had located Polanski at the Beverly Wilshire and given him a copy of the screenplay. Farrow was very interested, so, having completed negotiations for the rights from Hitchcock, it was up to Allen to find the remainder of the financing.

A couple of days later, on August 25, Allen wrote to agent Paul Kohner in Los Angeles, who represented stars from Henry Fonda to Ingrid Bergman, asking for casting and director suggestions for the play. "We would expect to make the film late spring or summer of 1976 and at this point we can be quite flexible as to a starting date." Four days later, on August 29, 1975, Allen wrote to Citron: "I am very pleased that Mr. Hitchcock is willing to accept my offer for the rights to *Mary Rose*. In as much as a considerable portion of the financing will come from private investment funds, which is to some extent a tax shelter, it would be helpful to me to have as large a portion of the initial $50,000 to be payable in the year 1976 as possible."

By October 31, Allen had outlined a budget for producer Bob Montgomery: "The budget should be $1.1 to $1.3. Mia Farrow is committed and there is a good opportunity to get a name male lead since one actor can play all three male leads, the father and the son, both being close to the same age when they appear and the father as an older man."

Allen also contacted John Terry, at the National Film Finance Corporation in London, who was involved in co-financing and producing Anglo Canadian films. In a letter dated December 6, 1976, Allen explained the back history of *Mary Rose* and how Hitchcock planned to shoot it at the original location in the Hebrides. "Lew Wasserman, for reasons of his own, never wanted Hitch to make the film and Hitch continually planned to make it after he left Universal. Since this never happened, and does not appear likely to happen, the picture has never been made. I should tell you in front that Jay and I both feel that the screenplay, only her second effort, still retains too much of the procenium arch and needs an additional rewrite to make it more cinematic. On the other hand, I do feel she has solved some of the dramatic problems and eliminated some of the excess sentimentality." John Terry studied the script and agreed that it had financial possibilities.

As well as looking to Canada for co-production financing, Brooke Allen remembers her parents making sporadic attempts to raise the finance of *Mary Rose* in Scotland, where the original story was set. "I remember in 1967 Jay went out to Scotland, and they were filming *Ring of Bright Water* and Jack Couffer was directing and starred Bill Travers and Virginia McKenna. She went around to all the islands and they were always enthusiastic about *Mary Rose*."

Both Jay and Lewis Allen tried to get Scottish Television interested in the play. STV had adapted *The Prime of Miss Jean Brodie* into a television series starring Geraldine McEwan, and when Jay visited Glasgow in May 1977, she wondered about STV making *Mary Rose* as a 1.5-hour television special using the same crew. Lewis Allen contacted Richard Bates of Scottish Television on May 24 and June 6, 1977, suggesting that he act as the line producer.

In another letter to John Daly of the Hemdale leasing corporation in New York, dated April 25, 1977, Allen suggested Jenny Agutter for the part of Mary Rose, as he feared that Farrow was getting too old for the role. Agutter had made a notable impression in *The Railway Children* (1970) and *Walkabout* (1971). He went on to say that the film could be done for $1 million.

After *Family Plot* was released in 1976, Allen wrote a letter to Hitchcock on March 31, "Congratulates Hitch on *Family Plot* . . . and I noted in a column in the trades that your favourite project was still *Mary Rose*, with the inference that you would like to do it with Barbara Harris." Even though the Allens still hadn't raised the capital to buy the story rights, they were gracious enough to defer to Hitchcock to make it. "I don't think anyone else really appreciates its potential or knows how to achieve it," Allen concluded in his letter.

On December 5, 1979, a memo shows that Scott Rudin of Edgar J. Scherick Associates, Burbank Studios, who went on to become a leading theatrical and features producer, read Jay's script for *Mary Rose* as well as Andrew Birkin's biography of J. M. Barrie. Both inspired Rudin to read the original Barrie play: "I thought it was lovely—charming and mysterious." In doing some research on the play, Rudin found out that Jay Allen had written an adaptation of it, which he located. "I think the screenplay is wonderful . . . I think with the right kind of elementing it could be made into a very good picture which might prove commercial." A mutual friend and associate was Ross Milloy, who went on to produce the 1990 remake of *Lord of the Flies* with Lewis Allen. He replied on December 13 informing Rudin of *Mary Rose*'s convoluted history, and that Mia Farrow wanted to play Mary Rose and that George Cukor, who is Mia's godfather, might direct the film.

In the 1980s, even after Hitchcock's death in April 1980, the Allens were still trying to acquire the *Mary Rose* script from his estate. A letter to Herman Citron from Lewis Allen dated November 17, 1983, offered "$5,000 option for one year renewable for a year against the $100,000 price. I would appreciate any comments you have on this." Hitchcock whilst he was alive wouldn't consider any option. Citron replied on December 20, 1983: "If you are prepared to make a deal for *Mary Rose* and to pay $100,000 for the rights, we will approach the Trustees to ascertain whether they are prepared to make the deal."

Allen was still trying to find a broadcaster to raise the $100,000 for the story rights. On March 6, 1984, Allen wrote a letter to Carol Greene of United Artists Classics. Greene was director of development and acquisitions. Allen informed her of the back history and that *Mary Rose* had been written about twenty years earlier and was in need of updating. "I neglected to tell you that there is no director set and I gather from Peter [Newman] that you might have some ideas on this. What would you think of Harold Pinter as director and he could also obviously contribute enormously to a rewrite."

He also approached Showtime/The Movie Channel and tried to interest them in *Mary Rose*, and received a reply on September 18, 1984. The general feeling was that it was "too gentle a tale for us, I'm afraid it would be very difficult to promote." That was the problem with *Mary Rose* all along. Although haunting and beautiful, it was considered just too un-commercial a project to attract investors, especially in the 1980s. As the years progressed, time was not kind to *Mary Rose*, the story becoming more old-fashioned, whimsical, and dated.

Peter Newman was a producer who moved into Lewis Allen's office space in 1982, at the time when Mike Nichols was moving out. He worked with Allen in the independent sector making small films such as *1918* (1985), starring a young Matthew Broderick, and *On Valentine's Day* (1986). "I read the *Mary Rose* script and I thought it was intriguing and well written," remembers Newman in 2012.[21] "Lewis would bring up the topic of *Mary Rose* in the 1980s along with some other plays. At the time, he was dealing with Texan investors in selling concepts for a group of movies, and *Mary Rose* was potentially available. He never portrayed it as if he had the rights, so it wasn't packaged. It was also mentioned infrequently though Lewis wasn't a high pressure kind of guy."

Newman agrees that $100,000 was a massive amount at the time to buy the story rights, and as *Mary Rose* wasn't a studio movie, there weren't too many independent production companies that could make it. He himself later went on to produce *The Secret of Roan Inish* in 1994, directed by John Sayles. The story is based on a Celtic tale, about selkies, seals that can shed their skin to become humans, and had many elements similar to those of *Mary Rose*, like humans living between two worlds. An old family legend says that Fiona, the main character, had a younger brother named Jamie, who was swept away as a child and raised by selkies. This is very similar to how Mary Rose vanishes on the island as a child.

By the late 1980s Lewis Allen had retired. After he had gone down the Showtime television and cable routes, there was nowhere else to take the screenplay. Hitchcock's story rights expired in 1987, and without that, *Mary Rose* would have been a difficult product to sell. "I saw *Mary Rose* a few years ago on the New York stage, and thought it was a wonderful play," remarks Brooke Allen. "It was so theatrical, philosophical, and creepy and it worked for me." The great tragedy of *Mary Rose* is that Hitchcock and the Allens failed to bring it to the screen.

But a final twist to the convoluted tale occurred. Tippi Hedren's daughter Melanie Griffith, and her husband Antonio Banderas, acquired the rights to *Mary Rose* through their company Green Moon Productions. At the time, they had a development deal with one of the Hollywood studios. In 2000 they hired Australian screenwriter Susan MacGillicuddy, who was working in Los Angeles on an American television series.

MacGillicuddy was given a copy of Jay Allen's script of *Mary Rose*, which was so faded it was barely legible. But she took it away and read it over the weekend. "It was beautifully written," remembers MacGillicuddy in 2013, "But like a lot of those British films from the 60s, every scene had long dialogue and were talking heads in rooms basically. So one of the things they said to me was to make it more commercial and accessible to modern audiences. More of a ghost story."[22]

MacGillicuddy heard the story about Hitchcock and Hedren's falling out and realized that she was holding onto a piece of Hollywood history. She also listened to the Hitchcock and Truffaut discussion of *Mary Rose*. "There was a quote from the interview that struck a chord in me; 'If the dead were to come back, what would you do with them?' Because at the time I was dealing with three people very close to me who had died in quick succession of each other within a year."

Griffith said she was "haunted" by the role and her mother had given her a copy of the play when she was a child and she had loved it. The challenge for MacGillicuddy when she was writing the screenplay was that Griffith wanted to play Mary Rose, but in 2000, she was 43 years old. MacGillicuddy's sister worked as a make up prosthetic expert, and had the opinion that Griffith could play five years younger, but no more than that. So MacGillicuddy gave the story a contemporary spin, and wrote Mary Rose as a strange lady who wasn't really someone of her time. For inspiration she put a picture of the alleged photograph of a ghost, "The Brown Lady of Raynham Hall" on the front of the script when she submitted it. Griffith reportedly was talking to Scottish actor Ewan McGregor to play the male lead, as well as Edward Norton. Banderas also wanted to direct it, but his latest movie *The Body* (2001) hadn't done so well at the box office. In the event, although a script was written, the project was shelved.

## CONCLUSION

*Mary Rose* undoubtedly struck a chord deep in Hitchcock, with his fears of ageing, time passing, and death. He had seen no other play or story like it before. Its themes about love and loss, of yearning and age and innocence, must have made a deep impression on the young Hitchcock when he saw the play at the age of twenty at the Haymarket theatre. He was mesmerized by the production, the lighting, the music, and the beauty of the central character played by Fay Compton, so for the next fifty years he tried to bring it to the screen.

As Albert Whitlock said, Hitchcock had a fear of growing old. Maybe at the age of sixty-five, Hitchcock was thinking about his own mortality and wanted to address his fears with *Mary Rose*, which would have been his ultimate meditation on timelessness, longing, and regret, surpassing even *Vertigo*. The idea of never growing old, remaining young and beautiful forever, intrigued Hitchcock, tempered with the problem of seeing your loved ones age and disappear. That's the dilemma of *Mary Rose*. We know one day that we are all going to die, but often we don't want anything we love to end, whether it be a book, a song or a play. Mary Rose herself had to let go in order to move on, as she's basically a spirit that is haunting her house. Barrie himself may have been haunted by his own loss.

The efforts of Lewis and Jay Allen show that they too shared Hitchcock's interest in adapting the play for film or television. But the failure of all three of them to do so was due in large part to the play's inherent attraction; its old-fashioned whimsicality and sentimentality made it an anachronism, which may have been better left on the page.

## NOTES

1. John Russell Taylor, "Surviving," *Sight & Sound* (Summer 1977): 174–76.

2. Interview with Andrew Birkin, Pwllheli, Wales, December 23, 2012.

3. Denis MacKail, *The Story of J.M.B* (London: Peter Davies, 1941), 443.

4. Unpublished correspondence: Nico Llewelyn Davies to Andrew Birkin, January 1, 1976.

5. Admiral Mark Kerr: letter to *The Sunday Times*, London, July 25, 1937.

6. J. M. Barrie, *Peter Pan and Other Plays* (Oxford: Oxford University Press, 1995), xxii.

7. Fay Compton, *Rosemary* (London: Alston Rivers, 1926), 196.

8. Compton, *Rosemary*, 197.

9. Barrie, *Peter Pan and Other Plays*, xxii.

10. Hitchcock to Truffaut, in *Hitchcock*, 1967.

11. Compton, *Rosemary*, 197.

12. Ivor Brown, *Observer*, "Ivor," April 25, 1920.

13. Michael Meyer, *Strindberg* (New York: Random House, 1985), 408.

14. Review of Mary Rose, *Tatler* 1010 (November 3, 1920).

15. Letter from J. M. Barrie to E. Lucas, http://www.jmbarrie.co.uk.

16. Charles Isherwood, "Reviving a Barrie Fantasy Not Called 'Peter Pan,'" *New York Times*, February 21, 2007.

17. "Where Film Men Cast No Shadows," *The Times*, November 26, 1963.

18. "Mr. Alfred Hitchcock's Zest for Cinema," *The Times*, June 24, 1964.

19. Hitchcock to Truffaut, 1966.

20. Irving Wardle, Review of Mary Rose, *The Times*, July 14, 1972.

21. Interview with Peter Newman, New York, July 7, 2012.

22. Interview with Susan MacGillicuddy, Brisbane, Australia, April 16, 2013.

## Chapter Eleven

# Through the Lens

> Hitchcock loved matte shots, he loved to make the audience wonder, "How did they get that shot?" Right after he died the technology changed. Too bad he missed it.
>
> —Hilton Green, Production Manager on *Marnie*

Hitchcock has been described as the most subjective of filmmakers, and Robert Boyle said that in *Marnie* he was "mostly interested in feelings." Hitchcock called subjective treatment "the purist form of cinema, putting the audience in the mind of the camera. *Rear Window* is the best example of that. Close up of the man, what he sees, he reacts to it. It can't be done in the theatre, or the novel, it's the purest form of cinema, the subjective treatment." With *Marnie*, he would reach the pinnacle of this subjective treatment, utilizing the camera to achieve a level of virtuosity unparalleled in his work.

Winston Graham made the remark that Hitchcock was more of a cameraman than a director. He said that Hitchcock never saw a story, he only saw a shot.[1] Indeed when Hitchcock met Graham in Claridges, London, in 1964 shortly after the release of *Marnie*, Graham remembers,"He never asked me if I enjoyed the film; he immediately went into the photographic side. Instead he said, did you see this shot with the lens when Strutt arrives, suggesting that he began as a photographer. He assumed that I did like the film but only wanted to talk about the photography."

Throughout the film, the camera is rarely still or objective. At every moment in *Marnie*, the camera is engaged in expressing the thoughts, feelings, and moods of the characters. Hitchcock's camera creates an extraordinary intimacy and articulation, from the extreme close-up kiss of Mark and Marnie during the thunderstorm, to the close up tracking shot of the gun as Marnie rushes to shoot her beloved horse.

Hitchcock used to say that the most difficult genre to him was melodrama. "That's why he was involved with melodrama, and as such, it had a theatrical connotation, and I don't think he cared that the film looked theatrical in some respects," said close friend and matte artist Albert Whitlock. Certainly *Marnie* is theatrical and melodramatic, with it's thunderstorms, red suffusions and painted backdrops, but for Hitchcock that didn't matter because he was mostly interested in subjective states.

The camera in *Marnie* is also a precursor of 1960s art cinema and its themes echo those of the Italian director Michelangelo Antonioni. As Richard Brody says in the *New Yorker*, "*The Birds* and especially *Marnie* are the work of an American Antonioni, whose psychological dramas are matched by architectural and symbolic ones, by a confrontation with the roiling chill of technological modernity."[2] With *Marnie*, Hitchcock was making a concerted push in the direction of European art house cinema, certainly in terms of camera style, where the camera echoes the character's feelings. Prior to making *The Birds* he watched films by Antonioni, Bergman, and Renais. The coastal setting in *The Birds* resembles *L'avventura* (1960), *La Notte* (1961), and *Through a Glass Darkly* (1960). As well as the sand dune scene of *The Birds* echoing *L'avventura* and Antonioni's next film, *La Notte*, it experiments with electronic music. In most of his late career, Hitchcock was interested in the dynamics of the human mind, exploring human psychology in *Vertigo*, *Psycho*, and *The Birds*. With *Marnie* he was "desperately trying to dig into the psyche of this woman," said Robert Boyle, which is why he got involved in all these tricky solutions. His camera work was exemplary and none of it would have been possible without the collaboration of Robert Burks.

## ROBERT BURKS

Hitch insists on perfection. You never have any trouble with him as long as you know your job and do it.

—Robert Burks

When Hitchcock moved to America, the cinematographers he worked with were the best in the industry, beginning with George Barnes, who filmed *Rebecca* (1940) and *Spellbound* (1945). Other cinematographers were Harry Stradling, Joseph Valentine, Glen MacWilliams, Lee Garmes, and Ted Tetzlaff; each worked with the master director more than once. When he returned to England for *Under Capricorn* and *Stage Fright*, he filmed with Jack Cardiff and Wilkie Cooper. But it was with Robert Burks that Hitchcock would attain levels of technical accomplishments like never before, and the two of them, with *Marnie*, would reach their greatest achievement with the camera.

It was when Hitchcock was preparing to make *Strangers on a Train* for Warner Brothers in 1950 that he first met Bob Burks. Born in Los Angeles in 1909 as Leslie Robert Burks, he started working at the Warner Brothers lab in 1928, at the age of nineteen. He learned from some of the top cinematographers at work in the industry's largest special effects facility on Stage 5 where he learned about emulsions, lenses, and camera movement. It was the best place for an apprentice to get his training because he learned everything from the ground up. Burks ascended quickly up the ranks and was soon working as an assistant to the best cinematographers. Special effects supervisor Byron Haskin, who later went on to direct 1953's *The War of the Worlds*, recommended Burks saying, "His work is thoroughly excellent in every respect. . . . [He is] straightforward, resourceful, and in the true sense, a gentleman." Burks became a full-time cinematographer in 1948 and his next two films, *The Fountainhead* (1949) with Gary Cooper and *The Glass Menagerie* (1950) with Kirk Douglas, both had the expressionist look that Hitchcock favored.

When Burks met Hitchcock in 1950, he proved to be the perfect cinematographer, as the director was always looking to use the camera for special effects and to evoke feelings. Hitchcock had recently experimented with long takes in *Rope* (1948) and *Under Capricorn* (1949) and appreciated Burks's comprehensive knowledge of effects and innovative camera work. Their first collaboration, *Strangers on a Train* (1951), earned Burks an Academy Award nomination for best black and white photography. One famous scene in which Bruno Anthony (Robert Walker) strangles Miriam Haynes (Laura Elliot) is shown as a distorted reflection in the victim's fallen glasses. For the sequence where the carousel spins out of control, Burks enlisted the help of fellow Stage 5 special effects supervisor Hans F. Koenekamp.

In the fourteen years that followed, Burks photographed eleven more of Hitchcock's films, including *I Confess* (1953), *Dial M for Murder* (1954, 3-D, Warner Color), *Rear Window* (1954, Technicolor), *To Catch a Thief* (1955, VistaVision, Technicolor), *The Trouble with Harry* (1955, VistaVision, Technicolor), *The Man Who Knew Too Much* (1956, VistaVision, Technicolor), *The Wrong Man* (1957, black and white), *Vertigo* (1958, VistaVision, Technicolor), *North by Northwest* (1958, VistaVision, Technicolor), *The Birds* (1963, Technicolor), and *Marnie* (1964, Technicolor).

Throughout all of these projects, Burks's camera operator was Leonard J. South, ASC, known to his colleagues as Lenny, who also started in the Warner Brothers Special Effects unit. Both men became close friends of the Hitchcock family. Burks was nominated for an Oscar for the color photography of *Rear Window* and won the following year for *To Catch a Thief*, a magnificent example of VistaVision technique. In a career spanning twenty-five years as a director of photography, Burks made fifty-five features.

"Bob Burks was a marvelous person," remembers Jim Brown. "A real fine cameraman, he was a real gentleman, the very best. We were very close because we did *The Birds* and *Marnie*, along with Bob Boyle. We had lunch almost every day when we were doing the preproduction, a real nice man. Bob almost invariably knew what Hitchcock wanted. A lot of times Hitch would say, 'What do you think Bob?' and Hitch said 'You got it.' There were times visually it was like one mind, Bob knew Hitchcock so well by then, he could anticipate what Hitchcock wanted."

Burks and the crew used a 35mm Mitchell BNC camera when filming *Marnie*, which was Hollywood industry standard. By the mid-1960s, wide-angle or short focal lenses less than 50mm, exaggerating and deepening depth relationships in a wide area, were available for 35mm filming. They were used, along with filters, for flashbacks by Hitchcock and Burks to represent Marnie's traumatic past. Hitchcock used a 50mm lens most of the time on 35mm cameras to make the film appear as it would to the human eye. A 50mm lens is called a normal lens because objects remain in perspective approximately as they do with your eye. According to his script supervisor Marshall Schlom, "He wanted the camera, being the audience all the time, to see as if they were seeing it with their own eyes."

Marnie is frequently filmed walking away from the camera, such as in the opening scene, into an exaggerated deep point perspective in which the focus remains crisp into a point far in the distance. Robert Burks had an innate understanding of Hitchcock's vision of what he wanted on the screen and their experiments with film became bold and avant-garde, especially with color. In *Marnie*, Hitchcock and Burks created a vibrant color palette, from the bright yellow handbag to the browns, russets, and greens of the Rutland house, to the red that afflicts Marnie. The color palette that they created was at the vanguard of 1960s art-cinema, especially preceding Antonioni's *Red Desert* (1966). That Hitchcock was aware of Antonioni is evidenced by his correspondence with Guilio Ascarelli, the head of Universal in Rome, in a memo to find out how Antonioni achieved the color in *Red Desert*.

## STORYBOARDS

As *Marnie* was mostly filmed inside the studio, there was little location work, except a few exteriors at the Golden Oak Disney Ranch, the American President Liner, Radnor Hunt, and the back projection plates for the car journeys and Marnie's horse riding. Hitchcock seldom storyboarded two-hander scenes of people talking, but these location scenes required the expertise of storyboard illustrator Harold Michelson.

Michelson was the main production illustrator on *The Birds* and it was his task to sketch almost all of the storyboards on that film. As Bob Boyle affirmed, "Harold has an extraordinary sense of film. He only draws what the camera sees. He reproduces storyboards of what the lens sees exactly. From his storyboard you could tell what lens you should use, what the angle of the camera was. Harold was a master of his technique and his storyboards always represented a shot that you could get with the camera."

Michelson's storyboards were essential for the production team as Hitchcock favored filming process plates as backgrounds. These had to be filmed on location so that Hitchcock could later use them in the studio with the actors. When Bob Boyle went to scout Atlantic City racetrack in the fall of 1963, he brought with him Michelson's storyboards (figure 1). "What I was doing was making background projection plates; most of this was shot in the studio—all of it, except the backgrounds, the horses racing, the stands, I did as a second unit," remembers Boyle. "What I would do, I knew that this would be in the studio, but the background. That's what we were doing."

Michelson also storyboarded the hunt sequence for Jim Brown to take with him to Pennsylvania (figure 2). The beginning of the hunt was shot in front of the house at Universal. "We were also shooting that house for the hunt sequence," says Boyle. "Where the hunt was, a few scenes at Disney Ranch, but we shot most of the big stuff out on the Philadelphia main line. The people who lived there followed the hounds. We had production shots with doubles where all the horses would gather together."

Boyle confirms that Hitchcock wasn't keen on location filming and never even went to Philadelphia. He also said that in keeping with Marnie's color palette, they kept the backgrounds muted. Everyone was trying to interpret Hitchcock's vision through the use of storyboards and Hitchcock encouraged this: "So Harold, myself, and all the others, including somebody who's sweeping the stage, we began to think like Hitchcock, because he allowed us to do that," says Boyle. Michelson agrees: "Many directors, particularly these days, seemed to be afraid to let other people in on the secret. You would draw a close up highly stylized. I would sweat over these portraits. Each one of these is a background, I would draw the girl left or right, or right or left, it's very mechanical. I would use photographs as resource materials, and would even trace it, if it was all there."

Albert Whitlock also remembers Hitchcock being very cavalier about the storyboarding and location filming, even to the point of forgetting to tell his art department if a shot was no longer needed. This was the case with the fox hunters in long procession riding away from the Rutland house which was going to be a matte in the background (figure 2):

Well, we got back [from the East Coast] and I painted the matte shots. I mean, Hitch wouldn't even say to me, "We don't need the matte shots so don't bother with that." I got the thing all finished, a lot of work, and I showed it to Hitch. He said, "Oh yeah. Well, we're not using that, you know, Al." So I said, "What do you mean?" So he said, "Well, it holds up the story. We don't need the hunt. After all, you know, a fox. We know it's a fox hunt, we don't have to." We had the fox! We could see the fox and everything. It was marvelous. We had chase scenes, and I painted all the backgrounds. I painted them all! A whole slew of matte shots. And Hitch said, "Well, the hunt's out. It's holding up the story." But further than that, while we were back in Pennsylvania. I'd come back early and the company was still there. Jim Brown was doing the second unit.[3]

Of the hunt sequence, Boyle said, "I guess I'm lucky. . . . We had two second units. I did the plates and stuff for the racetrack sequence, where she's at the racetrack. And Brown was in there with the hunt club doing the hunt. And Hitch didn't like that stuff. So Brown took the brunt, in Hitch's mind, for the whole thing. And he forgot all about the fact that I was also doing the second unit over with the other." He went on to say that Hitchcock was such a perfectionist that "the worst thing in the world was to accept a second unit from Hitch because it couldn't be right." Albert Whitlock continued,

They were still back there and I was here, and Hitch said to me, "You know, we're missing one scene. A car driving up to the house. There's that nice avenue. Why don't you go shoot the avenue and the car and paint the house in for me?" I said, "Well, I'll have to go all the way back to Pennsylvania to do it. It's just one shot." He said, "Well, never mind. They're there. So phone Jim Brown and tell him you're coming." Now, this is Friday, so I called Jim and he said, "You'll be traveling . . . were there being held back for me to arrive to shoot this shot. And so I went back there and I shot the scene and came back on Monday, walked into his office on Monday morning. All the way to Pennsylvania. It's halfway to Europe! So I walked into his office on Monday morning and I said, We've got a nice shot. Beautiful light, Hitch." He said, "What's that for?" So I said, "It's for the car driving up to the house." He said, "Oh, I cut that out." I said, "Wait a minute. When did you cut it out?" Well, it turned out he had cut it out on Friday! All this mish-mash, you know. I mean my traveling to Pennsylvania. Getting this shot and everything. He'd already cut it out long before I left. But I mean he's terribly cavalier. It just didn't occur to him to call me up and stop me from going and to bring the company back. This was Hitch. And he didn't do it with any intent, but it was just something he couldn't stop.

## COMPLEX POV

Part of Hitchcock's technique as a subjective director was his complex use of point of view (POV). This is most evident in *Marnie* when Marnie starts a job at the Rutland office and the camera shifts among multiple points of view. At Rutland's the power of the gaze becomes a struggle to own the point of view, as looks exchanged between Marnie and Mark maneuver for power, in this case access to the combination of the Rutland safe. Marnie spies on Susan, unaware that Mark is spying on her. There is a battle of control for the looks and "ownership" of the camera.

These office scenes were the first to be filmed, between Tuesday, November 26, and Friday, December 6. Linden Chiles was hired as Artie the office worker, who tries to tempt Marnie with a Danish. "I was under contract to Universal when I first heard that Hitchcock was going to shoot *Marnie*," Chiles remembers.[4] "I opened the soundstage door. It was completely dark and empty, or so it seemed. I thought I'd come to the wrong place. Usually these cavernous dens are a beehive of activity. But not this time. I stood there for a moment and as my eyes adjusted I could make out dozens of ghostly figures rushing about. The place was a beehive but you could've heard a pin drop. Right about then an AD showed up and introduced himself and took me over to meet Hitchcock. He gave me a soft pudgy handshake and we went right to work in the office set with Tippi and Mariette Hartley." Chiles's memories echo others that Hitchcock's sets were as quiet and orderly as a cathedral.

"Hitchcock and I hardly spoke another word," Chiles continues. "He was very quiet and had next to nothing to say about my performance, but he shot the hell out of those few pages. Covered every angle. I've never worked with a director who did such exhaustive coverage. And he never deviated from the script. Many directors like to 'mess around,' improvise, rework the dialogue, play with a scene, get the actors' input, not Hitchcock. We shot it word-for-word. I don't recall how many days we spent in that office—several as I recall. We only shot two or three pages a day. Everything was choreographed, every move, every line."

This view is confirmed by Hitchcock in an interview two years later. "Actually, I make a film entirely on paper. Not 'write it' but 'make it' on paper. I never experiment on the set, I never improvise. I improvise in the office seven or eight months before the shooting. I have the whole film in mind shot for shot, complete."[5]

When Mark Rutland sees Marnie for the first time in Ward's outer office, Hitchcock uses a forward-tracking subjective camera, one of his favorite devices. As Hitchcock said, "a subjective camera is the way you get a mental process going by use of the visual." On this occasion Hitchcock films Sean Connery in front and in close so that the audience identifies with him as he sees Marnie. The camera then precedes his character's movement, walking past Marnie, who lowers her skirt over her knees as if they were "a national treasure." Hitchcock then cuts to Rutland's reaction shot as he tries to place Marnie. When he does remember, it's told all through the visuals, with a reliance on Sean Connery's marvelous acting and expressions.

When Marnie spills the red ink on her blouse, Hitchcock sustains the mood by keeping his camera framed tightly on her face and following her as she gets up and runs to the washroom. He doesn't cut a wide shot because this would dissipate the mood, only allowing Marnie to disappear in long shot into the ladies' washroom. Later when Mark takes Marnie from the doorway to the armchair during the thunderstorm, the camera stays on a two shot. This represents the general way that Hitchcock handles mood, sustaining the emotion by never cutting back to a wide but keeping close.

## THE ROBBERY

In the first robbery of the Rutland safe, Hitchcock uses lighting and sound to effectively heighten the emotional tension and suspense. It's a Friday night, and in anticipation of robbing the safe Marnie waits in the ladies' toilets for her co-workers to clear the building. Hitchcock counterpoints sound and silence, as we first hear the chatter of the workers, followed by "goodnights," until eventually there is silence. The camera is fixed on a static shot of Marnie in a long take, her face partially hidden by shadows in the lower right corner of the frame. Only when she is certain that she is alone does she venture out of the stall. Hitchcock keeps the camera close on Marnie, following her to the desk where she retrieves her handbag and then to Susan's drawer to gain access to the safe combination, which precedes the famous long shot.

At the end of the ten days, on Friday, December 6, Hitchcock filmed Marnie's robbery of the Rutland safe. He had been planning the shot for over a year and had it firmly in his mind. During his interviews with Peter Bogdanovich in February 1963, he described the shot in detail: "I go to a full long shot, and around the corner comes a cleaning woman, with her back to us, swabbing the floor, and she comes down and down, no cuts with the camera, until she gets level with the glass partition. Then the girl closes the safe, bulging bag of money. Then she turns and sees the bent head. So she takes her shoes off and stuffs them in the pocket of her suit, close up of her feet, one shoe walking. She gets outside. The shoe drops with a clap. Woman still mopping away. Then the night watchman comes. While she's almost out of view, going down the stairs, he says (in a loud voice), 'How's your husband lately?' What a faux pas, what a bloomer. I can hear them now, critics and all."[6]

As always Hitchcock's remarks show that he was constantly thinking of the audience. He was also thinking about the architectural space of the Rutland office when he was designing that scene, including the glass partition that separated Susan's outer office from the long corridor where the cleaning woman appears. Hitchcock was also aware of the moral ambiguity of the scene. The audience knows that stealing is wrong and, what's more, won't help Marnie, who needs psychological help. As Hitchcock said, "This comes under the heading of rooting for the evildoer to succeed—because in all of us we have that eleventh commandment nagging us: 'Thou shalt not be found out.' The average person looking at someone doing evil or wrong wants the person to get away with it. There's something that makes them say, 'Look out! Look out! They're coming!' I think it's the most amazing instinct—doesn't matter how evil it is, you know. Can't go as far as murder, but anything up to that point. The audience can't bear the suspense of the person being discovered. 'Hurry up! Quick! You're going to be caught!'"

Harold Michelson made a sketch of the very low shot in *Marnie*, so that the camera was set a foot above the floor. In some ways it's likened to Ozu's low-angle shots in *Tokyo Story*. "I know that everything we did came out a discussion with Hitchcock," says Bob Boyle. "He was always talking. I think his driver had as much information as anyone, because he would talk to everybody and he would listen to everybody. He was always in control, but he was always very interested in the audience, he made movies for the audience, and he was an audience, so he would look up there on the screen and was seeing his movie and he was judging it, and he was judging it as an audience."

## THE KISS

Hitchcock's kissing scenes are known for creating intimacy by moving the camera around the actors in a 360-degree arc—most famously in *Vertigo*, *Notorious*, *Marnie*, and *Topaz*. The definitive Hitchcock moment would have to be the 360-degree kiss in *Vertigo*. It's been described as pure emotional cinema at its finest, the shot expressing Scottie's emotional state visually, which is, of course, the point of all Hitchcock movies. One of the most famous kissing sequences is in *Notorious*, where Hitchcock circumvented the rule of a maximum of 3 ½ second kisses by breaking Cary Grant and Ingrid Bergman up and then having them resume kissing.

Hitchcock's favorite sculptor was Rodin and he was proud to own one of his works. According to the biographer Charlotte Chandler, "Ideally, he would have liked to be a sculptor, like Rodin." He especially admired Rodin's "The Kiss."

Marnie has a particularly long and detailed kissing scene, filmed in extreme close-up, when Mark kisses Marnie during the thunderstorm in his office. The camera lingers all in response to Bernard Herrmann's surging romantic music. The scene was filmed on Stage 21 on Tuesday, December

3, 1963. Paul Jacobsen was a twenty-year-old electrician working on the set of the Rutland offices. In 2013 he remembers, "I was up high in the green beds or the deck where the lights are placed and operated. That was the first time we used spun glass infront of the lights which was a diffusion material that softened the harshness of the light beam. I had never seen that before because I was new to being a lamp operator." Jacobsen's job was to operate the machine that created the lightning effects during the thunderstorm in Mark's office. He also remembers working with Hitchcock and Bob Burks. "It was a time when younger directors were casually dressed working on television shows, but Hitchcock had a suit on and shiny black shoes, and a white shirt and a tie. I remembered the light shined off his balding head. He was treated like a king and he was definitely driving the boat. And after the director, the DOP was the highest paid crew member on the set."

During the thunderstorm, the camera dollies to an extreme close-up of their lips, which Hedren later describes as one of the sexiest kisses in screen history. The implication is clear; Marnie's mind is somewhere else during the kiss, terrified of thunder, the color red, and the lightning. When Peter Bogdanovich asked Hitchcock, "Are the kisses in Mark's point of view or Marnie's point of view or your point of view? They are remarkably romantic," Hitchcock paused for a moment before answering, "I think they are my point of view after all. A woman can be embraced with a man, and her mind can be somewhere else. I don't think the actual physical act of kissing always connotes emotional feeling."

## THE CRANE

In technique, *Marnie* also echoes *Notorious*, a firm favorite of Hitchcock. Hitchcock said it was the story of a girl who doesn't know who she is. "She is a psychotic, a compulsive thief, and afraid of sex, and in the end she finds out why. In terms of style, it will be a bit like *Notorious*," said Hitchcock to Peter Bogdanovich.[7]

That *Marnie* would be rather like *Notorious* in style is most evident in the party scene, which occurs in both films about three-quarters of the way through. As Hilton Green said, "In the preparation for *Marnie*, we looked at one of Mr. Hitchcock's other films, *Notorious*, beforehand. Bob Burks and everyone, and there was a shot where . . . it was a very famous shot of a crane shot down a staircase from high above, keep moving, moving, moving in on Ingrid Bergman and, uh, Claude Rains, which kept going and going right into her hand, and in her hand was the key to the basement wine cellar. And in *Marnie*, we had a similar, not exact, but a similar occasion of using that type of shot, where the party's going on, and he wanted the same feeling of coming in, coming in, coming in, and ending on a close shot of the character of Strutt, who had seen Marnie earlier and remembered the robbery in the office."

A team of grips was under Bob Burks's direction to achieve the impressive crane shot that occurs in *Marnie*'s party scene, which was filmed on Friday, January 17, 1964. Bob Burks starts the shot from a vantage point on the balcony overlooking the spacious foyer of the Rutland house. We hear the sound of the doorbell, a butler opens the door and guests enter. The camera starts to move in on the door in one fluid crane shot with modulated focus, twenty feet down to floor level and forty feet forward and ending on the unexpected face of Sidney Strutt. As Hitchcock said to Peter Bogdanovich, "The actual movement of the camera creates a suspense in the audience 'cause you know it's going somewhere. So, it's like, 'Where is he going? Where is he going? Where is he going?' And it ends up on a close-up of Strutt, and the audience says, 'Oh, my God.'"

Hitchcock's crane movements in *Notorious* and *Marnie* echo the subjective state of the audience. In *Notorious* he said it was a way of saying, you know, "Here's this party, and all these things are going on, and the whole crux of the matter is in the hand, a small object in the hand. And in this case, you could say the same thing. It's this, 'Where is it going?' Well, what could unmask her is this fellow that comes in the door. Again, it's visual storytelling. It's involving the audience, in both cases, kind of unconsciously."

## THE FLASHBACK

Hitchcock and Burks experimented with a special lens for *Marnie*'s childhood flashback, by using a very long focus and using the same technique of changing perspective as they had in *Vertigo*. The call sheet for filming the flashback on Tuesday, February 9, 1964, described it as a "Slum Room, foreground Baltimore Table, Cigarette, Pillow and Blanket, Photo effect, distorted perspective, b and white effect, zoom lens and dolly."

The lens that was used was similar to the one used in *Vertigo*, which has famously become known as the *Vertigo* shot. As Boyle recalls, "Bob Burks designed that lens. It was a big thing, in which it held the foreground, but let the background recede. He did that in *Vertigo*, when he had Jimmy Stewart looking down. He had it kind of fall away." Burks accomplished it by building a scale model that would lie on its side, and then combining a lens zoom forward while the camera was dollied back. Bob Burks designed a similar lens for Marnie's flashback—the lens was a fish eye with a reverse zoom. Instead of being a down shot like in *Vertigo*, it's a reverse zoom so that the background moves away. The flashback zoom lens gives the feeling of time distortion as Marnie remembers her past. Her memories recede back like the camera moving away from the background, a reverse zoom.

Peter Bogdanovich describes the shot as creating a "tremendous feeling of disorientation, which is what the character was feeling, by moving the camera back, then zooming forward, which will create a kind of disorientation. You don't know which way you're going." Hitchcock, as mentioned, said that he got the idea for the lens one night at the Chelsea Arts Ball in London. As Hitchcock said,

> First of all, we have to explain the perspective of various lenses. In other words, when you look through the finder of a 50mm lens—a two-inch lens—you see the perspective as roughly normal, as the eye sees it. Now the moment you go to a 35mm lens, the perspective begins to change, to elongate. Then you go to a 28mm. In other words, the wider the angle of lens, the more forced the perspective becomes. You've probably seen still photographs of interiors of rooms where the ceiling seemed to go up, especially if you're familiar with the room. It was on this basis that I'd gotten them to devise this movement. It's a changing of perspective from the normal to the abnormal—from the normal of a 50mm lens to the abnormal of the 22mm, say. The difficulty they had in doing it was that they found the sides moved, and I said, "The sides cannot move!" The sides nearest the camera must stay where they are. At one time many years ago, when I was frustrated in getting this effect, I had thought, why can't we get a still printed on rubber, and I'll make a little wire on the back and pull it. I got so desperate, I even suggested that. And at last, of course, they came up with the effect of dollying back while zooming forward.

Harold Michelson was on hand that day to assist with the lighting: "I remember that scene, I was standing there with the cameraman, and Hitch asked for a gobo (which makes abstract shadows on the wall), to be placed in front of the lights, to have with crazy shadows on the wall. I think I nailed it with a gobo on a bunch of sticks and I went there and set it up. Hitch came by and said, that's fine, shoot it. I looked at the cameraman and he said well, I said shoot it. It was a shot with a reverse zoom in a fish-eye lens. That was a lens that Bob Burks invented that kept the foreground stationary but the background moved away from the foreground."

Bruce Dern was on set during the filming of the flashback, which was on another stage away from the main stage where Connery and Hedren were working on. He remembers that they shot the flashback sequence with a huge lens. "It was a German lens that looked like a lightbulb, and what it did was it distorted everything in the foreground, but made everything in the background sharp focus. And so, it was neat because I had Mr. Hitchcock to myself. He had no other distractions except me. So, he really took time to get to know me a little bit."

As makeup man Howard Smit recalled, he used more fake blood than in any of his previous films for the flashback scene. "I remember the blood," says script supervisor Lois Thurman. "Hitch had the make up man put something in Bruce Dern's hair to make the blood run, and I remember watching it in the dailies."[8] The color scheme was subdued on the set, "We were trying to keep the background muted here on *Marnie* and saving it for blood," says Robert Boyle. Afterward the film was desaturated so that it had a grainy quality, and so contrasting the past of Marnie's memory with the present.

## THE HORSE ACCIDENT

Another example of time distortion occurs during the horse accident in *Marnie*, at a moment of sheer terror and anxiety. The camera treads over the same ground to convey a moment as time is agonizingly stretched. The props on the call sheet for two days on Friday, January 24, and Monday, January 27, 1964, were a trick horse that had been taught to lay down and roll over, dummy legs for the close-ups of Forio, dolly shot, hand-held camera, trampoline, and a gimbal. The sequence was filmed at the Disney Ranch with the use of a crane.

The horse accident in *Marnie* is another example of Hitchcock's use of montage, combined with deliberate cinematic distortion that stretches time. When asked if the horse accident was an expressionistic technique, Hitchcock's reply was, "Oh, yes. Sure. You see, when you deal with an accident of this sort, if you did it at its normal speed, it would happen so flashily that you'd never really realize what was happening; you wouldn't get the full benefit of it. Now for when the horse rears up, we built a low wall—I think it was only nine inches from the ground, and then we skimmed the ground with the camera, just leaving the grass out of the picture, and then we got a horse just to roll over. It was a trick horse that loved to roll. So all it was doing was rolling over a nine-inch bit of brick wall, that's all. The rest, when the girl was thrown into the air, was slow motion. We sat her on the arm of the crane and swung her through the air in an arc, in slow motion."

## THE PAINTED BACKDROP

The painted backdrop has already been discussed in detail in chapter 4. Boyle had made the decision to paint the reduced backing, but it didn't go well after Hitchcock decided to shoot the set from three different eye levels.

"I made the decision to do it with paint," remembers Boyle. "It should have been done with three dimensions but it was a painted brick, and one thing I didn't remember . . . I didn't realize. There was going to be rain, and the rain was in the set, and the rain got on these flat [and reflected all the lights]. And you couldn't see the bricks at all. All you could see was a flat shiny surface." Technical mishaps ensued from Boyle because he wasn't aware there would be rain on the set.

Michelson concurs: "But the cutouts that we had—because he wanted it at two feet, six feet, and eight feet, we had to pull the cutouts out and put it at a different eye level, we had to have the ship, which he wanted looming, because he had once seen a picture with a telephoto lens of a ship looming." Albert Whitlock reinforces Hitchcock's view of the looming ship from his childhood memories: "It's an early recollection, because he said to me, 'Do you remember when you walk down the East India Dock Road in London, and you do still today, you walk down among these awful sort of terraced houses, very low-grade houses, rows and rows of them, and you walk down them, Limehouse and that area, and you turn the corner and suddenly, there's a ship! It's in the street. You know it's actually at the end of the road. And Baltimore is the same way.'"

When Bob Boyle and Hitchcock went to Baltimore on their scout, they saw a looming ship and Hitchcock "loved it." He wanted this looming image because it was such an important memory from his childhood. Whitlock and the others tried to dissuade him from that perspective but Hitchcock was adamant and determined to get that image. In reality it would have been physically impossible, because a 1.85-meter man would only see the hull, and the image on camera would be black and totally unreadable. In the end Harold Michelson had to keep drawing it so that the superstructure came in, so that you could see the funnel, and then it was a ship—but the trouble was the perspective was now too small to look authentic.

On the stage, the ship didn't look too bad—but on Tuesday, February 6, 1964, when Bob Boyle saw the dailies on the screen he went to Bob Burks and said "Bob, I think we can change the surface on the houses and can we do certain things, let's try to get Hitch to retake this." And Bob said, "Yes. I can do a better job too. We won't have all that shine and all that." They went to Hitchcock appealing to reshoot it, but he said, "It seems all right to me." "But later when the critics pounced on it, then he would hardly speak to us," laughs Bob Boyle. If Hitchcock liked or disliked a shot, it was very difficult for you to argue with him or change his mind, as he was the final arbiter. As Boyle said, "But he's also willing to put up with technical flaws if he feels it does the trick for him."

When Jim Brown saw it in the dailies, he thought it didn't work. "I thought we have to reshoot this, but [Hitchcock] accepted it. To this day, looking at it didn't work. I was surprised he accepted it—it was a painting on a stage. Bob Boyle got someone to paint it—it was huge. I know Bob wasn't happy with it either."

In a later interview with Peter Bogdanovich, after the film was released, Hitchcock speaks about the looming ship and his childhood: "The ship—I had seen that years ago in England, although it wasn't well done in *Marnie*. I was fascinated years ago as a kid in London to go down to the docks. And there was an ordinary mean street, and right across the inn was a huge liner, with the smokestacks, ridiculous little low houses, almost disappeared. You almost had a ship on dry land. It didn't really come off the way I wanted it to. I've always had the feeling when you arrive in Southampton. The ship *Elizabeth* comes in so close into the town, so that when you stand near the front of the ship, all you can see are the bows of the ship and it always fascinates me."

## BACK PROJECTION

Just like the end of the filming of *The Birds*, the majority of the back projection was scheduled toward the end of the shoot, between Thursday, February 13, and Tuesday, February 18, 1964. These included process plates to cover Marnie's horseriding, the use of treadmill, and Forio or a double horse for the treadmill.

"He wanted to do, instead of process, sodium vapor, which was a process that Disney did in those days," remembers Bob Boyle. "And I went over to Disney a couple of times to get a mechanical horse and that's where I met Mr. Disney, but it didn't work for some reason so we did bluescreen—but that was bad because of the blonde hair and blowing; it just didn't look right, with a halo."

"I think the main reason why he chose to film the way he did without going on location was for the control," says Jim Brown. Although much criticized, it was necessary to use rear projection on a soundstage to capture Marnie's reaction and Hitchcock was mostly interested in feelings. "He wanted to create a feeling of the woman she was, with wind blowing in her hair. He was going for a feeling of being safe," remembers Evan Hunter. "In *Marnie*, where the girl is a compulsive thief, after every job she does, she goes to a farm in Maryland, and I suppose using some of the proceeds she goes to ride a horse," said Hitchcock. "Loves riding on a horse, in the open air, let her hair blow free, almost as if she is cleansing herself of the crime just committed."[9]

Much has been written about the intentional use of the back projection to convey Marnie's dreamlike state. In Robin Wood's book, *Hitchcock's Films Revisited*, he argues that "The back-projection gives a dream-like quality to the ride, but no sense of genuine release."[10] When Peter Bodganovich mentioned this to Hitchcock in their 1966 interview, he says, "back projection uses a purposeful artificial quality to Marnie's happiness on the horse. Do you think [Wood's] reading in or was it a planned effect? Hitchcock's reply was. "I think it's a very good idea," and then they both laugh. The assumption is that Hitchcock never thought of that when he was making the film and that Wood was overreaching in his intepretation. Bob Boyle also dismissed the theory when this author asked him in 2000.

## HARVARD TRIP

On July 14, 1966, Alfred Hitchcock's fiftieth film, *Torn Curtain*, had its world premiere in Boston. Hitchcock and Universal representatives were in attendance and in the afternoon they visited the Harvard Dramatic Club. The club was founded in 1908 and staged productions within Harvard University. Past students included Tommy Lee Jones, Stockard Channing, Tim Mayer, and Thomas Babe. Honor Moore was the first female president of the club at the time. "We knew that Hitch was coming to Boston, so we invented an award for him to come and collect," remembers Moore in 2013. "We completely invented the event to make publicity for our season. I went into town and asked a calligrapher to make up an award and I handed it to Hitch. We were beside ourselves that he had decided to come to our club."[11]

The club held a two-day festival on Hitchcock with screenings of *The Lodger*, *Shadow of a Doubt*, *Blackmail*, and *Psycho*. Honor also remembers a few other details that Thursday afternoon when she presented Hitchcock with the award. "I remember how short he was, and I think he must have been a little drunk after lunch. He wasn't overtly loaded I don't think." Hitchcock is likely to have just had lunch before arriving at the club and often enjoyed vodka with his meal. "It was in the daytime, it was very hot and the theater had no air conditioning," recalls Honor. "I felt he was completely undemonstrative, as if he was phoning it in; he didn't come out of himself. I was so shy myself. But apart from that, I didn't feel anything out of the ordinary from him."

After being given the award, Hitchcock attended a thirty-minute question and answer session held at the Radcliffe Graduate Center. Tim Hunter, film critic of *The Harvard Crimson*, chaired the questions. He later graduated in the class of 1968, and went on to become a director on American television with credits including *The Rivers Edge*, *Glee*, *American Horror Story*, and *Breaking Bad*.

As Hunter remembers, "It was hard to get Hitchcock to say anything beyond his usual repertoire of stories and about montage."[12] Indeed Hitchcock started the Q&A with familiar anecdotes explaining the difference between suspense, where the audience has all of the information, and mystery, when the audience knows very little: "Well, all detail in the literature of the camera applies to most situations. It is how you use the intimacy and detail. In *Potemkin*, of course, you have the perambulator going down the steps, and the incident is repeated several times at several angles—you remember that. Well, I think it's a matter of using the language of the camera, which is so flexible and free. The beauty of the camera is that you can photograph anything you want and make any comment you want." He also went on to describe his concept of pure cinema: "Unfortunately, you see, most of the films we see today are what I term "photographs of people talking." They aren't true pieces of cinema. Film was the newest part of the twentieth century, and what is it really—imagery and montage, pieces of film put together to create ideas."

What pleased Hunter, who was a fan of Hitchcock and a fevered auteurist, was that Hitchcock was willing to get very theoretical and technical about his films, discussing for example the use of reflected light in *Torn Curtain*. In talking about uses of color, Hitchcock said he had tried to convey the impression of East Germany's drabness by shooting lots of greys and blacks.[13]

Hitchcock himself, slightly inebriated or not, was pleased that many of the students were keen to ask him about *Marnie*. "I loved *Marnie* from the first day it was released," recalls Tim Hunter, "And saw it twice on the first day." We were big *Marnie* fans. Hunter actually got into Harvard by a successful college interview when he discussed the merits of *Psycho*.

Asked by the students why shots of the ship at harbor in *Marnie* so resembled cardboard the director explained that "they told me it wouldn't look that way in Technicolor. They were lying." They also asked him about the unreality of the riding sequences. Hitchcock replied, "That was a bad horse on a treadmill. The process in back of her was made on the actual field. It was made on a crane, it went that was correct. She was on a trained shot. They said when you get the final Technicolor print, it won't look like that. But they were lying. It was a bad shot."

In response to a question about whether the obvious unreality of the process and set-painting in *Marnie* could be interpreted as a sign of Marnie's world of illusion (which the students must have picked up from Robin Wood's book released the year before), Hitchcock's response was, "Yes. I think so." Throughout the interview Hunter said that Hitchcock was very gracious, enjoyed the interview, and clearly wanted the credit as an artist and auteur. "I think Hitchcock has been unbelievably influential to me. Today I use a kind of Hitchcockian breakdown of action. I work in a lot of TV these days where you have to distill the action into a short number of shots, and Hitchcock has helped me do that. I don't think there has been any filmmaker who has been more influential than Hitchcock."

After the talk Hitchcock very generously lent the Harvard Dramatic Club rare prints of *Rear Window* and *The Man Who Knew Too Much*, as well as *Under Capricorn*, which they were allowed to keep for a very long time. A month later, on August 16, 1966, Hitchcock was interviewed by Peter Bogdanovich as a follow-up and continuation of their 1963 meeting. Bogdanovich asked, "In your personal preference, how would you rate *The Birds*, *Marnie*, or *Torn Curtain*? In which order?" Hitchcock replied saying "I think they are entirely three different pictures. *Marnie* of course is gradually emerging in my trips east and back to London, I found that people were most appreciative. They talked of nothing but that when I went to Harvard. They put that right at the top of the list." Bogdanovich goes on to say that, "The killing of the horse was very emotional." And Hitchcock's reply is, "The horse was a symbol of the father, the loss of the father, the mythic father. She's killing of her father. Yes it worked out well I thought too."

Bogdanovich says he likes *Marnie* the best of the three because it had the most depth. So the Harvard trip undoubtedly pleased Hitchcock in the appreciation for his concept of pure cinema in *Marnie*.

## CONCLUSION

The collaboration of Alfred Hitchcock and Robert Burks sadly came to an end on *Marnie* and in many ways it's the pinnacle of their creative agreement. Hitchcock's style became increasingly abstract into montage with *Marnie* as he delved into areas that interested him. *Marnie* is a late period piece experimenting with montage, distilling action, and those challenges are what kept Hitchcock creatively alive. In addition to the color scheme, *Marnie*'s distinctive visuals can be seen in the wide angle and zoom lenses, especially in the climactic flashback scene.

Hitchcock invited Burks to be the cinematographer on his fiftieth feature, *Torn Curtain*, but Burks declined because Hitchcock still insisted on doing process plates. "I remember Bob kept saying to me, 'Al, he wants to do all this process.' By now, process was just too much for Bob," recalls Alfred Whitlock. "And he didn't want Bob to go to Germany to shoot the plates. 'That's all right, Bob, we'll send somebody over.' Well, Bob got so. . . . You remember Bob at the end."[14]

Bob Boyle agrees, "Yes, it was difficult for Bob. I remember Bob told me, he said he was getting up one morning, and he put one foot down and he didn't put the other one down. That was it." But it was more than creative differences over the use of back projection that terminated their relationship. Sadly on May 13, 1968, Burks and his wife, Elizabeth, died in a fire at their home. Hitchcock was devastated at the loss of his favorite cinematographer. But their remarkable collaboration and creative peak lives on in *Marnie.*

## NOTES

1. Interview with Andrew Graham, Oxford, England, February, 17, 2012.

2. Richard Brody, "Tippi Hedren and Alfred Hitchcock." *The New Yorker.* October 19, 2012.

3. Albert Whitlock, "Roundtable on *The Birds,*" *Cahiers du Cinema*, 1982.

4. Interview with Linden Chiles, Los Angeles, August 22, 2012.

5. Tim Hunter, "Alfred Hitchcock at Harvard," *Harvard Crimson*, October 14, 1966.

6. Hitchcock to Peter Bogdanovich, February 13, 1962.

7. Hitchcock to Peter Bogdanovich, *Who the Devil Made It?* (New York: Ballantine, 1998).

8. Interview with Lois Thurman, Los Angeles, April 17, 2012.

9. Alfred Hitchcock to Fletcher Markle, *A Talk with Hitchcock*, Telescope CBS documentary, 1964.

10. Robin Wood, *Hitchcock's Films Revisited*, revised edition (New York: Columbia University Press, 2002), 175.

11. Interview with Honor Moore, New York, January 10, 2013.

12. Interview with Tim Hunter, Toronto, January 13, 2013

13. Hunter, "Alfred Hitchcock at Harvard."

14. Whitlock, "Roundtable on *The Birds.*"

## Chapter Twelve

# Hitchcock Remembered

He was a pixie, a real pixie.

—Marshall Schlom on the set of *Psycho*

Two thousand and twelve was declared the year of Hitchcock. *Vertigo* was voted the number one film of all time by an international poll of 850 critics for *Sight and Sound* magazine.

"It's wonderful that *Vertigo* has been voted number one film," said its star Kim Novak. "It's only a shame that Hitch and Jimmy Stewart aren't here to know it, but at least I'm here. I think people respond to *Vertigo* because there are so many layers—there is always something new to see. It's not only a film that you never get bored watching, there are always new nuances to find. Hitch used to say, "That's why it's a mystery, he didn't know all the answers himself."[1]

Two biopics on Hitchcock's life released in 2012 offered different interpretations of the director. First, *Hitchcock* the movie, starring Anthony Hopkins as Hitchcock and Helen Mirren as Alma, was released theatrically. The film, based on Stephen Rebello's *Alfred Hitchcock and the Making of Psycho*, offered us a humorous portrait of an anxious, overeating Hitchcock, with a focus on Alma as the woman behind the director. The second, a BBC/HBO telefilm, *The Girl*, based on Donald Spoto's *Spellbound by Beauty*, portrayed him as an abusive, sadistic, domineering tyrant. So who was the real Alfred Hitchcock? In this chapter, colleagues and coworkers, especially from his late-period films, *Psycho*, *The Birds*, and *Marnie*, remember him in the year 2012. Those interviewed by the author include script supervisors Marshall Schlom and Lois Thurman, unit manager and assistant director Hilton Green, costume supervisors Helen Colvig and Rita Riggs, hairdresser Virginia Darcy, and actors Louise Latham, Mariette Hartley, Norman Lloyd, Kimberly Beck, Kim Novak, Alec McCowen, Karin Dor, and Eva Marie Saint.

## HITCHCOCK THE PIXIE

"What was he really like?" queries Marshall Schlom, Hitchcock's script supervisor on *Psycho*. "That's the question interviewers ask me more than any other. He had so many facets to his personality. I felt he was a pixie, a real pixie. On the one hand he could be one person, and the next moment he could be someone else."[2] This interpretation portrays Hitchcock as being changeable, whimsical, and mischievous, a practical joker and someone who didn't take himself too seriously. It then may account for the conflicting interpretations of the director as a sensitive collaborator or a sadistic Svengali, someone who was a different person to different people, especially during the production of *Marnie*. He showed one side of his personality to Diane Baker, another to Tippi Hedren, and yet another to Bob Boyle. Coworkers remarked that he was a very complicated character who liked to think of himself as simple, which was absurd.

Then there is the Alfred Hitchcock who was very orderly about his personal habits, especially his outward appearance and style of dress. "He liked to wear a dark suit," says Marshall Schlom, "And if it was a warm day, he would change that suit, it was his stock look. He quit at 5:30 P.M. every day. Even on location he would only stay until 7:00 P.M., that was his maximum." Hitchcock's style of dress was in keeping with his punctilious, orderly habits, and Jesuit upbringing. Underneath this rigid and fastidious wardrobe, there was Hitchcock the man. "First and foremost I believe he was an honest person," says Schlom. "Though he had a side to him that was nasty, which I never saw. I know of one incident when he was nasty to someone, he told me about it. He could be a little nasty." (Schlom wouldn't elaborate on what the incident was.)

"His life was divided into two halves," says producer and long-time friend Norman Lloyd. "The artist and the bourgeois. He liked to sit at the kitchen table and have a glass of white wine with chicken and read *Time* magazine. And he led his life like a bourgeois. And he didn't even have a swimming pool. He led a very simple life."[3]

As Eva Marie Saint says, "Each of us had a different experience with him. There were six of us Hitchcock blondes, and it's like we all were married to the man at one time or another and we all have a different take on him. Each actress was at a different stage of their life; we were different ages, some married, some not. My experience with Hitch was one of utter respect, warmth, friendliness, and humor, and *North by Northwest* was a glorious time in my life."[4]

## HITCHCOCK THE COLLABORATOR

Many who worked with Hitchcock remarked that his sets were detailed and orderly, and as quiet as the interior of a church. Louise Latham relished her time working with Hitchcock on the set of *Marnie*, which was her first Hollywood movie experience: "What he did to make things comfortable for the actors was just wonderful, the set was always calm and cool and quiet; he gave people the space to do their work. The set was just heaven. I was brought up in New York where discipline was numero uno. For me, to be on a set with a brilliant man, aware of everyone's work and why it's happening and to guide you in a very kindly way, he was a wonderful director."

Seven-year-old child actress Kimberly Beck played Jessie, the little girl whom Louise's character Bernice Edgar dotes on. "I got the part of Jessie because Mr. Hitchcock saw me in a 76 Union commercial," remembers Kimberly fifty years later.

> Mr. Hitchcock was memorable! He was very nice to me and a couple of things I remember clearly are he told me he liked to listen to music when he went to bed so he had a radio put into his pillow so as not to disturb his wife's sleep. I remember that my natural blonde hair needed to be darkened for the movie because Tippi was to be the only blonde. I remember the set so well! It was impressive and seemed gigantic to me. I have always loved the backdrops on sets and can't understand why people don't appreciate that art more. He wanted me to act territorial over Louise and wanted me to snub Tippi's character Marnie, like she was in the way of our time together. I do remember that she was asked to be loving to me and sort of cold to Marnie. Such complex emotions for a child to pay attention to, so I remember more the feelings than the words. She was told to like me more is what I took away from it. I worked with him also on his TV show and remember for many years, whenever I was on the lot at Universal, which was quite a bit because I was under contract, I would stop by and say hello to him. He was always very kind and genuinely interested in me, at least that is how I took his attention. A nice man, who moved slowly, spoke slowly, who seemed as though he didn't suffer fools yet was kind and patient with children.[5]

This view of Hitchcock as the sensitive collaborator is echoed by actors who worked with him post-*Marnie*. "Of all the directors I have worked with Hitchcock was my favorite," says Karin Dor, who played Juanita de Cordoba in *Topaz*. "I adored and loved him as a director. At the end of every filming day on *Topaz* he would come to my trailer with his secretary with German recipes because he knew that I liked to cook. We had a marvelous, immediate, simpatico relationship. It was one of my best experiences in movie-making."[6] The actors who appeared in *Frenzy* also enjoyed working with Hitchcock. He mostly chose trained, established actors from the theater for the roles. "I adored Hitch and making *Frenzy* was a wonderful time," says Barbara Leigh-Hunt, who played Brenda Blaney. "He went out of his way and was kindness personified, he knew I was exceedingly nervous. If I had a question he would always courteously explain something to me. Every day he would give me a lift home [to] where I was staying in Baker Street before going onto Claridges. Alma was of ill health, he was very concerned about her, but it impressed me how he was so considerate towards me at the time."[7]

Alec McCowen, the co-star on *Frenzy* who played Chief Inspector Oxford, agrees: "He gave me hardly any direction in the dialogue scenes. On two occasions he was very firm—when Jon Finch was found guilty, and there was a shot of him on his own. Hitch took this shot of me, and he said, 'It's up to your expression to keep the audience interested in the story.' We had to do the scene many times to get it right. And the other scene, at the end when he says, 'You're not wearing your necktie.' On the first take I said it more aggressively, coming on like Kirk Douglas. Hitch said to me, 'You know, Alec, this is the end of the film, there's no need to come on all tough, because you've got your man. I'd say it more quietly, but it's up to you.' He gave no particular direction in the scenes with Vivien Merchant. Many of the dialogue scenes only needed one take."[8]

Then there is the director infamous for his remarks "All actors are cattle" or "All actors should be treated like cattle." Jim Brown believes deep down that Hitchcock respected actors and that he may have said those words to shock or create publicity. "With Tippi he took her through every look, every move; he rehearsed prior, going on to the stage," remembers Brown. "They had long meetings. He spent a lot of time directing Tippi, long talks and discussions with her. The other actors he pretty much left them to do their work. So Tippi got his full attention and he hired competent actors for the rest. Sean Connery was an old pro, marvelous. If you're a top star and you have a problem, it wouldn't come out on the set, all the discussions would be in the dressing room." Lois Thurman, the script supervisor on *Marnie*, also echoes Brown's assessment of Hitchcock's working methods with actors. "Sean Connery was perfect, you couldn't fault him," she said. "He got along with Hitch. I remember once Sean wanted to change a line in the script, but he said it in a different way (to some other actors). I told Hitch and he said that its okay to change the line for Sean. So they got along fine."[9] Connery did admit, however, that he felt slightly abandoned in the role of Mark Rutland because of Hitchcock's lack of specific direction to him during filming, which is yet a further reason for the ambiguous nature of Mark Rutland's character.

"I think he was an actor's director," says Alec McCowen, "Especially when working with good actors like Cary Grant. He just left it to you, if he trusted you and he did a good job with the casting. For an actor to work with Hitch, I think you should have a sense of humor and trust him completely. I adored working for him and it was a great pleasure, and it was—I had seen most of his films. I've worked with George Cukor and they both had one thing in common. Just before a take, with the technicians you are often distracted and the make-up people, there's a lot of movement. Hitch and Cukor both said, 'Everyone keep out of the actors' eye-line.' This is very useful for theater actors and a good tip for working with actors."

## HITCHCOCK THE SVENGALI

More than ever, Hitchcock's reputation as a sadistic director was in the spotlight in 2012, as he was accused by the international press of sexual harassment, misogyny, and physical abuse. This was the result of a BBC/HBO dramatization about the making of *The Birds* and *Marnie* that was shown in the United States in October 2012 and then the rest of the world in the proceeding months. Following the BBC transmission of *The Girl* over Christmas in the United Kingdom, Alfred Hitchcock was labeled a pervert, a letch, a dirty old man, a monster, and a cruel misogynist.

"It's very difficult to get inside someone's head and really know what they are thinking and feeling, it's virtually impossible," said Tippi Hedren to this author in 1999. "So all we can do is say this is what he did, this is what he said, but talking about how someone felt is very difficult." But Hedren does remember that "he never felt that I should get married. It's very old-school thinking and it is very manipulative and possessive."

Tippi's engagement to Noel Marshall is a story that isn't told in *The Girl*, and how this interfered with Hitchcock's plans to make her a star, which is why he may have resorted to Svengali-like tricks by creating competition with Diane Baker. Hitchcock also spoke about Hedren and his ambitions for her to other directors, which took an exacting toll on him. "I was pouring myself into the girl," he told François Truffaut, "I taught her every expression, never a wasted one."

In a key interview with Peter Bogdanovich in February 1963, just before the release of *The Birds*, Hitchcock talks frankly about his problems in creating new stars: "There's a whole rhythm. It's like this girl Hedren. Until I have launched them, they belong to me, and they better face that fact. You can't run around with men, you can't start having babies, one thing at a time, get the career going and then start to have the babies."

The latter was a direct reference to Vera Miles, whom Hitchcock had been grooming for stardom just before Hedren. Unfortunately Miles doesn't give interviews today, but an archive interview in 1982 to promote *Psycho II* shows that, contrary to popular opinion, she bears no grudges toward Hitchcock.[10] "There was a great deal of respect between Hitchcock and me," said Miles. "He expected people to be good and never rehearsed them at all. When you signed a contract with Hitchcock it stipulated the number of hours a day you would work. . . . And as for playing casting couch in the role, I'd have told him to go to hell. Neither of us had time for that kind of thing."

Rita Riggs, costume supervisor on *The Birds* and *Marnie*, who was interviewed by the production team for *The Girl*, diplomatically has remained loyal to both Hitchcock and Hedren during the furore that followed the broadcast of the TV movie. "I respected Mr. Hitchcock as a professional and I respected Tippi as a personal friend," she says, "I hope he will be remembered as a film maker foremost. I've never known anyone who could manipulate a script or a scene so beautifully. Because of the extent of his career I have nothing but really kind words about Mr. Hitchcock . . . He was inspirational to all of us, our manners, our dress. Everything. We were really inspired by his sense of classicism." About the sadistic rumors, Riggs says, "It's like newspapers—it sells, and I never really thought that he was serious. He was a jokester and a prankster and I have good memories all through *The Birds*. We were talking about strawberries. There was a packet of wild strawberries from France and I remember when he shipped a whole load of potatoes to Tippi because she was losing so much weight. I was on the set all the time . . . I may be one of the very naive people that didn't see all of the Sturm and Dang." Hilton Green concurs, "You could feel the tension, but it didn't spill over into actual shooting."[11]

"Tippi and Hitch had their differences on *Marnie*," said Jim Brown. "There was some tension between the two of them that you could feel on the set and that permeated through the rest of the cast and crew. So maybe Tippi didn't get as much direction as she could of have." Later Brown worked as a producer on the night-time soap *Dallas*. "*Marnie* was a cinch compared to doing *Dallas*," said Brown, "Dealing with stars, because when I went in (in 1985) they were all well-established, well-paid multi-millionaires, and none of them wanted to come to work. They all wanted to go out and open grocery stores for $150,000 cash."

Of her part in *Marnie*, Mariette Hartley remembers, "I had such a limited time with [Hitchcock], it was the same size part as Linden's [Chiles], though mine was a little larger. I had none of those experiences with other directors so I have mixed feelings. I was new to film, it was my first experience. Hitchcock had seen me in *Gunsmoke* and hired me. He and I had a wonderful time, with great repartee. He was very funny and giving, showing me the storyboarding, exquisitely beautiful. I was so thrilled. Then he completely turned off and that was shocking to me. I knew Tippi was upset, but I didn't know how to approach her. I felt she was in her dressing room too long at some point, and she kept going back into her dressing room. My feelings about Hitch, if anything happened it would have been hidden, for him it would have all been innuendo."[12]

Was Hitchcock overconfident in his abilities as a director? Mariette Hartley thinks he may have been so. "Everyone in the creative league is vulnerable, you can't always make it work. It's coming out of your center if you're sensitive about it, and you may miss something. Hitch had his own outlook, but I feel so blessed that I was able to work with him and it was pretty amazing. There was also an innocence about Tippi, a naiveté, she was kind of an ordinary person and had been placed in a position that she was uncomfortable with. I felt that way and I identified with her."

Louise Latham didn't observe anything untoward on the set when it came to shooting her scenes in February 1964. "That [harassment] may happen to you at that age, when you're sexy and attractive," says Louise Latham. "Sometimes the messages one gives out are not always accurate and people leap to conclusions. I came out of New York theater, all those subtleties on stage, you're aware of early on. [Tippi] was pretty and dear, maybe she was just too vulnerable to the power. It's a very physical thing to be on the set with everyone revealing their feeling and emotions."

Virginia Darcy, Hedren's hairdresser, believes that you had to take Hitchcock with a pinch of salt. "If an actress had said, 'Alright, I'll meet you at the Beverly Hills hotel,' Hitchcock would have said, 'Okay, but I've got to get home by 5:30 P.M.!' He would say shocking things to me, but I laughed and said, 'You can't say those things, they're not nice, you can get into trouble.' He used to do a lot of things to get what he wanted out of people . . . For one thing he was so frustrated trying to get some emotion out of her, that's the way he tried to get it. He used to do things to Doris Day on *The Man Who Knew Too Much* to make her cry all the time. But that was his way. He's so involved in the making of his film."

"That's what he had, his fantasies, but as far as connected, no, they were just fantasies," said Hilton Green. "I feel they are just trying to exploit him today. The man is dead, he had a great career, he was a genius of a director, he was not in because he didn't go to parties, and I felt he was more of an introvert. He wanted to know his crews, he didn't want new faces. To me the man was a genius and a very creative person. Look at the positive side, look at what he brought to our industry. To go back and look at what he did or didn't do, why dig up things today?"

## HITCHCOCK THE PERFECTIONIST

Hitchcock the controlling Svengali is closely linked to his persona as a perfectionist on set, with his obsessive storyboarding and attention to detail, controlling all aspects of wardrobe, hairstyles, and set design. "Hitchcock is one of the great directors and one to be studied," says Kim Novak. "He was a perfectionist; he didn't make any short cuts. Nowadays directors do and it's a mistake. There wasn't a part of the movie he wasn't involved in."

"Hitchcock knew everything about making movies; it was his job to go to work and make movies," says Marshall Schlom. "I can tell you without a doubt, he knew more about making movies than any other director that I've been associated with. He ran a master class for me, that's the best way to describe it." "I liked him very much and appreciated him," says Lois Thurman, who succeeded Schlom as Hitchcock's script supervisor on *The Birds* and *Marnie*. "He was my favorite director because it was easy to know what he wanted. He wasn't going to do a lot of extra shots, so he was easier to work with than other directors. Every actor wanted to work with him because he would go home at 5:30 or 6:00 o'clock. He always told the cameraman what the shot was, what the coverage was going to be and what the script says."

"I enjoyed Mr. Hitchcock, I really did," says Virginia Darcy, who also describes herself as a perfectionist. "Hitchcock knew everything—he knew hair, he knew makeup, it was all sketched out before he went on the set. I was thrilled with Mr. Hitchcock and I was privileged to work with him and to be able to be friendly with him. On *The Birds* we conversed a lot and by *Marnie* we were very close. He never told me how to do Sean's [Connery] hair. He said Virginia is here, she'll know."

"He was very professional," says Hilton Green. "He knew exactly what he wanted and how to get it and there wasn't this guessing. There was none of that. He could tell you right down to the frame where he would cut the movie." Some of the actors on *Marnie* complained that he never gave them much direction and had a tendency to ignore them on the set. "He did that with all his actors," says Green. "If they were doing it the way he thought they should play the part he didn't bother them. They got their direction, the actors, in preproduction when they would have readings and he would explain. They would get their part down, and he expected them not to need a lot of direction. Sean was coming off his first movie, *Dr. No*, and may have felt that way. And that's why he wanted to work."

Hitchcock could also be very particular about detail, Green remembers. "On a television show with Laurence Harvey, with the prop man, he was very particular with meals or anything with serving food and stuff like that, and he had it in for the prop man, because he didn't like his attitude, so he thought the prop man was wrong and let him have it, and he told me 'Let's have a new prop man tomorrow.' He didn't tell him!"

## HITCHCOCK THE SENSITIVE MAN

The film *Hitchcock* starring Anthony Hopkins depicts the director as a man who allowed his conflicted emotions to interfere with him on the set. One man who knew him better than anyone was Hilton Green. "I was with him a long time, I was very close to Hitch and I never ever saw him as the way they portrayed him. When he came on the set and blurted out and raised his voice, that never happened. The only instance when I saw him raise his voice was when we were filming the swinging light bulb in *Psycho*. He wanted a flash across the lens, but it took two different shooting days to get it. The camera operator kept saying he'd got it, but he hadn't and Hitchcock was angry with me."

"He didn't bring to the set his problems, if there were problems," says Green. The only time he saw Hitchcock emotionally upset was when he found out that Alma had cancer. People often get physically upset by an emotional set, and this was the case with Hitchcock, as Norman Lloyd also recalled.

> I remember a period, Hitch had gone dry and nothing was happening. And I remember Alma during this period, because he had, like a lot of people . . . something would come over him and he couldn't work. And she said, "Perhaps, Norman, if you come across anything you might be interested in?" He couldn't settle on a property, he was lethargic and not creative. It was a vivid spot in my memory because this man who I idolized suddenly found himself in this predicament. On *Marnie* he actually fell ill and he discussed with me about stepping in and then he changed his mind—he was going to plough through, which he did. In retrospect I wonder if he had anything to do with Tippi. I think Hitch, as people often do, [would] get physically upset by an emotional upset, and I don't know why but at that moment he discussed my taking over but then dropped it.

The production archives corroborate Lloyd's memory of Hitchcock falling ill on the set of *Marnie*. A memo from Morris David to Jerre Henshaw was sent on January 28, 1964, enquiring about Sean Connery's contract on Marnie: "There have been some delays in production due to a virus infection with the principals and Mr Hitchcock and Jim Brown, his production manager."

A flu bug had already affected Sean Connery, Tippi Hedren (as also evidenced in the David Golding publicity memo), and Jim Brown. Hitchcock caught the bug too. As it came to it, Hitch was able to recover from the bug and carry on filming, but the physical upset he had may have contributed to his emotional distress with the Hedren fall out.

Then there is Hitchcock the overeater as portrayed in the *Hitchcock* movie, raiding the refrigerator and gorging on ice cream in the middle of the night. "He would gain a lot of weight," acknowledges Green. "And before liposuction he would have a similar technique done to him. He would come back not trim, but a lot different, and within six months he would be back to his weight again. It didn't make him better."

"He had no compulsion about his looks," says Virginia Darcy. "He knew what he looked like. And what was underneath everything he had a drive inside that he was a handsome being. He had a lot of good points and was good to a lot of people. Yes, he went over the side sometimes, but I don't know anybody who doesn't. And what a talent, that meant everything to him. Inside he thought he was Cary Grant, and if people didn't react that way it was like 'What's the matter with them?' I saw that inside, and that's why I could talk to him."

Not many people recognized this, but Hitchcock was a very shy man. He himself said in an interview to Peter Bogdanovich in February 1963 just before the release of *The Birds*: "I don't know anyone in Hollywood. I don't suppose I've spoken to another director ever about filmmaking, never had. The only man I've ever known to talk to is Mervyn LeRoy because I meet him at the racetrack. I don't know any writers; I'm shy about this sort of thing, I really am. I never mix with anyone. Why do I like working in Hollywood? Because I can get home at 6 o'clock every evening, that's all. [And] Hollywood always has had the best facilities."

His two assistant directors on *Marnie* agree that Hitchcock was shy and remarked what a privilege it was to get to know him. As Hilton Green says, "I spent quite a few years with him and got very close to him, and I truly, sincerely loved the man, I respected him so much. I could see why people would get upset with him sometimes; basically he was an introvert, he wasn't snubbing people, but he wasn't outgoing, he was very reserved. Mr. Hitchcock had a great warmth to him, but he was cold to a lot of people because he was a very reserved man." Jim Brown agrees with this assessment: "He didn't vocalize his inner thoughts very well, as a matter of fact he was a very shy person," said Brown. "I had the pleasure of getting as close to him as anyone else ever has, because we worked on both pictures back to back. He talked about his life growing up and some personal things. But when it came to work, he kept pretty much inside." Did Hitchcock lose control and interest on the set of *Marnie*? According to Brown:

> I think possibly there is some truth. I thought some of the things expressed about Hitchcock were highly overexaggerated. I think Hitchcock became a little upset with Tippi because she wasn't fulfilling the star qualities that he thought she had or was looking for. I think Hitchcock got bored on the set of most of his pictures, his creativity and enthusiasm came in the preparation, and after the preparation he was just fulfilling the obligation, and you can see that in the photo of all three of us falling asleep as we were waiting for the rear projection to be set up and rewound. We were shooting things that took physical time.

Although Brown conceded that Hitchcock got a little bored toward the end of filming, he didn't see that much difference between his behavior on *Marnie* and *The Birds*. "*Marnie* was a much simpler picture to make than *The Birds* because we didn't have a lot of location work and children," said Brown.

> I didn't like working on the stage that much. I was much more pleased with the conclusion of *The Birds*, whereas I didn't feel that *Marnie* was that special a project. I certainly wouldn't rate *Marnie* as one of his better projects. I don't think it's something that he was all that proud of and I just don't think it was that good of a project, not comparable to other projects he'd done like *Rear Window*. I thought Tippi and Sean did a marvelous job, but the way it was shot, the process photography, the backdrops, it was a time when television and commercials were far more interesting and motion pictures were shot on the lot and locations, different techniques. And the techniques for its time were too old fashioned. There was a breakthrough at the time where television itself was more exciting than that type of motion picture.

Brown said that although he thought *Marnie* wasn't superior Hitchcock, the director still felt an obligation to Universal and himself to make pictures that were successful.

## CONCLUSION

Pixie, perfectionist, sensitive collaborator, or sadistic Svengali, Hitchcock showed a different side of his persona to different people. What all his cast and crew members agree with, however, was that Hitchcock was a great teacher who inspired many other people in the film industry. How he achieved his aims, and the ethics behind them, is debatable. But what is undeniable, is that in a career spanning sixty years, he received five Oscar nominations for best director and elicited a further nine nominations for his actors.

## NOTES

1. Interview with Kim Novak in Los Angeles, August 31, 2012.
2. Interview with Marshall Schlom in Los Angeles, November 30, 2012.
3. Interview with Norman Lloyd in Los Angeles, November 30, 2012.
4. Interview with Eva Marie Saint in Los Angeles, October 16, 2012.
5. Interview with Kimberly Clark in Los Angeles, January 19, 2012.
6. Interview with Karin Dor in Germany, July 10, 2012.
7. Interview with Barbara Leigh-Hunt in Stratford-upon-Avon, England, July 14, 2012.
8. Interview with Alec McCowen, London, England, July 18, 2012.
9. Interview with Lois Thurman in Los Angeles, March 2, 2013.
10. "Perkins, Miles Return in *Psycho II*," *Spartanburg Herald-Journal*, June 24, 1983.
11. Interview with Hilton Green, Pasadena, California, December 3, 2012.
12. Interview with Mariette Hartley, Los Angeles, December 3, 2012.

# Afterword

Fifty years after its release, *Marnie* still fascinates and troubles. No other Hitchcock film polarizes the audience so deeply. There are those who believe the film to be sadistic, offensive, and misogynistic; others recognize it as one of Hitchcock's most important films, providing a tableaux for the thorough working out of issues of gender, identity, and sexuality within our culture. For the latter the film remains a significant work because of Hitchcock's acumen toward the sexual relationships between men and women and his dramatization of the conflicts and pressures imposed on Marnie by patriarchal society.

*Marnie* was one of Hitchcock's most deeply personal films, and his identification with the feminine impulse is keenly felt, initiating some important questions about violence against women in our culture. A reading of the film suggests that Hitchcock *was* Marnie. He identified strongly with the character, her open pleas for love and acceptance, her shyness, repression, fear of sex, and her hang-ups about class. Hitchcock was much more like Marnie than Mark. She was a mass of contradictions and complexities just like the director was.

As a child, Hitchcock, like Marnie, invented stories and identities and lived in his own dream world. Just like Marnie uses her horse riding for retreat, Hitchcock escaped to cinema and theatre. And Hitchcock, like Marnie, had a terrible fear of the police. "Will I go to jail?" asks Marnie at the end of film. "No," she is reassured by Mark. "Not after what I have to tell them."

Hitchcock often cited the terrible moment when he was five years old and his father, to punish him for some infraction, sent him down to the chief of police, with a note asking that he be put in a jail cell for five minutes to teach him a lesson. This was long before the days of identified child abuse, and Hitchcock himself told the story to explain his lifelong fear of the police. Certainly that trauma could have been more far-reaching and may have been in the director's mind when he made *Marnie*. With this film Hitchcock was on a quest for his own identity.

In an interview in 1973 Hitchcock said, "I think it will be interesting to talk about fear and how it first came to one. Psychiatrists will tell you that if you have certain psychological problems and if you can trace them back to your childhood, all will be released. And of course, I don't believe this to be true at all . . . And so my father sent me with a note to the local chief of police and led me to a corridor and I was locked in a cell for five minutes, and then he let me out and said that's what we do to naughty boys. It was the clang of the door, the solidity of that bolt."

The tentative end of *Marnie* doesn't suggest that Marnie is cured, nor that her childhood release will solve all her problems. As critic Robin Wood noted perceptively, the child in the flashback is already neurotic and disturbed as a result of her mother's behavior. "It was just that I was so young, Marnie," says Bernice Edgar movingly at the end of the flashback. "I never had anything of my own."

"I am not like other people, I know what I am!" insists Marnie to Mark. Maybe Marnie felt that she was incapable of loving or being loved. And not wanting to psychoanalyze Hitchcock, maybe because of his physique, which throughout his life he was unhappy about as he mentioned to colleagues like Jim Brown, he felt that he was different from other people too. Yet Marnie does find love with Mark despite the terrible problems in her past. In Jay Presson Allen's and Hitchcock's script, love becomes a tangible reality for Marnie at the end, which is assuring for those who have been wounded by life's miseries and the disappointment of love. Hitchcock's *Marnie* charts the unfathomability of love and it elusiveness and that touched a chord deep within Hitchcock.

As William Rothman writes in a whole new chapter devoted to *Marnie* in his second edition of *The Murderous Gaze*, "One reason I feel justified in devoting so many pages to *Marnie* is the fact that almost a half century after its release this singular and beautiful film still stands in need of defending. No one these days doubts *Psycho*'s stature. But *Marnie*, although it has its supporters, remains widely maligned, denigrated and dismissed, even though it is one of Hitchcock's greatest achievements."[1]

Many artists who subsequently respond to *Marnie* relate to the heroine as being an outlaw in a society given to repressing those who do not configure to the accepted norm, or have some way been damaged by the mysteries of love. Hitchcock, far from being out of touch with contemporary audiences, as criticized by early reviewers, was very much in tune with the problems of young people in both maintaining family relationships and seeking out a potential partner. In an interview in 1969, Hitchcock remarked, "Well, naturally

I am pro-young. I wrote my first script at the age of twenty-two and directed my first film at twenty-five. So I'm for the young. And when people today say I'm seventy. I say that's a confounded lie. I'm twice thirty-five, that's all. Twice thirty-five."

Hitchcock said little publicly after *Marnie* was released, upset about the negative reaction toward a project that he had nurtured for three years. The initial failure of *Marnie* dissuaded him from directly exposing his emotional concerns on screen again. In his remaining films, he returned to more familiar formulae such as the spy thriller. "Not many people know this, but Hitchcock was easily hurt," remarked Joseph Stefano. "He did not like to be unloved. He lived in almost a dream world, where no one ever told him he was wrong, and the only people who criticized him were the film critics."

Aside from the Bogdanovich interviews, Hitchcock's most documented comments about *Marnie* arise from an interview in late July 1966, when he again met François Truffaut and Helen Scott to complete the publication of their collaborative book. In Hitchcock's mind, the fetish idea, which was his reasoning for making the film, didn't come across as effectively as it had in *Vertigo*:

> To put it bluntly, we'd have had to have Sean Connery catching the girl robbing the safe and show that he felt like jumping at her and raping her on the spot. . . . What really bothered me about *Marnie* were all the secondary characters. I had the feeling that I didn't know these people, the family in the background. Mark's father, for instance. And I wasn't convinced that Sean Connery was a Philadelphia gentleman. You know, if you want to reduce *Marnie* to its lowest common denominator, it is the story of the prince and the beggar girl.[2]

For Hitchcock the film required a real gentleman, like Laurence Olivier, in a story that was linked to the class-consciousness that prevailed in the past. "It's a real Victorian, late Edwardian type of hero, very strong," said Hitchcock in a 1964 interview.[3]

In another interview, Hitchcock also confirmed the expressionistic nature of the Baltimore backdrop, with the ship looming at the end of the street. He said that he had seen it years ago in England, linking it to a direct childhood experience:

> I was fascinated as a kid in London to go down to the docks—there was an ordinary street and right across the end was a huge liner with a smokestack. Well, it seemed ridiculous: these little, low houses in front, they almost disappeared—so they really had the effect of a ship on dry land. It didn't come off the way I wanted it to in *Marnie*. I've always had the same feeling arriving at Southampton. The ship, the *Elizabeth*, comes so close into town that when you stand at the front of the ship, you don't see any water at all. All you see is the bow and rooftops everywhere. This ship at the end of the street has always fascinated me. Haven't really brought it off yet.[4]

For Hitchcock, the looming ship was a symbol of his childhood. "I wanted to show something that had always fascinated me—I think I'd seen it in Copenhagen and London, as well as in Baltimore, where *Marnie* takes place—a row of houses and suddenly a ship looming above them."[5]

Aside from this paucity of anecdotes, why the reticence toward *Marnie*? Alma Hitchcock once described a cancer operation she had and the devastating consequences it had on her husband:

> This is a difficult experience for any devoted husband to live though, but for a man with Hitch's phobia about suspense, it was like being impaled on a torture rack. He couldn't work at all during the few weeks when my condition was at the most suspenseful stage. Finally I underwent surgery, and Hitch went to a restaurant near the hospital to drown his jitters in coffee. The operation was a complete success, and I'm happy to say that my health today is excellent. Hitch, however, refuses to set foot in the restaurant again. In fact, one night when friends were driving us in that direction, he demanded that they take a detour. In Hitch's mind the restaurant is indelibly associated with a night of goose pimples. Therefore, he wants it blotted out of his life.[6]

Hilton Green also remembers when Hitchcock found out about Alma's diagnosis when they were filming "A Dip in the Pool," an episode of *Alfred Hitchcock Presents* in 1958. "I was the assistant on the show and [Hitchcock] had tears in his eyes and he couldn't go on. He had just found out that Alma had cancer. That was the only time I saw him emotionally upset. And he left that afternoon. He told me to carry on and he just left."

Similarly, Hitchcock's reluctance to talk about *Marnie* could be explained by his wanting to erase the production from his mind. Truffaut later confided that Hitchcock urged him to keep the section on *Marnie* in his book to the minimum, mainly because he wanted to avoid discussing his failed personal and professional falling out with Tippi Hedren. By concentrating on the flaws of Mark Rutland and the fetishist element, Hitchcock could avoid talking about Hedren altogether. In their initial meeting in August 1962, Hitchcock had spoken enthusiastically and at length about his plans for *Marnie* as a psychological character study and a showcase for Hedren, and his plans to make her a star, but at his request, none of these preproduction comments appear in the final book.

When Winston Graham saw the film, he felt that there were "many nuances of the story missed and . . . drastic oversimplifications that took place. Of course the screen is the medium of broad brush strokes, and Hitchcock's films are noted for their emphatic structure."[7] He liked Sean Connery in the part, calling him a "first rate actor," but had reservations about Tippi Hedren. "It's difficult because I had my mind set on Grace Kelly," said Graham generously. He went to see the film when it was released in London with his son Andrew, who was less magnanimous than his father: "She was no Grace Kelly, absolutely as well as comparatively. I was incredibly disappointed. I thought the acting was wooden and the Hedren and Connery relationship not at all convincing. The whole treatment at the end, when Marnie goes to see her mother, was messy. The bad backdrop looked bloody awful, you could see the cardboard. I'm amazed that it's become so successful and that in time it's considered to be one of Hitchcock's significant films."[8]

Of the writers who were involved in *Marnie*, Jay Presson Allen felt the most disappointed in seeing the finished product:

> I certainly don't think it's the worst film that Hitch ever made, but in his degrading of power, I think it's in the lower third. And of mine I would say at the bottom. I think a good deal of the script was long, which I don't think I would be guilty of today. But I understand why the critics didn't go for it; it seemed perfectly obvious to me the first time I saw it. I thought Tippi was wrong for the part, but if I had been a more skillful screenwriter, I may have been able to help her appear more vulnerable. She has a very brittle, edgy quality. Hitchcock had a fancy for icy blondes, but for the lead character to be a liar and a cheat, they also needed to be deeply vulnerable to arouse sympathy in an audience, and Tippi doesn't have that quality. Hitchcock took chances with the backdrops, which he needn't have taken. All those things worked against it. My feelings about the movie have nothing to do with the events surrounding it. I adored working with Hitch. He was a great teacher, and I would probably have never gone into screen-writing if I hadn't worked with him.

Allen's remarks, like Hitchcock's, are characteristically self-deprecating. Her reluctance to ingrain *Marnie* with any social or cultural significance should not be taken as evidence that the film is lacking in these elements. In fact, Allen's dismissal of *Marnie* is more to do with a heartfelt novice approach:

> It is a very flawed movie, for which I have to take a lot of the responsibility—it was my first script. Hitch certainly didn't breathe on me. He loved the script I did, so that he did not make as good a movie as he should have made. I think one of the reasons that Hitch was fond of me and filmed a lot of the stuff I wrote was that I am frequently almost crippled by making everything rational. Hitch was enormously permissive with me. He fell in love with my endless linear scenes and shot them. In point of fact, he loved what I wrote, he shot what I wrote, and he shouldn't have. I'd had whatever training I'd had in the theater, and the theater that long ago was very sequential. It didn't get really cut up and able to move it around the way it's done like a movie, the way it's done today, until Arthur Miller's play (about his marriage to Marilyn). In any event, that was the first play I ever saw that behaved like a movie. So all I knew was to bring somebody on stage, have them say their thing, have their little whatever, and get them off. So clearly a movie was very, very far indeed.[9]

Evan Hunter, like Allen, marks *Marnie* as the start of the director's decline: "When I first met Hitch, he told me he was at the peak of his career; he was brimming with ideas and talking about future projects all the time." Hunter, although having been dismissed from the project, gained no satisfaction when *Marnie* opened to negative reviews. Joseph Stefano, who wrote the original treatment, was one of the few who liked the film: "When I first saw it, I wrote to Hitch to tell him how much I admired the things that he was doing. I thought it was a very tomorrowish movie. Hitch had once again taken enormous strides with some of his backdrops. I thought he wanted me—the audience—to know they were backdrops and it seemed he was saying many things simply in the way he staged the movie."

In many ways, *Marnie* is the corollary of Hitchcock's obsession with control and what happens when he loses that control. Hitchcock was a perfectionist who valued order foremost, but during the production of *Marnie* he lost control of the finished product. Hitchcock investigated the loss of such control, the loss of power and the impotence, which is echoed in male and female relations in some of his greatest films, particularly *Rebecca*, *Notorious*, and *Vertigo*.

Unfortunately, the greatness of *Marnie* gets caught up in a conflict about Hitchcock's film technique that repeatedly deprives the film of much of its social resonance. This view has been compounded by Hitchcock's posthumous reputation arising from biographies, which in turn has led to further printed distortions by the media. This was particularly the case in 2012, as a result of the BBC/HBO dramatization that aired around the world, bringing the Hitchcock and Hedren working relationship into the international spotlight.

The critical and commercial failure of *Marnie* was something that disappointed Hitchcock and from which he never fully recovered. It wasn't just the critical failure, as he had others, but also his personal failure to make Tippi Hedren a star. "He once said, I can make anyone a star," said Virginia Darcy. It was his ego at work more than anything. After the tremendous success of *Psycho* he thought he was invincible. Only the critics could hurt him and only the critics could prove him wrong.

Moreover, he had just had a similar experience with Vera Miles, whom he was grooming for stardom. She starred in *The Wrong Man* and he cast her in *Vertigo*. "This was to be the definitive contract that would put Vera Miles over, I spent a lot of money on her, but this is the thing that you run into with these women, they are impossible people," said Hitchcock to Peter Bogdanovich in February 1963. "It didn't seem to bother her [that she lost out on the role because she became pregnant]. She said afterwards 'When am I going to work again?' I said wait a minute. There's a whole rhythm. It's like this girl Hedren, until I have launched them, they belong to me, and they better face that fact. You can't run around with men, you can't start having babies, one thing at a time, get the career going and then start to have the babies."[10] Hitchcock went on to say in the same conversation that he thought Grace Kelly was more sensible, because she put her work first before her private life. "That's really the dreadful thing about developing these women," Hitchcock continued.

> With this girl [Hedren] I'm about halfway along with her, if it goes into *Marnie*, which will be my biggest headache of all. It's a very exacting role. This girl is really a psychotic character. First of all, she is a calculating thief, she's attractive to men, she becomes frigid, and fights the sex, but she's gotta look sexy. And then her husband talks her to going to the psychiatrist, which she plays in high comedy and gradually through the treatment, he begins to uncover her, and she calls him a filthy old man. He begins to uncover and she begins to crack. And the last scene when she goes back home, and finds her mother dead and goes through the effects and finds that her mother instead of being a bible-thumping woman, telling her to keep clean of men, was a prostitute. This child was constantly being taken out of the bed. And it all takes place during a thunderstorm; in the middle of the picture she has to go berserk. So you get a girl being attacked, told the past, while being under the dreadful influence of the effects of thunder on her.

Hitchcock's words show just how much of a headache the filming of *Marnie* would turn out to be. As Norman Lloyd described him, Hitch was a man who was very much affected by what was happening emotionally. "He never talked about it after *Marnie*," says close friend Hilton Green.

> I don't know why Tippi did that [collaborated with the TV drama], because I like Tippi, she's a wonderful person, and I sat next to Tippi at his funeral. I don't know what went on when I wasn't there, but I was with him in preparation and on the set, but he went home and I didn't see the other side. Maybe there was something, I don't know, but it didn't happen on the set. He gave Tippi a lot of direction, because she needed it—it was a very dramatic part, the emotional end of it, the character, her flashbacks to when she was a young girl, she needed it. She was young and inexperienced and working with Mr. Hitchcock was . . . and as he did he always wanted to build his stars. And I do believe that with Vera Miles when she became pregnant, he was going to make her a big star and in his mind she let him down. And he never forgave her for that. And I can believe that.

In the TV drama, *The Girl*'s version of events is told emphatically through the eyes of Tippi Hedren. As part of the extensive publicity campaign in America and Britain, Hedren endorsed the view of the film and was thanked in the end credits. In interviews she said, "It's a terrible thing to be the object of some-one's obsession. He made a demand on me that was so awful, it was the end of filming *Marnie*. I remember the scene when Sean Connery pulls me out of the pool and revives me from drowning and we finished that scene, and I asked him for two days off so that I could go to New York to accept an award on the *Tonight Show*. He thought that was outrageous and then he made this demand on me, 'You will do whatever I want, whenever I choose.'"[11]

If Hitchcock indeed said those words, was he talking sexually? Or did he refer to his proprietorial sense of Hedren's contract, as evidenced by his earlier interview with Peter Bogdanovich when he remarked, "Until I have launched them, they belong to me."? Only Hedren knows, and will ever know, the exact dialogue that took place that day. Also did the incident take place before or after filming of the drowning scene, as the TV dramatization contradicts the source material on which it was based?[12]

There are two sides to every story, but Hitchcock's side so far has been untold. As detailed in chapter 4, the memo from Universal publicity man-ager David Golding on January 31, 1964, advised Hitchcock that it was impractical for Hedren to fly to New York to accept the *Photoplay* award, as the ceremony was scheduled to take place midweek on Wednesday, Febru-ary 5, rather than over a weekend as commonly cited. He emphasized Sean Connery's imminent departure at the end of February as evidence of the tremendous pressure that the production was under to complete the filming on schedule. The award ceremony also clashed with the filming of powerful flashback sequences as the call sheets held at the Margaret Herrick library testify, and Hitchcock did not want Hedren to break the mood for her charac-ter. But all these points are ignored in *The Girl*, which opts to portray Hitch-cock as a sadistic and mean ogre.

In addition to consulting Tippi Hedren, the TV drama claims the screenplay is based on extensive interviews with the surviving crew members. The writer interviewed three additional people—the late Jim Brown, Rita Riggs, and Diane Baker. When this author asked Brown in 2000 about the harassment charges, as already mentioned, he said on tape, "Some of the things that are expressed about him are highly overexaggerated. I think Hitch became upset because he thought Tippi wasn't fulfilling the star quality that he thought she had or was looking for." Brown died in July 2011 before shooting on *The Girl* began, but after the film's release, his widow, Nora Brown, publicly complained to the *Daily Telegraph*: "From my conversations with my husband Jim Brown, I doubt that he would have endorsed any of the sexual allegations against Alfred Hitchcock. He had nothing but admiration and respect for Hitch, understood his clever cockney sense of humour, and thought the man a genius. If he was here today, I doubt that he would have any negative comments and would be saddened by the image portrayed of his friend and mentor."[13]

In response to the media accusations, wardrobe supervisor Rita Riggs remarked in 2012, "I told the BBC when they came to interview me, 'I will not do dish,' and I think that's what they were looking for. . . . He could be a total Jekyll and Hyde but I never saw that. I think Hitch did many things to get performances from [Tippi], particularly in *Marnie*, because he didn't depend on her with acting technique, he may have shocked her with all manner of his techniques. I'm disappointed if the BBC has taken that line [of the sadistic tyrant]. I hoped they would do better than that."

Riggs conceded that Hitchcock may have been controlling of Hedren, "Partly because he had a plan for her, she was an investment for him. We spent $40,000 on clothes just to send her to Monaco (for the Cannes Film Festival)." Her words echo those of Hitchcock's when he referred to the expense he spent on Vera Miles. For him, these women he groomed were a business investment.

Virginia Darcy, Hedren's hairdresser, wasn't interviewed for the TV drama, but was invited by Hedren for a private screening of the film in July 2012, for thirty of her friends, which Darcy subsequently declined. "I loved that man (Hitchcock). I loved him and put my arms around him, he loved that, he never had that from his mother. He was a fabulous director. I was there all the time with Tippi and Hitch. He had delusions of romance, but it never came to anything. He went home every night to Alma." Darcy, like Riggs, tried to maintain good relations with both Hitchcock and Hedren, instead of taking sides. She went on to say, "I love Tip and everything but there are only certain types of roles she can play, because she's not a varied actress like Grace who can do *The Country Girl* and then *High Society*. What I know of [Hitchcock's] technique, what he did with Doris Day to get her to cry all the time that's his technique with actresses to get what he wants out of them. He could have used any other actress other than Tippi and that made him mad as he told everyone that he could make her an actress. It was his ego. He was mad that she wasn't giving everything."

Darcy also felt that Hitchcock greatly appreciated displays of affection from his female stars, such as the kiss Grace is reported to have given him on the lips mimicking her character in *To Catch a Thief.* "Grace knew what she was doing, and knew how far to go. And that little kiss was enough to keep him happy, you didn't have to make a big issue."

It was during the production of *Marnie* that the sexual harassment charges are most evident in the BBC drama. Louise Latham's response to the media's portrayal of Hitchcock when interviewed in 2012 was, "I find some of the allegations hard to believe. My observations are so far from what Tippi claims, and I'm a rather observant person, and was trained in the theater. She's a lovely woman, but I don't think Tippi should have said those things about Hitch. If you have some guy come on to you, and it happens all the time, a bright woman knows how to deal with it. Because she was so ambitious and dependent on Hitch she didn't dare to say 'What are you doing?' But I wasn't aware of her being hassled on the set." Latham also expressed reservations about Hedren's experience as an actress and her suitability for such a demanding role. "I truly think that a young person who didn't really have that much experience, but was gorgeous-looking and photographed like a dream, a very nice girl, but to consider such demands and expectations from a very limited performance I always thought was crazy. There were actresses from all over New York and London doing very difficult things with difficult roles. Then suddenly this girl, who's very dear, photographs like a dream, is something major." Latham concluded by saying, "For Hitchcock to go down as this monstrous thing, to the degree that [Tippi] was vulnerable, is not accurate."

Although they had passed away before the broadcast of *The Girl*, the writers Jay Presson Allen and Evan Hunter were also questioned about the Hitchcock and Hedren relationship. Hunter's reply was that he didn't know, as Hitchcock never talked about it, only referring to Hedren as "The Girl" in his company. Allen, on the other hand, vociferously defended Hitchcock. Even though she was present during the preproduction meetings with Hitchcock and Hedren, she was absent for most of the filming—two months in Africa— before returning at the end of January 1964 to begin work on *Mary Rose* and to comment on *Marnie*'s editing. When asked repeatedly about what exactly happened, Allen's response was, "All I know is that he was really pissed off with her at the end of filming."

John Russell Taylor, Hitchcock's official biographer, also gives an indication of what may have happened, which is markedly different than *The Girl*'s version of events:

> When I was first going to the studio [in the 1970s], the people around him, particularly Peggy [Robertson] said, don't mention *Marnie* because it's a sore point. It was one of my favorite movies and I told him that. Obviously it had left painful memories and he seemed to be pleased, I liked it and praised him. In some ways it was very close to his heart. I knew about the famous quarrel and I heard both sides, because I subsequently talked to Tippi about it. After about two-thirds of the film had been shot, they had this quarrel, consequent to which they had a flaming row on set, after which they didn't speak directly to each other for about a week. "Would you ask Mr. Hitchcock?" "Would you ask Miss Hedren?" which I'm sure contributed to the extraordinary atmosphere about the film. So I asked Hitchcock about it, and he said, oh we had this row, and she said something that no-one is permitted to say to me, "Well, she, hem, referred to my weight."[14]

Hitchcock was deeply sensitive about his weight and also hated and avoided confrontation whenever he could, as evidenced when Roy Thinnes confronted him in Jack's restaurant in San Francisco about why Hitchcock had fired him from *Family Plot* (William DeVane replaced him). Hitchcock could only look at him, speechless, and the whole incident was very traumatic for the director.

Hitchcock's co-workers have been quoted extensively because they suggest another version of events not discussed in the media. Are they being truthful? Or are they simply defending Hitch? Many concede that Hedren was very nice on the set, professional and private, but none of them, aside from Diane Baker, suggested any ill treatment toward her. Is it all a big cover-up to protect Hitchcock or are they simply stating what they observed? Could Hitchcock the pixie have deceived such intelligent collaborators as Evan Hunter, Jay Presson Allen, and Robert Boyle to the point that they were oblivious to the sexual harassment that he would be later accused of?

At the end of the day, whatever transpired between Hitchcock and Hedren was done in private, in his office, with no witnesses, and only Hedren knows or will ever know the truth. Yes, Diane Baker was used as a tool to create competition for Hedren, a Svengali trick for sure, but neither actress rose to Hitchcock's challenge, and they remain friends to this day.

Another assertion in the media in 2012 was that as a result of the Hitchcock-Hedren falling out, after *Marnie* was edited in the spring of 1964 and there were screenings, there was talk of Hedren receiving a nomination for the Academy Awards. But Hitchcock allegedly put an immediate stop to any of that. How likely is this scenario? A previous member of the Academy Advisory Board was interviewed on October 31, 2012, in response to these allegations:

> It's hard to imagine that an effort like that by Hitchcock would not have been a scandal. He himself had never won an Oscar, to the dismay of many critics and fans. For him to campaign against one of his own with movies would have been unlikely to say the least. Hedren's performance was received unkindly, with a lot of the blame placed on Hitchcock. A win for her would have been vindication for him. There should at least be backup for this remarkable claim. Also, the actors' branch was, and is, to a lesser extent, by far the largest Academy branch, with thousands of members. They are solely responsible for the nominations; the whole membership, of course, votes on the Best Actor Awards. What influence could they have tried to exert over so many people without a major scandal?

It's also of importance to note that the 1964 winner for best actress was Julie Andrews for *Mary Poppins*, at the height of her career. She would go on to succeed Hedren as the next Hitchcock heroine in *Torn Curtain* (1966). Other nominees that year were Anne Bancroft in *The Pumpkin Eater*, Sophia Loren in *Marriage Italian Style*, Debbie Reynolds in *The Unsinkable Molly Brown*, and Kim Stanley in *Séance on a Wet Afternoon*. The best picture was *My Fair Lady*, and runners up were *Dr. Strangelove*, *Mary Poppins*, and *Zorba the Greek*. *Marnie* was not nominated in any category.

The publicity campaign for *The Girl* also repeatedly claims that Hitchcock discouraged other directors from hiring Hedren after *Marnie*. In particular the director François Truffaut is cited as wanting her for his film *Fahrenheit 451*, which is the only film he made while Hedren was still under contract to Hitchcock in 1965. Hitchcock reputedly said, "She's not available." When interviewed, daughter Laura Truffaut denies her father wanting to hire Hedren for the role:

> I did some research through my father's correspondence and biography, as well as through a very well-researched book on his work based on his very extensive archives (*François Truffaut au Travail*, by Carole Le Berre). I also asked my mother about whether she had ever heard my father's mentioning Tippi Hedren as a possible part of the cast of *Fahrenheit 451*. She was just as surprised as I was. My parents had a close relationship and it is extremely unlikely, in my view, that my father seriously entertained this project without sharing it with my mother or mentioning it to us in later years. I am all the more confident about this as my father was not secretive about the other actors who were considered for casting in that film. The only other actress seriously considered was Jean Seberg. I remember my father telling me about how Tippi Hedren was shooting scenes for the [Charlie] Chaplin film at the same time and in the same studio [in London] where *Fahrenheit 451* was being made. Surely he would have mentioned having considered her for his own film in that context during this same conversation if this had been the case? In one of my father's published letters to Helen Scott, his collaborator on the Hitchcock book, he refers jokingly to the possibility of offering a seven-year contract to an actress (generic, not a specific person). He also refers in another letter to Hitchcock's professional and personal disappointment with Miss Hedren, but without any further comment.[15]

Brooke Allen, the daughter of the film's producer, Lewis Allen, also denies the claim. "First I've ever heard of Tippi Hedren being up for the role in *Fahrenheit 451*. My father produced that movie and never mentioned any such thing. They were very excited about working with Julie Christie."[16] The casting files of Lewis Allen for *Fahrenheit 451*, held at the Harry Ransom Center, University of Texas at Austin, corroborate this. They include correspondence for Julie Christie, Jane Fonda, Mia Farrow, and Florence Henderson, but there is no mention of Tippi Hedren.

Norman Lloyd also disagrees that Hitchcock would have stooped so low as to try to ruin Hedren's career. "She claims that he had her blackballed, I think she uses the word. He could never have done that. He wouldn't have had that influence. If someone wanted to hire her, they would have hired her."[17]

These claims that Hitchcock tried to ruin Hedren's career have also been dismissed by the film historian Brian Hannan in his new book *Hitchcock's Hollywood Hell*.[18] Hannan persuasively argues for a more tangled scenario of contract disputes, diminishing box office returns and the poor reception of *Marnie* which contributed to Hitchcock's break with Hedren: "*Marnie* was not the success Hitchcock had predicted, nor Hedren as easy to deal with as he expected, especially with the string pulling behind the scenes by her new husband Noel Marshall, an ambitious television producer," writes Hannan.

Eventually Hedren was released by Hitchcock from her contract in early 1966 after he sold it to Universal. When she refused to appear in a television series, after having already appeared in two for Universal in 1965, *Kraft Suspense Theatre* and *Run for Your Life*, her contract was dissolved by the studio by mutual agreement. Two weeks later, she received a phone call from Charlie Chaplin. Chaplin had seen her in *Marnie* and offered her a part in what turned out to be his last film, *A Countess from Hong Kong* (1967), starring Marlon Brando and Sophia Loren. But, disappointingly, it turned out to be little more than a cameo, as Hedren appears in only four scenes.

Hitchcock himself said little publicly about Tippi Hedren afterward. "He never talked about it," said Hilton Green. But there are at least two instances on record. In 1972, he was interviewed by the journalist Janet Maslin. In response to his attempt to make a star out of Hedren, Hitchcock said, "I later turned her over to Universal, because you can't have the same woman in every picture . . . they offered to renew her contract if she would agree to do television, which she didn't want to do." In answer to Maslin's question of whether he would consider doing it again if he found somebody else in another commercial, Hitchcock said, "Well I don't know, it takes a lot . . . you know, to build a person up it costs a lot of money. With the Hedren girl, I had a special wardrobe made by Edith Head, special tests. I even brought Martin Balsam in from New York to play opposite her, just for a test, and I took a scene out of *To Catch a Thief* for that test. Building a girl up, it takes a lot. We don't have the system any more—in the old days of MGM, boy, they put them through school practically, they had a whole roster of stars. But those days are gone."

Aside from the challenges of casting, as a filmmaker, Hitchcock was more interested in emotion than technological perfection. Sometimes he would ask more of the technology than could be provided at the time. Robert Boyle stated, "I know from Hitch's standpoint, he felt this film very deeply and expected it to be accepted more than it was. He saw the physical environments of his films and tried to attain these visions clearly, always worked out from the standpoints of his own feelings. He felt very strongly about this movie. He had many personal fears and was able to put these fears on film."

Hitchcock was strongly influenced by German expressionism, and *Marnie* is very much an expressionistic film. The central aim of expressionism, a tradition compatible with the Hollywood melodrama, is the projection of emotional states by means of imagery. With *Marnie,* Hitchcock strips away the intricacies of personal psychology to reveal fundamental human drives, such as pain and fear, in the most intense way possible. The forceful projection of such violent feelings is a feature common to many great works of art, and what may be regarded as simplistic and ugly can also be seen as a stripping away to what is truly essential. In a speech made to the Screen Producer's Guild on March 7, 1965, Hitchcock remarked:

> There is one impression with which I wish to leave you, and I want it to be unmistakable. It is this: that the recipient of this award aims to create emotion in an audience, not through subject matter, but through technique. Working in the genre of the suspense picture, he always insists on treating his material with humor. He is not interested in making a film that is merely photographs of people talking, but strives always to tell his stories in a way that no other medium can—in strictly cinematic terms.

The preponderance of the evidence—the film itself and the documentary record—indicates that Hitchcock was being expressionistic throughout the making of *Marnie.* The entire film was deeply and hopelessly personal, as evidenced by the London aspect of the Baltimore ship and row of houses. Subsequently, *Marnie* emerges as one of Hitchcock's finest, most intense, and disturbing works. The director was able to use all of his early experiences and turn misery, unhappiness, and distorted problematic occurrences into an art form that has withstood the test of time and will continue to be more important as time passes.

## NOTES

1. William Rothman, *The Murderous Gaze*, 2nd edition (Albany: State University of New York Press, 2012), xiv.

2. François Truffaut, *Hitchcock* (New York: Simon & Schuster, 1985), 301.

3. Alfred Hitchcock to *Telescope* television programme, 1964.

4. Peter Bogdanovich, *Who the Devil Made It?* (New York: Ballantine Books, 1998), 538.

5. Hitchcock interviewed by Charles Thomas Samuels, 1972.

6. Mrs. Alfred Hitchcock as told to Martin Abramson, "My Husband Alfred Hitchcock Hates Suspense," *Coronet* (August 1964): 12–17.

7. Winston Graham, *Memoirs of a Private Man* (London: Macmillan, 2003), 140.

8. Interview with Andrew Graham, Corfu, August 18, 2012.

9. Jay Presson Allen at the Hitchcock Centennial conference in New York, October 1999.

10. Hitchcock to Peter Bogdanovich, unpublished interview, February 14, 1963.

11. Tippi Hedren to *Huffington Post Live*, October 2012.

12. Donald Spoto, *Spellbound by Beauty* (London: Arrow, 2008), 187.

13. Anita Singh, "Alfred Hitchcock Drama *The Girl* Sparks Angry Backlash," *Daily Telegraph*, October 22, 2012.

14. Interview with John Russell Taylor, London, England, December 20, 2012.

15. Interview with Laura Truffaut, Berkeley, California, October 3, 2012.

16. Interview with Brooke Allen, Connecticut, October 21, 2012.

17. Interview with Norman Lloyd, Los Angeles, November 30, 2012.

18. Brian Hannan, *Hitchcock's Hollywood Hell* (Glasgow: Baroliant Press, 2013).

# Appendix A
## Marnie *Cast and Crew*

### CAST

Marnie—Tippi Hedren
Mark—Sean Connery
Lil—Diane Baker
Strutt—Martin Gabel
Mrs. Edgar—Louise Latham
Mr. Rutland—Alan Napier
Cousin Bob—Bob Sweeney
Susan Clabon—Mariette Hartley
Sailor—Bruce Dern

### CREW

Director—Alfred Hitchcock
Screenplay—Jay Presson Allen
Based on the novel *Marnie* by Winston Graham
Director of Photography—Robert Burks, A.S.C.
Editor—George Tomasini, A.C.E.
Production Designer—Robert Boyle
Production Manager—Hilton Green
Assistant Director—James H. Brown
Miss Hedren's hairstyles—Alexandre of Paris
Hairstyles—Virginia Darcy
Miss Hedren's and Miss Baker's costumes—Edith Head
Wardrobe—Rita Riggs
Musical composition—Bernard Herrmann

# Appendix B
## Marnie *Timeline*

January 8, 1961: Winston Graham's *Marnie* is published in the United States
January 15, 1961: Hitchcock buys story rights to Winston Graham's *Marnie*
October 13, 1961: Hitchcock sees Tippi Hedren in commercial
November 8, 1961: Tippi Hedren's screen test
March 3, 1962: Principal filming of *The Birds*
March 18, 1962: Palace announces that Grace Kelly will play the lead
June 7, 1962: Grace Kelly withdraws from negotiations to play Marnie
June 7, 1962: Hitchcock offers Tippi Hedren the part of Marnie
April 10, 1963: Evan Hunter is fired from *Marnie*
May 29, 1963: Jay Presson Allen starts writing the script
November 22, 1963: JFK is assassinated in Dallas
November 25, 1963: National day of mourning delays production
November 26, 1963: Principal photography begins
February 3, 1964: Hitchcock and Hedren have a falling out
February 5, 1964: *Photoplay* award in New York
February 28, 1964: Wrap party for Sean Connery
March 11, 1964: Principal photography ends
July 8, 1964: *Marnie* premieres in London
July 23, 1964: *Marnie* premieres in New York
July 2014: Fiftieth anniversary of *Marnie*

# Appendix C

## *The Films of Alfred Hitchcock*

**SILENT**

*The Pleasure Garden* (1925)
*The Mountain Eagle* (1926)
*The Lodger* (1927)
*Downhill* (1927)
*Easy Virtue* (1927)
*The Ring* (1927)
*The Farmer's Wife* (1928)
*Champagne* (1928)
*The Manxman* (1929)

**SOUND**

*Blackmail* (1929)
*Juno and the Paycock* (1930)
*Murder!* (1930)
*The Skin Game* (1931)
*Number Seventeen* (1932)
*Rich and Strange* (1932)
*Waltzes from Vienna* (1933)
*The Man Who Knew Too Much* (1934)
*The 39 Steps* (1935)
*Secret Agent* (1936)
*Sabotage* (1936)
*Young and Innocent* (1938)

*The Lady Vanishes* (1938)
*Jamaica Inn* (1939)
*Rebecca* (1940)
*Foreign Correspondent* (1940)
*Mr. and Mrs. Smith* (1941)
*Suspicion* (1941)
*Saboteur* (1942)
*Shadow of a Doubt* (1943)
*Lifeboat* (1944)
*Spellbound* (1945)
*Notorious* (1946)
*The Paradine Case* (1947)
*Rope* (1948)
*Under Capricorn* (1949)
*Stage Fright* (1950)
*Strangers on a Train* (1951)
*I Confess* (1953)
*Dial M for Murder* (1954)
*Rear Window* (1954)
*To Catch a Thief* (1955)
*The Trouble with Harry* (1955)
*The Man Who Knew Too Much* (1956)
*The Wrong Man* (1957)
*Vertigo* (1958)
*North by Northwest* (1959)
*Psycho* (1960)
*The Birds* (1963)
*Marnie* (1964)
*Torn Curtain* (1966)
*Topaz* (1969)
*Frenzy* (1972)
*Family Plot* (1976)

# Select Bibliography

Allen, Richard, and S. Ishi Gonzalés, eds. *Alfred Hitchcock Centenary Essays*. London: British Film Institute, 1999.

Asquith, Cynthia. *Portrait of Barrie*. London: Robert Cunningham & Sons, 1954.

Aulier, Dan. *Hitchcock's Notebooks*. New York: Avon, 1999.

Bogdanovich, Peter. *Who the Devil Made It?* New York: Ballantine, 1997 (hardback edition); 1998 (paperback edition).

Chandler, Charlotte. *It's Only a Movie: Alfred Hitchcock, A Personal Biography*. Australia: Simon & Schuster, 2005.

Dunbar, Janet. *JM Barrie: the man behind the image*. London: Collins, 1970.

Graham, Winston. *Memoirs of a Private Man*. London: Macmillan, 2003.

Hannan, Brian. *Hitchcock's Hollywood Hell*. Glasgow: Baroliant Press, 2013.

Hitchcock, Alfred. *Hitchcock on Hitchcock: Selected Writings and Interviews*. Edited by Sidney Gottlieb. Berkeley: University of California Press, 1995.

Hunter, Evan. *Me and Hitch*. London: Faber & Faber, 1997.

Hunter, Tim. "Alfred Hitchcock at Harvard." *The Harvard Crimson*, October 14, 1966.

Kapsis, Robert E. *Hitchcock: The Making of a Reputation*. Chicago: University of Chicago Press, 1992.

Mackail, Denis. *The Story of JMB*. London: Peter Davies, 1941.

McBride, Joseph. "Alfred Hitchcock's Mary Rose: An Old Master's Unheard Cri de Coeur." *Cineaste* 26.2 (24–26), 2001.

Modleski, Tania. *The Women Who Knew Too Much: Hitchcock and Feminist Film Theory*. London: Methuen, 1988.

Morrison James. "On Burkes." *Film Comment*, Vol. 8. No. 2. New York, 1972.

Raubicheck, Walter and Walter Srebnick. *Scripting Hitchcock*: Psycho, The Birds, and Marnie. Illinois: University of Illinois Press, 2011.

Rebello, Stephen. *Alfred Hitchcock and the Making of* Psycho. New York: Dembner, 1990.

Rothman, William. *Hitchcock: The Murderous Gaze,* 2nd ed. New York: SUNY Press, 2012.

Spoto, Donald. *The Dark Side of Genius: The Life of Alfred Hitchcock.* Boston: Little, Brown, 1983.

Taylor, John Russell. *Hitch: The Life and Times of Alfred Hitchcock.* New York: Pantheon Books, 1978.

Truffaut, François. *Hitchcock.* New York: Simon & Schuster, 1967 (original edition); 1985 (revised edition).

Turner, George. "Robert Burks, ASC, and Alfred Hitchcock." *The American Society of Cinematographers*, 1998.

Wood, Robin. *Hitchcock's Films Revisited.* New York: Columbia University Press, 1989 (original edition); 2002 (revised edition).

Zizek, Slavoj. *Everything You Always Wanted to Know about Lacan (But Were Afraid to Ask Hitchcock).* London: Verso, 1992.

# Index

277

# About the Author

**Tony Lee Moral** is a documentary filmmaker and writer. He is the author of two other books on Alfred Hitchcock: *The Making of Hitchcock's* The Birds (2013) and *Alfred Hitchcock's Movie Making Masterclass* (2013). He lives in London and Los Angeles.